iPad®
ALL-IN-ONE
FOR
DUMMIES®
5TH EDITION

by Nancy Muir

WILEY

John Wiley & Sons, Inc.

iPad® All-in-One For Dummies? 5th Edition

Published by
John Wiley & Sons, Inc.
111 River Street
Hoboken, NJ 07030-5774

www.wiley.com

Copyright © 2013 by John Wiley & Sons, Inc., Hoboken, New Jersey

Published by John Wiley & Sons, Inc., Hoboken, New Jersey

Published simultaneously in Canada

Library of Congress Control Number: 2012954398

ISBN 978-1-118-49696-1 (pbk); ISBN 978-1-118-54098-5 (ebk); ISBN 978-1-118-54100-5 (ebk); ISBN 978-1-118-54187-6 (ebk)

Manufactured in the United States of America

10 9 8 7 6 5 4 3 2 1

WILEY

About the Author

Nancy Muir is the author of over 100 books on technology and business topics. In addition to her writing work, Nancy runs a website on technology for seniors called `TechSmartSenior.com` and a companion website for her iPad books in the *For Dummies* series, `iPadMadeClear.com`. She writes a regular column on computers and the Internet on Retirenet.com. Prior to her writing career Nancy was a manager at several publishing companies, and a training manager at Symantec.

Dedication

To the Elf, for taking care of everything while I worked.

Author's Acknowledgments

I was lucky enough to have Blair Pottenger, the absolute best editor in the world, assigned to lead the team on this book and as usual he did a stellar job. Thanks also to Rebecca Senninger, the book's project editor, Dennis Cohen for his able work as technical editor, and to John Edwards, the book's copy editor, for checking all the details. Last but never least, thanks to Kyle Looper, an outstanding Acquisitions Editor, for hiring me to write this and many other books.

Publisher's Acknowledgments

We're proud of this book; please send us your comments at http://dummies.custhelp.com. For other comments, please contact our Customer Care Department within the U.S. at 877-762-2974, outside the U.S. at 317-572-3993, or fax 317-572-4002.

Some of the people who helped bring this book to market include the following:

Acquisitions and Editorial

Project Editor: Rebecca Senninger, Blair J. Pottenger

Acquisitions Editor: Kyle Looper

Copy Editor: John Edwards

Technical Editor: Dennis Cohen

Editorial Manager: Kevin Kirschner

Editorial Assistant: Leslie Saxman

Sr. Editorial Assistant: Cherie Case

Cover Photo: © SelectStock/iStockphoto.com

Cartoons: Rich Tennant (www.the5thwave.com)

Composition Services

Project Coordinator: Katherine Crocker

Layout and Graphics: Jennifer Creasey, Joyce Haughey

Proofreaders: Debbye Butler, Lauren Mandelbaum, Evelyn Wellborn, The Well-Chosen Word

Indexer: BIM Indexing & Proofreading Services

Publishing and Editorial for Technology Dummies

    Richard Swadley, Vice President and Executive Group Publisher

    Andy Cummings, Vice President and Publisher

    Mary Bednarek, Executive Acquisitions Director

    Mary C. Corder, Editorial Director

Publishing for Consumer Dummies

    Kathleen Nebenhaus, Vice President and Executive Publisher

Composition Services

    Debbie Stailey, Director of Composition Services

Contents at a Glance

Table of Contents

Introduction

*A*pple turned the computing world on its ear when it introduced the iPad. This small wonder, which weighs less than a pound-and-a-half, sold many millions of units in its first few years for good reason: It's well designed and feature rich, and it opens up a world of apps and media viewing in a highly portable format.

About This Book

iPad All-in-One For Dummies, 5th Edition, has one aim: to be the ultimate reference on the coolest digital device of the day. If you're reasonably computer savvy, you can use this book to get up to speed quickly the day you buy your iPad, and then you can pick up the book again anytime you feel like taking your knowledge of the iPad to the next level. Even if you've been puttering with your iPad for a while, you'll still find things between these covers that you didn't know about.

Though the iPad is relatively simple to use, a lot is packed in there, and you can get even more from it by downloading apps to do seemingly everything under the sun. The book approaches the iPad from every angle: from the basics to powerful road-warrior tools and from productivity apps to ultra-cool games and media.

You can read step-by-step instructions for basic tasks, hot tips for getting the most out of iPad, and reviews of apps to steer you to the best of the best.

How This Book Is Organized

This book consists of easily read chunks of chapters that are organized into six minibooks. Each minibook covers a different facet of using the iPad, such as having fun or getting work done. Most material is relevant whether you have an original iPad, iPad 2, iPad mini, or a third- or fourth- generation iPad, though I strongly recommend that you update to iOS 6, which is quick and easy to do (see Book I, Chapter 2), because it's the operating system I based this book on.

You don't have to read the chapters in this book in sequence, but if you're new to iPad, consider starting with the basic concepts in Book I. The following sections give you a synopsis of the topics covered in each minibook.

Book I: iPad Basics

This minibook starts with an overview of new features in iPad mini and third-and fourth-generation iPad and iOS 6 such as the fast A5X (third-generation iPad and iPad mini) and A6X (fourth-generation iPad) processor, Retina display, Dictation, Siri, and iSight camera. It's also where you discover what items come supplied in the iPad box, get an overview of all the preinstalled apps that come with your iPad, and discover how to set up iPad and sync it with your computer, including how to open an iCloud account and back up and share content with other devices. I provide an overview of preinstalled apps and tell you how to acquire more apps. You become acquainted with the iPad touchscreen and cameras, and you see how to make settings that control how iPad works, including accessibility settings. You also get going with the built-in Safari browser and set up your e-mail account, as well as explore some advice about how to take care of your iPad. Finally, I provide some troubleshooting and maintenance advice to protect your investment.

Book II: Just for Fun

Why wait until later in the book to get to the fun stuff? iPad is a fun device, but the music, videos, photos, and e-books you can view or listen to on it are a big part of its appeal. In fact, iPad is considered by many people to be primarily a content-consuming machine. The front- and rear-facing video and still cameras take advantage of useful apps such as FaceTime for video chatting and Photo Booth for adding way-out effects to snapshots as you take them. You discover how Twitter and Facebook are integrated into several apps and find out all about iMessage for instant messaging. Become expert at using the iBooks and other e-reader apps to read all kinds of books, and explore Newsstand to subscribe to and read publications. And don't forget games: Some absolutely awesome games are out there that you may have played on your phone, but they roar to life on the iPad's outstanding screen.

Book III: iPad on the Go

If you travel for business or pleasure, one huge attraction of iPad is its portability (taken to the max with the .68 pound iPad mini) and long battery life (10 hours for all models), and the chapters in this minibook help take you on the road with your iPad. Using a Wi-Fi or 3G/4G connection (or a personal hotspot for tethering), you can stay in touch with others and your home office or connect with clients by using video and FaceTime. This minibook also covers the benefits of using iPad when traveling, from finding directions in the Maps app to making travel arrangements or finding that classic hotel or restaurant or the nearest ATM as you roam. Finally, the last chapter in this book covers Siri, a great feature new to the iPad with iOS 6 that allows you to ask your iPad just about anything, from the date of the next solar eclipse to the name of the restaurant that makes the best hot dog in town, and she'll give you an answer.

Book IV: Getting Productive with iWork

Some reviewers claim that the iPad isn't useful for getting work done, but they're wrong. Some of the apps that are available help you perform the typical office suite functions, including iWork from Apple. In this minibook, you find out about the iWork for iOS apps, including how to share your work on iWork.com. You also can read how to use Pages for word processing, Numbers to crunch numbers, and Keynote for creating power presentations.

Book V: Using iPad to Get Organized

Several built-in apps in iPad can help you organize your life. You'll find the usual Calendar and Contacts apps to keep your schedule and people in line, as well as a handy Notes app for jotting down quick messages or records for yourself. In this minibook, I advise you on file management on iPad: syncing files to your computer, storing documents online, and printing hard copies. You can also find out about the Reminders app and Notification Center.

Book VI: Must-Have iPad Apps

Throughout this edition of *iPad All-in-One For Dummies,* I mention apps that can broaden your iPad horizons, but this minibook is the one that's strictly dedicated to apps. In a variety of categories, such as business, travel, social networking, news, finance, and entertainment, I offer reviews of some of the hottest apps out there. If you want to go beyond the built-in functionality of iPad to a world of possibilities, this is the minibook for you!

Foolish Assumptions

To offer you a book that gives you insight into the powerful ways you can use iPad, I have to assume that you're computer and mobile phone literate. You don't have to be an iPhone user to use this book (though iPhone has a great many similarities to iPad and shares many apps with it). You don't even have to be a Mac-oriented person — PC people do just fine with iPad.

I also assume that you want to take iPad to the next level by getting helpful tips and advice as well as discovering apps that are useful in expanding your iPad experience. You may use iPad for personal pleasure or to get your work done — or both. If you travel a great deal or use iPad to work, you'll find extra benefits in the material covered in Book VI.

Icons Used in This Book

Little pictures often found in the margin of technical books help you quickly find certain types of information, such as tips or warnings. Here are the icons you should look for in *iPad All-in-One For Dummies,* 5th Edition:

The Tip icon points to a tiny advice column about the current topic or other useful strategies for advancing your iPad experience to the next level.

The Remember icon signals either a pertinent fact that relates to the topic you're reading about (but is also mentioned elsewhere in the book) or a reiteration of a particularly important piece of information that's, well, worth repeating.

The Warning icon alerts you to potential pitfalls, so don't ignore it. Ignoring the Warning icon might leave you with lost data, a broken iPad, or a lost connection.

For the latest and greatest features of iPad mini and third- and fourth-generation iPad and iOS 6, hunt for the New icon. If you own a first-generation iPad or iPad 2, this information can help you understand where your model might differ in its functionality. (Don't worry: Except for the first-generation model not having built-in cameras and the third- and fourth-generation's Retina display and faster processors, the differences aren't that great if you have the current iOS.)

The Technical Stuff icon marks iPad information that ventures beyond the basics.

Where to Go from Here

After you read this book's introduction, it's time to jump into all things iPad. I hope that when you turn to any chapter in this book, you'll find something you didn't know about iPad that will increase your enjoyment of your new device.

Start by checking out the basic concepts and instructions in Book I (you might be surprised at what you discover, even if you've been tinkering with your iPad for a bit) and then jump to any minibook that addresses where you want to go next — to have fun, get work done, or explore more apps, for example.

Wherever you dive in, you're likely to find some advice or information that will make your iPad experience even more rewarding.

The first step you should take (and this is covered in Book I, Chapter 2) is to update to the latest operating system for iPad — iOS 6, at the time this book went to press. All steps in this book are based on iOS 6. I provide information on changes to the iOS or iPad hardware on my website (at `www.ipadmade clear.com`), so you can continue to use this book even if changes are introduced after you buy it. Also, if a change is very substantial, I may add an update or bonus information that you can download at this book's companion website, `www.dummies.com/go/ipadaio`. Please check both websites periodically as Apple makes software and hardware updates to iPad now and then.

Book I
iPad Basics

*I*f you're looking for basics on buying, setting up, and using features of your iPad, you've come to the right part of this book. Here you get to explore what's in the box and register your iPad. You start to get a feel for how you interact with iPad by playing around with its camera, the touchscreen, and the onscreen keyboard. This is also where I introduce you to the preinstalled apps that come with your iPad (each of which is covered in detail in later books). I also help you explore iPad settings, many of which can make for an even better iPad experience, including a chapter on accessibility settings for those who need help with vision, hearing, or dexterity challenges when using an iPad.

This part provides basics on getting connected to the Internet and using the Mail e-mail app, as well as getting set up to sync your iPad with iTunes or by using iCloud, the great service from Apple that automatically pushes content to all your iOS devices. Finally, I provide advice about troubleshooting and maintaining your iPad to keep it running for years to come.

Chapter 1: Buying Your iPad

*Y*ou've read about it. You've seen news reports about the lines at Apple Stores every time a new generation iPad is released. You know you can't live without your own iPad to have fun, explore the online world, read e-books, organize your photos, and more.

Trust me; you've made a good decision because the iPad does redefine the computing experience in an exciting new way.

This chapter is for those of you who don't already have an iPad. Here is where you discover the different iPad models and their advantages, as well as where to buy this little gem and the accessories you can purchase to trick out your iPad.

Discovering What's New in iOS 6.0

iPad gets its features from a combination of hardware and its software operating system, with the most current operating system being iOS 6.0, though small updates appear all the time, so by the time you're reading this, you might have 6.1, 2, or 3. If you've seen the original iPad in action or own one, it might be helpful to understand what new features the third- and fourth-generation iPad brought to the table (which are all covered in more detail in this book). In addition to features on the original iPad and iPad 2, the third- and fourth-generation iPads offer

⮕ **Retina display:** This awesomely crisp display provides 3.1 million pixels, which trust me, is a lot.

⮕ **An improved dual-core A5X chip on third-generation and iPad mini; an A6X chip on fourth-generation iPad:** These chips give your iPad much faster performance and quad-core graphics, with the A6X being the faster of the two.

✒ **An improved 5-megapixel iSight camera:** The rear-facing iSight camera offers advanced optics, an illumination sensor, a face detection feature that makes people you capture clearer, and the ability to capture video in 1080 pixels, all discussed in more detail in Book II, Chapter 4.

✒ **Dictation:** You can use the Dictation feature to speak into your iPad rather than typing. This comes in handy in apps like Maps, Mail, and Notes.

✒ **Available 4G LTE:** Whereas the original iPad and iPad 2 were offered in a 3G version, the third- and fourth-generation iPad and iPad mini can take advantage of 4G and even *4G LTE,* the latest in cellular communication technology, which simply means you can get a very fast, strong connection to the Internet if you're near a 4G-enabled locale. Unfortunately, because this is a relatively recent technology, right now you have to live near a major city to take full advantage of it. However, the fourth-generation iPad brought with it more LTE bands to give you a better chance to take advantage of LTE.

✒ **An improved FaceTime HD camera in fourth-generation iPad:** The front-facing camera on both the third- and fourth-generation iPad is perfect for making video calls using FaceTime. The fourth-generation iPad brought with it some improvements to the quality of that camera and allows you to capture HD-quality video.

Throughout this book, I point out any features that are only available on certain models of iPads, so you can use this book no matter which version of the device you own.

Any iPad device can use iOS 6.0 if you update the operating system (discussed in detail in Chapter 2 of this minibook); this book is based on version 6.0 of iOS.

This update to the operating system adds a few new features, including

✒ **Brand-new Maps:** The Maps app has been totally rebuilt in iOS 6.0. Graphics are crisper, and you have more control over panning, tilting, and zooming. You can use Maps to get spoken turn-by-turn navigation, as well as traffic information in real time.

✒ **Siri:** This is a technology that was introduced with iPhone 4S and appeared first on iPad's third-generation models. You can talk to Siri and ask questions from the practical (Where's the nearest gas station?) to the fun (Where can I buy a used sailboat?). See Book V, Chapter 6 for all things Siri.

✒ **Sharing:** You can share photos with your Facebook friends, share links from Safari, share high scores from Game Center, or update your status using Notification Center or Siri.

✔ **Shared photo streams:** The Photo Stream feature isn't new to iOS 6.0 but the ability to share photos with a select group of people is. This approach uses iCloud to share with other Apple devices, or to share photos with anybody online.

✔ **FaceTime over cellular:** You can now use the FaceTime video calling feature to call others over cellular networks (if you have a 3G/4G iPad model) as well as over Wi-Fi.

✔ **Guided Access:** This accessibility feature allows you to focus your iPad to just certain sites or apps to help you or those you're helping to have an easier learning experience.

✔ **Find My Friends:** You can use this feature to share your location with others and receive alerts when friends leave or arrive at a certain location.

✔ **Better-than-ever apps:** Several apps such as Mail, Safari, and Apple's online stores have been spiffed up to offer a few neat features.

Choosing the Right iPad for You

Though there are slight differences in thickness and weight among the different generations of the larger iPad model, if you pick up an iPad (see Figure 1-1), you're not likely to be able to tell one model from another on first glance, except that some are black and some are white. Although the four generations have slightly different heft and the original iPad is the only one without cameras, their differences are primarily under the hood.

Figure 1-1: A white iPad could become your newest BFF.

If you're in the market for a new iPad, Apple currently offers iPad 2s (at a discounted price), third- and fourth-generation iPads, and the iPad mini. iPad minis and third- and fourth generation models have three variations:

- ✔ Black or white
- ✔ Amount of built-in memory
- ✔ Method used for connecting to the Internet: Wi-Fi only; Wi-Fi and 3G (iPad2); or Wi-Fi and 4G (third- and fourth-generation iPad and iPad mini)

In addition, the fourth-generation iPad has a faster processor, a better FaceTime camera, and a new kind of connector called a *Lightning Connector* which has a smaller plug on the end of the connector that slots into the iPad itself. For my money the biggest advantage to you about the Lightning Connector is that it plugs into your iPad no matter which way you hold it.

Your options in the first item in this list are pretty, well, black and white, but if you're confused about the other two, read on as I explain these variations in more detail in the following sections.

If you're of the opinion that smaller is better, then you might want to opt for the new 7.9" display iPad mini. This model is 23% thinner and 53% lighter than the third- or fourth-generation iPad. Otherwise, its specs pretty much match the iPad 2 in terms of screen resolution and processor power.

Some people feel that the white model is less effective at taking advantage of the Retina display. The black model in effect disappears, letting the crisp image really pop. Still, color selection is subjective, so I say get the one that appeals to you.

Because Apple upgrades the software and releases new versions of the hardware on a somewhat regular basis (a practice that keeps tech writers on their toes), I've avoided getting too specific on memory specifications and pricing in this chapter. However, you can go to www.apple.com/ipad to check out the latest details at any time.

Deciding how much memory is enough

You know that computer *memory* is a measure of how much information — for example, movies, photos, and software applications, or *apps* — you can store on a computing device. Memory can also affect your iPad's performance when handling tasks, such as streaming favorite TV shows from the World Wide Web or downloading music.

With video and audio streaming, you can enjoy a lot of content online without ever downloading the full content to your hard drive or iPad flash memory, and given that the iPad has a relatively small amount of memory in any of its models, that's not a bad idea. See Book II, Chapters 1–3 for more about getting your music and movies online.

Your memory options with an iPad are 16, 32, or 64 gigabytes (GB). You must choose the right amount of memory because you can't open the unit and add to it, as you usually can with a desktop computer. There is also no way to directly insert a flash drive (also known as a USB stick) to add backup capacity because iPad has no USB port — or CD/DVD drive, for that matter. However, Apple has thoughtfully provided *iCloud,* a service you can use to save space by backing up content to the Internet. (You can read more about that in Chapter 5 of this minibook.)

With an Apple Digital AV Adapter accessory, you can plug into the iPad to attach an HDMI-enabled device, such as an external hard drive for additional storage capacity. See Book II, Chapter 3 for more about using these AV features (most of which have not yet hit the market — but they're coming!). As of this writing, ViewSonic is offering three new HDMI projectors, DVDO is offering an HD Travel Kit for smartphones and tablets, and Belkin has introduced a new line of tools for HDTV streaming, for example.

So how much memory is enough for your iPad? Here's a good rule: If you like lots of media, such as movies or TV shows, and you want to store them on your iPad (rather than experiencing or accessing this content online on sites such as Hulu or Netflix or from your Mac/PC using an app like Air Video), you might need 64GB. For most people who manage a reasonable number of photos, download some music, and watch heavy-duty media such as movies online, 32GB is probably sufficient. If you simply want to check e-mail, browse the web, and write short notes to yourself, 16GB *might* be enough, but for my money, why bother?

You can't expand memory in an iPad. Memory resides on a *micro-SIM card* (a smaller version of the SIM card in your cellphone), which is fine for saving your contacts' addresses and similar data but doesn't lend itself to video storage. Apple is banking on you wanting to stream and sync content via iTunes or iCloud. Only you can decide whether that will work for you.

What's the price for larger memory? For the third- and fourth- generation iPad, a 16GB Wi-Fi unit (see the next section for more about Wi-Fi) costs $499; 32GB jumps the price to $599; and 64GB adds another $100, setting you back a whopping $699. If you buy an iPad mini you're looking at $329, $429, and $529 for the three levels of memory.

Determining whether you need Wi-Fi only or Wi-Fi and 3G/4G

Another variation on price and performance for the iPad is whether your model has Wi-Fi or Wi-Fi and 3G/4G. Because the iPad is great for browsing online, shopping online, e-mailing, and so on, obviously having an Internet connection for your device is pretty essential. That's where Wi-Fi and 3G/4G come in. Both are technologies used to connect to the Internet, and in case you need a refresher course, here's a quick summary:

- *Wi-Fi* is what you use to connect to a wireless network at home or at your local coffee shop or an airport that offers Wi-Fi. This type of network uses short-range radio to connect devices to the Internet; its range is reasonably limited — so if you leave home or walk out of the coffee shop, you can't use it. (These limitations are changing as some towns are installing community-wide Wi-Fi networks.)

- *3G and 4G* cellphone technologies allow an iPad to connect to the Internet via a cellular network that's widespread. You use it in much the same way you make calls from just about anywhere using your cellphone. 3G is available on iPad 2; 4G is available on third- and fourth-generation iPad as well as iPad mini, and as the latest cellular connection technology, it may not be available in every location. You'll still connect to the Internet when 4G service isn't available, but without the advantage of the superfast 4G technology.

You can buy an iPad with only Wi-Fi or one with both Wi-Fi and 3G or 3G and 4G capabilities. Getting a 3G/4G iPad costs an additional $130, but it also includes GPS so that you can get more accurate driving directions. You have to buy an iPad model that fits your data connection provider — either AT&T or Verizon in the United States, as of this writing.

Also, to use your 3G/4G network, you have to pay AT&T or Verizon a monthly fee. The good news is that neither carrier requires a long-term contract, as you probably had to commit to with your cellphone and its data connection — you can pay for a connection the month you travel to Hong Kong and then get rid of it when you return home. But each carrier has slightly different plans. AT&T offers prepaid and postpaid options, but Verizon offers only a prepaid plan. AT&T offers plans that top out at 5GB of data per month per connection, whereas Verizon offers several levels, including 3GB, 5GB, and 10GB of data per month. Check out these plans before buying your iPad because you have to buy either an AT&T or Verizon version. Note that if you intend to *stream* videos (watch them on your iPad from the Internet), you can eat through these numbers quickly. Recently, Sprint joined the ranks of those offering both iPhones and iPads. Check out its website (http://sprint.com) when you're ready to sign up to see what Sprint has to offer.

If you have a Wi-Fi network available and a smartphone for calling over 3G/4G, you might consider just getting a Wi-Fi iPad model and save the rather high cost of provider data plans.

Of course, AT&T and Verizon could change their pricing and options at any time, so go to these links for more information about iPad data plans: AT&T is at www.att.com/shop/wireless/devices/ipad.jsp, and Verizon is at www.verizonwireless.com/b2c/splash/ipad.jsp.

You can use the hotspot feature on a smartphone, which allows iPad to use your phone's 3G or 4G connection to go online if you pay for a higher-data-use plan that supports hotspot usage with your phone service carrier. Check out the features of your phone to turn on hotspot. See Book III, Chapter 3 for more about this feature.

So how do you choose? If you want to wander around the woods or town — or take long drives with your iPad continually connected to the Internet — get 3G/4G and pay the price. But if you'll use your iPad mainly at home or using a Wi-Fi *hotspot* (a location where Wi-Fi access to the Internet is available, such as at an Internet café or a library), don't bother with 3G/4G. And frankly, you can now find *lots* of hotspots out there, including restaurants, hotels, airports, and more.

Because 3G and 4G iPads are GPS devices, they know where you are and can act as a navigation system to get you from here to there. The Wi-Fi–only model uses a digital compass and triangulation method for locating your current position, which is less accurate; with no constant Internet connection, it won't help you to get around town. If getting accurate directions when you're on the go is one iPad feature that excites you, get 3G/4G and then see Book III, Chapter 2 for more about the Maps app.

Knowing what you need to use your iPad

Before you head off to buy your iPad, you should know what other devices, connections, and accounts you'll need to work with it optimally. At a bare minimum, you need to be able to connect to the Internet to take advantage of most of iPad's features. You can open an iCloud account to store and share content online, or you can use a computer to download photos, music, or applications from non-Apple online sources such as stores or sharing sites like your local library and transfer them to your iPad through a process called *syncing*. You can also use a computer or iCloud to register your iPad the first time you start it, although if you have an Apple Store nearby you can have them handle the registration for you.

Can you use iPad without owning a computer and just use public Wi-Fi hotspots to go online (or a 3G/4G connection if you have one of those models)? Yes. However, to be able to go online using a Wi-Fi–only iPad and to use many of its built-in features at home, you need to have a home Wi-Fi network available or be lucky enough to live in a town that offers town-wide Wi-Fi (or at least Wi-Fi in your neighborhood). You also need to use iCloud or sync to your computer to get updates for the iPad operating system.

Apple's *iPad User Guide* recommends that you have

- A Mac or PC with a USB 2.0 or USB 3.0 port and one of the following operating systems:
  - Mac OS X version 10.5.8 or later
  - Windows 8, Windows 7, Windows Vista, or Windows XP Home or Professional with Service Pack 3 or later
- iTunes 10.6 or later, available at `www.itunes.com/download`
- An Apple ID and iTunes Store account
- Internet access
- An iCloud account

Apple has set up its iTunes software and the iCloud service to give you two ways to manage content for your iPad — including movies, music, or photos you've downloaded — and specify how to sync your calendar and contact information. Chapter 4 in this minibook covers those settings in more detail.

Getting Your Hands on an iPad

As of this writing, you can buy an iPad at the Apple Store and from several brick-and-mortar stores such as Best Buy, Wal-Mart, Sam's Club, and Target, and at online sites such as MacMall. You can also buy 3G/4G models, which require an account with a phone service provider, from the data providers AT&T and Verizon.

If you get your iPad from Apple, either at one of its retail stores or through its online store, here's the difference in the buying experience.

The brick and mortar Apple Store advantage is that the sales staff will help you unpack your iPad and make sure it's working properly, register the device (which you have to do before you can use it), and help you learn the basics. There are also occasional workshops offered to help people learn about iPads, and Apple employees are famous for being helpful to customers.

However, Apple Stores aren't on every corner, so if visiting one isn't an option (or you just prefer to go it alone), you can go to the Apple Store website (`http://store.apple.com/us/browse/home/shop_ipad/family/ipad`), as shown in Figure 1-2, and order one to be shipped to you (and even get it engraved, if you wish). Standard shipping typically is free, and if there's a problem, Apple's online store customer service reps are very helpful — they will help you solve the problem or possibly replace your iPad.

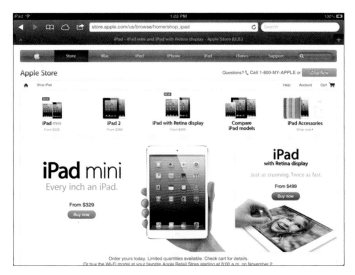

Figure 1-2: iPad model options are spelled out on Apple's site.

Considering iPad Accessories

Accessories for your iPad can make your computing life easier. You can get them from Apple or explore the broad and ever-growing world of third-party accessories.

Apple's stable of accessories

At present, Apple offers a few accessories you might want to check out when you purchase your iPad (or you can purchase them down the road), including:

 iPad Smart Case/Smart Cover: Your iPad isn't cheap and, unlike a laptop computer, it has an exposed screen that can be damaged if you drop or scratch it. Investing in the iPad Smart Case or Smart Cover (note that the Smart Cover and Smart Case don't work with the first generation iPad) is a good idea if you intend to take your iPad out of your house — or if you have a cat or grandchildren. The iPad Smart Cover covers only the front of your device and costs about $40 for polyurethane and $70 for leather, and the Smart Case, which completely surrounds your iPad, costs $49. Other cases vary in price depending on design and material. Look for iPad mini cases to appear from various vendors as this brand new size iPad begins to show up everywhere.

The official Apple iPad Smart Cover and Case have an ingenious little slot on the back. You can flip the front cover back and tuck it into the slot to make the case rest on your desk or counter at a very handy angle for viewing and typing. You can also prop up the case in a kind of U-shaped configuration to give presentations to others.

✔ **iPad Camera Connection Kit:** Because there's no USB port on an iPad, you can't use a USB connection to upload photos from your digital camera or media card to your iPad. If you want to add this functionality, you can use this handy kit. It will set you back about $30 for the privilege.

✔ **Apple iPad Dock/Apple iPad 2 Dock:** The iPad is light and thin, which is great, but holding it all the time can get tedious. The iPad 2 Dock (see Figure 1-3) lets you prop it up so you can view it hands-free while you charge the battery and sync content to your computer. At about $30, it's a good investment for ease and comfort. Be sure to get the dock that matches your iPad model.

Figure 1-3: The simple, but useful, iPad 2 Dock.

✔ **iPad Keyboard Dock:** The iPad provides an onscreen keyboard that's passable, especially if you position it to view things in landscape orientation. However, if you're a touch typist who wants to write long notes or e-mails, or you want to use the iPad as a primary computing device, the iPad Keyboard Dock or a wireless keyboard could be a must-have. You get some dedicated keys for brightness and volume control, a lock key, and some iPod controls. However, you can use the Keyboard Dock with your iPad only in portrait mode and only with an original iPad. You can also use an Apple Wireless Keyboard or any Bluetooth keyboard with your iPad, which costs about $70 as well. You can also explore Bluetooth keyboards from other manufacturers.

✔ **Apple Earphones with Remote and Mic:** There are two versions of these: in-ear and not-so in-ear. They both offer remote control of your audio.

✔ **Apple Digital AV Adapter:** To make use of the Thunderbolt technology that allows you to connect devices to output high-definition media as well as using HDMI connections, you can buy this adapter (see Figure 1-4) for about $30. Although there are hardly any devices out there that use this technology, they're coming soon.

Figure 1-4: Send media to other devices using this adapter.

✓ **Apple Component AV Cable/Apple Composite AV Cable:** These accessories sell for about $40 each and let you connect your iPad 2 or third- or fourth-generation iPad to certain TV or stereo systems.

✓ **Printers:** Several printers from companies such as Hewlett-Packard, Canon, and Epson work with iPad's native printing capability to handle wireless printing. These printers range in price from about $100 to about $250, and you can browse all models at the online Apple Store (`http://store.apple.com`). AirPrint Activator 2 and Printopia are Macintosh apps that can make any printer shared on a network accessible to your iPad.

It's a good idea to have a spare cable available to charge your iPad in case one gets mislaid. Note that if you bought an iPhone 5, the cables are no longer interchangeable as they once were.

Checking out what others have to offer

If you want to explore third-party accessories, there are many, and more appear all the time. Just perform a search for *iPad accessories*. You'll find that there are suede, leather, neoprene, aluminum, and canvas cases; a variety of stands; carrying bags; screen protectors; and external batteries to supplement iPad's impressive ten-hour battery life. LEVO even offers an iPad stand through several online retailers, such as Amazon, so you can lie down and view the screen without having to use your hands; this, I assume, is for those days when you are *really* tired or suffering from carpal tunnel syndrome.

Want to stand out from the crowd by carrying your iPad around in a case with character? The Macally microsuede case is a good option that folds like the Apple Case so you can use your iPad as a presentation unit. If you're made of money, the Louis Vuitton model at about $400 will make you the envy of your friends. And eBags offers some nice canvas bags if your tastes, and budget, are more down-to-earth.

A good alternative to Apple's Keyboard Dock is Macally's BTKey, a fully extended keyboard with a number pad, which you can use with your iPad device in portrait or landscape mode. This neat device also works with your iPhone and most Macs and Bluetooth-enabled PCs.

There are even a few clothing companies coming up with duds that can hold an iPad. (Steve Wozniak is on the board of SCOTTEVEST, as shown in Figure 1-5, which offers a line of iPad-holding clothes.) iClothing and iPad Suit are following suit — excuse the pun.

Don't bother buying a wireless mouse to connect with your iPad via Bluetooth — the iPad recognizes your finger as its primary input device, and mice need not apply. However if you're finger-clumsy, you can also get a stylus for touch input. The Wacom Bamboo is among those that I like.

Figure 1-5: Wear your iPad with style.

Chapter 2: Getting Started with iPad

In This Chapter

- ✔ Discovering what's in the box
- ✔ Getting your first look at the gadget
- ✔ Charging the battery
- ✔ Powering on your iPad and registering it
- ✔ Using the touchscreen
- ✔ Getting familiar with the split keyboard
- ✔ Making sure your operating system is up to date
- ✔ Discovering multitasking gestures
- ✔ Taking a first look at iPad's camera
- ✔ Understanding how to customize the side switch
- ✔ Becoming familiar with the Status bar
- ✔ Locking your iPad, turning it off, and unlocking it

After you get your hands on an iPad, you can explore what's in the box and get an overview of the buttons and slots you'll encounter — luckily, there are very few of them.

You also need to get comfortable with the touch-screen. If you have an iPhone or iPod touch, you're ahead of the game here, but even if you do, you should take a little time to get comfortable with using the larger-format screen.

iPads (with the exception of the original iPad) have two cameras and a customizable side switch. In addition, iPad has native printing ability, all of which I introduce you to here.

Finally, after a tough day of playing with your new gadget, you need to know how to put it to sleep. I cover all these iPad basics in this chapter.

Exploring What's in the Box

When you fork over your hard-earned money for your iPad, you're left holding one box about the size of a package of copy paper. Here's what you'll find when you take off the shrink wrap and open the box:

- ✒ **iPad:** Your iPad is covered in two plastic sheets you can take off and toss. (Unless you think there's a chance you'll return it, in which case you might want to keep all packaging for 14 days — Apple's return period.)

- ✒ **Documentation (and I use the term loosely):** You find a small white envelope under the iPad itself, about the size of a half-dozen index cards. Open it, and you'll find

  - *A tiny, useless pamphlet:* This pamphlet, named Important Product Information Guide, is essentially small print (that you mostly don't need to read) from folks like the FCC.

  - *A mysterious label sheet:* This contains two white Apple logo stickers. (Not sure what they're for, but my husband and I use one of these stickers to differentiate my iPad from his.)

  - *A small card containing the actual documentation (sort of):* This displays a picture of the iPad and callouts to its buttons on one side, and the other side contains about three sentences of instructions for setting it up and info about where to go online to find out more.

- ✒ **Lightning to USB Cable (fourth-generation iPad and iPad mini)/Dock Connector to USB Cable (all other iPad models):** Use this cord (see Figure 2-1) to connect the iPad to your computer, or use it with the last item in the box, which is the . . .

- ✒ **10W USB Power Adapter:** The power adapter (see Figure 2-1) attaches to the Lightning to USB Cable (or the Dock Connector to USB Cable) so you can plug it into the wall and charge the battery.

That's it. That's all there is in the box. It's kind of the typical Apple study in Zen-like simplicity.

Lightning to USB Cable   10W USB Power Adapter

Figure 2-1: Some pretty simple gadgets for power and USB connections.

Taking a First Look at the Gadget

The little card contained in the documentation (see the preceding section) gives you a picture of the iPad with callouts to the buttons you'll find on it. In this section, I give you a bit more information about those buttons and some other physical features of the iPad. Figure 2-2 shows you where each of these items is located.

Here's the rundown on what these things are and what they do:

✔ **(The all-important) Home button:** Before the 4.2 update to iOS, you had to go back to the Home screen to do just about anything. If you were browsing online and wanted to open the calendar, you pushed the Home button and you'd exit the web browser and end up on the Home screen, where you could tap one of the application icons, such as the Calendar app (or whatever app you wanted to use), to open it. After iOS 4.2 added the ability to *multitask* (have various apps open at the same time and switch among them), you didn't have to use the Home button to first return to the Home screen and then open another app; rather, you display a multi-tasking bar of apps and choose one from there. However, it's still the case that no matter where you are or what you're doing, you can push Home and you're back to home base.

Figure 2-2: There are probably fewer gizmos to get used to on an iPad than on your cellphone.

✔ **Sleep/Wake button:** You can use this button to power up your iPad, put it in sleep mode, wake it up, or power it down (more about this in the final section of this chapter).

✔ **Lightning Connector (fourth-generation iPad and iPad mini)/Dock Connector slot (all other iPad models):** This is where you plug in the Lightning to USB Cable/Dock Connector to USB Cable to charge your battery or sync with your computer (which you find out more about in Chapter 5 of this minibook). Also use this slot for the Camera Connection Kit or to connect various AV adapter cables.

✔ **Cameras:** iPads (except for the original iPad) offer front- and rear-facing cameras that you can use to shoot photos or video. The rear one is on the top-right corner, and you need to be careful not to put your thumb over it when taking shots. (I have several very nice photos of my thumb already.)

✓ **Silent/Screen Rotation Lock switch:** In case you hadn't heard, the iPad screen rotates to match the angle you're holding it at. If you want to stick with one orientation even if you spin the iPad in circles, you can use this little switch to lock the screen, which is especially handy when reading an e-book. (Note that some apps can override this functionality if they require one orientation or the other.) You can also customize the function of this switch using iPad General Settings to make the switch mute sounds instead of locking the screen rotation.

✓ **(A tiny, mighty) mono speaker:** One of the nice surprises I had when I first got my iPad was the great little sound system it has and how much sound can come out of this little speaker. The speaker is located on the bottom edge of the screen below the Home button.

✓ **Volume:** This is a volume rocker you use like any other volume rocker: Tap up for more volume and down for less. With iOS 5 and iOS 6, you can use this rocker as a camera shutter button when the camera is activated.

✓ **Headphone jack and microphone:** If you want to listen to your music in private, you can plug a 3.5mm minijack headphone and some ⅛" headphones in here (including an iPhone headset, if you have one, which gives you bidirectional sound). There's also a tiny microphone that makes it possible to speak into your iPad to do things like make phone calls using the Internet, video calling services, or other apps that accept audio input.

Charging the Battery

You've heard about the awesome ten-hour battery life on your iPad, and it's all true. My iPad showed up almost fully charged from the Apple Store, but even if you got yours shipped, it should've been at least partially charged. But all batteries run down eventually (the little battery icon in the iPad Status bar will tell you when you're running low), so one of your first priorities is to know how to recharge your battery. This is a pretty obvious procedure, given the few items that come with your iPad, but just in case you need help, you can follow these steps to get that battery meter up to 100 percent:

1. **Gather your iPad, connector cord, and power adapter.**

2. **Gently plug the USB end of the Lightning to USB Cable (or the Dock Connector to USB Cable) into the USB Power Adapter.**

3. **Plug the other end of the cord (see Figure 2-3) into the Lightning Connector (or Dock Connector slot) on the iPad.**

Attach the USB connector . . .

to the power adapter.   Then plug this end into the iPad.

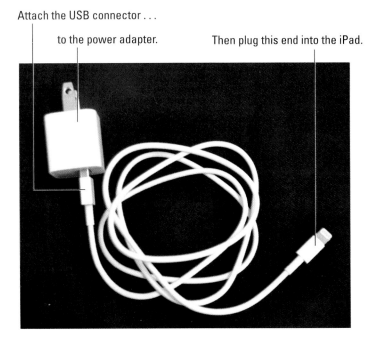

Figure 2-3: Assembling the connector cord and power adapter to charge the iPad battery.

4. **Unfold the two metal prongs on the power adapter (refer to Figure 2-3) so they extend from it at a 90-degree angle, and plug the adapter into an electrical outlet.**

If you buy the iPad Dock or the iPad Keyboard Dock accessory ($29.99) for an original iPad, you can charge your iPad while it's resting in the dock. Just plug the larger end of the connector cord into the back of the dock instead of the bottom of the iPad.

Turning iPad On and Registering It

Apple has done a pretty nice job of getting folks to sign up for its services, such as iTunes and iCloud, whether Apple product owners want to. In fact, the first time you turn on your iPad, you have to register it using either a connection to a computer with the latest version of iTunes installed before you can get it to do anything at all, or you can use Apple's new iCloud service to register PC Free. This section covers both methods.

Registering iPad using a computer

After you have an iTunes account (Chapter 5 in this minibook provides details of getting set up with an iTunes account if you don't have one), hold the iPad with one hand on either side, oriented like a pad of paper, and then follow these steps to register it:

1. **Press and hold the Sleep/Wake button on the top of your iPad until the Apple logo appears.**

   In another moment a screen appears, asking whether you want to register via iCloud or use iTunes. If you choose via iCloud, you can simply follow directions to register. If you want to use iTunes, tap the iTunes option and proceed. (If you prefer to register using iCloud instead, see the next section.)

2. **Plug the Lightning to USB Cable (or the Dock Connector to USB Cable) that came with your device into your iPad.**

3. **Plug the other end into a USB port on your computer.**

   Both your computer and iPad think for a few moments while they exchange some data.

4. **Sign in to your iTunes account in the dialog that appears on your computer's screen, and then follow the simple onscreen instructions to register your iPad and choose what content is automatically downloaded when you connect your iPad to your computer.**

   (You can change these settings later; see Chapter 4 in this minibook.)

   During registration you also get to choose a language and country; choose a network; agree to terms and conditions; choose to use the Find My iPad service; choose to use the Siri feature (available only on third- and fourth-generation iPads and iPad mini); select whether to automatically send information about your iPad to Apple; and choose whether to allow location services to use your current location. (If you're not sure about these options, you can accept or decline any of them, and then you can change these settings later using various settings discussed throughout this book.) When you're done, your iPad Home screen appears, and you're in business.

5. **Unplug the Lightning to USB Cable (or the Dock Connector to USB Cable).**

If you buy your iPad at an Apple Store, the Apple Store representatives register it for you, and you can avoid getting an iTunes account right away and in fact skip this whole process (though you'll probably want to get an iTunes account to get at the treasure trove of content and apps, some of which are free).

You can choose to have certain items transferred to your iPad from your computer when you sync, including music, videos, downloaded apps, contacts, calendars, e-books, podcasts, and browser bookmarks. You can also transfer to your computer content you download directly to your iPad using the iTunes and App Store apps as well as content you gather through the

Newsstand, iBooks, Podcasts, and iTunesU apps. See Book II, Chapter 1 for more about these features.

Registering PC Free using iCloud

In Step 1 of the preceding section, you might choose to register your device via iCloud. In that case, to use iCloud, you need to have access to a Wi-Fi hotspot or have a 3G or 4G iPad so you can connect directly to the Internet.

When you make this choice, rather than signing into iTunes, you provide an Apple ID. If you don't have an Apple ID, you're offered the option of creating one right then and there. That ID will be associated with your iCloud account, and you will use it for various iCloud-supported activities.

You'll also be asked to respond to various questions, such as your preferred language and country. When you finish answering these questions, your iPad is registered without ever having plugged it into a computer.

Meeting the Multi-Touch Screen

When your Home screen appears (see Figure 2-4), you'll see a pretty picture in the background and two sets of icons. One set appears in the Dock along the bottom of the screen. The *Dock* contains the Safari browser, Mail, Photos, and Music app icons by default, though you can add up to two other apps to it. The Dock appears on every Home screen. (You start with one Home screen, but adding new apps creates additional Home screens — up to 11 in all.)

Other icons, the app icons, appear above the Dock and are closer to the top of the screen. (I give you an overview of the functionality of all these icons in Chapter 3 of this minibook.) Different icons appear in this area on each Home screen.

This may or may not need saying, but the screen is made of glass and will smudge when you touch it and break if you throw it at the wall, and contrary to Apple's boasts, can also scratch. So, be careful and treat it nicely.

Connecting with the touchscreen

The iPad touchscreen technology allows you to swipe your finger across the screen or tap it to provide input to the device just as you use a mouse or keyboard with your computer. You read more about that in the next section, but for now, go ahead and play with it for a few minutes. Just as you may have become used to with your mobile phone, you use the pads of your fingertips (not your fingernails) and do the following:

1. Tap the Settings icon.

The various settings (which you read more about throughout this book) appear. (See Figure 2-5.)

Application icons   The Dock

Figure 2-4: Icons for various apps live in the Dock or on a Home screen.

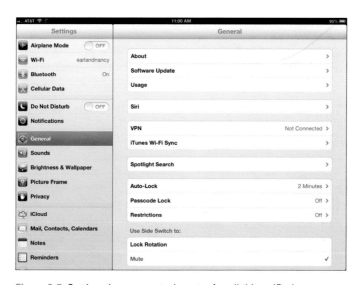

Figure 2-5: Settings is your control center for all things iPad.

2. **To return to the Home screen, press the Home button.**

3. **Swipe a finger or two from right to left on the screen.**

   Because the iPad has a few additional Home screens available (11, to be exact) that you can fill up with all the apps you'll be downloading, the screen shifts slightly to the left. (If you have more apps downloaded, filling additional Home screens, this action moves you to the next Home screen.)

   With multiple Home screens in use, you get little dots at the bottom of the screen above the Dock icons, indicating which of the Home screens you're on. You can tap to the right or left of the dots to move one screen in either direction.

4. **To experience the rotating screen feature, while holding the iPad firmly, turn it sideways.**

   The screen flips to a horizontal orientation. If it doesn't, check the Screen Orientation Lock to make sure it's not active.

5. **To flip the screen back, just turn the device so it's oriented like a pad of paper again.**

6. **Tap Music in the Dock.**

7. **Practice multitasking by double-tapping the Home button.**

   All running apps appear in a bar along the bottom of the screen.

8. **Swipe to scroll through the apps and tap one to jump to it without going back to the Home screen.**

You can customize the Home screen by changing the wallpaper and brightness. Read about making these changes in Chapter 8 of this minibook.

Goodbye click-and-drag, hello tap-and-swipe

If you're like me, you'll fall in love with the touchscreen interface that iPad sports. It's just so intuitive using your finger as a pointing device — something you're probably already doing on your iPhone or other mobile device.

There are several methods you can use for getting around and getting things done in iPad using its Multi-Touch screen, including:

✏ **Tap once:** To open an application on the Home screen, choose a field such as a search box, select an item in a list, select an arrow to move back or forward one screen, or follow an online link, tap the item once with your finger.

✏ **Tap twice:** Use this method to enlarge or reduce the display of a web page (see Chapter 6 in this minibook for more about using the Safari web browser) or zoom in or out in the Maps app.

✔ **Pinch and unpinch:** As an alternative to the tap-twice method, you can pinch or unpinch your fingers on the screen (see Figure 2-6) when you're looking at photos, maps, web pages, or e-mail messages to quickly reduce or enlarge them, respectively.

Figure 2-6: Pinch to zoom in or out on a page.

You can use a three-finger tap to zoom your screen to be even larger or use Multitasking Gestures to swipe with four or five fingers. (See "Exploring Multitasking Gestures," later in this chapter.) This is handy if you have vision challenges. Go to Chapter 3 in this minibook to discover how to turn on this feature using Accessibility features.

✔ **Drag to scroll (known as *swiping*):** When you press your finger to the screen and drag to the right, left, up, or down, you move around the screen. (See Figure 2-7.) Swiping to the right on the Home screen moves you to the *Spotlight screen,* Apple's term for the iPad search screen. Swiping up while reading an online newspaper moves you down the page, while swiping down moves you back up the page.

✔ **Flick:** To scroll more quickly on a page, quickly flick your finger on the screen in the direction you want to move.

✔ **Tap the Status bar:** To move quickly to the top of a list, web page, or e-mail message, tap the Status bar at the top of the iPad screen.

Figure 2-7: Swiping gets you around a screen quickly.

✔ **Press and hold:** If you're in any application where selecting text is an option, such as Notes or Mail, or if you're on a web page, pressing and holding near text will select a word and bring up editing tools that allow you to select, cut, copy, or paste text, and more. You can also use this method to reposition the insertion point under the magnifying glass icon that appears.

Note that since iOS 5's introduction of the Notification Center, you can swipe down from the top of the screen with one finger to display the center, which lists all messages, mail, calendar events, and more in one handy spot.

If you feel like a practice session, try out these actions by following these steps:

1. **Tap the Safari button to display the web browser. (You may be asked to enter your Wi-Fi network password to access the network to go online.)**

2. **Tap a link to move to another page.**

3. **Double-tap the page to enlarge it; then pinch your fingers together on the screen to reduce its size.**

4. **Drag one finger around the page to scroll up or down or side to side.**

5. **Flick your finger quickly on the page to scroll more quickly.**

6. **Press and hold your finger on black text that isn't a link.**

   A magnifying glass icon appears.

7. **Release your finger.**

   The item is selected, and a Copy/Define tool displays, as shown in Figure 2-8.

The Copy tool

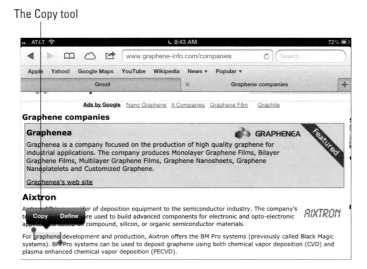

Figure 2-8: Copy text and paste it into an e-mail or document using the Copy tool.

8. **Press and hold your finger on a link or an image.**

   A menu appears with commands that allow you to open the link or picture, open it in a new page, add it to your Reading List (see Chapter 6 in this minibook), or copy it. The image menu also offers a Save Image command.

9. **Put your fingers slightly apart on the screen and then pinch your fingers together to reduce the page.**

10. **Press the Home button to go back to the Home screen.**

Displaying and using the onscreen keyboard

Part of the beauty of iPad is that it's highly portable, but that portability comes at a price: a physical keyboard. You can use a wireless or Bluetooth keyboard, but for short text entry, you don't really need either. That's where the onscreen keyboard comes into play, allowing you to enter text as you may have done on a touchscreen mobile phone screen.

iPad's built-in keyboard appears whenever you're in a text-entry location, such as in a Search field or when writing an e-mail. Follow these steps to practice using the onscreen keyboard:

1. **Tap the Notes icon on the Home screen to open this easy-to-use notepad.**

2. **Tap the note.**

   The onscreen keyboard appears.

3. **Type a few words using the keyboard or, if you own a third- or fourth-generation iPad or iPad mini, you can tap the Dictation key (see Figure 2-9) to activate the Dictation feature, and then speak your input. This requires an active Internet connection as the translation is done on Apple's servers.**

   To get the widest keyboard display possible, rotate your iPad to be in landscape (horizontal) orientation, as shown in Figure 2-9.

4. **If you make a mistake (and you may when you first use it), use the Delete key (the key in the top-right corner with a little *x* on it) to delete text to the left of the insertion point.**

5. **To create a new paragraph, press the Return key, just as you would on a regular computer keyboard.**

6. **To type numbers and some symbols, press one of the number keys (labeled .?123) located on either side of the spacebar (refer to Figure 2-9).**

   Characters on the keyboard change. To return to the letter keyboard at any time, simply tap one of the letter keys (labeled ABC) on either side of the spacebar.

   If you type a number in the number/symbol keyboard and then tap the spacebar, the keyboard automatically returns to the letter keyboard.

Tap in the note...

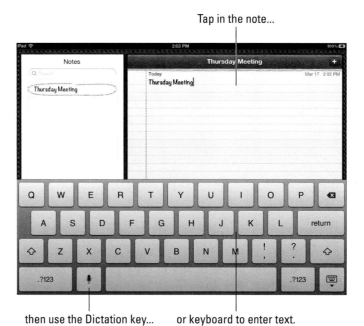

then use the Dictation key...   or keyboard to enter text.

Figure 2-9: The onscreen keyboard is handiest to use in landscape orientation.

7. **Use the Shift keys just as you would on a regular keyboard to type uppercase letters or alternate characters.**

   Tapping this once causes just the next letter you type to be capitalized.

8. **Double-tap the Shift key to turn on the Caps Lock feature so that all letters you type are capitalized until you turn the feature off. Tap the Shift key once to turn it off.**

   You can control whether this feature is available in iPad General Settings under Keyboard.

9. **To type a variation on a symbol (for example, to get alternate currency symbols when you hold down the dollar sign on the numeric keyboard), press the key and hold it until a set of alternate symbols appears (see Figure 2-10).**

   Note that displaying variations on symbols works only on some symbols.

A set of alternate symbols

Figure 2-10: Only some symbols offer alternatives when you press and drag them.

10. **Tap the Dictation key (refer to Figure 2-9) to activate the Dictation feature, and then speak your input.**

    This works in several apps, such as Mail, Notes, and Maps. Tap the Dictation key again (or tap in the note) to turn off the Dictation feature.

11. **To hide the keyboard, press the Keyboard key in the bottom-right corner.**

12. **Tap the Home button to return to the Home screen.**

You can unlock the keyboard to move it around the screen. To do this, press and hold the Keyboard button on the keyboard and, from the pop-up menu that appears, choose Unlock. Now by pressing the Keyboard button and swiping up or down, you can move the keyboard up and down on the screen. To dock the keyboard again at the bottom of the screen, press and hold the Keyboard button and choose Dock from the pop-up menu.

To type a period and space, double-tap the spacebar.

Using the split keyboard

With iOS 5 came the *Split Keyboard* feature. This allows you to split the keyboard so that each side appears nearer the edge of the iPad screen. For those who are into texting with their thumbs, this feature makes it easier to reach all the keys from the sides of the device. The feature is on by default, but if it doesn't work for you it may have been turned off. Use the Keyboard options in iPad's General Settings to turn it on.

1. **Open an application, such as Notes, where you can use the onscreen keyboard.**

2. **Tap in an entry field or page, which displays the onscreen keyboard.**

3. **Place two fingers in the middle of the onscreen keyboard and spread them toward the left and right.**

    The keyboard splits, as shown in Figure 2-11.

4. **Hold the iPad with a hand on either side and practice using your thumbs to enter text.**

Figure 2-11: A split keyboard makes thumb entry quicker.

5. **To rejoin the keyboard, place two fingers on each side of the keyboard and swipe to join them together again.**

When the keyboard is docked and merged at the bottom of your screen, you can also simply press the Keyboard key and swipe upward simultaneously. This undocks and splits the keyboard. To revert this, press and swipe the Keyboard key and swipe downward. The keyboard is docked and merged.

Flicking to search

Can't find that song you downloaded or an e-mail from your boss? You'll be relieved to know that a search feature in iPad called *Spotlight* helps you find photos, music, e-mails, contacts, movies, and more. This search feature can be found on the screen to the left of the default Home screen.

Follow these steps to access and use Spotlight:

1. **Press and drag from left to right on the Home screen, or tap the small magnifying glass symbol farthest to the left at the bottom of the Home screen, to display the Spotlight screen.**

   You can also, from the primary Home screen, tap the left side of the Home button to move one screen to the left.

2. **Tap in the Search iPad field.**

   The keyboard appears. (See Figure 2-12.)

Tap here...

then enter a search term.

Figure 2-12: Use the familiar search box to enter search terms.

3. Begin entering a search term.

In the example in Figure 2-13, I typed the letter *S,* and it came up with a couple of apps, some music I had downloaded, as well as a few e-mail messages. As you continue to type a search term, the results are narrowed down to match.

Figure 2-13: Narrow your search by typing more letters.

4. Tap an item in the search results to open it in the associated app.

To close the app and go back to the search screen, tap the Home button and then tap the left side of the Home button to display the search screen again.

5. To enter a different search term, tap in the search box and tap the circled X at the right end of the box or the Delete key on the keyboard to delete the current term and then enter another.

You can use some standard search techniques to narrow your search. For example, if you want only the e-mails that include both Bob Smith and Jane Jones, enter *"Smith, Jones"* or *"Bob, Jane"* as your search term. To change the search language, tap the key on the onscreen keyboard that looks like a little globe to cycle through available languages.

Updating the Operating System

This book is based on the latest version of the iPad operating system at the time, iOS 6.0. If you have an iPad, to make sure you get the latest and greatest features in iPad, it's a good idea to update right now (and periodically, no matter which model of iPad you have, to receive minor upgrades to 6.0) to the latest iOS. If you've set up an iCloud account on your iPad, updates will happen automatically, or you can update over a Wi-Fi or 3/4G connection by going to Settings⇨General and tapping Software Update.

The iPad may charge itself when connected to certain computers, so if you're updating the iOS from a laptop, plug it in so the battery doesn't drain before the update is complete.

Here's how to update the iOS via a connection with your computer:

1. **Plug the Lightning to USB Cable (or the Dock Connector to USB Cable) into your iPad, and plug the USB end into your computer.**

2. **When iTunes opens on your computer, look for your iPad name in the Devices section in the Source List on the left side of the screen (see Figure 2-14).**

3. **Click your iPad name and then click the Summary tab if it's not already displayed.**

4. **Read the note next to the Check for Update button to see whether your iOS is up to date; if it isn't, click the Check for Update button.**

   iTunes checks to find the latest iOS version and walks you through the updating procedure.

Click on your iPad... then click the Summary tab.

Figure 2-14: Go to the Summary tab to find out whether you need to update iOS.

A new iOS introduces new features for your iPad. If a new iOS appears after you've bought this book, go to the companion website, `www.ipad-madeclear.com`, for updates on new features.

Understanding Multitasking Basics

Multitasking means that you can easily switch from one app to another without closing the first one and returning to the Home screen. You do this by means of a handy little scrolling menu along the bottom of the iPad screen. Follow these steps to multitask:

1. **Open an app.**

2. **Double-tap the Home button.**

3. **On the horizontal bar that appears beneath the Dock at the bottom of the screen (see Figure 2-15), flick to scroll to the left or right until you find the second open app you want to switch to.**

Figure 2-15: The multitasking bar.

4. **Tap the app to display it.**

At the left end of the multitasking bar (you may have to scroll to the left to see them) are controls for volume and playback, as well as a button that locks and unlocks screen rotation so that the screen changes based on how you are holding your iPad or mutes the sound, depending on which feature you've set up for the side switch to activate (you do that in the General Settings).

Exploring Multitasking Gestures

Multitasking involves jumping from one app to another. Introduced in iOS 5 were some gestures you can tell the system to activate so you can use four or five fingers to multitask. You can turn on these gestures by tapping Settings on the Home screen, and then in the General Settings, tap the On/Off button for Multitasking Gestures.

Here are the three gestures you can then use:

✔ Swipe up with four or five fingers on any Home screen to reveal the multitasking bar.

✔ Swipe down with four or five fingers to remove the multitasking bar from the Home screen.

✔ With an app open, swipe left or right using four or five fingers, and you move to another app.

Examining Your iPad Cameras

iPad 2 introduced front- and rear-facing cameras to the iPad hardware feature list. You can use the cameras to take still photos (covered in more detail in Book II, Chapter 4) or shoot videos (covered in Book II, Chapter 4). The fourth-generation iPad introduced a higher quality FaceTime front-facing camera useful for making video calls. For now, take a quick look at your cameras by tapping the Camera app icon on the Home screen. An image appears, as shown in Figure 2-16.

There's good news and bad news. The good news is that the third-generation iPad introduced a super-clear Retina display and 5-megapixel rear-facing iSight camera for viewing and taking the best iPad-generated photos and video yet. The fourth-generation and iPad mini also offer this super great display. The bad news is that if you own a first-generation iPad, you have no cameras at all.

Controls located around the screen allow you to

✔ Switch between the front and rear cameras.

✔ Change from a still camera to a video camera operation using the Camera/Video slider.

✔ Take a picture or start recording a video.

✔ Turn on a grid to help you autofocus on still photo subjects.

✔ Open the previously captured image or video.

When you view a photo or video, you can use several features to do things like send the image by posting it to Facebook or send it by e-mail or as a tweet, print an image, use a still photo as wallpaper or assign it to a contact, and run a slideshow or edit a video. See Book II, Chapters 3 and 4 for more details about using iPad cameras.

Take photo or start recording.

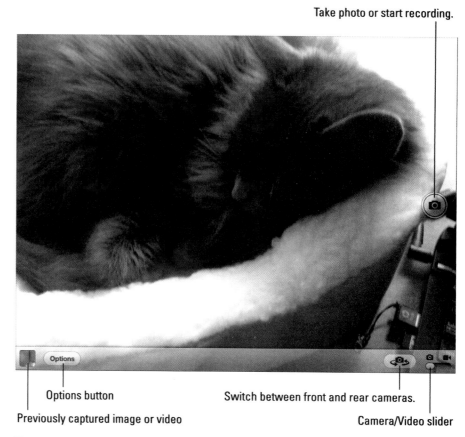

Options button

Previously captured image or video

Switch between front and rear cameras.

Camera/Video slider

Figure 2-16: Simple tools let you start and stop a recording or switch between cameras.

Customizing the Silent/Screen Rotation Lock Switch

Starting with iOS 4.3, you had the ability to customize the switch on the top-right side of your iPad (holding it in vertical orientation). Use these steps to set it up to either control the screen orientation or mute sound:

1. **From the Home screen, tap the Settings icon.**

2. **Under General Settings, tap either the Lock Rotation or Mute option under the Use Side Switch To section to choose which feature you want the switch to control.**

3. **Tap the Home button to return to the Home screen.**

4. **Move the side switch up or down to toggle between the settings you chose: screen rotation locked or unlocked, or sound muted or unmuted.**

If you choose to use the side switch to mute or unmute system sound, you can use an icon on the multitasking bar (double-tap the Home button to display this and flick to scroll all the way to the left side of the bar) to lock and unlock the screen rotation. This works the same way if you have set up the switch to handle screen rotation and want to mute or unmute the sound using the multitasking bar.

Exploring the Status Bar

Across the top of your iPad screen is a Status bar. (See Figure 2-17.) Little icons in this area can provide some useful information, such as the time, your battery charge, or the status of your wireless connection. Table 2-1 lists some of the most common items you'll find on the Status bar.

Though it doesn't sport an icon you can swipe down on the Status bar to display the Notification Center. This handy drop down window shows you all your alerts, updates, and appointments and more in one place.

iPad 🛜 📶   3:30 PM   🔄 ▶ 79% 🔋

Figure 2-17: The Status bar provides some handy info about your iPad.

Table 2-1		Common Status Bar Icons
Icon	*Name*	*What It Indicates*
🛜	Wi-Fi	You're connected to a Wi-Fi network.
✳️	Activity	Something's in progress, such as a web page loading.
2:55 PM	Time	You guessed it: the time.
🔄	Screen Rotation Lock	The screen is locked and will not rotate when you turn the iPad.
▶	Play	A media element (such as a song or video) is playing.
100% 🔋	Battery Life	The percentage of charge your battery has left. (It changes to a lightning bolt when the battery is charging.)

If you have GPS, 3G or 4G, Bluetooth devices, and/or a connection to a virtual private network (VPN), symbols appear on the Status bar when these are active. The GPS and 3G icons appear only with 3G/4G-enabled iPad models. If you have a 3G/4G model but no 3G/4G available, you may see an icon for EDGE. If you're out of range of 3G/4G and EDGE, you see GPRS. Essentially, iPad tries for the best connection and then jumps to a lesser connection if the best isn't available. Note that 3G and EDGE are the only ones of the three that allow both voice and data transmission.

Locking iPad, Turning It Off, or Unlocking It

You've seen how simple it is to turn the power on for your iPad earlier in this chapter. Now it's time to put it to *sleep* (the iPad screen goes black, but iPad can quickly awaken again) or turn off the power to give your new toy a rest. Here are the procedures you can use:

✔ **Press the Sleep/Wake button.** iPad goes to sleep, and the screen goes black. If iPad is asleep, pressing the Sleep/Wake button does its wake-up thing. If you set up a Passcode Lock under iPad's General Settings you would have to provide a passcode to wake your iPad up.

 If you bought a Smart Cover or Smart Case with your iPad, just fold the cover over the front of the screen, and iPad goes to sleep; open the cover to wake up the iPad. See Chapter 1 in this minibook for more about iPad accessories.

✔ **Press the Home button and then use the Slide to Unlock bar.** This wakes up iPad. Swipe the onscreen arrow on the Slide to Unlock bar (see Figure 2-18) to unlock the iPad.

Figure 2-18: Use the Slide to Unlock bar to wake up iPad.

 Wondering about that little flower symbol (refer to Figure 2-18) in the lower-right corner of a sleeping iPad's screen? That's the Slideshow button. Tap it if you want a cool slideshow of the images in Photos displayed on the sleep screen. The Slide to Unlock area disappears, but you can get it back by pressing the Home button on your iPad. See Book II, Chapter 4, for more about working with Photos.

✓ **Press and hold the Sleep/Wake button until the Slide to Power Off bar appears at the top of the screen, and then swipe the bar.** You've just turned off your iPad.

✓ **Use the Smart Cover or Smart Case accessory.** When you attach the Smart Cover and close it over your screen, iPad goes to sleep automatically.

TIP

iPad automatically goes into sleep mode after a few minutes of inactivity. You can change the time interval at which it sleeps by adjusting the Auto-Lock feature in Settings. (I tell you how to do that in Chapter 8 of this minibook.)

Chapter 3: iPad Accessibility Settings

In This Chapter

✓ Setting brightness and changing the wallpaper

✓ Using zoom, inverting screen colors, and displaying larger text

✓ Setting up VoiceOver and Speak Auto-text

✓ Adjusting volume and settings to help you hear more easily

✓ Using the touchscreen with ease

✓ Utilizing the Dictation feature

✓ Focused learning with Guided Access

*i*Pad users are all different; some face visual, dexterity, or hearing challenges. If you're one of those folks, you'll be glad to hear that iPad offers some handy accessibility features.

To help you read your screen more easily, a Zoom feature lets you enlarge the screen even more than the standard unpinch gesture on the touchscreen does. There's even an Invert Screen Colors option, which offers a photo-negative effect producing a dark background with white lettering that some people find helpful when reading text. You can also set up a VoiceOver feature to read onscreen elements out loud. iPad uses the Speak Auto-text feature to tell you whenever text you enter in any iPad application is autocorrected or capitalized. You can also set a larger text size for your iPad to bring text into better focus.

If hearing is your challenge, there's a setting for Mono Audio that's useful when you're wearing headphones or playing sound through an attached speaker system. Rather than breaking up sounds in a stereo effect, this setting puts all the sound in each ear. If you have more trouble hearing in one ear than in the other, this option can help make sounds clearer.

For those who struggle with using the touchscreen and gestures, you can take advantage of the AssistiveTouch control pane. If typing text is painful or difficult for you, consider the Dictation feature (not available on the original iPad or iPad 2), which enables you to speak text instead of typing.

Finally, the Guided Access feature introduced with iOS 6 provides help for those who have difficulty focusing on one task and also provides a handy mode for showing presentations of content in settings where you don't want users to flit off to other apps, as in school or a public kiosk.

In this chapter, you get some highlights of the accessibility settings you're likely to need most often and advice for how to use them.

Features to Help You See Better

You might as well set up the visual side of iPad first so your interaction with the device is easy on the eyes and battery power. There are two such settings that fall together as one category in the Settings: Brightness & Wallpaper dialog. In addition, you discover other settings that change how iPad appears and interacts with you using sound rather than visuals.

Setting brightness

Especially when using iPad as an e-book reader, you may find a little less brightness in the display reduces strain on your eyes. Also, reducing the brightness can save a little on your iPad's battery life.

To adjust screen brightness, follow these steps:

1. **Tap the Settings icon on the Home screen.**

2. **In the Settings pane, as shown in Figure 3-1, tap Brightness & Wallpaper.**

Figure 3-1: Brightness and wallpaper settings are combined in one dialog.

3. **To control brightness manually, tap the Auto-Brightness On/Off button (refer to Figure 3-1) to turn it off.**

4. **Tap and drag the Brightness slider to the right to make the screen brighter or to the left to make it dimmer.**

5. **Tap the Home button to close the Settings dialog.**

If glare from the screen is a problem for you, consider getting a screen protector. This thin film not only protects your screen from damage, but can also reduce glare. These are available from a wide variety of sources (just search for *iPad screen protector*) and cost anywhere from $2 to $24 each.

In the iBooks app, you can set a sepia tone for book pages, which might be easier on your eyes. See Book II, Chapter 7 for more about using iBooks.

Changing the wallpaper

Just as your desktop computer or laptop can display a pretty picture or pattern as a desktop background called a *wallpaper,* your iPad can display an image on the Home screen and another picture when your iPad is locked.

The picture of a blue pool of water that's the default iPad image may be pretty, but it may not be the background that's best for you. Choosing different wallpaper may help you to see all the icons on your Home screen, or just allow you to display an image that appeals to your artistic sensibilities.

To change the wallpaper, do this:

1. **Tap the Settings icon on the Home screen, and then, in the Settings pane, tap Brightness & Wallpaper.**

2. **In the Brightness & Wallpaper settings that appear, tap the arrow to the right of the iPad images displayed in the Wallpaper section (refer to Figure 3-1).**

3. **In the screen that appears (see Figure 3-2), tap Wallpaper to display all the built-in wallpaper images.**

You can also use your own picture for your wallpaper. Instead of choosing Wallpaper, tap Camera Roll, Photo Stream, or Photo Library or choose any listed photo album to browse your saved photos, select the picture you want to assign, and then resume with Step 5.

Figure 3-2: Tap to reveal Wallpaper settings.

4. **In the Wallpaper pane (see Figure 3-3), tap a wallpaper image.**

A preview of that wallpaper appears onscreen.

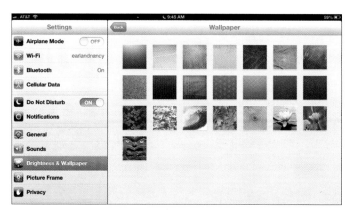

Figure 3-3: Choose from various built-in wallpapers.

5. **Tap Set Lock Screen (the screen that appears when you lock the iPad by tapping the power button), Set Home Screen (to use as the wallpaper), or Set Both.**

6. **Tap the Home button.**

You return to your Home screen with the new wallpaper set as the background.

Turning on Zoom

Normally, you can increase the size of things on your screen by double-tapping with two fingers. However, the Zoom feature enlarges the contents displayed on the iPad screen even more when you double-tap the screen with three fingers.

To turn on the Zoom feature, follow these steps:

1. **Tap the Settings icon on the Home screen and then tap General.**

2. **In General Settings, swipe upward to find Accessibility and then tap it.**

   The Accessibility pane shown in Figure 3-4 appears.

Figure 3-4: The Accessibility pane.

3. **Tap Zoom.**

4. **In the Zoom pane, as shown in Figure 3-5, tap the Zoom On/Off button to turn on the feature.**

Tap to turn on Zoom.

Figure 3-5: Tap and drag the Zoom On/Off button to turn it on or off.

5. **Double-tap the screen using three fingers to enlarge it.**

6. **Press three fingers on the screen and drag to move around it.**

7. **Double-tap with three fingers again to go back to regular magnification.**

8. **Tap the Home button to close Settings.**

This Zoom feature works pretty much everywhere in iPad: in Photos, on web pages, in Mail, and in Music and Videos. Give it a try!

Turning on Invert Colors

Invert Colors is an accessibility setting that reverses colors on your screen so that backgrounds are black and text is white. This can help people with particular vision challenges to read text more easily.

To turn on this feature:

1. **Tap the Settings icon on the Home screen and then tap General.**

2. **Tap Accessibility.**

3. **In the Accessibility pane, as shown in Figure 3-6, tap the Invert Colors On/Off button to turn it on.**

   The colors on the screen invert, as shown in Figure 3-7.

Tap to invert colors.

Figure 3-6: Turning on the Invert Colors setting can help you read text more easily.

The Invert Colors feature works great in some places and not so well in others. For example, in the Photos application, pictures appear almost as photo negatives. Your Home screen image will likewise look a bit strange. And don't even think of playing a video with this feature turned on! However, if you need help reading text, Invert Colors can be very useful in several applications.

Figure 3-7: The effect of turning on the Invert Colors setting.

Turning on Large Text

If having larger text in apps such as Contacts, Mail, and Notes would be help-ful to you, you can turn on the Large Text feature and choose the text size that works best for you. To turn on Large Text, follow these steps:

1. **Tap the Settings icon on the Home screen.**

2. **Under the General Settings, tap Accessibility.**

3. **In the Accessibility pane, tap the Large Text button to turn on the feature.**

4. **In the list of text sizes, as shown in Figure 3-8, tap the one you prefer.**

Figure 3-8: Choose your text size here.

Setting up VoiceOver

VoiceOver reads the names of screen elements and settings to you, but it also changes the way you interact with iPad. In Notes, for example, you can have VoiceOver read the name of the Notes app button to you, and when you enter Notes, it reads any words or characters you've entered, and tell you whether features such as Auto-Correction are on.

To turn on the feature, follow these steps:

1. **Tap the Settings icon on the Home screen and then tap General.**

2. **Tap Accessibility.**

3. **In the Accessibility pane, as shown in Figure 3-9, tap the VoiceOver button.**

Tap this option.

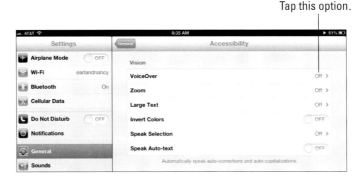

Figure 3-9: VoiceOver reads onscreen elements to you.

4. **In the VoiceOver pane, as shown in Figure 3-10, tap the VoiceOver On/ Off button to turn it on.**

   The first time you turn on the feature, you see a dialog noting that turning on VoiceOver changes gestures used to interact with iPad. Tap OK once to select it and then tap OK twice to proceed.

5. **Tap the VoiceOver Practice button to select it, and then double-tap to open VoiceOver Practice.**

   This is the new method of tapping that VoiceOver activates.

6. **Practice using gestures, such as pinching or flicking left.**

   VoiceOver tells you what action each gesture initiates.

Tap to turn on Voice Over.

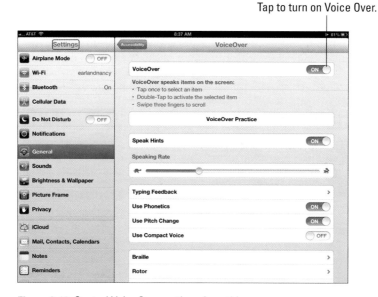

Figure 3-10: Control VoiceOver settings from this pane.

It's important that you first single-tap to select an item such as a button, which causes VoiceOver to read the name of the button to you. Then double-tap the button to activate its function. (VoiceOver reminds you to do this if you turn on Speak Hints, which is a help when you first use VoiceOver but gets annoying after a short time.)

7. **Tap the Done button and then double-tap it to return to the VoiceOver pane.**

8. **Tap the Speak Hints field so that VoiceOver speaks the name of each tapped item; double-tap the slider to turn off Speak Hints.**

   If you find the rate of the voice too fast or slow, double-tap the slider and move the slider to the left to slow it down or to the right to speed it up.

9. **If you want VoiceOver to read words or characters to you (for example, in the Notes app), tap and then double-tap Typing Feedback.**

10. **In the Typing Feedback dialog, tap to select the option you prefer.**

    The Words option will read words but not characters such as $ (dollar sign). The Characters and Words option reads both.

You can now press the Home button and start to use other apps with the VoiceOver feature enabled. Be sure to review the next section to find out how to navigate your iPad now that you have turned on VoiceOver.

You can change the language that VoiceOver speaks. In General Settings, choose International, then Language, and select another language. This will, however, also change the language used for labels on Home screen icons and various settings and fields in iPad.

You can use the Set Triple-Click Home Accessibility setting to help you more quickly turn the VoiceOver or Invert Colors feature on and off. In the Accessibility pane, tap Triple-Click Home. In the dialog that appears, choose what you want a Home button triple-click to do: turn on Guided Access (the default); toggle VoiceOver on or off; toggle Invert Colors on or off; toggle the Zoom feature on or off; or toggle the AssistiveTouch Control Panel. Now a triple-click with a single finger on the Home button provides you with the option you selected wherever you go in iPad.

Now that VoiceOver is turned on, you need to know how it works. I won't kid you; using it is a bit tricky at first, but you'll get the hang of it! Here are the main onscreen gestures you should know:

- Tap an item to select it, and VoiceOver speaks its name.
- Double-tap a selected item to activate it.
- Flick three fingers to scroll.

Table 3-1 provides additional gestures that will help you use VoiceOver. I suggest that, if you want to use this feature often, you read the "VoiceOver" section of the iPad online User Guide, which goes into a great deal of detail about the ins and outs of using VoiceOver.

Table 3-1	VoiceOver Gestures
Gesture	*Effect*
Flick right or left.	Select next or preceding item.
Tap with two fingers.	Stop speaking current item.
Flick two fingers up.	Read everything from the top of the screen.
Flick two fingers down.	Read everything from the current position.
Flick up or down with three fingers.	Scroll one page at a time.
Flick right or left with three fingers.	Go to next or preceding page.
Tap three fingers.	Speak the scroll status (for example, line 20 of 100).
Flick four fingers up or down.	Go to first or last element on a page.
Flick four fingers right or left.	Go to next or preceding section (as on a web page).

Check out some other settings for VoiceOver, including a choice for Braille, Language Rotor for language choices, the ability to navigate images, and a setting to have iPad speak notifications.

Utilizing iPad's Speak Auto-text

Speak Auto-text is a feature that speaks autocorrections and autocapitalizations (you can turn on both these features using Keyboard settings). When you enter text in an application, such as Pages or Mail, and the app then makes either type of change, Speak Auto-text lets you know what change was made.

To turn on Speak Auto-text, follow these steps:

1. **Tap the Settings icon on the Home screen and then tap General.**
2. **In the General Settings pane, tap Accessibility.**
3. **In the Accessibility pane, as shown in Figure 3-11, tap the Speak Auto-text On/Off button to turn on the feature.**

Tap to turn on Speak Auto-text.

Settings	General	Accessibility	
Airplane Mode	OFF	Vision	
Wi-Fi	earlandnancy	VoiceOver	Off >
Bluetooth	On	Zoom	Off >
Cellular Data		Large Text	Off >
Do Not Disturb	OFF	Invert Colors	OFF
Notifications		Speak Selection	Off >
General		Speak Auto-text	OFF
Sounds		Automatically speak auto-corrections and auto-capitalizations.	

Figure 3-11: Let iPad speak to you.

Why would you want iPad to tell you when an autocorrection has been made? If you have vision challenges and you know you typed "ain't" when writing dialogue for a character in your novel, but iPad corrected it to "isn't," you'd want to know, right? Similarly, if you typed the poet's name "e.e. Cummings" and autocapitalization corrected it (incorrectly), you need to know immediately so you can change it back again!

Hearing Better

In the hearing category, you can do two things: adjust the volume level for all apps on your iPad and modify how sounds play when you're using headphones or an attached speaker system.

Adjusting the Volume of Ringer and Alerts

Though individual applications, such as Music and Videos, have their own volume settings, you can set your iPad system volume higher to control the level of system sounds and sounds in apps that don't have their own volume control. This system setting is the max against which Music volume settings work; if you set volume to 80 percent here, for example, Music's 100 percent volume setting will actually be the maximum system volume, or 80 percent.

You can simply press the volume rocker controls on the top-right side of your iPad (when it's in portrait orientation) to increase or decrease volume. However, this doesn't change the volume of Ringer and Alerts unless you change one additional setting. To adjust the system volume from the Settings app, tap Sounds. In the Sounds pane that appears (see Figure 3-12), tap and drag the slider to the right to increase the volume, or to the left to lower it.

Adjust iPad volume.

Figure 3-12: Use this familiar volume slider to adjust your system's volume.

In the Sounds pane, you can turn on or off the sounds that iPad makes when certain events occur (such as receiving new mail or Calendar alerts). These sounds are turned on by default. Conversely, if you need the audio clue and this feature has been turned off, just tap the On/Off button for the item to turn it back on.

Using Mono Audio

Stereo used in headphones breaks up sounds into two channels so that you hear a portion in one ear and a portion in the other to simulate the way your ears actually process sounds. However, if you're hard of hearing or deaf in one ear, you're getting only a portion of a sound in your hearing ear, which can be problematic. If you have hearing challenges and wear headphones, turn on Mono Audio, and iPad plays all sounds in each ear.

Follow these steps to turn on Mono Audio:

1. **Tap the Settings icon on the Home screen and then tap General.**

2. **Tap Accessibility.**

3. **In the Accessibility pane, as shown in Figure 3-13, tap the Mono Audio On/Off button to turn it on.**

Tap to turn on Mono Audio.

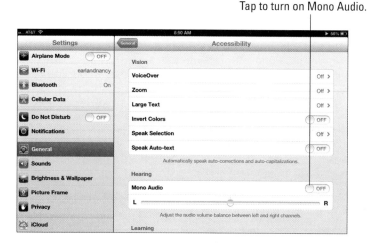

Figure 3-13: Mono Audio helps people who hear better in one ear than the other.

4. **Tap and drag the slider to L for sending sound to only your left ear or R for only your right ear.**

If you have hearing challenges, another good feature that iPad provides is support for closed-captioning. In the Videos player, you can use a closed-captioning feature to provide onscreen text for dialogue and actions in a movie as it plays if the movie format supports closed-captioning. For more about playing videos, see Book II, Chapter 3.

Using AssistiveTouch

The AssistiveTouch Control Panel helps those who have challenges working with the touchscreen to provide input to iPad using custom gestures. When turned on, this feature makes onscreen menus of common tasks available to you to get things done with a single tap.

To turn on AssistiveTouch, follow these steps:

1. **Tap Settings on the Home screen and then tap General and Accessibility.**

2. **In the Accessibility pane, tap AssistiveTouch.**

3. **In the pane that appears, tap the On/Off button for AssistiveTouch to turn it on.**

   Note the gray square that appears in the lower-right corner of the pane. This square now appears in the same location in whatever apps you display on your iPad.

4. **Tap the AssistiveTouch Control Panel to display options, as shown in Figure 3-14.**

5. **You can tap Gestures, Favorites, or Device on the panel to see additional choices, or tap Home to go directly to the Home screen.**

   After you choose an option, tapping the Back arrow takes you back to the main panel.

Table 3-2 shows the major options available in the AssistiveTouch Control Panel.

Figure 3-14: These options help you perform actions with a simple tap or two.

Table 3-2	AssistiveTouch Controls
Control	*Purpose*
Gestures	Chooses the number of fingers to use for gestures on the touchscreen.
Favorites	Displays a set of gestures with only the Pinch gesture preset; you can tap any of the other blank squares to add your own favorite gestures.
Device	You can rotate the screen, lock the screen, turn volume up or down, mute or unmute sound, or shake iPad to undo an action using the presets in this option.
Home	Sends you to the Home screen.

Utilizing the Dictation Feature

Dictation is a simple but powerful feature that allows you to tap a button on the onscreen keyboard and speak text rather than typing it in several apps, including Mail, Notes, Contacts, Calendar, Messages, and Reminders. The Dictation feature is not available on the original iPad or the iPad 2, and it requires an Internet connection as your speech is sent to an Apple server to be translated into text. Dictation also can use your Contacts data to improve its recognition of names stored there.

If you find speaking text to be useful, check out Siri in Book 5, Chapter 6. This personal assistant feature can respond to spoken requests and commands.

1. **With an app where you want to enter text open, tap in the text entry area to display the onscreen keyboard.**

2. **Tap the Dictation key on the keyboard.**

   The Dictation icon, as shown in Figure 3-15, appears.

Dictation key

Dictation icon indicating Dictation feature is active

Figure 3-15: Speak to your iPad with the tap of the Dictation key.

3. **Speak the text you want to include in the document.**

   Keeping to about a paragraph of text at a time is a good rule.

4. **Tap the Dictation icon to stop recording.**

   Wait a moment, and the text appears in your document.

Dictation will accept spoken punctuation such as "comma" and "period"; however, it accepts only limited directions such as "new paragraph" to move to the next line in the document. You may find that you have to edit a few things after dictating. For example, I dictated "item two" and got "item to" in one instance.

Focus Learning with Guided Access

Guided Access is a new feature of iOS 6. You can use it to limit a user's access to iPad to a single app, and even limit access to that app to certain features. This is considered useful in several settings ranging from a classroom, to use by someone with attention deficit disorder, and even in a public setting such as a kiosk where you don't want users to be able to open other apps.

Follow these steps to turn on Guided Access:

1. **Tap Settings and then tap General.**

2. **Tap Guided Access.**

   On the screen that follows (see Figure 3-16), tap Guided Access to turn the feature on.

3. **Tap Set Passcode to activate a passcode so that those using an app cannot return to the Home screen to access other apps.**

   In the Set Passcode dialog that appears, as shown in Figure 3-17, enter a passcode using the number pad. Enter the number again when prompted.

Tap to turn on Guided Acccess.

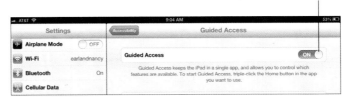

Figure 3-16: With Guided Access on you can control access across iPad.

Figure 3-17: Remember your password so you don't lock yourself out!

4. **Press the Home button and tap an app to open it.**

5. **Triple-tap the Home button.**

   You are presented with three choices along the bottom of the screen:

   - *Hardware Buttons:* You can tap to turn this Always On or Always Off. If you don't want users to be able to adjust volume using the volume toggle on the side of the iPad, for example, use this setting.

   - *Touch:* If you don't want users to be able to use the touchscreen, turn this off.

   - *Motion:* Turn this setting off if you don't want users to move the iPad around, for example, to play a racecar driving game.

   At this point, you can also use your finger to circle areas of the screen that you want to disable, such as a Store button in the Music app.

6. **Triple-tap the Home button and then enter your passcode, if you set one, to return to the Home screen.**

Chapter 4: Overview of Bundled Apps

In This Chapter

- Getting the most out of the Internet with Safari, Mail, and Messages
- Using cameras and organizing and sharing your photos
- Getting organized with Calendar, Contacts, Notes, and Reminders
- Going places with Maps
- Using built-in apps for playing music and videos
- Shopping for content at iTunes and apps at the App Store
- Reading periodicals with Newsstand
- Playing around with Game Center
- Making video calls with FaceTime
- Using fun photo effects with Photo Booth

*i*Pad comes with certain functionality and applications (which you probably know as *apps,* for short) already installed. When you look at your Home screen (1 of 11 possible Home screens you can fill with other apps), you'll see 16 icons for apps, plus 1 for accessing iPad Settings. Four icons are displayed across the bottom in iPad's Dock: Safari, Mail, Photos, and Music. The other apps (Messages, Calendar, Notes, Reminders, Maps, Clock, Videos, Contacts, Game Center, iTunes, App Store, Newsstand, FaceTime, Camera, Photo Booth, and Settings) are nearer the top of your screen and include apps for organizing your time and contacts, playing videos and reading periodicals, snapping pictures, gaming, and shopping for content and yet more apps. The Dock icons appear on every Home screen. The others appear on the first Home screen unless you move them elsewhere. Note that you can add up to two apps to the Dock, if you wish to have them available on every Home screen.

This chapter gives you a quick overview of what each bundled app does. You'll find out more about every one of them as you move through the chapters in this book.

Settings isn't exactly an app, but it's an icon you should know about: It's the central location in iPad where you can adjust settings for various functions, change settings for how apps function, and perform administrative tasks like setting up e-mail accounts or a password. Read more about using Settings in Chapter 8 of this minibook. There is also advice about using settings for various apps in Books II, III, and V, and information about e-mail settings in Chapter 7 of this minibook.

Another built-in feature (but not an app on your Home screen) to check out is Siri, new with iOS 6.0 on iPads (except for the original iPad and iPad 2). See Book V, Chapter 6 for more about this cool new personal assistant that does everything from finding the nearest Italian restaurant to providing the latest stock quotes.

Getting Online with iPad

iPad would kind of be an expensive calendar, address book, and music player if you couldn't go online to browse, buy things, get e-mail, stream video and audio, and more. Two bundled apps, Safari and Mail, help to connect your iPad to many of the Internet's resources.

Going on Safari

Safari is Apple's web browser. If you've owned a Mac computer, iPhone, or iPod touch, you've already used Safari (see Figure 4-1) to navigate around the Internet, create and save bookmarks of favorite sites, and add web clips to your Home screen so you can quickly visit favorite sites from there.

Figure 4-1: Find what you need on the web with Safari.

If you've been a Windows user in the past, you may also have used Safari, or you may be more familiar with browsers such as Internet Explorer or Firefox. If you haven't used Safari, don't worry; the browser should be pretty easy for you to get the hang of, with its familiar address field, Search field, tabs, navigation buttons, and bookmarks.

Using a browser on iPad is a lot of fun because of the touchscreen functionality and the ability to zoom in or out on a page by flicking two fingers inward or outward. Tabbed browsing allows you to move easily among open web pages. You can read more about using Safari in Chapter 6 of this minibook.

Be sure to check out iCloud tabs, new to Safari with iOS 6.0. If you have several Apple devices, you can use iCloud tabs to pick up where you left off searching on one device on another.

You can get much of what you want to do on your iPad done using Siri. This personal assistant, which you learn more about in Book V, Chapter 6, can help you go to a web page, create and send an email, enter an event in Reminders or Calendar, and more.

Getting Mail

iPad lets you get all your mail in one place through the Mail app — the program you use to access e-mail accounts you set up in iPad. You can set up accounts you have with popular e-mail providers such as Gmail, Yahoo!, AOL, and Windows Live Hotmail. You can also access accounts through iCloud or Microsoft Exchange. (Your work e-mail account might use Microsoft Exchange, for example.) Most any IMAP- or POP3-type account (the two most common mail protocols) is supported. You can also arrange to access the e-mail accounts you have with your Internet service provider (ISP).

After you set up an account, when you tap the Mail icon, your e-mail will display without you having to browse to the site or sign in. Then you can use tools to move among a few preset mail folders, read and reply to mail, and download attached photos to iPad. You can also use the Print feature in Mail to print your e-mail messages to a wireless printer. You can read more about setting up and using e-mail accounts in Chapter 7 of this minibook.

In portrait orientation, e-mails are displayed full screen, and you can use a drop-down menu to view your inbox. In landscape orientation, the inbox stays put on the left side of your screen.

iPad users (except those with an original iPad or iPad 2) can use the Dictation feature to enter e-mail addresses and messages in Mail by speaking them. See Chapter 3 in this minibook for more about the Dictation feature.

Using iMessage to connect

With iOS 5 came an instant messaging app called Messages. This app allows you to use the iMessage service to swap text messages with others in real time using a cellphone number or e-mail address. You can forward your conversations to others as well.

You can use Messages settings to turn the app on or allow others to get a read receipt when you've read their messages. You can also use the data in your Contacts app to make addressing messages quick and easy.

Shooting and Organizing Photos

iPads (except for the original iPad) include front- and rear-facing cameras. You can use the cameras to take still photos or shoot videos (both of which are covered in Book II, Chapter 4). To review and play around with photos you snap or bring onto iPad from another source, there's the Photos app.

Examining the iPad cameras

The third-and fourth-generation iPads have a super-clear Retina display and 5-megapixel rear-facing iSight camera for viewing and taking the best iPad-generated photos and video yet.

Take a quick look at your camera's features by tapping the Camera app icon on the Home screen.

You can use the controls in the Camera app to

- Switch between the front and rear cameras.
- Change from still-camera to video-camera operation by using the Camera/Video slider.
- Take a picture or start recording a video.
- Turn on a grid to help you autofocus on still photo subjects.
- Open previously captured images or videos.

When you view a photo or video, you can use an iPad feature to send the image via a tweet or e-mail, post it to your Facebook or Flickr account, print images, use a still photo as wallpaper or assign it to represent a contact, or run a slideshow or edit a video. See Book II, Chapters 4 and 6 for more detail about using the iPad cameras.

Perusing your photos

Photos isn't exactly Photoshop or any other sophisticated photo-imaging program — it's just a pretty simple app for organizing and viewing photos with a few very simple editing tools. Still, although it doesn't do much, what it does, it does in a very cool way.

Photos (see Figure 4-2) allows you to organize pictures in folders; e-mail, message, or tweet photos to others or post photos to Facebook; use a photo as your iPad wallpaper; or upload someone's picture to a contact record. You can use tools to rotate, enhance, remove red-eye, or crop photos. You can also run slideshows of your photos. You can open albums, pinch or unpinch to shrink or expand photos, and scroll through photos with a swipe.

 With iOS 6, use the Photo Stream feature to share photos among your friends. In addition, iOS 6 brought with it the ability to share photos and other content using Twitter or Facebook from right within several apps, including Photos.

The sexy part of Photos is the way you interact with the photos with your fingers on the touchscreen. You can also use Photos to convert iPad into a digital photo frame while you have it docked or charging, and you can run slideshows of your photo albums as well. If Photos sounds like fun (and it is), read more about how it works in Book II, Chapter 6.

Figure 4-2: A simple but fun way to view your photos.

Using Apps to Stay Organized

Scheduling your time, tracking contacts, jotting down notes — they're all a part of keeping organized in today's hectic world. iPad offers five apps to help you do just that: Calendar, Contacts, Reminders, Clock, and Notes.

 Note that from iOS 4.2 on, iPads have native print capability. In Photos, that means that you can select a photo or photos, tap to display the main menu, tap the Print option, select your printer, and print. You have to have a printer that supports AirPrint wireless printing to use this method. See Book V, Chapter 1 for more about printing.

 Version 4.2 and later of the iOS for iPad also made multitasking available. That means that you don't have to return to the Home screen every time you want to switch among all these great apps. As on the iPhone, multitasking is dead simple. With one app open, just double-tap the Home button or place five fingers on the screen and pinch them together. A horizontal bar with app icons for any open apps appears along the bottom of the screen. Scroll to find the one you want, tap it, and it displays. You can also use four fingers and swipe to the left or right to move through any currently running apps or apps you've used recently.

Tracking your schedule with Calendar

What would any computing device today be without a calendar feature, given our busy lives? If the calendar features on your computer and mobile phone don't already keep you on track, try iPad's Calendar. This app provides a handy onscreen daybook you can use to set up appointments and send alerts to remind you about them. You can also sync Calendar with other calendars you maintain online such as Google, Yahoo!, iTunes, or iCloud.

See Chapter 5 in this minibook for more about syncing and Book V, Chapter 3 for details on using Calendar.

Keeping in touch with Contacts

Today, it's all about who you know and staying in touch. Contacts is the built-in address book feature (see Figure 4-3) for iPad that lets you do just that. You can use Contacts to enter contact information (including photos, if you like, from your Photos app) and share contact information via e-mail. You can also use a search feature to find contacts easily.

Figure 4-3: Keep the basics about all your contacts in this handy app.

Contacts is another app you can sync with your iPhone or computer to save you tedious reentry of information. Read more about this in Book V, Chapter 5.

Want to find your contact in the real world? Tap that person's address in Contacts, and the iPad Maps app shows you how to get there! You can also tap an address you find in Maps and add it to Contacts.

Making Notes

Notes is a simple notepad app where you can enter text or cut and paste text from a website or e-mail. You can't do much except create and edit your notes or e-mail or print them — there are no features for formatting text or inserting objects. You'll find Notes handy, though, for simple notes on the fly.

You'll feel right at home with the familiar yellow pad interface that Notes sports. The default font has a casual look, and the icons along the bottom are pretty straightforward, though you can switch among three fonts by changing Notes options in iPad Settings. You can move to the previous note, e-mail a note, trash a note, or move to the next note. You can even tap the Dictation key on the onscreen keyboard of an iPad (except for the original iPad and iPad 2) and speak your Notes' content!

If this simple note-keeper appeals to you, read more about the Notes app in Book V, Chapter 2.

You can enter info into Notes using Dictation or the onscreen keyboard. If you are a heavy note taker and dictating notes has no appeal, consider buying a compatible Bluetooth keyboard for easier typing.

Keeping yourself on track with Reminders

Reminders is an app that was introduced in iOS 5. This is a handy electronic to-do list where you can enter tasks or pull tasks from the Calendar app. You can organize reminders into custom categories and see them in a list or organized by date, which also displays a useful monthly calendar on one side of the screen.

Of course, an obvious feature of an app called Reminders is that you can set it up to remind you of an event. Location-based reminders (which work most efficiently with the always-on 3G or 4G connection on iPad 3G/4G models) prompt your iPad to remind you about an event based on your location; for example, set a reminder to buy milk when you get to a specific location, and you receive the alert when you arrive at the market. This feature uses Location Services to track your whereabouts at any point in time.

Staying on time with Clock

This app, new to the iPad with iOS 6, is a simple but useful utility and is especially useful to all you world travelers. Clock allows you to display clocks from around the world side by side, so if you're in Paris, you can easily see what time it is in New York as well.

Clock also has a feature that lets you set alarms to keep your day on schedule. Finally, you can use timer and stopwatch features. The timer lets you do things like time the cookies you just put in the oven, while the stopwatch lets you add up the minutes of your morning jog or workout.

Going Places with Maps

The Maps app is reimagined in iOS 6.0. You can view classic maps or aerial views of addresses; get directions from one place to another by car, foot, or public transportation; and check on traffic in larger cities.

If you own a Wi-Fi–only iPad, a less sophisticated system than 3G/4G can identify your current location and help you find directions from there to other places. 3G/4G iPad owners enjoy a much more targeted location system using GPS, but all models can take advantage of the ability to bookmark or share locations, or add an address to Contacts.

See Book III, Chapter 2 for step-by-step procedures for using the Maps app.

Being Entertained by iPad

One of the joys of iPad is its use as a media consumption tool. Playing music and watching videos are very entertaining uses of iPad, indeed. The bundled Music and Videos apps make playing media easy to do.

Playing around with Music

Unless you've been living in a cave without 3G/4G or satellite TV for the last several years, you know perfectly well that iPod is the Apple-preferred player. On your iPad, the Music app is your media player with a heavy emphasis on music. You can use Music to play music, podcasts, or audiobooks.

One of the nicest things about Music on iPad is the fact that iPad comes with a very nifty sound system and mono speaker, so the experience of listening with or without headphones will be a pleasing experience for everyone who's addicted to MP3 listening devices. You can also browse your music by a variety of criteria, such as artist, album, song, or genre.

You can also use the Videos app to play TV or movies, and it offers some great features for controlling video playback.

Watching videos

The Videos app is a media player like Music, but it specializes in playing videos and offers a few more features, such as chapter breakdowns and information about movie plots and casts for media you got from iTunes. You can move between widescreen and full-screen display, and it shines at showing high-definition content, especially with the third- and fourth-generation iPad's awesome Retina display. See Book II, Chapter 3 for more on the Videos app.

Going Shopping at iTunes and the App Store

The iTunes app takes you to the iTunes Store, where you can shop 'til you drop (or your iPad battery runs out of juice) for music, movies, TV shows, and audiobooks and then download them directly to your iPad. You can also preview content before you download it. See Chapter 5 in this minibook for more about how to buy apps, and Book VI for a listing of some of the very best apps out there.

Ready for more shopping? Tapping the App Store icon takes you directly to an Apple online store, where you can buy and download apps that do everything from enabling you to play games to building business presentations. At last count, more than 550,000 apps were available for iPad, with more being added all the time. Some were created for iPhone/iPod touch and run on iPad; some were created especially for the iPad. And some are even free!

Check out the new iTunes U app that gives you access to hundreds of great online courses from sources such as major universities as well as the Podcasts app for listening to podcasts.

Reading Periodicals with Newsstand

Newsstand is a handy interface for subscribing to and reading magazines, newspapers, and other periodical apps. Publications you subscribe to are laid out in neat rows on a virtual bookcase, and there's a handy Store button to shop for more periodicals.

Are you more into books than magazines? Then you'll be glad to know about iBooks, an e-reader application that isn't supplied with iPad out of the box. It's free (like many other apps out there), but you have to download it from the App Store. Because iPad has been touted as a great e-reader, definitely consider getting the iBooks app and/or another e-reader app, such as Kindle or Stanza, as soon as possible. For more about downloading apps for your iPad, see Book II, Chapter 1, and to work with the iBooks' e-reader app itself, go to Book II, Chapter 7.

Playing with Game Center

Game Center is a way to essentially browse game apps in the App Store by bestselling titles. Tap Game Center on your Home screen and tap one of the sets of colorful icons that appears on the Game Center screen, and you're taken to the App Store, with information about a game displayed.

From then on, it's about obtaining the game (either free or for a price through your iTunes account) and playing it. You can add friends to build your gaming social network and play and track scores for interactive games. See Chapter 5 in this minibook for more about buying apps, and Book II, Chapter 8 for more about gaming with your iPad.

Facing Up to Things with FaceTime

iPads (with the exception of the original iPad) ship with front- and rear-facing cameras, which unleash all kinds of possibilities. One of the coolest is an app called FaceTime. The FaceTime video calling app lets you use the iPad's video cameras to talk face-to-face with someone who has an iPad (except an original iPad); Mac (running OS X 10.6.6 or later); fourth-generation iPod touch; or iPhone 4, 4S, or 5. (See Figure 4-4.) You can call someone via his or her iPhone cellphone number or e-mail address. As of iOS 6, FaceTime even works directly over a cellular connection, though you'll pay for it eating up your data allotment.

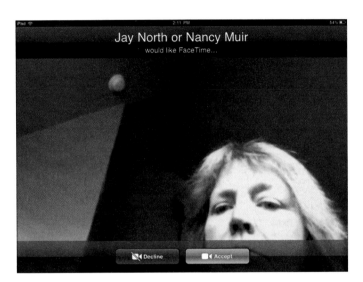

Figure 4-4: Talk face-to-face using FaceTime.

You'll want to start trying FaceTime with all your friends who own a compatible Apple device, so head straight to Book II, Chapter 4, to get up to speed on FaceTime features.

Exploring Fun Photo Effects with Photo Booth

The very fun Photo Booth app has been included with Mac OS X for some time, and it came to the iPad with the release of iOS 5. It lets you take photos with weird and wonderful results. (See Figure 4-5.) You can use the built-in effects, such as Kaleidoscope, Mirror, and Thermal Camera, along with your iPad camera to take photos that turn out unlike any others.

Figure 4-5: Manipulate photos in a variety of ways with Photo Booth.

The photos you take using Photo Booth are stored in your Camera Roll album of Photos. You can easily share them with others or use iPad's native printing capability to print them to an AirPrint-compatible wireless printer.

Chapter 5: Setting Up iTunes to Sync and Buy Apps

In This Chapter

- Getting connected to the Internet
- Downloading iTunes and creating an account
- Making iPad settings in iTunes
- Syncing iPad to your computer
- Using iCloud
- Purchasing apps from the App Store
- Updating your apps

Apple made its iTunes desktop application one way for you to manage settings for how your iPad *syncs* with your computer so you can share information and content such as calendar events, pictures, music, movies, and contacts. Before you can use iTunes to sync from a PC, you have to download the software, and if you want to make purchases from the store, you need to open an iTunes account, both of which I cover in this chapter. You can also use the new iCloud service to store and share content online using a Wi-Fi connection. In this chapter, I cover how to set up an iCloud account and make settings to back up and share content in the cloud.

Some apps, such as Contacts and Videos, come pre-installed on your iPad. But as you know if you're an iPhone user, a world of other apps is out there, including many that you can get for your iPad. After you set up iTunes, you can buy apps (or download free ones) in the App Store using your iTunes account. Some are free, such as iBooks, and some you can get for a price (typically from 99 cents to about $10, though a few go up to $50 or more).

In this chapter, I tell you how to connect to the Internet (you need an Internet connection to access the App Store) and then I tell you how to set iTunes and iCloud to sync your iPad with other devices and how you can acquire apps for your iPad through the App Store.

After you have an iTunes account, you can also shop iTunes for music, videos, audiobooks, and more. See Book II, Chapter 1, for more about shopping for multimedia content.

Connecting to the Internet

In order to browse the web, access Mail, and shop online, you have to first be connected to the Internet, so I'm putting this information right up front. How you connect to the Internet depends on which iPad model you own:

- The **Wi-Fi–only iPad** connects to the Internet via a Wi-Fi network. You may already have set up this type of network in your own home using your computer and some equipment from your Internet provider. You can also connect through public Wi-Fi networks *(hotspots)*. You probably have already noticed how many hotspots your town or city has: Look for Internet cafés, coffee shops, hotels, libraries, and transportation centers such as airports or bus stations. In fact, after you start looking, you'll notice lots of signs alerting you to free Wi-Fi locations — they're everywhere.

- If you own a **Wi-Fi and 3G- or Wi-Fi and 4G-enabled iPad,** you can still use a Wi-Fi connection (which is usually much faster if you have a good connection), but you can also use a paid data network through AT&T, Sprint, or Verizon to connect via a cellular network just about anywhere you can get cellular phone coverage. If you have a 3G or 4G model, you don't have to do anything; with a contract for coverage, the connection is made automatically wherever cellular service is available, just as it is on your cellphone.

See Chapter 1 in this minibook for more about the capabilities of different iPad models and the costs associated with a cellular network.

When you're in range of a hotspot, a pop-up may display automatically; if it doesn't, tap Settings, tap Wi-Fi, and then tap a network in the Choose a Network category, or tap Other. (Note that secure networks, which require a password, will display a little padlock icon.) If access to several nearby networks is available, tap a network name to select it. After you select one (or if only one network is available), you see a message similar to the one shown in Figure 5-1 if a password is required. Enter a network password and then tap the Join button.

Free public Wi-Fi networks typically don't require passwords. However, it's therefore possible for someone else to track your online activities over these unsecured networks. No matter how much you might be tempted, you might want to avoid accessing financial accounts or sending unencrypted sensitive e-mail when connected to a public hotspot.

Enter the network password...

then tap Join.

Figure 5-1: Joining a Wi-Fi network.

Setting Up iTunes

Think of iTunes as Apple's version of the Mall of America. It's both one place from which you can manage your iPad settings for syncing content and a great big online store where you can buy content and apps for your Mac or PC, iPod touch, iPhone, and iPad. It's also the place where you can make settings for several of these devices to control how they download and share content. Even if you find some other sources of content for your iPad, it's worth having an iTunes account, if only to use the settings it provides.

Before you can use iTunes to manage your iPad, you have to download the latest version of iTunes by going to `www.apple.com/itunes`. You should also create an iTunes account, providing a payment method so that you can use iTunes on your computer or use the iTunes app on your iPad to purchase apps and content.

You can use an iTunes account or an Apple ID and iCloud to register your iPad when you first buy it before you can use it. In my case and perhaps in yours, the nice man at the Apple Store activated my iPad before I left the store with it, so I set up my own iTunes account the first time I wanted to buy a hot movie title.

Making Settings and Syncing

Remember that great photo of your promotion party you have on your hard drive? How do you get that onto iPad so you can show it off at the next family reunion? Or how about that audiobook on career success you bought and downloaded to your laptop on your last business trip? It would sure be handy to get that sucker onto your iPad. Never fear: By making a few easy settings and syncing with your computer, you can bring all that content over in a (pardon the term) flash.

Remember that you can also sync content using iCloud. See the next section for more about that option.

Making iPad settings using iTunes

When you plug your Lightning to USB Cable (the Dock Connector to USB Cable for third-generation iPads, iPad 2s, and original iPads) into your iPad and computer and then open iTunes, a whole group of settings becomes available. These help you determine how content will sync between the two devices.

Note that you can sync wirelessly to your computer by tapping Settings on the Home screen, opening General Settings, and tapping iTunes Wi-Fi Sync. In the dialog that appears, tap Sync Now. This works only if your iPad is plugged in and both iPad and your computer are connected to the same Wi-Fi network.

Here's how to use the iTunes settings for your iPad:

1. **Connect your iPad to your computer using the Lightning to USB Cable.**

   Plug the Lightning end of your cable (the smaller end) into your iPad and plug the other end of the cord into a USB port on your computer.

2. **Open your iTunes software.**

   On a Mac, click the iTunes icon in the Dock; on a Windows computer, choose Start⇨All Programs⇨iTunes or double-click the shortcut for iTunes on your desktop.

   iTunes opens, and your iPad is listed in the Devices section of the Source List.

3. **Click the name of your iPad in the Devices section of the Source List.**

   A series of tabs displays, as shown in Figure 5-2. The tabs offer informa-tion about your iPad and settings to determine which content such as music, movies, or podcasts to download, and for some content types, when to download. (You can see the simple choices on the Music tab in Figure 5-3.) The settings relate to the kind of content you want to down-load and whether you want to download it automatically when you sync or do it manually. See Table 5-1 for an overview of the settings that are available on each tab.

4. **Make all settings for the types of content you plan to obtain on your computer and sync to your iPad, and then click the Sync button in the bottom-right corner to sync files with the iPad.**

Click on your iPad. . .   to display this series of tabs.

Figure 5-2: The various tabs you can use to control iPad from iTunes.

☐ **Sync Music**

⦿ Entire music library
○ Selected playlists, artists, and genres

☑ Include music videos
☑ Include voice memos

Figure 5-3: Settings to control how music syncs to your iPad.

Table 5-1	iPad Settings in iTunes
Tab Name	*What You Can Do with These Settings*
Summary	Perform updates to iPad software and set general syncing options.
Info	Specify which information to sync: Contacts, Calendars, E-mail accounts, Bookmarks, or Notes.
Apps	Sync apps and data you've downloaded to your computer to iPad and manage the location of those apps and folders.
Tones	Choose to sync selected or sync all tones
Music	Choose which music to download to your iPad when you sync.
Movies	Specify whether to automatically download movies.
TV Shows	Choose which shows and episodes to sync automatically.
Podcasts	Choose which podcasts and episodes to sync automatically.
iTunes U	Sync all, a specified number of unplayed courses, or a specified number of recent items in all or selected collections.
Books	Choose to sync all or only selected audio and electronic books to your iPad.
Photos	Choose the folders from which you want to download photos or albums.

Be alert to warnings when you sync your iPad and computer because, depending on your settings, you may overwrite or erase content you've downloaded when you sync. You may want to copy content you've downloaded to your iPad directly to your iTunes library before syncing so your computer doesn't erase what you've downloaded during the sync.

For Photos folders, on a Mac, you can sync through iPhoto or Aperture rather than through Photos folders, and on a Windows computer, you can go through Photoshop Elements version 8 or later.

Syncing iPad to your computer

After you specify which content to download in iTunes (see the preceding section), you use the Lightning to USB Cable to connect your iPad and computer to sync info like contacts and calendar settings. Note that Wi-Fi syncing takes place when iPad is asleep and plugged into power.

With iTunes installed on your computer and an iTunes account set up, follow these steps to sync to your iPad:

1. **Plug the Lightning end (the smaller end) of your Lightning to USB Cable into your iPad.**

2. **Plug the other end of the Lightning to USB Cable into your computer.**

iTunes opens and shows an iPad item in the Source List. (See Figure 5-4.) Your iPad screen shows the words *Sync in Progress.*

When the syncing is complete, the Lock screen returns on the iPad, and iTunes shows a message indicating that the iPad sync is complete and that you can disconnect the cable. Any media you chose to transfer in your iTunes settings, and any new photos on your computer, have been transferred to your iPad.

3. **After syncing, unplug the Lightning to USB Cable from your iPad and your computer.**

Syncing wirelessly

You can also use the iTunes Wi-Fi Sync setting to allow cordless syncing if you are within range of a Wi-Fi network that has a computer connected to it with iTunes installed.

Follow these steps to make Wi-Fi syncing settings:

1. **Tap Settings⊏⟩General⊏⟩iTunes Wi-Fi Sync.**

2. **In the dialog shown in Figure 5-5, tap Sync Now to sync with a computer connected to the same Wi-Fi network.**

Your iPad is listed here.

Figure 5-4: Syncing connects your computer and iPad so you can share data.

Figure 5-5: Set up your iPad to sync using the nearest Wi-Fi network.

Understanding iCloud

You have an alternative to syncing content by using iTunes. At the time that Apple launched iOS 5, it also introduced iCloud, a service that allows you to back up all your content and certain settings, such as bookmarks, to online storage. That content and those settings are then pushed automatically to all your Apple devices through a wireless connection.

All you need to do is get an iCloud account, which is free, and then make settings on each device for which types of content you want to have pushed to each device. After you've done that, any content you create or purchase on one device — such as music, apps, books, and TV shows, as well as documents created in Apple's iWork apps, photos, and so on — can be synced among your devices automatically.

When you get an iCloud account, you get 5GB of free storage; content you purchase through Apple (such as apps, books, music, and TV shows) are not counted against your storage. If you want additional storage, you can buy an upgrade from one of your devices. 10GB costs $20 per year; 20GB is $40; and 50GB is $100 a year. Most people will do just fine with the free 5GB of storage. Note that items you've purchased from iTunes, which include any music such as ripped CDs that you've synced across devices using the iTunes Match service, doesn't count toward your data storage.

To upgrade your storage, go to iCloud in Settings, tap Storage & Backup, and then tap Manage Storage. In the dialog that appears, tap Buy More Storage. Tap the amount you need and then tap Buy.

You can make settings for backing up your content to iCloud in the iCloud section of Settings. You can have content backed up automatically, or back it up manually. See Chapter 9 in this minibook for more about this topic.

Getting an iCloud account

Before you can use iCloud, you need an iCloud account, which is tied to the Apple ID you probably already have. You can turn on iCloud when first setting up your iPad or use Settings to sign up using your Apple ID. Follow these steps:

1. **When first setting up your iPad (except for an original iPad), tap Use iCloud in the sequence of screens that appears (see Figure 5-6).**

2. **In the next dialog, tap Backup to iCloud.**

   Your account is now set up based on the Apple ID you entered earlier in the setup sequence.

Figure 5-6: Set up iCloud while setting up your iPad.

Here are the steps to set up iCloud on your iPad if you didn't do so on first setting up iPad:

1. **Tap Settings and then tap iCloud.**

2. **Tap the On/Off button to turn on iCloud.**

3. **Enter your Apple ID and password and then tap the Sign In button (see Figure 5-7).**

   If you don't have an Apple ID, tap the Get a Free Apple ID button and follow the instructions to get your ID.

   A dialog appears, asking whether you want to merge your iPad calendars, reminders, and bookmarks with iCloud.

Figure 5-7: Use your Apple ID to access iCloud.

4. **Tap OK.**

   A dialog may appear asking whether you want to allow iCloud to use the location of your iPad. Tap OK.

   Your account is now set up.

Making iCloud sync settings

When you have an iCloud account up and running (see the preceding section), you have to specify which type of content should be synced with your iPad via iCloud. Note that content that you purchase and download is synced among your devices automatically via iCloud. Follow these steps:

1. **Tap Settings and then tap iCloud.**

2. **In the iCloud settings, as shown in Figure 5-8, tap the On/Off button for any item that's turned off that you want to turn on (or vice versa).**

   You can sync Mail, Contacts, Calendars, Reminders, Safari, and Notes.

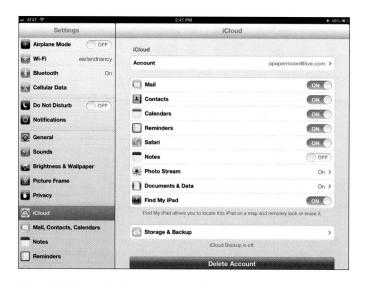

Figure 5-8: Choose the items you want to have synced with your iPad here.

3. **To turn Photo Stream, Documents & Data, or Storage & Backup on or off (so you can sync photos, documents created in iWork, or settings data, respectively), tap those options in the list (refer to Figure 5-8) and then tap the On/Off button for each particular setting in the subsequent screen.**

4. **To enable automatic downloads of music, apps, and books, tap Store in the Settings pane.**

5. **Tap the On/Off button for Music, Apps, or Books to set up automatic downloads of any of this content to your iPad via iCloud.**

If you want to allow iCloud to provide a service for locating a lost or stolen iPad, tap the On/Off button in the Find My iPad field to activate it. This service helps you locate, send a message to, or delete content from your iPad if it falls into other hands.

Buying Apps or Downloading Free Apps

Apps provide all kinds of functionality, from the ability to plan travel, manage finances, and find local restaurants and gas stations to hard-core business productivity and serious gaming fun. By buying and downloading apps, you can assemble a custom computing experience.

Most iPhone apps will work on your iPad, so if you own the trendy mobile phone and have favorite apps on it, you might want to use them on your iPad! Also, for more about my recommended apps, see Book VI.

Searching the App Store

Apple isn't one to miss a profit opportunity, so naturally, one of the iPad built-in apps is the App Store. This is the apps portal that will get you to thousands of great apps for everything from games to bean counting.

If you want to get non-Apple apps, such as Google Voice, you can join the estimated 4 million people who have done what's called *jailbreaking* to liberate their iPhones or iPads from the tyranny of getting apps solely through iTunes. Check out this article for details about jailbreaking, but be forewarned that jailbreaking voids your iPad warranty, impedes your access to Apple updates, opens you up to the dangers of malware, and could even make it hard to download and use legitimate Apple-approved apps: `http://gizmodo.com/5530906/jailbreaking-your-ipad-how-you-can-and-why-you-should`.

Here's your quick introduction to using the App Store to obtain whatever apps your heart desires:

1. **Tap the App Store icon on your iPad Home screen.**

   The site shown in Figure 5-9 appears.

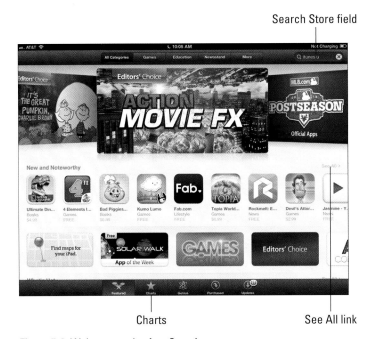

Figure 5-9: Welcome to the App Store!

2. **At this point, you have several options for finding apps:**

    *   *Tap in the Search Store field,* enter a search term, and tap the Search button on the onscreen keyboard to see results.

    *   *Tap and swipe the screen* to scroll down to see more selections.

    *   *Tap the tabs such as Games, Education, or Newsstand* at the top of the screen to see a category of apps.

    *   *Tap the Charts button* at the bottom of the screen to see which free and paid apps other people are downloading most.

    *   *Tap the Purchased button* to view apps you've already purchased, as shown in Figure 5-10.

Figure 5-10: Find the apps that fit your needs.

Getting apps from the App Store

Getting free apps or buying apps requires that you have an iTunes account, which I cover earlier in this chapter. After you have an account, you can use the saved payment information there to buy apps or download free apps. I strongly recommend that you install the free iBooks app, so in this section, I walk you through the steps for getting it:

1. **With the App Store open, tap the Search field, enter** iBooks, **and then tap the Search button on the onscreen keyboard.**

2. **Tap the price button (which in this case reads** *Free***) for iBooks in the results that appear, as shown in Figure 5-11.**

Tap this button.

Figure 5-11: Tap the app you need.

Note that to get a paid app, you'd tap the price button, which displays the cost of the app.

The price button changes to read Install App (or in the case of a paid app, the button changes to read Buy App).

3. **Tap the Install (or Buy) App button.**

   You may be asked to enter your iTunes password and tap the OK button to proceed.

   The app downloads; if you purchase an app that isn't free, at this point your credit card is charged for the purchase price or your Store credit is reduced by the amount of the purchase price.

Out of the box, only preinstalled apps are located on the first iPad Home screen of your iPad by default. Apps you download are placed on additional Home screens, and you have to scroll to view and use them. See the next section for help in finding your newly downloaded apps using multiple Home screens.

If you've opened an iCloud account, anything you purchase on your iPad can be set up to automatically be pushed to other Apple iOS devices, your PC, or Mac. See earlier sections in this chapter for more about iCloud.

If you're a road warrior, you'll be glad to hear that the travel industry is all over apps to help you get around, as the iPad is such a logical travel companion. Lonely Planet has released country guides for the iPad, and iPhone apps for travelers are being re-created for iPad. See Book III, Chapter 3, if you're someone who hits the road on a regular basis and wants to make the most of your iPad.

Organizing your apps

iPad can display up to 11 Home screens. By default, the first contains prein-stalled apps; other screens are created to contain any apps you download or sync to your iPad. At the bottom of any iPad Home screen (just above the Dock), a magnifying glass icon represents the Search screen to the left of the primary Home screen; dots that appear to the right of the magnifying glass icon indicate the number of Home screens, as shown in Figure 5-12.

You can use some very nice features in iTunes to organize apps on your con-nected iPad, but you can also organize things right on the iPad using a few different methods.

Here's some advice on how to organize your apps:

1. **Tap the Home button to open the last displayed Home screen.**

Dots indicating the number of screens

Magnifying glass icon

The screen you're currently viewing

Figure 5-12: Finding apps on the various iPad Home screens.

2. **Flick your finger from right to left or tap either end of the Home screen dots to move to the next or previous Home screen.**

   Note that the dots near the bottom of the screen indicate which Home screen you're on. To move back, flick from left to right.

3. **To reorganize apps on a Home screen, press and hold any app on that page.**

   The app icons begin to jiggle, and any apps you installed will sport a Delete button (a black circle with a white X on it). (See Figure 5-13.)

4. **Press, hold, and drag an app icon to another location on the screen to move it.**

5. **Tap the Home button to stop all those icons from jiggling!**

Figure 5-13: Move an app to another location on a Home screen.

To move an app from one page to another, while things are jiggling, you can press, hold, and drag an app to the left or right to move it to the next Home screen. You can also manage what app resides on what Home screen and in which folder from iTunes when you've connected iPad to iTunes via a cable or wireless sync, which may be easier for some.

You can also manage your apps from iTunes with your iPad connected using the settings on the Apples tab. You can even reorder the home screens there.

Organizing apps in folders

As with iPhone, iPad lets you organize apps in folders (if you have iOS version 4.2 or later). The process is simple and specific to each device. For iPad, follow these steps to get more organized:

1. **Tap and hold an app 'til all apps do their jiggle dance.**

2. **Drag an app on top of another app.**

   A bar appears across the screen showing the two apps and a folder name field that contains a placeholder name. (See Figure 5-14.)

3. **To delete the placeholder name and change the folder name, tap in the field at the end of the placeholder name.**

   The placeholder text is deleted, and the keyboard appears.

Figure 5-14: Collect apps in logical folders to help you save Home screen space.

4. **Tap the Delete key to delete the placeholder name and then type one of your own.**

   If you change your mind and want to put the app back on the Home screen, you can easily drag it out of the folder.

5. **Tap anywhere outside the bar to save the name.**

6. **Tap the Home button to stop all that jiggling!**

   The folder appears on the Home screen where you began this process.

To get to the items stored in your folder, just double-tap it.

Deleting apps you no longer need

Not all apps are endlessly entertaining or useful. When you no longer need an app you have installed, it's time to get rid of it to save some space on your iPad. (Note, however, that you can't delete apps that were preinstalled on the iPad such as Notes, Calendar, or Photos.) If you use iCloud to push content across all Apple iOS devices, note that deleting an app on your iPad won't affect that app on other devices.

To send an app on its way, do this:

1. **Display the Home screen that contains the app you want to delete.**

2. **Press and hold the app until all apps begin to jiggle.**

3. **Tap the Delete button for the app you want to delete (see Figure 5-15).**

Delete buttons

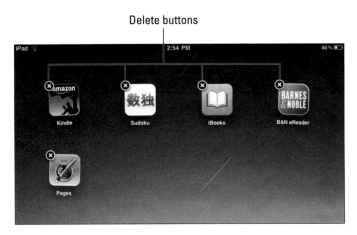

Figure 5-15: Tap Delete on the jiggling app.

4. **In the confirmation dialog, as shown in Figure 5-16, tap Delete to proceed with the deletion.**

   A dialog asking you to rate an app before deleting it appears.

Figure 5-16: Tap Cancel if you have regrets; otherwise, tap Delete to send the app on its way.

5. **Tap the Rate button to rate the app or No Thanks to opt out of the survey.**

   If you have several apps to delete, you can delete them by using iTunes connected to your iPad, making the process a bit more streamlined.

   Don't worry about wiping out several apps at once by deleting a folder. You can't delete full folders, only individual apps within them.

Updating apps

App developers update their apps all the time to fix problems or add new features, so you might want to check for those updates. The App Store icon on the Home screen displays the number of available updates in a red circle. Tap the App Store icon when you have some apps with updates ready.

Now you can proceed with these steps to update your apps:

1. **Tap the Updates icon to access the Updates screen (see Figure 5-17) and then tap any item you want to update.**

   To update all, tap the Update All button.

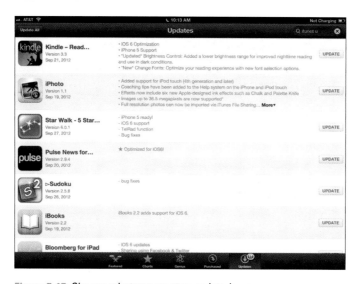

Figure 5-17: Choose what you want to update here.

2. **On the app screen that appears, tap Update.**

   You may be asked to confirm that you want to update, or to enter your Apple ID password and then tap OK to proceed. You may also be asked to confirm that you are over a certain age or agree to terms and conditions; if so, scroll down the Terms dialog (reading all items as you go, of course) and at the bottom, tap Agree.

In iOS 5, Apple introduced the capability to download multiple apps at once. If you choose more than one app to update instead of them downloading sequentially, all items are downloaded simultaneously.

If you have an iCloud account and update an app on your iPad, it's also updated on any other Apple iOS devices automatically, and vice versa.

Chapter 6: Browsing the Web

In This Chapter

✓ Discovering Safari

✓ Creating and utilizing bookmarks

✓ Using Safari Reading List and Reader

✓ Saving web clips to the Home screen

✓ Adding an image to your Photos library

✓ E-mailing a link to a website

✓ Making private browsing and cookie settings

✓ Printing from Safari

✓ Using iCloud tabs

Getting on the Internet with your iPad is easy, using its Wi-Fi or 3G/4G capabilities. After you're online, the built-in browser, Safari, can take you all around the web. Safari will be familiar to you if you've used an Apple device before or used the browser on your Mac or PC. On iPad, you're actually using a hybrid of the mobile version of Safari also used on iPhone and iPod touch and the desktop Safari.

If you've never used Safari, this chapter helps you get up to speed quickly. In this chapter, you discover how to connect your iPad to the Internet and navigate among web pages using tabbed browsing and how to use iCloud tabs to share your browsing history among devices. Along the way, you see how to place a bookmark for a favorite site or web clip on your Home screen. You can also view your browsing history, save online images to your Photos library, post photos to sites from within Safari, and e-mail a hotlink to a friend. You explore the Safari Reader and Safari Reading List features including the ability to save links and web pages to Reading List, and find out how to keep yourself safer while online using private browsing. Finally, you review the simple steps involved in printing what you find online.

Exploring Safari

If you need to know how to connect to the Internet, see Chapter 5 in this minibook. After you're connected, you're ready to browse with Safari.

Just in case you've never used Safari, here's a quick rundown of how it works on your iPad. It offers all the typical browser tools, but an important iPad feature is how you can use gestures on the touchscreen to manipulate pages and navigate the web.

Though Safari is a fine browser, you aren't limited to it. You can download other browsers to iPad, such as Atomic Web Browser, iCab, and Duo Browser. Check out the App Store for the latest available browsers.

Try the following steps to practice using Safari:

1. **After you're connected to a network, tap the Safari icon on the Home screen.**

   Safari opens, probably displaying the Apple iPad home page the first time you go online. (See Figure 6-1.)

Figure 6-1: These tools will be familiar to you from almost any browser you may have used.

2. **Put two fingers together on the screen and swipe outward to enlarge the view, as shown in Figure 6-2.**

3. **Double-tap the screen with a single finger to restore the default screen size.**

Using the pinch method (see Chapter 2 in this minibook) to enlarge or reduce the size of a web page on your screen allows you to enlarge or reduce the screen to various sizes, giving you more flexibility and control than the double-tap method.

Figure 6-2: Double-tapping enlarges the screen so you can read the fine print.

4. **Put your finger on the screen and flick upward to scroll down the page.**

5. **To return to the top of the web page, put your finger on the screen and drag downward, or tap the Status bar at the top of the screen.**

When you enlarge the display, you gain more control using two fingers to drag from left to right or from top to bottom on the screen. On a reduced display, one finger works fine for making these gestures.

Navigating among web pages

I expect that you have entered URLs and used the Next and Previous buttons in a browser to navigate around the web. However, the iPad's onscreen keyboard differs slightly from a standard keyboard, and it might help you to run through how you navigate with the mobile version of Safari.

Follow these steps for a bit of navigating practice:

1. **Tap in the Address field.**

   The onscreen keyboard appears, as shown in Figure 6-3.

   Note that this keyboard doesn't include the Dictation key.

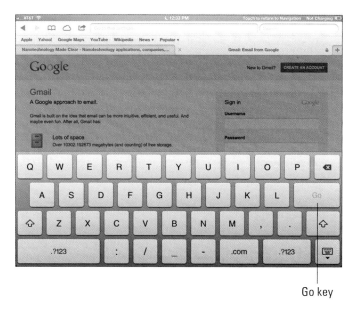

Go key

Figure 6-3: This keyboard requires you to do a few unique things to use numbers and symbols.

2. **To clear the field, press the Delete key on the keyboard. Enter a web address, using the .com key to make entry faster.**

   Hold down the .com key to access options like .edu, .gov, and .net.

   If you have no website in mind, go to this book's companion site, www.ipadmadeclear.com.

   If you entered this particular address before or have it bookmarked, AutoFill may fill in the address for you. By default, AutoFill is turned on in iPad, causing entries you make in fields such as the Address field to automatically display possible matching entries. You can turn off AutoFill by using iPad Settings for Safari.

3. **Tap the Go key on the keyboard (refer to Figure 6-3).**

   The website appears.

   • If, for some reason, a page doesn't display, tap the Reload icon at the end of the Address field.

- If Safari is loading a web page and you change your mind about viewing the page, you can tap the Cancel icon (the *X)* that appears at the end of the Address field during this process to stop loading the page.

4. **Tap the Previous arrow to go back to the last page Safari displayed.**

5. **Tap the Next arrow to go forward to the page you just came from.**

6. **To follow a link to another web page, tap the link with your finger.**

   To view the destination web address of the link before you tap it, just touch and hold the link, and a menu appears that displays the address at the top, as shown in Figure 6-4.

The link's web address

Figure 6-4: You can open a link in a new page using this menu.

You probably know that Apple doesn't support Flash, the technology that *lots* of sites use to play videos. That's because Apple considered Flash a poor technology, and who am I to disagree with Apple? You have a couple of options for getting content. There are some sites posting non-Flash versions of content, and you can search for these using the keywords *non-Flash movies.* You can stream content using a conversion app such as AirVideo with AirVideo Server on your Mac or PC. Or you can convert a Flash, AVI, or MPG files to mp4 format to use it on an iPad. To do this, you can download a free tool, such as one of these:

- **HandBrake:** www.handbrake.fr

- **swf>>avi:** www.avi-swf-convert.com

- **SWF to Video Scout:** http://tinyurl.com/28a4g7f

Using tabbed browsing

Safari includes a feature called *tabbed browsing,* which allows you to have several web pages open at once on separate tabs so you can move easily among those sites. You may have used tabbed browsing in other popular browsers, such as the desktop version of Safari, Internet Explorer, or Mozilla Firefox. This is a welcome feature of Safari that's worth exploring.

To add a tab, follow these steps:

1. **With Safari open, tap the plus icon near the upper-right corner of the screen (refer to Figure 6-1).**

   A new tab opens and the address field becomes active and the onscreen keyboard appears. (See Figure 6-5.)

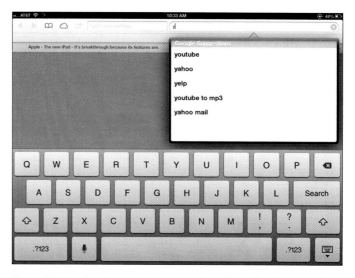

Figure 6-5: Here's where you can enter the address for the new tab you created.

2. **Tap an item from a recent search, tap in the search field and enter the name of a site to open, or tap the Dictation key and say a search term.**

   The site opens on a new tab.

3. **Switch among open sites by tapping another tab.**

Using tabbed browsing, you can not only place a site on a tab but also place a search results screen on a tab. If you recently searched for something, those search results will be on your Recent Searches list. Also, if you're displaying a search results page when you tap the plus icon to add a tab, the first ten suggested sites in the results will be listed there for you to choose from.

Viewing browsing history

As you know, when you move around the web, your browser keeps a record of your browsing history. This record can be handy when you visit a site that you want to view again but you've forgotten its address. (Everyone's done it.) On your iPad, you use the Bookmarks menu to get to your history.

Follow these steps to browse your browsing history:

1. **With Safari open, tap Bookmarks.**

2. **In the menu, as shown in Figure 6-6, tap the History tab in the middle of the bottom menu.**

   Alternatively, tap and hold the Previous button to quickly display a list of your browsing history.

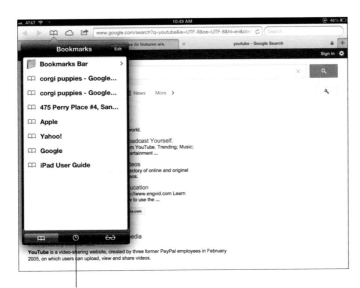

Tap to go to your History list.

Figure 6-6: In addition to bookmarks, this menu is your gateway to your browsing history.

3. **In the History list that appears (see Figure 6-7), tap a date if available and then tap a site to navigate to it.**

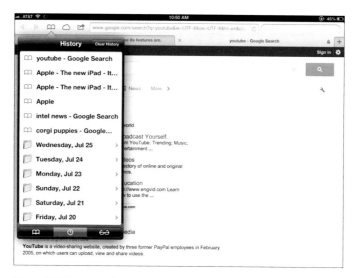

Figure 6-7: Use your finger to scroll down to view more of this list.

To clear the history, tap the Clear History button. (Refer to Figure 6-7.) This button is useful when you don't want your spouse or children to see where you've been browsing for birthday or holiday presents!

Searching the web

If you don't know the address of the site you want to visit (or you want to do research on a topic or find information you need online), get acquainted with Safari's Search feature on iPad. By default, Safari uses the Google search engine.

You can use Siri or Spotlight Search to search the Web without having opened Safari first. With Siri, you simply speak a request such as "Search the web for information on dogs". You can use Spotlight by entering a search term and then tapping Search Web. You can also use the Find on Page bar across the top of the keyboard to search within the currently active site.

1. **With Safari open, tap in the Search field (see Figure 6-8).**

   The onscreen keyboard appears.

2. **Tap one of the suggested sites or enter a search word or phrase, and then tap the Search key on your keyboard.**

3. **In the search results that are displayed, tap a link to visit that site.**

Search field

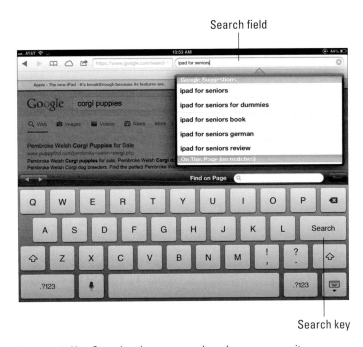

Search key

Figure 6-8: Use Search to locate a word or phrase on any site.

You can change your default search engine from Google to Bing or Yahoo!. In iPad Settings, tap Safari and then tap Search Engine. Tap Yahoo! or Bing, and your default search engine changes.

You can browse for specific items such as images, videos, or maps by tapping the corresponding link at the top of the Google results screen. Also, tap the More button in this list to see even more options to narrow your results, such as searching for books or YouTube videos on the subject.

Adding and Using Bookmarks

Bookmarks, which you have probably used in other browsers, are a way to save sites you visit often so that you can easily go to them again. Follow these steps to add bookmarks:

1. **With a site you want to bookmark displayed, tap the Menu icon.**

2. **On the menu that appears (see Figure 6-9), tap Bookmark.**

Tap to add a bookmark.

Figure 6-9: Choose to add a bookmark in this menu.

3. **In the Add Bookmark dialog, as shown in Figure 6-10, edit the name of the bookmark (if you want) by tapping the name of the site and using the onscreen keyboard to edit its name.**

Enter the name here.

Figure 6-10: Give your bookmark a name that makes sense to you.

4. **Tap the Save button.**

5. **To go to the bookmark, tap Bookmarks.**

6. **On the Bookmarks menu that appears (see Figure 6-11), tap the book-marked site you want to visit.**

   If you want to save a web location to your desktop, read Adding Web Clips to Your Desktop later in this chapter.

Tap a bookmarked site to visit it.

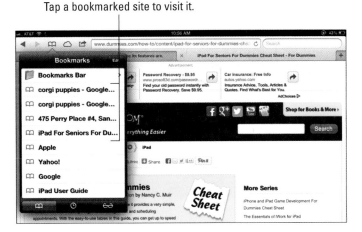

Figure 6-11: Tap to go to a favorite bookmark.

If you want to sync your bookmarks on your iPad browser to your computer, connect your iPad to your computer and make sure that the Sync Safari Bookmarks setting on the Info tab is activated.

When you tap Bookmarks, you can use the Bookmarks Bar New Folder option to create folders to organize your bookmarks. First, turn on the Always Show Bookmarks Bar in iPad Settings for Safari. When you next add a bookmark, you can then choose, from the dialog that appears, to add the new bookmark to any folder by tapping Bookmarks.

Using Safari Reading List

Remember when you were in school and had lots of reading assignments to keep track of from all your classes? Well, after graduation, reading lists don't go away; whether staying up to date in your chosen field or just keeping up with the latest articles and information, being able to assemble a list of online reading can be a great help. The Safari Reading List provides a way to save links to content you want to read at a later time so you can easily visit them again.

With iOS 6, you can save not only links to sites but also sites themselves, which allows you to read the content even when you're offline.

To use Reading List, follow these steps:

1. **With a site you want to add to your Reading List displayed, tap the Bookmarks icon.**

2. **On the menu that appears, tap the Reading List tab.**

3. **Tap the + symbol in the upper-right corner.**

The site is added to your list.

4. **To view your Reading List, tap Bookmarks and then tap Reading List.**

5. **On the Reading List that appears (see Figure 6-12), tap the content you want to revisit and resume reading.**

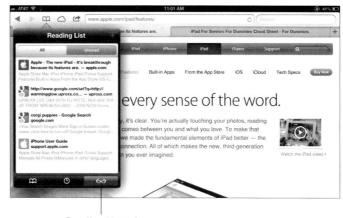

Reading List tab

Figure 6-12: It's so easy to find where you left off reading with Safari Reading List.

If you want to see both the Reading List material you've read and the material you haven't read, tap the All tab in the Reading List pane. (Refer to Figure 6-12.) To see just the material you haven't read, use the Unread tab. Be aware, however, that with websites that change content frequently, the content you placed on your Reading List may not be available at a later date.

To save an image on a web page to your Reading List, tap and hold the image until a menu appears and then tap Add to Reading List. To delete an item, with the Reading List displayed, swipe left or right, and a Delete button appears. Tap this button to delete the item from Reading List.

Utilizing Safari Reader

Reading content on the web isn't always user-friendly. The ads, sidebars, and various distractions can take away from your reading experience. Happily, the Safari Reader feature now gives you an e-reader type of experience right within your browser, removing other stories and links as well as those distracting advertisements.

1. **Tap the Reader button (see Figure 6-13) on the right side of the Address field when you're on a site where you're reading content such as an article.**

   The content appears in a reader format. (See Figure 6-14.)

   Reader button

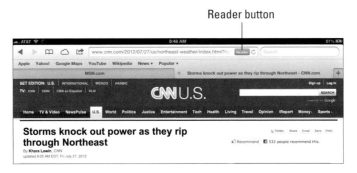

Figure 6-13: The Reader button appears when the feature is available for the page you're viewing.

Figure 6-14: At last . . . an easy-on-the-eyes reading experience on the web!

To enlarge the text in Reader, tap the large *A* in the top-left corner. (Refer to Figure 6-14.)

2. **Scroll down the page.**

   The entire content is contained in this one long page.

3. **When you finish reading the material, just tap the Reader button in the Address field again to go back to the material's source.**

If you're holding iPad in landscape orientation, the Reader window doesn't fill the screen, and you can tap on either side of the Reader window to go back to the source material.

If there's a video contained in an article you're perusing in Reader, it still appears with the standard Play button. Tap the button, and the video plays right within Reader.

Adding Web Clips to the Home Screen

The Web Clips feature allows you to save a website as an icon on your Home screen so that you can go to the site at any time with one tap. You can then reorganize those icons just as you can reorganize apps icons. (See Chapter 2 in this minibook for information on organizing apps on Home screens.)

Here are the steps for adding web clips:

1. **With Safari open and displaying the site you want to add, tap the Menu icon.**

2. **On the menu that appears (refer to Figure 6-9), tap Add to Home Screen.**

3. **In the Add to Home dialog that appears (see Figure 6-15), you can edit the name of the site to be more descriptive (if you like) by tapping the name of the site and using the onscreen keyboard to edit its name.**

Edit the name here.

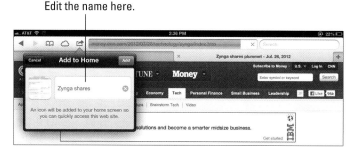

Figure 6-15: Give your web clip a descriptive name or use the site's URL.

4. **Tap the Add button.**

   The shortcut to the site is added to your Home screen.

You can have up to 11 Home screens on your iPad to accommodate all the web clips and apps you download (though there is a limit to how many will fit). You can also use folders to organize your web clips and save space on your Home screens. If you want to delete an item from your Home screen for any reason, you can connect your iPad to iTunes and deal with the process there, or press and hold the icon on the Home screen until all items on the screen start to jiggle and Delete badges appear on all items except preinstalled apps. Tap the Delete button on the item you want to delete, and it's gone. (To get rid of the jiggle, tap the Home button again.)

Saving an Image to Your Photos Library

Have you found a photo you like online? Maybe your BF's Facebook image, or a picture of your upcoming vacation spot? You can easily save images you find online to the iPad Photos app library. Here's how:

1. **Display a web page that contains an image you want to copy.**

2. **Press and hold the image.**

   The menu in Figure 6-16 appears.

http://money.cnn.com/news/specials/gasp
rices/?iid=EL

Open

Open in New Tab

Add to Reading List

Save Image ———— Tap this option.

Copy

Figure 6-16: Quickly saving an online image into Photos.

3. **Tap the Save Image option (refer to Figure 6-16).**

   The image is saved to your Photos library.

Be careful about copying images from the Internet and using them for business or promotional activities. Most images are copyrighted, and you may be violating that copyright if you use an image in (say) a brochure for your association or a flyer for your community group. Note that some search engines offer the option of browsing only for images that aren't copyrighted.

Posting Photos from Safari

Before iOS 6, you had to post photos from within apps such as Photos. Now you can post photos on your iPad to sites such as eBay, Craig's List, or Facebook from within Safari, rather than going through Photos or Videos. Follow these steps:

1. **To get an idea of how this works, go to Facebook and sign in.**

2. **Click an Add Photo/Video or similar link, like the one shown in Figure 6-17.**

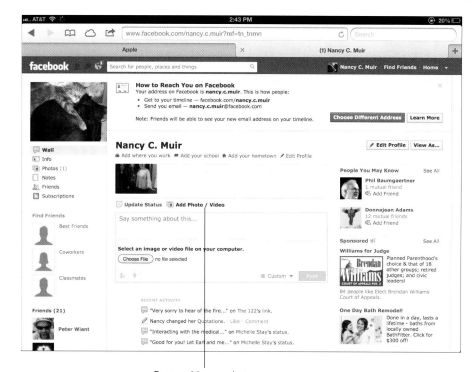

Post a video or photo.

Figure 6-17: Posting photos without leaving Safari is so convenient!

3. **Tap Upload Photo/Video and then tap Choose File.**

4. **Tap Choose Existing to get a photo on your iPad.**

   If you'd rather take a picture or record a video at this point, you would tap Take Photo or Video (see Figure 6-18).

5. **Tap on a photo source such as Camera Roll or My Photo Stream, and then tap the photo or video you want to post.**

6. **Tap Post to post the photo or video.**

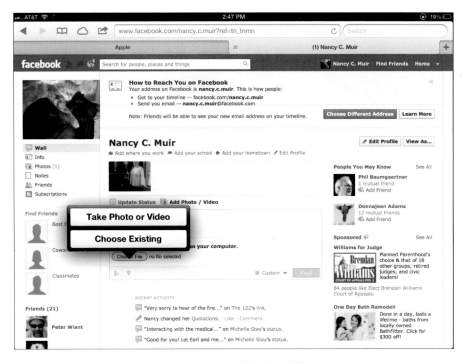

Figure 6-18: Find that great shot of Uncle Ernie or The Grand Canyon right here.

Sending a Link

If you find a great site that you want to share, you can do so easily by sending a link in an e-mail. Follow these steps to do so:

1. **With Safari open and the site you want to share displayed, tap the Menu icon.**

2. **On the menu that appears (refer to Figure 6-9), tap Mail.**

3. **In the message form that appears (see Figure 6-19), enter a recipient's e-mail address, a subject, and your message.**

4. **Tap Send.**

   The e-mail goes on its way.

Figure 6-19: Use this simple e-mail form to send an image and message.

The e-mail is sent from the default e-mail account you have set up on iPad. For more about setting up an e-mail account, see Chapter 7 in this minibook.

When entering text in any online form, such as an e-mail message or search box, you can take advantage of Safari's AutoFill feature. Turn this on in the Safari area of iPad's Settings. Safari can then use information from iPad's Contacts app and remember names and passwords you've entered before to offer options for completing text entries as you type.

To tweet the link using your Twitter account, in Step 2 of the preceding steps, choose Tweet, enter your tweet message in the form that appears, and then tap Send. For more about using Twitter with iPad, see Book II, Chapter 5.

A four-finger swipe from right to left on your screen gets you back to Safari from either Mail or Twitter.

Making Private Browsing and Cookie Settings

Apple has provided some privacy settings for Safari that you should consider using. Private Browsing automatically removes items from the download list, stops Safari from letting AutoFill save information used to complete your entries in the search or address fields as you type, and doesn't save some browsing history information. These features can keep your online activities more private. The Accept Cookies setting allows you to stop the downloading of *cookies* (small files that document your browsing history so you can be recognized the next time you go to or move within a site) to your iPad.

You can control both settings by choosing Safari in the Settings pane. Tap to turn Private Browsing on or off. (See Figure 6-20). Tap the arrow on Accept Cookies and choose to never save cookies, always save cookies, or save cookies only from visited sites (the default setting).

You can also use those two settings to clear your browsing history, saved cookies, and other data manually. (Refer to Figure 6-20).

Turn on Private Browsing.

Make cookie settings here.

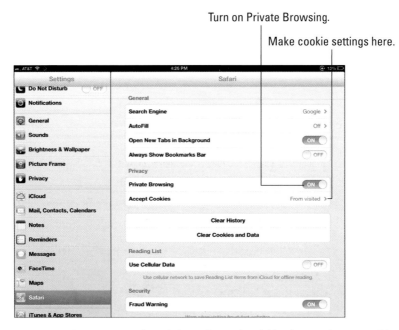

Figure 6-20: Protect your private information and activities from prying eyes with these settings.

Printing from Safari

If you have a wireless printer that supports Apple's AirPrint technology (most major manufacturers such as HP, Epson, Lexmark, Canon, and Brother offer at least one AirPrint model at this point), you can print web content using a wireless connection. Here's how:

1. **With Safari open and the site you want to print displayed, tap the Menu icon.**

2. **On the menu that appears, tap Print.**

3. **In the Printer Options dialog that appears (see Figure 6-21), tap Select Printer.**

4. **In the list of printers that appears, tap the name of your wireless printer.**

Tap this option.

Figure 6-21: Print directly from your iPad if you have a compatible wireless printer.

5. **Tap either the plus or minus button in the Copy field to adjust the number of copies to print.**

6. **Tap Print to print the displayed page.**

The apps Printopia and AirPrint Activator 2 make any shared or network printer on your home network visible to your iPad. Printopia has more features, but is more expensive, whereas AirPrint Activator is free.

If you don't have an AirPrint–compatible wireless printer or don't wish to use an app to help you print wirelessly, just e-mail a link to the web page to yourself, open the link on your computer, and print from there.

Understanding iCloud Tabs

iCloud Tabs are new with iOS 6. What this feature allows you to do is to access all browsing history among your different devices from any device. If you begin to research a project on your iPad before you leave home, you can then pick up where you left off as you sit in a waiting room with your iPhone.

Follow these steps to use iCloud Tabs:

1. **Check to make sure that both devices are using the same iCloud account by going to Settings⬚iCloud and checking the account name.**

2. **Open Safari on your iPad and click the iCloud Tabs button shown in Figure 6-22.**

   All items in your other device's browsing history are displayed (in the case of 6-22, the history is for my iPhone).

Figure 6-22: Pick up where you left off on another device using iCloud Tabs.

Chapter 7: Working with E-mail in Mail

*W*hat use would an iPad be if you couldn't stay in touch with your friends online? You can access an existing e-mail account using the handy Mail app supplied with your iPad, or you can sign into your e-mail account using the Safari browser. Using Mail involves adding one or more existing e-mail accounts using iPad Settings. Then you can use Mail to write, format, retrieve, and forward messages from any e-mail accounts you added to iPad.

Mail offers the capability to mark the messages you've read, delete messages, and organize your messages in folders, as well as use a handy Search feature. New with iOS 6 comes the ability to create a VIP list so that you are notified when that special person sends you an e-mail. In this chapter, you find out about Mail and its various features.

If you're wondering about IM (instant messaging) and iPad, check out Book II, Chapter 5 to discover the IM app, Messages, available with iOS 5 and later.

Adding an Account

To use the Mail app to access e-mail on iPad, you first have to make settings for an existing e-mail account on your iPad. You can add one or more e-mail accounts using iPad Settings, including any e-mail account that you've associated with an iCloud account. If you set up multiple accounts, you can then switch between accounts by tapping an account name in the upper-left corner of the displayed inbox, and then tapping Accounts and choosing which account to display. Or you can use the consolidated inbox and check your mail from all active accounts on one page.

If you have an iCloud, Gmail, Yahoo!, Windows Live Hotmail, or AOL account, iPad pretty much automates the setup. Here are the steps to get you going with any of these e-mail providers:

1. **Tap the Settings icon on the Home screen.**

2. **In the Settings pane, tap Mail, Contacts, Calendars.**

   The settings shown in Figure 7-1 appear.

3. **Tap Add Account.**

   The options shown in Figure 7-2 appear.

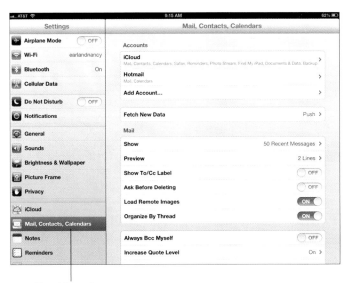

Tap this option.

Figure 7-1: Mail settings allow you to set up multiple e-mail accounts.

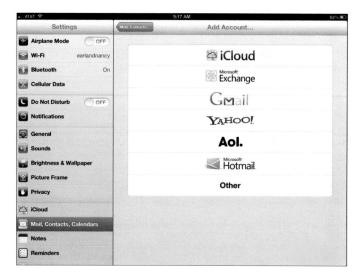

Figure 7-2: Choosing built-in e-mail providers is a quick way to get set up, if you have an account with one.

4. **Tap iCloud, Gmail, Yahoo!, AOL, or Windows Live Hotmail and then enter your account information in the form that appears (see Figure 7-3).**

5. **After iPad takes a moment to verify your account information, tap any On/Off button to have Mail, Contacts, Calendars, or Reminders from that account synced with iPad.**

6. **When you're done, tap Save.**

   The account is saved, and you can now open it using Mail.

Enter your account info.

Figure 7-3: Enter your name, e-mail address, and password, and iPad finds your settings for you.

TIP

If you have a Microsoft Exchange or iCloud account, you can also sync to your computer to exchange contact and calendar information as well as e-mail. See the *iPad User Guide* for more about these options. See Book III, Chapter 1, for more about working with Microsoft Exchange accounts.

Setting Up a POP3 E-Mail Account

You can also set up most e-mail accounts, such as those available through Earthlink or a cable provider, by obtaining the host name from the provider. To set up an existing account with a provider other than Gmail, Yahoo!, Windows Live Hotmail, or AOL, you have to enter the account settings yourself.

Follow these steps to set up an IMAP or POP3 account:

1. **Tap the Settings icon on the Home screen.**
2. **In Settings, tap Mail, Contacts, Calendars and then tap Add Account.**
3. **In the screen that appears (refer to Figure 7-2), tap Other.**
4. **In the screen that appears (see Figure 7-4), tap Add Mail Account.**

Tap this option.

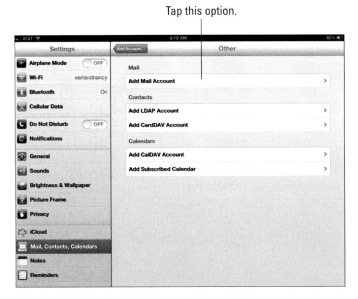

Figure 7-4: Proceed by choosing to add an e-mail account on this screen.

5. **In the form that appears, enter your name, the account address, password, and description, and tap Next.**

   iPad takes a moment to verify your account and then returns you to the Mail, Contacts, Calendars pane with your new account displayed.

   iPad will probably add the outgoing mail server information for you, but if it doesn't, tap SMTP and enter this information.

6. **To make sure the Account field is set to On, under Settings, tap Mail, Contacts, Calendars and then tap the account. In the dialog that appears, tap the On/Off button and then tap Done to save the setting.**

   You can now access the account through Mail.

You can have more than one active account set to On for receiving e-mail; tap the account name in Settings. When you do, you can then open different accounts to view their inboxes from within the Mail app. If you don't want a particular account's e-mails to be downloaded, you can turn off any active e-mail account by opening it in Settings and tapping the On/Off button.

If you turn on Calendars in the Mail account settings, any information you've put into your calendar in that e-mail account is brought over into the Calendar app on your iPad and reflected in the Notification Center (discussed in more detail in Book V, Chapter 4).

Opening Mail and Reading Messages

The whole point of e-mail is to send and receive messages. Mail offers a pretty simple interface for reading your e-mail. It displays an open message and a pane that you can use to show inbox contents or change to a different folder. In landscape orientation, the Mailboxes/Inbox pane is always displayed, but in portrait orientation, you display it by tapping the Inbox button.

When you tap the Mail app to open it, it automatically heads out and checks for any new e-mail. (If you use Microsoft Exchange or iCloud, you can turn on push settings to have your e-mail host send messages to your iPad automatically.)

Here are some common actions in Mail:

- **To follow a link in a message,** simply tap it. Note that tapping web links opens them in Safari, and tapping address links opens the Maps app with a map to that address displayed.

- **To open an attachment,** tap it, and it downloads and opens in the appropriate iPad app or viewer. If you have more than one app that could open that type of file, Mail presents you with a menu to select the one you want to use to open it.

✔ **To open a meeting invitation,** tap the meeting icon (what it looks like depends on the originating application; for example, Windows Live Hotmail uses a little calendar symbol).

iPad supports many common file types — including those that run on multiple platforms, such as PDF and text; those available on Macs, including iWork Pages and Numbers; those familiar to Windows users (though also available in Mac versions), including Microsoft Word and Excel; as well as most common graphics and audio file formats.

When your iPad gets an e-mail, it alerts you with a chime. If those e-mail–received alerts are driving you nuts, you can go to Settings and under General⇨Sounds, use the slider to lower the volume or tap the On/Off button to turn off the chimes.

These steps take you through the simple process of using Mail to open and read e-mails if you have a single e-mail account set up on iPad:

1. **Tap the Mail app icon on the Home screen (see Figure 7-5), which displays the number of unread e-mails in your inbox in a red circle.**

Tap this icon.

Figure 7-5: Without having to open Mail, you can see how many unread messages you have.

2. **If you have only one e-mail account set up on your iPad, a list of messages displays (see Figure 7-6); if the list doesn't display, tap the arrow-shaped button to the right of the words All Inboxes (refer to Figure 7-6) to display a list of inboxes. Tap the inbox whose contents you want to display.**

3. **Tap a message to read it.**

The message opens, as shown in Figure 7-7.

Use gestures such as double-tapping and pinching to reduce or enlarge e-mail.

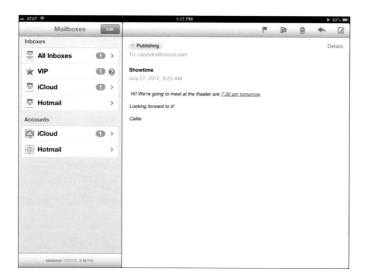

Figure 7-6: Open your Inbox and view its contents.

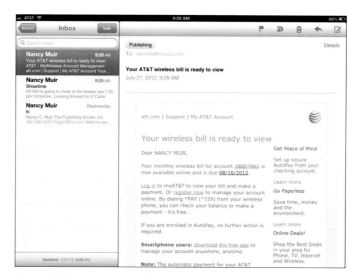

Figure 7-7: Open your e-mail and read it.

4. If you need to scroll to see the entire message, place your finger on the screen and flick upward to scroll down.

You can swipe right while reading a message in portrait orientation to open the Inbox list of messages, and then swipe left to hide the list.

Tap the Hide button (top-right corner of a message) to hide the address details (the To field) so more of the message appears on your screen. To reveal the field again, tap the Details button (which becomes the Hide button when details are displayed).

If you have multiple e-mail accounts set up, you can choose which inbox to display. From the inbox that appears when you open Mail, tap the Back button to view the list of your mailboxes. (See Figure 7-8.)

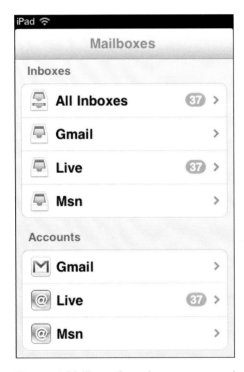

Figure 7-8: Mailboxes for various accounts and the consolidated inbox are listed here.

With several accounts set up, in addition to each account listed on the Mailboxes screen, there's an All Inboxes item listed. Tapping this takes you to a consolidated inbox containing all messages from all accounts in one place.

E-mail messages you haven't read are marked with a blue circle in your inbox. After you read a message, the blue circle disappears. If you like, you can mark a read message as unread. This can help remind you to read it again later. With a message open, tap the Flag button on the toolbar above a message and then tap Mark as Unread. To flag a message — which places a little flag next to it in your inbox, helping you to spot items of more importance or to read again — tap the Flag button and then tap Flag.

To refresh your inbox so that you can view new e-mails, simply swipe downward on the Mail screen. This handy feature arrived with iOS 6.

Replying to or forwarding e-mail

Replying to or forwarding e-mails is pretty darn easy with iPad as well. In fact, there's a handy button for replying or forwarding. There's also a Print command on this menu to make printing your e-mails to a compatible wireless printer easy.

One thing you need to know right now: You can't attach anything to new e-mail messages when you create, reply to, or forward them. Instead, you can use features in apps such as Photos, Contacts, Notes, iWork Pages, and Maps to share individual documents via e-mail.

Here's how to use the simple Reply/Forward functions in iPad:

1. **With an e-mail open (see the preceding section), tap the Reply/Reply All/Forward/Print button, as shown in Figure 7-9.**

Tap the Reply/Reply All/Forward/Print button.

| Reply |
| Reply All |
| Forward |
| Print |

Figure 7-9: The Reply/Reply All/Forward/Print button sports a left-pointing arrow.

2. **Do one of the following:**

   • *Tap Reply to respond to the message sender.* The reply message form shown in Figure 7-10 appears. Tap in the message body and jot down your inspired thoughts.

   • *Tap Reply All to respond to the sender and all other recipients.* A message form appears with all those folks included in the To field. You can now add your response for all to see.

   • *Tap Forward to send the message to somebody else.* If the e-mail has an attachment, you can choose Include or Don't Include in the dialog that appears. The form in Figure 7-11 then appears. Enter a recipient in the To field, and then tap in the message body and enter a message.

   To find out how to print an e-mail, see "Printing E-Mails," later in this chapter.

Tap here to enter a reply.

Figure 7-10: What you reply is up to you!

Tap here to enter a message.

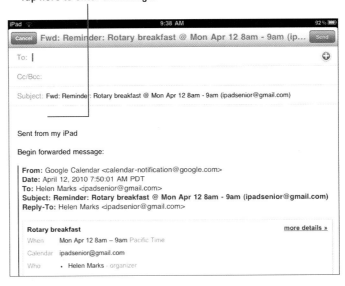

Figure 7-11: When you forward a message, all previous contents are included.

3. **Tap Send.**

   The message goes on its way.

If you want to copy an address from the To field to the Cc/Bcc field, tap and hold the address and drag it to the other field.

Although you can include whether to keep original attachments when *forwarding* an e-mail, any attachments to the original e-mail can't be included in a *reply.*

Creating and sending a new message

You're probably an old pro at creating and sending e-mail messages, but it's worth a quick trip through iPad's Mail feature and its approach to writing an e-mail using the onscreen keyboard.

Note that, by default, your e-mails have a signature that says, "Sent from my iPad." This will definitely impress your geekiest friends, but if you want to change it to something a little more useful, just go to Settings. In the Mail settings, choose Signature. You can then enter any signature text you want.

Follow these steps to create and send e-mail:

 1. **With Mail open, tap the New Message icon.**

    A blank message form (see Figure 7-12) appears.

Figure 7-12: A very basic e-mail message form.

 2. **Enter a recipient's address in the To field either by typing, or by tapping the Dictation key on the iPad's onscreen keyboard (except for the original iPad and iPad 2) and speaking the address.**

    If you have saved addresses in Contacts, tap the plus sign (+) in an address field to choose an addressee from the Contacts list that appears.

 3. **If you want to copy other people on the message, enter other addresses in the Cc/Bcc field.**

    When you tap the Cc/Bcc field, both Cc and Bcc fields are displayed.

 4. **Enter a subject for the message in the Subject field.**

 5. **Tap in the message body and type your message.**

 6. **Tap (you guessed it) Send.**

You can also use Siri to address an email to a person for whom you've created a record in your Contacts app that includes an email address. Just press and hold the Home button and say something like "E-mail Joe Smith, confirming the contact, and then filling out the form that appears via either Dictation or the keyboard.

Want to shout at somebody in an e-mail (not, of course, a practice I advocate)? You can activate Caps Lock when using the onscreen keyboard on your iPad by double-tapping either Shift key. To turn off Caps Lock, tap either Shift key once. To use this functionality, first be sure to use the General⇨Keyboard settings to enable Caps Lock.

Formatting E-Mail

A new feature that arrived with iOS 5 was the capability to apply formatting to e-mail text. You can use bold, underline, and italic formats, and indent text using the Quote Level feature. Follow these steps to do so:

1. **Tap and hold the text in a message and choose Select or Select All to select a single word or all the words in the e-mail.**

   Note that if you select a single word, handles appear that you can drag to add adjacent words to your selection.

2. **To apply bold, italic, or underline formatting, tap the BIU button (see Figure 7-13).**

3. **In the toolbar that appears (see Figure 7-14) tap Bold, Italics, or Underline to apply the respective formatting.**

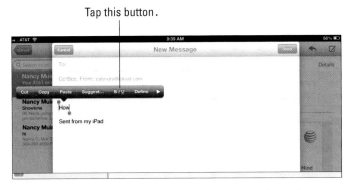

Figure 7-13: Use BIU to add standard styles or emphasis, such as italicized book titles.

Make your selection here.

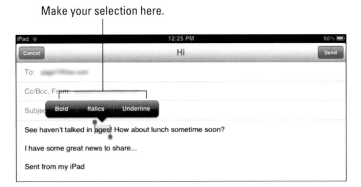

Figure 7-14: Choose the style that works for your message.

4. **To change the indent level, tap at the beginning of a line and then tap the arrow at the far end of the toolbar shown in Figure 7-13.**

5. **In the toolbar that appears, tap Quote Level.**

6. **Tap Increase to indent the text or Decrease to move indented text farther toward the left margin.**

To use the Quote Level feature, make sure that it's on using the iPad Settings. Tap Mail, Contacts, Calendars, and then tap the Increase Quote Level On/Off button.

Searching E-Mail

I'm sure you've never mislaid an e-mail, but some people do it all the time. What if you want to find all messages from a certain person or that contain a certain word in the Subject field. Of course you can enter a name or term into Spotlight Search and results will include any emails that match the search term as well as contacts, songs, and so on. Or, you can use Mail's handy Search feature to find that e-mail. You can search To, From, and Subject fields.

Follow these steps to practice using Mail's Search feature:

1. **With Mail open, tap an account to display its inbox.**

2. **In the inbox, tap in the Search field.**

   The onscreen keyboard appears.

3. **Enter a search term or name, as shown in Figure 7-15.**

Enter a search term here. Search results

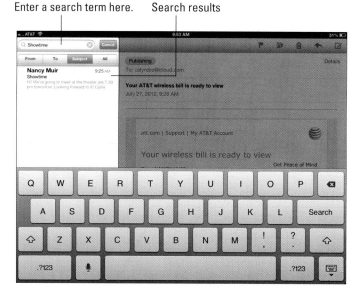

Figure 7-15: Tapping in the Search inbox field opens the onscreen keyboard.

If you have an e-mail account set up to download messages to your device instead of accessing them from the mail server, you can use Mail to search the entire content of the messages in that account.

4. **Tap the From, To, or Subject tab to view messages that contain the search term in one of those fields, or tap the All tab to see messages in which any of these three fields contains the term.**

Matching e-mails are listed in the results.

To start a new search or go back to the full inbox, tap the Delete key in the upper-right corner of the onscreen keyboard to delete the term, or tap the Cancel button.

Printing E-Mails

As of iOS version 4.2, iPad has had native printing capabilities that can be used by certain apps, including Mail. You need an AirPrint-compatible wireless printer setup to use this feature. For more about other options for printing from your iPad, see Book V, Chapter 1.

With an e-mail message open, follow these steps to print:

1. **Tap the Reply/Forward/Print button and then tap Print (refer to Figure 7-9).**

2. **In the Printer Options dialog that appears (if you haven't used this feature with your printer before), tap Select Printer.**

   iPad searches for any available printers.

3. **Tap your printer to select it.**

4. **Tap Printer Options to return to the Printer Options dialog and use the + or – buttons in the Copies field to adjust the number of copies.**

5. **Tap Print.**

   Your print job goes on its way.

Deleting an E-Mail

I have friends who never delete e-mails, but that, frankly, drives me nuts (plus at some point their mailbox fills up and new emails are rejected). When you no longer want an e-mail cluttering up your inbox, you can delete it. When you delete an e-mail on your iPad, it's gone from your inbox, including the inbox you access through your mobile phone or computer. However, for a time, you can retrieve it if your e-mail provider offers a Trash folder for your e-mail account and if your settings for your account with that provider don't cause e-mails to be deleted from their server on download.

Here's how to delete those e-mails you no longer want:

1. **With the inbox displayed, tap the Edit button.**

   Circular check boxes display to the left of each message. (See Figure 7-16.)

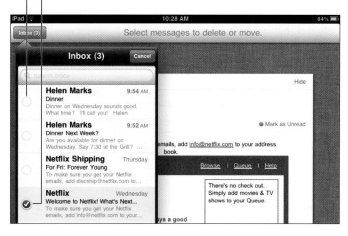

Figure 7-16: Delete several messages at once using the Delete feature.

2. **Tap the circle next to the message you want to delete.**

   You can tap multiple items if you have several e-mails to delete. Messages marked for deletion show a check mark displayed in the circular check box. (Refer to Figure 7-16.)

3. **Tap the Delete button.**

   The message(s) moves to the Trash folder.

Depending on your e-mail provider, Mail may keep a copy of all deleted messages for a time in a Trash folder. To view deleted messages, go to the list of all mailboxes. Tap the account name in the Accounts list in the Mailboxes panel, and a list of folders appears. Tap the Trash folder, and all deleted messages display.

You can also delete an open e-mail by tapping the trash can icon in the toolbar that runs across the top of Mail or by swiping left or right on a message displayed in an inbox and tapping the Delete button that appears.

Organizing E-Mail

I won't kid you; the message-management features in Mail aren't super-robust. In most e-mail accounts (iCloud and Gmail being the exceptions), you can't create your own folders, though I'm hoping that will be a feature added to the next version of iPad. Here's what you can do: Depending on your e-mail provider, you may be able to move messages into any of a few predefined folders in Mail. With the folder containing the message you want to move (for example, the Trash or Inbox if you have a Windows Live Hotmail account) displayed, tap the Edit button. Circular check boxes display to the left of each message. (Refer to Figure 7-17.)

Follow these steps to move any message into another folder:

1. **Tap the circle next to the message you want to move.**

2. **Tap the Move button.**

3. **In the Mailboxes list that appears (see Figure 7-17), tap the folder where you want to store the message.**

   The message is moved.

If you get a junk e-mail, you might want to move it to the Spam or Junk E-mail folder. After you do, any future mail from that same sender is placed automatically in that folder.

If you have an e-mail open, you can move it to a folder by tapping the Folder icon on the toolbar that runs along the top. The Mailboxes list displays; tap a folder to move the message.

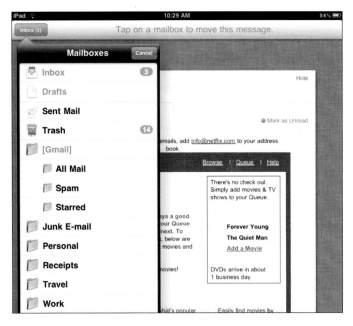

Figure 7-17: There aren't many folders here, but you'll probably make do.

Creating a VIP List

iOS 6 brings a new feature to Mail called VIP List. This is a way to create a list of senders; when any of these senders sends you an e-mail, you're notified through the Notifications feature of iPad. Be sure that in Notifications settings you have set up your Mail accounts to use Notification Center for VIP mail. Then, in the Mailboxes list of Mail, tap the arrow to the right of VIP (see Figure 7-18), and follow these steps to designate a contact as a VIP:

Tap to find your VIP e-mail.

Figure 7-18: Tap here to access the new VIP feature.

1. **Tap Add VIP and your Contacts list appears.**
2. **Tap a contact to add that person to the VIP list shown in Figure 7-19.**

VIP list

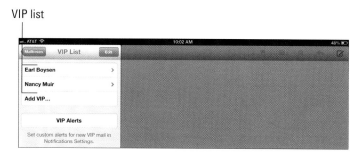

Figure 7-19: To add a VIP, that person must first be added to the Contacts app.

3. **Tap the Home button and then tap Settings.**
4. **Tap Notifications and then tap Mail.**
5. **In the settings that appear, shown in Figure 7-20, tap VIP.**

Set VIP settings.

Figure 7-20: Because VIP List displays information in Notifications, that's the setting category you work with.

6. **Tap the Notification Center On/Off button to turn on notifications for VIP mail.**
7. **Tap an alert style and choose whether a badge icon, sound, or preview should occur.**

   You can also choose to have the notification displayed on your lock screen (see Figure 7-21).

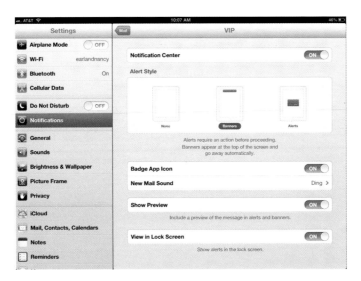

Figure 7-21: Choose from several options for how VIP List alerts happen.

8. Tap the Home button to close Settings.

New mail from your VIPs now appear in Notifications when you swipe down from the top of the screen, and depending on the settings you chose, may cause a sound to play or a note to appear on your lock screen, or a blue star icon to appear to the left of these messages in inbox in Mail.

Chapter 8: Managing iPad Settings

In This Chapter

✏ **Setting brightness and changing the wallpaper**

✏ **Managing Picture Frame settings**

✏ **Controlling General settings**

✏ **Managing iCloud**

✏ **Getting an overview of apps settings**

*i*Pad Settings is a control center for the device, offering settings that let you adjust things like the screen brightness and wallpaper, sound volume, and security features. You can also set up e-mail accounts (which I tell you about in Chapter 7 of this minibook) and control how the Calendar and Contacts apps manage their respective details. Finally, you find settings for each of the individual preinstalled apps, as well as many apps designed for the iPad that you've downloaded to your device.

Check out settings for the Siri personal assistant feature of iPad in Book V, Chapter 6.

In this chapter, you get some highlights of the settings you're likely to need most often, and advice for how to use them.

Making Brightness and Wallpaper Settings

You might as well set up the visual side of iPad first so your interaction with the device is easy on the eyes and battery power. Two such settings fall together as one category in the Settings pane: Brightness & Wallpaper.

Setting brightness

Especially when using iPad as an e-book reader, you may find that a dimmer screen reduces strain on your eyes. Also, reducing the brightness can save a little on your iPad's battery life.

To modify the brightness setting, follow these steps:

1. **Tap the Settings icon on the Home screen.**

2. **In the Settings pane, as shown in Figure 8-1, tap Brightness & Wallpaper.**

Tap this option ...   then adjust brightness.

Figure 8-1: Brightness and wallpaper settings are combined in one pane.

3. **To control brightness manually, tap the Auto-Brightness On/Off button (refer to Figure 8-1) to turn it off.**

4. **Tap and drag the Brightness slider to the right to make the screen brighter, or to the left to make it dimmer.**

5. **Tap the Home button to close Settings.**

If glare from the screen is a problem for you, consider getting a screen protector. This thin film not only protects your screen from damage, but can also reduce glare. These are available from a wide variety of sources (just search for *iPad screen protector*) and cost about $2 each.

In the iBooks app, you can set a sepia tone for book pages, which might be easier on your eyes. See Book II, Chapter 7 for more about using iBooks.

Changing the wallpaper

Just as your desktop computer or laptop can display a pretty picture or pattern as a desktop background called a *wallpaper,* your iPad can display an image on the Home screen and another picture that displays when your iPad is locked.

The picture of blue water that's the default iPad image may be pretty, but it may not be the background that's most appealing to you. Choosing different wallpaper may help you to see all the icons on your Home screen, or just allow you to display an image that appeals to your artistic sensibilities.

To change the wallpaper, do this:

1. **Tap the Settings icon on the Home screen, and then, in the Settings pane, tap Brightness & Wallpaper.**

2. **In the Brightness & Wallpaper settings that appear, tap the arrow to the right of the iPad images displayed in the Wallpaper section.**

3. **In the pane that appears, tap Wallpaper to display all the provided wallpaper images.**

   You can also use your own picture for your wallpaper. Instead of choosing Wallpaper, tap Camera Roll (Saved Photos on an original iPad) or choose a Photos library to browse your saved photos, select the picture you want to assign, and then resume with Step 5.

4. **In the Wallpaper pane (see Figure 8-2), tap a wallpaper image.**

   A preview of that wallpaper appears onscreen.

Figure 8-2: Choose from various built-in wallpapers.

5. **Tap Set Lock Screen (the screen that appears when you lock the iPad by tapping the power button), Set Home Screen (to use as the wallpaper), or Set Both.**

6. **Tap the Home button.**

   You return to your Home screen with the new wallpaper set as the background.

Controlling the Picture Frame

The *Picture Frame* is a feature of iPad that allows you to play a slideshow of images from the Lock screen. When the Lock screen is displayed, you just tap the little flower-like icon in the bottom-right corner to start the show. It's a great way to show a presentation to a customer or dazzle somebody with the pictures from your latest vacation.

To turn on Picture Frame and select the images it displays, follow these steps:

1. **Tap the Settings icon on the Home screen.**

2. **From the Settings pane, tap Picture Frame.**

   The settings shown in Figure 8-3 appear.

Tap this option.

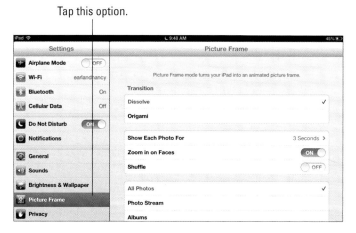

Figure 8-3: Choose how Picture Frame will display your pictures here.

3. **Tap either Dissolve or Origami to choose a transition style.**

   • *Dissolve:* Has one picture fade away, and another replaces it.

   • *Origami:* Displays several pictures on the screen and folds them together in an interesting way to change the picture display.

4. **Tap the Show Each Photo For feature to choose a time increment.**

   You can set this for 2, 3, 5, 10, or 20 seconds.

5. **Tap the Zoom in on Faces feature to have iPad zoom in on faces that appear in images.**

This mode allows iPad to work with iPhoto-captured images on which you have used your computer's photo-imaging software facial recognition feature.

6. **Tap Shuffle to move randomly among the pictures in your library.**

   Without shuffle, Picture Frame moves through the pictures in sequence.

7. **Tap All Photos, Photo Stream, or Albums to choose which photos to display.**

   If you tap Albums, all the albums in Photos appear in a list, and you can tap to select or deselect the ones you want to include.

8. **From the Lock screen, tap the pretty flower icon and watch your slide-show play back in Picture Frame.**

Note that if you enable Passcode Lock to allow your iPad to be turned on only when you enter a passcode (see the "Handling security" section, later in this chapter, for more about this), you can choose to enable or disable the Picture Frame.

To pause a slideshow, just tap the screen. Tap it again to resume. To stop the show, drag the slider, which unlocks iPad.

Managing General Settings

A great many of the iPad settings are tucked into the General category. These include sounds, network, security, and settings for things like date and time, keyboard, and accessibility.

Here's a rundown of settings you'll find tucked under the General category in Settings.

Handling security

Because you're likely to take your iPad on the road on a regular basis, it's a good idea to consider a few security features. Some save battery life and protect your data or access to certain apps.

Security settings involve three features, which you access through the General Settings:

- **Auto-Lock:** Turns off your display to save battery power. You can set the amount of time you want to expire before Auto-Lock locks your iPad.

- **Passcode Lock:** Assigns a passcode to the Lock screen. You can set a passcode, turn it on or off, change the passcode, and set the time interval at which your passcode is required. This is useful if you don't want to bother with a passcode for only brief periods of locking your iPad. Finally, you can use the Erase Data after Ten Failed Passcode Attempts setting so that multiple failed attempts to access your device results in your iPad erasing all data on it. This could protect, for example, your contacts' information or map data that shows your location from prying eyes. Note that if Simple Passcode is turned on (the default setting), you're limited to a four-digit passcode. If you turn off the Simple Passcode setting, you can use a longer, stronger, password using a combination of letters and numbers,

✓ **Restrictions:** Allows you to restrict access to certain apps and content using a passcode. (See Figure 8-4.) This is useful if you don't want your kids to access a particularly adult app or simply don't want them browsing with Safari or buying things with iTunes, for example.

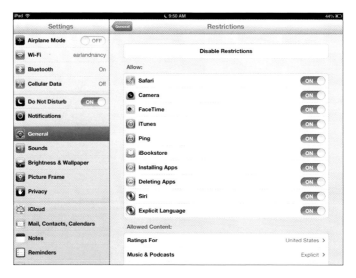

Figure 8-4: Choose the apps or content you want to restrict in this pane.

If you forget a passcode, the only thing to do is restore iPad software, which can be a headache. The obvious advice here: Don't forget your passcode!

Setting the date and time

By default, your iPad is set to Cupertino time — Cupertino, California, that is, home to Apple Computer. If you have occasion to reset the time zone or date and time, either because you live somewhere other than Apple headquarters or you travel around with your iPad, here's how you control the time setting on your iPad:

1. **Tap the Settings icon on the Home screen.**

2. **Tap General.**

3. **Tap Date & Time.**

   The settings shown in Figure 8-5 appear.

4. **Do any of the following:**

   • *Tap the Off button to turn 24-hour time on.* This is military time, so that 2 p.m. is 1400, and so on.

   • *Tap the On/Off button for Set Automatically.* This feature sets your time and date based on your current location.

   • *Tap Time Zone, and a text entry field displays along with your onscreen keyboard.* Press the Delete key to delete Cupertino, and type your location. (If you type a major city near you and in the same time zone, it comes up on a list as you type, and you can just tap to select it.)

Figure 8-5: Choose the time format or time zone, or let iPad set things up for you.

Controlling keyboard settings

Your keyboard is one of the most important ways you interact with iPad, so it's helpful if you have all the onscreen keyboard settings just the way you want them. You can access these under the Keyboard option in the General Settings (see Figure 8-6), and they include the following:

✓ **Auto-Capitalization and Auto-Correction:** Allow iPad to help you avoid mistakes by automatically suggesting corrections to what it perceives as spelling errors, based on a built-in dictionary, or correcting capitalization mistakes you make after you finish entering a sentence.

✓ **Check Spelling:** If you want iPad to automatically check spelling, turning on this feature causes two things to happen: A jagged red line appears under text in apps such as Notes and Mail; and as you type a word with a misspelling, a suggested correct spelling appears in a little bubble. If you also have Auto-Correction turned on, the word is corrected automatically when you finish typing it and add a space or punctuation mark such as a period. Note that you can use the Undo key on the onscreen keyboard with numbers displayed to undo automatic changes.

✔ **Enable Caps Lock:** Activates a feature that lets you double-tap the Shift key to activate Caps Lock. Note that when Caps Lock is activated, the Shift key on the onscreen keyboard is blue and you tap the Shift key to turn Caps Lock off. This setting is turned off by default.

✔ **"." Shortcut:** Turning this on activates a shortcut that allows you to enter a period and a space by double-tapping the spacebar.

✔ **Keyboards:** Gives you access to a choice of built-in keyboards styles such as QWERTY and AZERTY. You can also choose from nine country keyboard layout options, including German, Italian, Russian, Spanish, and my personal favorite, Belgian.

✔ **Split Keyboard:** Turns on a feature that allows you to break the onscreen keyboard into two pieces, one on each side of your screen, to make a more texting-like experience for those who like to type mainly with their thumbs.

✔ **Shortcuts:** Use these two settings to have iPad automatically convert common texting phrases such as "on my way" into shortcuts, or add new shortcuts to its repertoire.

Figure 8-6: Set up your keyboard to work the way you want it to.

Working with the Reset feature

If only life had a reset button to put some things back the way they were. Well, life doesn't, but iPad does. The last item under General settings is Reset. When you tap it, you get options for resetting the following:

- **Reset All Settings:** Every one of the preferences and settings are reset, though information you've added to apps like Calendar and Contacts doesn't change at all.

- **Erase All Content and Settings:** This one both resets your settings and erases information you've added to apps like Calendar and Contacts. This is useful if you plan to sell your iPad.

- **Reset Network Settings:** By choosing this, any networks you've set up are removed. iPad also turns off Wi-Fi and then turns it on again, which disconnects you from any network you're connected to. Note that the Ask to Join Networks setting stays on.

- **Reset Keyboard Dictionary:** When you turn down iPad suggestions of words as you type, you can add words to the keyboard dictionary. You do this by tapping a suggested word, which rejects it but adds the current spelling of the word to the dictionary. If you don't want to keep all those added words, use this reset option.

- **Reset Home Screen Layout:** If you want to get back to the original Home screen you saw when you took iPad out of its box, choose this reset option.

- **Reset Location & Privacy:** When you use an app like Maps that checks your location, it asks you whether it's okay to do that. When you tap OK two times to let it proceed, it stops asking. If you want it to start asking again, tap this reset option.

Managing Sounds

In the Sounds category, you can do two things: adjust the volume level for all apps on your iPad and modify whether system sounds play for events such as new e-mail, calendar alerts, and keyboard clicks.

Adjusting the volume

Though individual applications such as Music and Videos have their own volume settings, you can set your iPad system volume as well to control the level of system sounds and sounds in apps that don't have their own volume control. This system setting is the max against which Music volume settings work; if you set volume to 80% here, for example, Music's 100% volume setting will actually be the maximum system volume, or 80%.

You can simply press the volume rocker controls on the top-right side of
your iPad (when it's in portrait orientation) to increase or decrease volume.
However, this doesn't change the volume of ringers and alerts unless you
change one additional setting. To adjust the system volume from the
Settings pane, tap Sounds. In the Sounds pane that appears (see Figure 8-7),
tap and drag the slider to the right to increase the volume, or to the left to
lower it.

Adjust ringer and alert volume here.

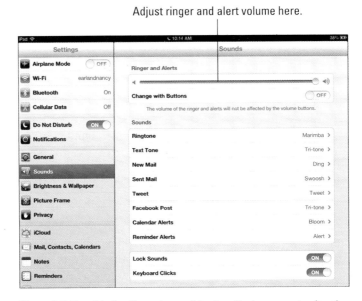

Figure 8-7: Use this familiar volume slider to adjust your system's volume.

Under General settings, make a choice from the Use Side Switch To settings
to set the side switch on your iPad to mute all sounds. If you prefer to use
that switch to lock screen rotation, another way to mute your iPad is to hold
down the volume switch (below the side switch on the top-right corner of
the device) until the sound is effectively off. This method assumes you have
set this switch to control volume.

Turning system sounds on and off

In my experience, people are either big fans or big haters of system sounds
on computers. You know, that annoying bleep you get when a new e-mail
arrives or whatever? iPad also makes sounds when certain events occur, if
you want it to. You can turn on and off the following system sounds:

- Ringtone
- Text Tone

⊯ New Mail

⊯ Sent Mail

⊯ Tweet

⊯ Calendar Alerts

⊯ Reminder Alerts

⊯ Lock Sounds

⊯ Keyboard Clicks

To turn these off or on or choose different system sounds, from the Settings pane, tap Sounds and use the On/Off feature or choose a different sound for any of these.

You can control the Apple Push Notification Service, used to push alerts to your Apple device, via the Notifications item in Settings. This lets you control the alerts sent to you. You can turn alerts on and off, for example, which can save your battery life. You can also control alerts in a specific app's settings.

Making Network and Bluetooth Settings

You can set a few settings for your networks and Bluetooth under the Settings: ones for virtual private networks (VPNs) under General settings, ones for Wi-Fi networks, and finally, settings for 3G/4G network cellular data.

You may have read in the news that your iPad and iPhone save a record of your every move. If you don't like that idea, plug your iPad or iPhone into your computer and, when iTunes opens, click on your device. Then, with the Summary tab selected, click the Encrypt iPhone/iPad Backup option. Apple can't find you anymore!

Another setting you can make in Privacy Settings is to turn Location Services on or off. Turning this on lets apps like Maps find your current physical location. If you turn this feature off and an app needs Location Services to function, it prompts you to turn it on.

If you want to have iTunes use Wi-Fi Sync to sync to your iPad over a Wi-Fi network without having to plug a cable into your iPad and computer, first connect you iPad to your computer and in iTunes enable Wi-Fi syncing. Then you can tap the iTunes Wi-Fi Sync item under General Settings and then tap Sync Now for future syncs.

A *virtual private network* (VPN) allows you to access a private network, such as one at your office or home, over the Internet. A VPN lets you make such a connection securely, and your iPad allows you to make settings for activating your connection through General settings.

For more about connecting to your company network remotely and configuring a VPN, see Book III, Chapter 1.

The Wi-Fi settings include simply turning Wi-Fi on or off, choosing which network to connect to, and activating a feature that joins recognized networks automatically.

I can't forget 3G and 4G. If you have a 3G or 3G/4G iPad, you can make some settings for your 3G/4G connections by tapping the Settings icon and then tapping Cellular Data. See Book III, Chapter 1 for more about these settings.

Note that you can also use Airplane mode settings to turn your Wi-Fi and Bluetooth signals off when in flight, and quickly turn them back on again when you're safely on *terra firma.*

Managing iCloud Settings

Book I, Chapter 5 takes you through the steps in setting up an iCloud account, one of four things you can do using the iCloud item in Settings. (See Figure 8-8.) Here are the other three things you can control for Apple's online storage and sharing service from within Settings:

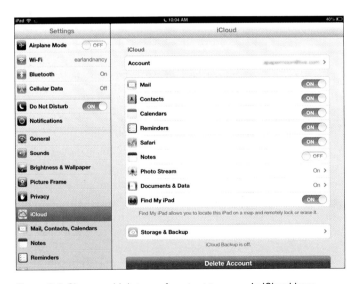

Figure 8-8: Choose which type of content to sync via iCloud here.

✔ **Turn various apps on or off for inclusion in iCloud syncs.** For example, you can set Contacts to sync contacts stored in e-mail accounts, set Calendars to sync with online calendars, sync Photos via Photo Stream, and set Documents and Data to back up and share content via iCloud.

✔ **Control Storage & Backup.** This includes checking your available storage, buying additional storage, or turning iCloud Backup on or off.

✔ **Delete an account.** You'd do this if you no longer want to use a certain iCloud account or want to change accounts.

Settings for Individual Apps

Most bundled apps have a corresponding group of settings in iPad. Rather than bore you by taking you through each and every one, I provide Table 8-1, which gives you an overview of the types of settings you can control. If you like to work with a particular app often, it's worth your while to explore the settings for it to see whether one might make your life with that app a bit easier.

Table 8-1	Built-In Apps Settings Overview
App	*Types of Settings*
Mail	Add Accounts, Fetch New Data Frequency, and Display Settings (how many messages to show, font size, and so on)
Contacts	Display Settings (sort order and display order)
Calendars	Turn on Alerts, Time Zone, and Default Calendar
Maps	Settings for Voice Navigation, Volume, Distance measurements in miles or kilometers, and map label language and size
FaceTime	Turn On/Off and Set Email Account
Safari	Search Engine, Turn AutoFill On/Off, Show Bookmarks Bar, and Security and History
Messages	Turn On/Off, Make Receive Settings, and Show/Hide Subject Field
Music	Sounds and Volume Settings and Display Lyrics and Podcast Information
Videos	Start Playing (where you left off or from the beginning), Closed Captioning, Widescreen On/Off, and Type of TV Signal
Photos & Camera	Slideshow Settings
Notes	Set Font
Reminders	Sync Reminders and choose the Default List of Reminders to use when a list isn't specified

Also note that apps that you download, which have been designed for iPad, often appear in Settings under the Apps heading. Non-iPad apps (for example, iPhone apps) don't seem to appear. The settings vary based on the app, so go exploring and see what you find!

Chapter 9: Maintaining and Troubleshooting

In This Chapter

- ✔ Taking care of your iPad
- ✔ Solving common iPad problems
- ✔ Finding technical support
- ✔ Finding a missing iPad
- ✔ Backing up to iCloud

*i*Pads don't grow on trees — they cost a pretty penny. That's why you should know how to take care of your iPad and troubleshoot any problems that it might have so you get the most out of it.

In this chapter, I provide some advice about the care and maintenance of your iPad, as well as tips about how to solve common problems, update iPad system software, and even reset iPad should something go seriously wrong. In case you lose your iPad, I even tell you about a feature that helps you find it — or even disable it if it's fallen into the wrong hands. Finally, you get information about backing up your iPad settings and content using iCloud.

Maintaining Your iPad

You have a great gadget and an investment to protect in your iPad. A few simple precautions can keep it damage-free — at least until you rush out and buy the next version.

It's wise to keep the screen clean and safe from damage, as well as maximize your battery use. The following sections tell you how.

Keeping the iPad screen clean

If you've been playing with your iPad, you know — despite Apple's claim that iPads have fingerprint-resistant screens — that iPads are fingerprint magnets. They're covered with an oil-resistant coating, but that definitely doesn't mean they're smudge-proof.

Here are some tips about cleaning your iPad screen:

- **Use a dry, soft cloth.** You can get most fingerprints off with a dry, soft cloth such as the one you use to clean your eyeglasses or a cleaning tissue that's lint- and chemical-free. Or try products used to clean lenses in labs, such as Kimwipes or Kaydry, which you can get from several major retailers such as Amazon.

- **Use a slightly moistened soft cloth.** To get the surface even cleaner, very slightly moisten the cloth before you use it to clean the screen. Again, make sure that whatever cloth material you use is lint-free.

- **Remove the cables.** This may go without saying, but I'll say it anyway: If you don't want a fried iPad, turn it off and unplug any cables from it before cleaning the screen with a moistened cloth.

- **Avoid too much moisture.** Avoid getting too much moisture around the edges of the screen where it can seep into the unit.

- **Never use any household cleaners on your iPad screen.** They can degrade the coating that keeps the screen from absorbing oil from your fingers.

Do *not* use premoistened lens-cleaning tissues to clean your screen. Most of these wipe products contain alcohol, which can damage the screen's coating.

Protecting your gadget with a case

Your screen isn't the only element on the iPad that can be damaged, so consider getting a case for it so you can carry it around the house or around town safely. Besides providing a bit of padding if you drop the device, a case makes the iPad less slippery in your hands, offering a better grip when working with it.

Several types of cases are available, and more are showing up all the time. You can choose the Smart Cover from Apple which covers the screen, for example ($39 for polyurethane finish or $69 for leather), the Smart Case from Apple which wraps around the iPad completely ($49), or covers from other manufacturers, such as Tuff-Luv (www.tuff-luv.com) and Griffin Technology (www.griffintechnology.com), that come in materials ranging from leather (see Figure 9-1) to silicone. (See Figure 9-2.)

Cases range in price from a few dollars to $70 or more for leather; some will cost you hundreds of dollars. Some provide a cover (refer to Figure 9-1), and others protect only the back and sides or, in the case of Smart Cover, only the screen. (Refer to Figure 9-2.) If you carry around your iPad much at all, consider a case with a screen cover to provide better protection for the screen or use a screen overlay, such as the invisibleSHIELD from ZAGG (www.zagg.com).

Figure 9-1: A lovely leather case, with a built-in stand mechanism for better viewing.

Figure 9-2: A less-expensive option is a silicone skin.

Extending your iPad's battery life

The much-touted, ten-hour battery life of the iPad is a wonderful feature, but you can take some steps to extend that battery life even further. You can estimate how much battery life you have left by looking at the Battery icon in the far-right end of the Status bar at the top of your screen. Here are a few tips to help that little icon stay full up:

✔ **Use a wall outlet to charge.** Though it can vary depending on your computer model, generally when connected to a Mac computer, iPad can slowly charge; however, some PC connections don't provide enough power to prevent battery drain. Even so, the most effective way to charge your iPad is to plug it into the wall outlet using the Lightning to USB Cable (Dock Connector to USB Cable for non–fourth-generation iPads) and the 10W USB Power Adapter that came with your iPad. (See Figure 9-3.)

Figure 9-3: The provided cord and power adapter.

✔ **Turn off the iPad.** The fastest way to charge the iPad is to turn it off while charging it.

✔ **Avoid USB ports on keyboards.** Your battery may lose some power if you leave it connected to the USB port on a keyboard or other device.

The best way to charge your iPad is with the included cord plugged into an electrical outlet. Using your computer to charge it can take a great deal longer. There are also power strips and adapters now available that have USB ports so you can charge several USB devices at once.

✔ **Limit the screen's impact on the battery.** Turn off the screen when not in use because the display eats up power. Also, reduce the screen brightness in Settings to save power.

✔ **Turn off Wi-Fi.** If you're not using Wi-Fi, turn it off under Settings. Constantly maintaining a Wi-Fi connection or searching for a signal can use up a bit of power.

Your iPad battery is sealed in the unit, so you can't replace it as you can with many laptops or your cellphone battery. If the battery is out of warranty, you have to fork over the money, possibly more than $100, to get a new one. If you use your iPad a great deal, consider getting the AppleCare service contract for free replacement. See the "Getting Support" section, later in this chapter, to find out where to get a replacement battery.

Apple has introduced AppleCare+. For $99, you get two years of coverage, which even covers you if you drop or spill liquids on your iPad. If your iPad has to be replaced, it costs only $50, rather than the $250 it used to cost with garden-variety AppleCare (but only for two instances). You can also purchase it when you buy your iPad or within a month of the date of purchase. See www.apple.com/support/products/ipad.html.

Troubleshooting Your iPad

Though everyone wants to think that his or her iPad is a perfect magical machine, unburdened with the vagaries of crashing Windows PCs and system software bugs, that's not always the case.

Here are some common issues that can come up with iPad, and ways around them.

Dealing with a nonresponsive iPad

If your iPad goes dead on you, it's most likely a power issue, so the first thing to do is to plug the Lightning to USB Cable (Dock Connector to USB Cable for non–fourth-generation iPads) into the 10W USB Power Adapter, plug the 10W USB Power Adapter into a wall outlet, plug the other end of the Lightning to USB Cable (or Dock Connector to USB Cable) into your iPad, and charge the battery.

Another thing to try — especially if you think that an app might be hanging up the iPad — is to press the Sleep/Wake button for a few seconds. Then, press and hold the Home button. The app you were using should close.

You can always try the old reboot procedure, which in the case of an iPad means pressing the Sleep/Wake button on the top until the red slider displays. Drag the slider to the right to turn off your iPad. After a few moments, press the Sleep/Wake button to boot up the little guy again. Be sure your battery has a decent charge because this procedure can eat up battery power.

If the situation seems drastic and none of these ideas works, try to reset your iPad. To do this, press the Sleep/Wake button and the Home button at the same time until the Apple logo appears onscreen.

Troubleshooting keyboard woes

When you're using a Bluetooth keyboard, your onscreen keyboard won't appear. The physical keyboard has, in essence, co-opted keyboard control of your device. To use your onscreen keyboard with a Bluetooth keyboard connected, you have a few options: You can turn off the Bluetooth keyboard, turn off Bluetooth in iPad's General settings, switch off the keyboard, or move the keyboard out of range. Your onscreen keyboard should reappear. Are you accidentally tapping extra keys on the onscreen keyboard as you type? Wearing a wrist support can keep you from hitting extra characters with your wrists. Also, it's much easier to use the onscreen keyboard in landscape mode where it's just plain wider.

Updating software

Just as software manufacturers provide updates for your main computer, Apple occasionally updates the iPad system software to fix problems or offer enhanced features. If you're not using the iCloud feature, which updates your iOS automatically, occasionally check for an updated version (say, every month). You can do this by opening Settings, tapping General, and then tapping Software Update.

Note that if you've chosen to back up and restore iPad via iCloud when you first set up the device or later using Settings, restoring and updating your device happens automatically (see Chapter 5 in this minibook for more about iCloud).

If you choose not to use iCloud, follow these steps to update the iPad system software using a connection to your computer:

1. **Connect your iPad to your computer.**

2. **On your computer, open iTunes.**

   See Chapter 4 in this minibook for more about this topic.

3. **Click your iPad's name in the iTunes Source List on the left.**

4. **Click the Summary tab, as shown in Figure 9-4.**

5. **Click the Check for Update button.**

   iTunes displays a message telling you whether a new update is available.

6. **Click the Update button to install the newest version.**

Select your iPad ...   then click the Summary tab.

Figure 9-4: Get system updates for iPad through your iTunes account.

If you're having problems with your iPad, you can use the Update feature to try to restore the current version of the software. Follow the preceding set of steps, and then click the Restore button instead of the Update button in Step 6. Typically, restoring an OS to another version does run the risk of going back to original settings, so be aware of that going in.

Restoring sound

Coincidentally, the very morning I wrote this chapter, my husband was puttering with his iPad. Suddenly, the sound stopped. We gave ourselves a quick course in recovering sound, so now I can share these tips with you. Make sure that

- **You haven't touched the volume control keys on a physical keyboard connected to your iPad via Bluetooth.** They're on the right side of the top-right side of your iPad when holding it in portrait orientation. Be sure not to touch one and inadvertently lower the sound 'til it's essentially muted.

- **You haven't flipped the Silent switch.** If you have the Screen Rotation/Silent switch set to control sound, moving the switch mutes sound on your iPad.

- **The speaker isn't covered up.** Make sure you haven't covered up the speaker in a way that muffles the sound.

- **A headset isn't plugged in.** Sound won't play through the speaker and the headset at the same time.

✔ **The Volume Limit is set to Off.** You can set up the Volume Limit in Music Settings to control how loudly the Music app can play (which is useful if your partner's into loud rap music). Tap the Settings icon on the Home screen, and then on the left side of the screen that displays, tap Music and use the Volume Limit controls (see Figure 9-5) to turn down the Volume Limit.

Set Volume Limit to Off.

Figure 9-5: Volume Limit lets your iPad get only so loud.

If all else fails, reboot. That's what worked for us — just press the Sleep/Wake button until the red slider appears. Press and drag the slider to the right. After iPad turns off, press the Sleep/Wake button again until the Apple logo appears, and you may find yourself back in business sound-wise. If you're also an iPhone user, and Siri or Voice Control stop understanding you, this reboot trick works for them, as well!

Getting Support

As you may already know if you own another Apple device, Apple is known for its great customer support, so if you're stuck, I definitely recommend that you try them. Also, be aware that every new iPad comes with a year's coverage for repair of the hardware and 90 days of free technical support. Here are a few options you can explore for getting help:

✔ **The Apple Store:** Go to your local Apple Store if one is handy to find out what the folks there might know about your problem.

✔ **The Apple iPad Support website:** Visit this site at www.apple.com/support/ipad. (See Figure 9-6.) Here you find online manuals, discussion forums, downloads, and the Apple Expert feature, which enables you to contact a live support person by phone.

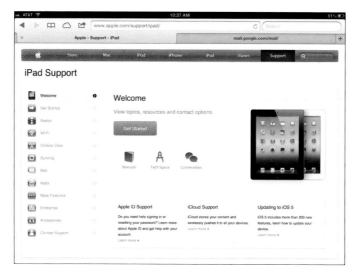

Figure 9-6: Don't forget to check out the manuals and discussions for help.

✔ **The *iPad User Guide:*** You can use the bookmarked manual in the Safari browser or visit `http://manuals.info.apple.com/en_us/ipad_user_guide.pdf`. This is a more robust version of the bookmarked User Guide. You can also download the manual and read it in most popular e-reader programs.

✔ **The Apple battery replacement service:** If you need repair or service for your battery, visit `www.apple.com/batteries/replacements.html`.

Note that your warranty provides free battery replacement if the battery level dips below 50 percent and won't go any higher during the first year you own it. If you purchase the AppleCare service agreement, this is extended to two years. Also note that Apple recommends that the iPad battery should be replaced only by an Apple Authorized Service Provider.

Finally, here are a few useful non-Apple discussion forums that may help provide some answers:

✔ **MacRumors** at `http://forums.macrumors.com/forumdisplay.php?f=137`

✔ **The iPad Guide** discussions at `www.theipadguide.com/forum`

✔ **ipad.org** provides several useful threads at `http://ipad.org/forum`

Finding a Missing iPad

You can take advantage of the Find My iPad feature to pinpoint the location of your iPad. This is a very handy feature if you forget where you left your iPad or somebody walks away with it. Find My iPad not only lets you track down the critter, but also lets you wipe off the data contained in it if you have no way to get the iPad back.

Follow these steps to set up this feature:

1. **Tap the Settings icon on the Home screen.**

2. **In the Settings pane, tap iCloud.**

3. **In the iCloud settings that appear, tap the On/Off button for Find My iPad to turn on the feature (see Figure 9-7).**

Turn on Find My iPad.

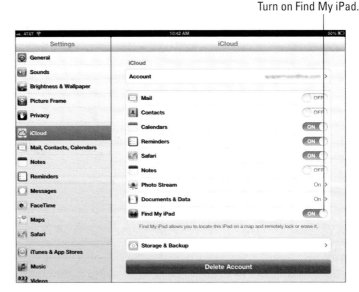

Figure 9-7: Turn the feature on or off to locate your iPad from your computer.

4. **Tap Allow on the Find My iPad dialog that appears.**

If your iPad is ever lost or stolen, go to `http://iCloud.com` and enter your ID and password. The Find My iPad screen appears with your iPad's location noted on a map.

Additionally, if you feel like your iPad is in the hands of someone who might misuse the data on it, you can use this feature to lock the device and even delete all data you've added to your iPad manually or by syncing. Just know, though, that the latter isn't reversible. To wipe information from the iPad, click the Remote Wipe button. (See Figure 9-8.) To lock the iPad from access by others, click the Remote Lock button. Remember that this erases all content, such as contacts, music, notes, and so on for good.

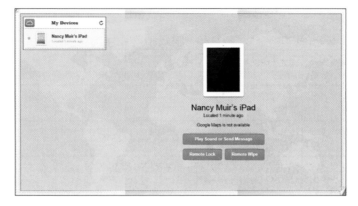

Figure 9-8: To protect data on your iPad, as a last resort you can wipe it clean.

You can also tap Display a Message or Play a Sound to send whoever has your iPad a note saying how to return it to you — or a note that the police are on their way if it's been stolen! If you choose to play a sound, it plays for two minutes, helping you track down your iPad or anybody holding it within earshot.

Backing Up to iCloud

You used to be able to back up your iPad content using only iTunes, but with iCloud, you can back up via a Wi-Fi network to your iCloud storage. You get 5GB of storage (not including iTunes-bought music, videos, apps, and electronic books or content pushed automatically among your Apple devices by iTunes Match) for free, or you can pay for increased levels of storage (10GB for $20 per year, 20GB for $40 per year, or 50GB for $100 per year).

To perform a backup to iCloud, follow these steps:

1. **Set up an iCloud account and then tap Settings on the Home screen.**

   See Chapter 5 in this minibook for details on creating an iCloud account.

2. **Tap iCloud and then tap Storage & Backup (see Figure 9-9).**

Tap this option to use iCloud.

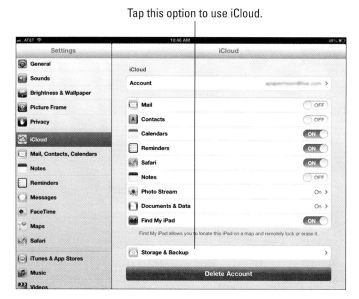

Figure 9-9: Backing up to the cloud.

3. **In the pane that appears (see Figure 9-10), tap the iCloud Backup On/ Off switch to enable automatic backups, or to perform a manual backup, tap Back Up Now.**

A progress bar shows how your backup is moving along.

Set this to On.

Figure 9-10: Automatic backups ensure your data is saved.

Book II
Just for Fun

The iPad is made for soaking up media and other fun stuff, so in this part, the focus is on fun. First, you explore how and where to buy content from music to movies. After you have music on your iPad, you get to try out the iPad music player (the Music app). Movie time? Play around with the Videos app and the built-in video camera. You can even videoconference using FaceTime.

In this part, you also find out all about the iPad camera and the Photos app, as well as how to get wonderful photo effects with Photo Booth. To round out the fun, I introduce you to using your iPad as an e-reader for both books and periodicals, and playing some very cool games on your very magical device.

Chapter 1: Buying Content at iTunes and Beyond

*i*Pad is set up with a preinstalled iTunes app that makes it easy to shop for music, movies, TV shows, audiobooks, and podcasts at Apple's iTunes Store.

In this chapter, you discover how to use your iPad to find content on the iTunes website. That content can be downloaded directly to your iPad, or to another device and then synced to your iPad. In addition, I cover a few options for buying content from other online stores and how to download purchases automatically using iCloud.

I cover opening an iTunes account and downloading iTunes software to your computer in Book I, Chapter 5. If you need to, go back and handle those two tasks before digging into this chapter.

Exploring the iTunes Store

Whether it's your favorite shopping source or not, the iTunes Store is set up to be your most convenient source for content on your iPad at the moment. Sure, you can get content from other places, but the iTunes app comes preinstalled on your iPad — and Apple makes it easy to access it from various Apple devices or your PC.

So, it's time you get to know the iTunes Store: the easiest way to grab all those movies, TV shows, and music that you love for viewing and listening to on your iPad.

Visiting the iTunes Store

Using the iTunes Store from your iPad is easy with the built-in iTunes app. You just tap the iTunes icon on the Home screen.

Now you can roam around trying different options. You have music, movies, TV shows, and audiobooks to choose from. If you begin to purchase or rent an item and you're not already signed in with your Apple ID, the dialog shown in Figure 1-1 appears, asking for your Apple ID and password. Enter your ID and password (you may have created one when you set up your iPad or may have already had one) and tap OK.

Tap here and enter your password

Figure 1-1: Log in to the iTunes Store.

Start exploring musical selections by tapping the Music button in the row of buttons at the bottom of the screen, if it's not already selected, to view selections as shown in Figure 1-2. Tap the See All link to display more music selections.

Tap the Music button in the upper-left corner to go back to the featured Music selections, and then tap the More button at the top of the screen. This step displays a list of music categories that you can choose from. Click one. Items in the category are organized by criteria, such as New and Noteworthy Albums and Top Songs. Tap any listed item to see more detail about it, as shown in Figure 1-3.

The navigation techniques in these steps work essentially the same in any of the content categories (the buttons at the bottom of the screen), which include Music, Movies, and TV Shows. Just tap one to explore it.

Podcasts and iTunes U (courses) used to be accessible through the iTunes Store, but now you have to install separate apps for them to get them and run them on your iPad (you can still shop for all these items in the iTunes Store from your computer). Go to the App Store and search for Podcasts and iTunes U, and install these free apps to get access to this additional content.

See All link

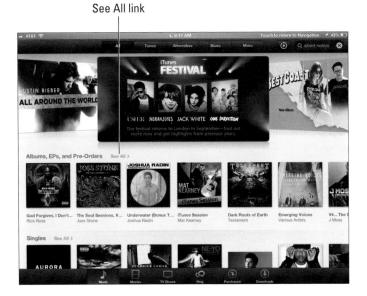

Figure 1-2: Browse selections in the iTunes Store.

Figure 1-3: Detailed information may include the genre,
release date, and song list.

Finding a selection

You can look for a selection in the iTunes Store in several ways. You can use the Search feature, search by genres or categories, or view artists' pages. Here's how these work:

- ✔ **Search:** Tap in the Search field shown in Figure 1-4 and enter a search term using the onscreen keyboard. Tap the Search button on the keyboard or, if one of the suggestions given appeals to you, just go ahead and tap it. Search results are divided into categories such as Music and Podcasts. Flick down to scroll through them and find what you need.

Enter a search term here.

Figure 1-4: Search by composer, artist, or album title.

- ✔ **Category:** Tap a category button at the top of the screen, or tap the More button. A list of genres/categories like the one shown in Figure 1-5 appears.

- ✔ **Link:** In a description page that appears when you tap a selection, you can find more offerings by the people involved. For example, for a music selection, tap the artist's name to follow a link to a page showing all of that artist's selections. For a movie, tap the name of someone in the movie credits to see more of that person's work, as shown for Robert Downey, Jr. in Figure 1-6.

If you find a selection you like, tap the Menu button on its description page to share your discovery with a friend via e-mail, Message, Twitter, or Facebook. A message appears with a link your friend can click to view the selection. Enter an address in the To field and tap Send or Post. Your friend is now in-the-know.

Want to see every option? When displaying items on the Featured tab for any type of content, tap the See All link to see all the featured selections rather than only the top New and Noteworthy selections.

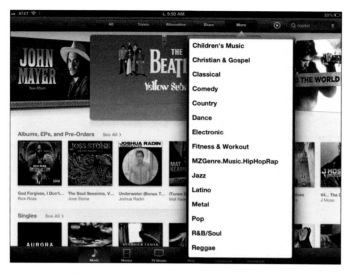

Figure 1-5: Find a genre of music to help you narrow down your search.

Figure 1-6: If you have an artist you favor, search for him.

Previewing music, a movie, or an audiobook

Because you've already set up an iTunes account (if you haven't done so yet, see Book I, Chapter 5), when you choose to buy an item, it's automatically charged to the credit card you have on record or against a store credit if you have one.

However, you might just want to preview an item before you buy it to be sure it's a good fit. If you like it, buying and downloading are then easy and quick.

Follow these steps to preview your content:

1. **Open iTunes and locate a selection you might want to buy using any of the methods I outline in earlier sections.**

2. **Tap the item to see detailed information about it, as shown in Figure 1-7.**

Preview button

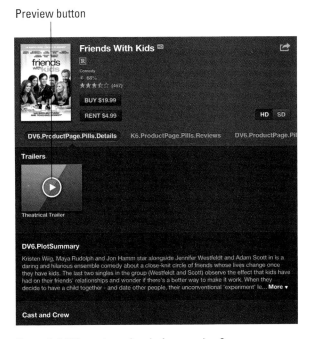

Figure 1-7: Why not preview before you buy?

3. **For a movie or audiobook selection, tap the Preview button (refer to Figure 1-7) to play a preview.**

   If you're looking at a music selection, tap the track number or name of a selection, as shown in Figure 1-8.

If you like what you hear or see, you're ready to buy. Which brings you to the next section.

Tap a track number or name to listen to a preview.

Name		Time	Popularity	Price
1	I Loves You, Porgy (Stereo) Nina Simone	2:33	▮▯▯▯▯	$0.99
2	Mississippi Goddam (Stereo) Nina Simone	4:54	▮▮▯▯▯	$0.99
3	The Other Woman Bobby Hamilton, Lisle Atkinson, Nina Simone & Rudy Stevenson	3:06	▮▯▯▯▯	$0.99
4	Sinner Man (Stereo) Nina Simone	10:22	▮▮▮▯▯	ALBUM ONLY
5	Ne me quitte pas Nina Simone	3:37	▮▯▯▯▯	$1.29
6	See Line Woman (Stereo) Nina Simone	2:38	▮▮▯▯▯	$0.99
7	I Put a Spell on You Nina Simone	2:38	▮▮▮▯▯	$1.29
8	Break Down and Let It Out Nina Simone	2:39	▮▯▯▯▯	$0.99
9	Four Women	4:27	▮▯▯▯▯	$1.29

The Best of Nina Simone
Nina Simone ›
Jazz
12 Songs
Released 1969

$9.99

DV6.ProductPage.Pills.Songs | K6.ProductPage.Pills.Reviews | DV6.ProductPage.Pill

Figure 1-8: You can also preview movies before you rent or buy.

Buying a selection

Free content is out there, but for all but movie selections that you can also rent, other types of content often require that you buy what you want to consume. Buying involves authorizing the purchase and downloading the content to your iPad (which is done automatically after the purchasing part is complete).

Buying and downloading a movie while running your iPad on a 3G/4G network can eat up your data allocation and take a while, if such a large file can download at all. You're better off doing this while connected to a Wi-Fi network.

When you find an item you want to buy, here's how to make your purchase:

1. **Tap the button that shows either the price (if it's a selection available for purchase; see Figure 1-9) or the word *Free* (if it's a selection available for free).**

   The button label changes to Buy *X,* where *X* is the particular content you're buying, such as a song or album.

2. **Tap the Buy *X* button.**

   The iTunes Password dialog appears. (Refer to Figure 1-1.)

Tap a price button to make a selection ...

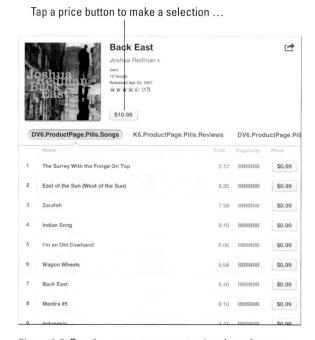

Figure 1-9: Buy the content you want using these buttons.

3. **Enter your password and tap OK, or if you have a credit, tap the Redeem link and enter the code provided.**

The item begins downloading (see Figure 1-10 to see a movie download in progress) and is automatically charged to your credit card or against a store credit. When the download finishes, you can view the content using the Music or Videos app, depending on the type of content you bought.

The selection being downloaded

Figure 1-10: iTunes shows you the progress of your download.

If you want to buy music, you can open the description page for an album and click the album price, or buy individual songs rather than the entire album. Tap the price for a song, and then proceed to purchase it.

Note the Redeem button on many iTunes screens. Tap this button to redeem any iTunes gift certificates you might have gotten from your generous friends, or from yourself.

If you don't want to allow purchases from within apps (for example, Music or Videos) but rather want to allow purchases only through the iTunes Store, you can go to the General settings, tap Restrictions, then tap Enable Restrictions, and enter a passcode. After you set a passcode, you can tap individual apps to turn on restrictions for them, as well as for actions such as deleting apps or using Siri.

If you have a 3G/4G-model iPad, you can allow content to be downloaded over your 3G cellular network. Be aware, however, that downloading larger items such as video or audiobooks could incur hefty data charges with your provider. However, if you aren't near a Wi-Fi hotspot, it might be your only option. Go to Settings⇨Store, and tap the On/Off button for the Cellular setting.

Renting movies

In the case of movies, you can either rent or buy content. If you rent, which is less expensive, you have 30 days from the time you rent the item to begin to watch it. After you have begun to watch it, you have 24 hours remaining from that time to watch it as many times as you like. To rent a movie, follow these steps:

1. **With the iTunes app open, tap the Movies button.**

2. **Locate the movie you want to rent and tap to open it, as shown in Figure 1-11.**

3. **Tap the Rent button.**

   The gray Rent button changes to a green Rent Movie button (see Figure 1-12). At this point you may be asked to enter your Apple ID and password.

4. **Tap the Rent Movie button to confirm the rental.**

   The movie begins to download to your iPad immediately, and your account is charged the rental fee.

5. **To check the status of your download, tap the Downloads button.**

   The progress of your download displays. After the download is complete, you can use either the Music or Videos app to watch it. (See Chapters 2 and 3 in this minibook to read about how these apps work.)

Some movies are offered in high-definition versions. These HD movies look great on that crisp, colorful iPad screen, especially if you have a third- or fourth-generation iPad with Retina display. It's best to download these over a Wi-Fi connection as a 3G/4G connection could incur hefty charges.

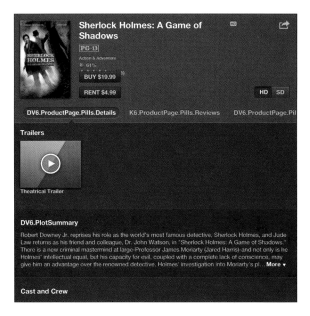

Figure 1-11: To rent, start by viewing details about the content.

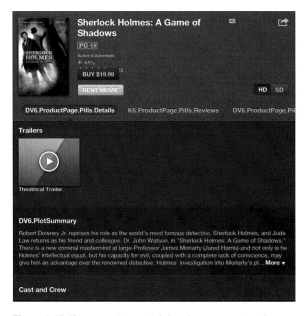

Figure 1-12: If you want to watch it only once, rent and save money.

You can also download content to your computer and sync it to your iPad. See Book I, Chapter 5 for more about this process.

Shopping Anywhere Else

As mentioned earlier in this chapter, one feature that's missing from iPad is support for Flash, a format of video playback that many online video-on-demand services use. Many content stores are hurriedly adding iPad-friendly videos to their collections, so you do have alternatives to iTunes for your choice of movies or TV shows. You can also shop for music from sources other than iTunes, such as Amazon.

You can open accounts at these stores by using your computer or your iPad's Safari browser and then following a store's instructions for purchasing and downloading content. Keep in mind that costs will vary. For example, one such provider is Hulu. (See Figure 1-13.) To get iPad-friendly content from Hulu, you have to sign up for Hulu Plus service and pay $9.99 a month. Then, download the app directly from Hulu and start watching content.

**Book II
Chapter 1**

**Buying Content at
iTunes and Beyond**

Figure 1-13: Hulu has jumped on the iPad wagon through its paid Hulu Plus service.

Here are some of the other online stores that are looking at offering iPad-compatible content, with more coming all the time:

- **Clicker** (www.clicker.com) is working on providing its online television and movie content to iPad.

- **Ustream** (www.ustream.tv) has a mobile app for streaming sports and entertainment programs to mobile devices.

✔ **ABC** (http://abc.go.com) and **CBS News** (www.cbsnews.com) stream live TV programming to the iPad.

✔ **Netflix** (www.netflix.com) makes non-Flash movies and TV shows available that can be played on iPad.

✔ PBS (www.pbs.org) the king of documentary and artsy movie programming has several apps for iPad including NOVA Elements iPad App, PBS KIDS iPad app, and PBS for iPad for other programming.

Additionally, if you can get Flash-based content onto your Mac or Windows machine, you can stream it to your iPad using Air Video and Air Video Server, and it will do an on-the-fly conversion. For more information, go to www.inmethod.com/air-video/index.html. Another free utility that converts most video to an iPad-friendly format is HandBrake. Go to http://handbrake.fr for more information.

There are also apps that stream content if you pay a subscription fee or are an existing customer. Two good ones are Xfinity TV from Comcast and TWCable from Time Warner.

Enabling Autodownloads of Purchases from Other Devices

With iCloud, after you set up an iCloud account, either during the initial setup of your device or through iPad Settings, you can make a purchase or download free content on any of your Apple devices and have those purchases automatically copied onto all your Apple devices. To enable this autodownload feature on iPad, follow these steps:

1. **Tap Settings on the Home screen.**

   To use iCloud, first set up an iCloud account. See Book I, Chapter 5 for detailed coverage of iCloud, including setting up your account.

2. **Tap iTunes & App Stores.**

3. **In the options that appear, tap the On/Off button to turn on any category of purchases you want to autodownload to your iPad from other Apple devices: Music, Apps, or Books (see Figure 1-14).**

At this point, Apple doesn't offer an option of autodownloading video content using these settings, probably because video is such a memory hog. You can always download video directly to your iPad through the iTunes app or sync to your computer using iTunes to get the content or through the iTunes U app for educational content.

Figure 1-14: Authorize purchases from an app by turning it on here.

Chapter 2: Playing Music on iPad

In This Chapter

✔ **Creating playlists**

✔ **Searching for audio**

✔ **Playing music and other audio**

✔ **Shuffling music**

✔ **Using AirPlay**

✔ **Playing around with GarageBand**

*A*lmost everybody on Earth has heard of the iPod — that small, portable, music-playing device from Apple that's seemingly glued into the ears of many. iPad includes an iPod-like app called Music that allows you to take advantage of the iPad's pretty amazing little sound system to play your favorite style of music or podcasts and audiobooks.

In this chapter, you can get acquainted with the Music app and its features that enable you to sort and find music and control playback from your iPad. You also get an overview of the AirPlay feature, which you can use to play music on your iPad over a home network; and GarageBand, an app that lets you take the spotlight as musician, composer, or arranger.

Looking over Your Library of Music

In Chapter 1 of this minibook, I guide you through the process of getting content onto your iPad. After you have some audio content in the form of music, podcasts, or audiobooks, it's organized into collections, and you can find that content by categories such as artist or genre with predefined category buttons along the bottom of the Music app screen.

Viewing the library contents

You can easily view the contents of your library collections, which you may have synced from your computer, pushed to your device through iCloud, or downloaded directly using iPad's Wi-Fi (or 3G or 4G, if you have a 3G or a 4G+LTE iPad) capability. (See Chapter 1 in this minibook for details.)

Take a tour of your Music library collections by following these simple steps:

1. **Tap the Music app icon located in the Dock on the Home screen.**

   The Music library appears. (See Figure 2-1.)

Tap a criteria to use.

Figure 2-1: The Music library showing your music.

2. **Tap the Playlists, Songs, Artists, or Albums button at the bottom of the library to view your music according to these criteria (refer to Figure 2-1).**

3. **Tap the More button (see Figure 2-2) to view music by genre or composer, or to view any audiobooks you've acquired.**

   The Purchased button appears only if you've already obtained content on iTunes.

iTunes has several free items you can download and use to play around with the features in Music, including music and podcasts. You can also sync content stored on your computer or other Apple devices to your iPad and play it using the Music app. See Book I, Chapter 5 for more about syncing.

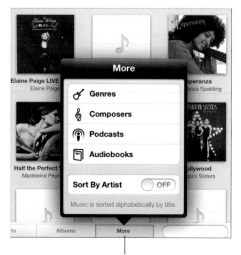

Tap to find more categories.

Figure 2-2: View selections by various criteria using the More button.

Apple offers a service called iTunes Match (www.apple.com/itunes/itunes-match). You pay $24.99 per year for the capability to match the music you've bought from other providers or ripped from CDs (and stored on your computer) to what's in the iTunes library. If there's a match (and there often is), that content is added to your iTunes library at 256 Kbps. If there's audio that isn't a match, it's uploaded to iCloud and synced to your iPad. Then, using iCloud, you can sync the content among all your Apple devices.

You can use the iTunes Summary tab to make a setting to sync music at 128 Kbps. Doing this saves space on your iPad if you're an avid music downloader. You can also make a setting for whether to download album covers in iTunes.

Creating playlists

Everybody loves *playlists*. They let you compile your very own music mix to match your mood or the occasion. You can easily create your own playlists with the Music app to put tracks from various sources into collections of your choosing.

With the Music app open, follow these steps to create your own playlists:

1. **Tap the Playlists button at the bottom of the iPad screen.**

2. **Tap New.**

3. **In the dialog that appears, enter a name for the playlist and tap Save.**

4. **In the list of selections that appears (see Figure 2-3), tap the plus sign next to each item you want to include.**

   Selected items turn gray.

Tap this symbol to include a song in the playlist.

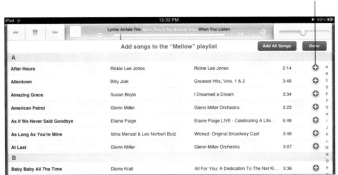

Figure 2-3: Personalize your Music experience with custom playlists.

5. **Tap the Done button, and then tap Done again on the list of songs that appears.**

6. **Tap the Playlists button.**

   Your playlist appears in the Library list, and you can play it by tapping the list name and then the Play button.

You can use the Genius Playlist feature in iTunes to set up playlists of recommended content in your iTunes library. Based on items you've purchased, iTunes suggests other purchases that would go well with your collection. Okay, it's a way to get you to buy more music, but if you're building your music collection, it might be worth a try! Visit the iTunes site at www.apple.com/itunes for more information.

Searching for audio

If you can't find what you want by going through collections or categories, you can search for an item in your Music library by using the Search feature. You can enter an artist's, author's, or composer's name or a word from the item's title in the Search field to find what you're looking for.

You can also ask Siri to play a selection, or use the Spotlight Search feature from the Home screen to search for music.

With the Music app open, tap in the Search field in the lower-right corner. (See Figure 2-4.) The onscreen keyboard opens.

Tap here to search for audio.

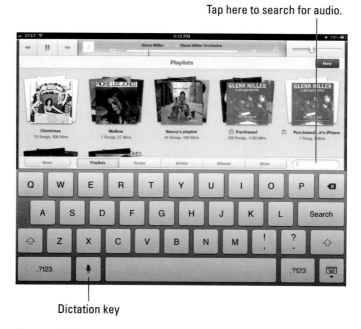

Dictation key

Figure 2-4: Enter your search terms and see what you find!

Enter a search term in the Search field. Or, tap the Dictation key (refer to Figure 2-4) on the onscreen keyboard of an iPad (the Dictation key is not present on the original iPad or iPad 2) to speak the search term, and then tap the Search button on the keyboard. Results display, narrowing the search as you type. Results of a search with the Songs tab selected are shown in Figure 2-5. Now just tap any item in the Search results to play it.

Results display as you type.

Figure 2-5: Music search results.

Playing Music and Other Audio

You have all that music and other audio content to listen to, and beyond downloading and organizing your selections, that's what Music is mainly for. You'll find the typical playback tools in the Music app, but in case you want a refresher, here's the quick rundown on how to use Music as a player.

Playing your tunes

Playing an audio file is simple, and you'll be glad to hear Music can continue to play in the background while you go about using other apps. If you're browsing in Safari, for example, with music playing in Music, you can double-tap the Home button and a mini toolbar opens where you can control playback without leaving the browser. If your iPad is showing the lockscreen, you can also use controls displayed there to control music playback for currently playing selections.

The procedure for playing music is to basically find what you want to play, and then use the playback tools to play it. Here's how:

1. **Locate the item you want to play using the methods I describe in previous sections of this chapter.**

2. **Tap the item you want to play from the list that appears (see Figure 2-6).**

   It begins playing.

3. **Tap the musical note symbol to the right of the playback tools to display the album cover full screen.**

Tap an item to play it.

Figure 2-6: Choose your musical poison here.

4. **If you want to go a specific item, such as a song in the album that's playing, tap the item you want to play from the list that appears.**

   It begins to play.

5. **Use the Previous and Next buttons that display when you tap the top of the screen, shown in Figure 2-7, to navigate the audio files.**

   The Previous button takes you back to the beginning of the item that's playing or the previous track if nothing's playing; the Next button takes you to the next item.

Previous Pause Next   Progress bar   Genius Volume slider

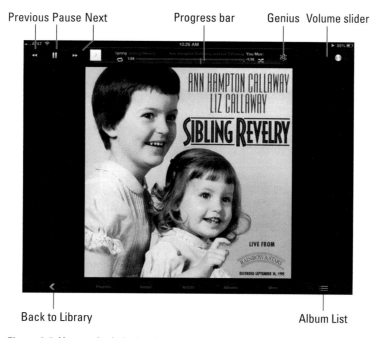

Book II
Chapter 2

Playing Music
on iPad

Back to Library   Album List

Figure 2-7: Your typical playback tools displayed in the Music app.

6. **Tap the Pause button to pause playback.**

7. **Tap and drag the line that indicates the current playback location on the Progress bar left or right to "scrub" to another location in the song.**

8. **Don't like what's playing? Tap the Back to Library arrow in the bottom-left corner to return to the Library view, or tap the Album List button in the bottom-right corner to show other tracks in the album that's playing and make another selection.**

You can use Siri to play music hands-free. Just tap and hold the Home button and when Siri appears, say something like, "Play Take the A Train" or "Play The White Album."

Shuffling music

If you want to play a random selection of the music you've purchased or synced through iCloud or from your computer to your iPad, use the Shuffle feature. With the Music app open, tap the Music, Playlist, or Purchased button in the Source List on the left and then tap the Songs button on the bottom of the screen.

Tap the Shuffle button shown in Figure 2-8. Your content plays in random order.

Tap to shuffle your music.

Figure 2-8: Shuffle your music for a varied musical experience.

Adjusting the volume

Music offers its own volume control that you can adjust during playback. This volume is set relative to the system volume you control using iPad's Settings; if you set it to 50% it will play at 50 percent of the system volume setting.

With Music open, tap a piece of music or a podcast to play it. In the controls that appear onscreen (see Figure 2-9), press and drag the button on the Volume slider to the right for more volume or to the left for less volume. To mute iPad's speaker at any time, press the Mute button or, if it's set up to control volume, slide the Silent switch on the side of your iPad to the mute setting.

Use the Volume slider to adjust the volume.

Figure 2-9: Louder or softer, just use the slider to get the effect you want.

If you have volume set at high and you're still having trouble hearing, consider getting a headset. These devices cut out extraneous noises and should improve the sound quality of what you're listening to, as well as adding stereo to iPad's mono speaker setup. I recommend that you use a 3.5mm stereo headphone (a 1⁄8" headphone also works fairly well) and insert it in the headphone jack at the top of your iPad. You can also use Apple's iPod or iPhone EarPods, which work just fine with iPad. The iPhone EarPods include a microphone as well.

Using AirPlay and Home Sharing

AirPlay and Home Sharing are two methods of sharing music among devices.

AirPlay gives you the ability to stream audio to externally powered speakers that are included on your wireless network as well as home entertainment centers that include an Apple TV unit. Several speaker manufacturers are building AirPlay hardware into their systems. AirPlay streaming technology is built into the iPhone, iPod touch, and iPad, as well as being available to iTunes. With AirPlay, you can send media files from one device to be played on another. You can send (say) a movie you purchased on your iPad or a slideshow of photos to be played on your TV — and control the playback from your iPad. You can also send music to be played over speakers.

There are a few ways to do this. You can purchase an Apple TV and stream video, photos, and music to the TV, or you can purchase AirPort Express and attach it to your speakers to play music. Finally, if you buy AirPlay-enabled wireless speakers, you can stream audio directly to them. Because this combination of equipment varies, my advice — if you're interested in using AirPlay — is to visit your nearest Apple Store or certified Apple dealer and find out which hardware combination will work best for you.

If you get a bit antsy watching a long movie, one of the beauties of AirPlay is that you can still use your iPad to check e-mail, browse photos or the Internet, or check your calendar while the media plays.

Home Sharing is a feature of iTunes you can use to share music and video among devices that have home sharing turned on. To use the feature, each device has to have the same Apple ID on your network. After it is set up via iTunes, you can stream music and videos to any of the devices, and even click and drag content between devices using iTunes. For more about home sharing, visit this site: www.apple.com/support/homesharing.

Playing around with GarageBand

GarageBand is a music composition and playing app that has been prein-stalled on Mac computers for a while, and now it's available for iPad, so I just have to give you a glimpse of what you can do with it. You have to buy the app for about $5 from the App Store. After you install it, you can start making music as follows:

1. **Tap GarageBand on the Home screen where it appears.**

   A menu of virtual instruments appears, as shown in Figure 2-10. Swipe left or right to scroll through them.

Figure 2-10: What instrument did you study in high school? Pick it from this list.

2. **Tap an instrument name, such as Keyboard, to display it (as shown in Figure 2-11).**

   Each instrument has slightly different options, but all allow you to record what you play on the virtual instrument; you can also play it back, visit any songs you've saved, control volume, and return to the main menu of Instruments.

   Tap the Instruments button to change to a different instrument.

Instrument Settings

My Songs button   Playback and recording options   Song Settings

Instruments button   Volume slider

Figure 2-11: The options allow you to be a musician, composer, or arranger.

3. **Tap the Instrument Settings button to control settings such as echo and reverb (see Figure 2-12), or tap the Song Settings button to add sounds or adjust the tempo (see Figure 2-13).**

Figure 2-12: Give your music cool effects.

Play button   Record button

Figure 2-13: Keep your song jumping by adjusting the tempo.

4. **With the instrument displayed, tap it (whether it's a drum or keyboard) to produce sounds.**

5. **If you want to record what you're playing, tap the Record button to start playing, and tap it again when you're done.**

6. **Play back what you've recorded by tapping My Songs, tapping an item, and then tapping the Play button.**

There's no room here for an exhaustive tutorial on using all GarageBand instruments, but feel free to play with this fun app. You can't break anything, and the great built-in help system can help you figure out most features!

Chapter 3: Watching Videos

In This Chapter

✔ Playing movies, podcasts, or TV shows with Videos

✔ Going to a movie chapter

✔ Deleting a video item from iPad

*I*n this chapter, I cover the pre-installed app called Videos. The Videos app is a player with which you can watch downloaded movies, TV shows, as well as media you've synced from iCloud or your Mac or PC. If you like to view things on a bigger screen, you can use iPad's AirPlay technology and Apple TV, a device that will cost you $99, to send your iPad movies and photos to your TV, which requires that you get the component and composite connectors, $39 accessories.

Note that iPads (except the original iPad) sport two video cameras you can use to capture your own videos. By purchasing the iMovie app (a longtime mainstay on Mac computers), you add the capability to edit those videos. You find out about both of these features in Chapter 4 of this minibook.

In this chapter, I explain all about watching, rating, deleting, and sharing video content from a variety of sources. You might want to refer to Chapter 1 in this minibook first to purchase or download one of many free TV shows or movies you can practice with.

Finding Videos

Note that you can get video content through iTunes and some third-party companies that support iPad, including Netflix and ABC TV. You can also use an app such as Air Video to send content from your Mac or PC to your iPad via a wireless connection, or use the EyeTV app from your Mac to send live TV or recordings. Some of the content you find online is free, and some shows or movies will cost you a few bucks.

You can also view videos you stream from a Home Sharing iTunes library over a home network, which can really save space on your iPad because the content can be stored on another device (such as a hard drive attached to your Mac or PC). Turn on Home Sharing in the Video section of iPad Settings.

This chapter focuses mainly on the bundled Videos app, but you should also note that more and more online content providers are making it possible to view videos on their sites. For example, you can go to Flickr and use its HTML5 player for video playback.

See Chapter 1 in this minibook for more about buying or renting movies or TV shows using the iTunes Store.

Playing Movies or TV Shows

Did you realize your iPad is a miniature home entertainment center? The built-in Videos app can play TV shows and movies.

When you first open the Videos app, you may see relatively blank screens with a note that you don't own any videos and a link to the iTunes Store. After you purchase TV shows and movies or rent movies, you see tabs for the different kinds of content you own. Use the steps in Chapter 1 of this minibook to download video content to your iPad. After you download content, use these steps to work with Video's pretty familiar playback tools to play it:

1. **Tap the Videos app icon on the Home screen to open the application.**

2. **On a screen like the one shown in Figure 3-1, tap the Movies or TV Shows tab, depending on which one you want to watch.**

Figure 3-1: Choose the type of content you want to view.

3. **Tap an item to open it.**

   A description appears, as shown in Figure 3-2.

4. **Tap the Play button.**

   The movie or TV show opens and begins playing. The progress of the playback displays in the Progress bar, showing how many minutes you've viewed and how many remain. (See Figure 3-3.) If you don't see this bar, tap the screen once to display it briefly along with a set of playback tools at the bottom of the screen.

Play button

Figure 3-2: You can get information about the media on this opening screen.

Done button   Progress bar

Volume slider   Go to Next Chapter button

Go to Previous Chapter button   Pause/Play button

Figure 3-3: Use the standard playback controls to play your content.

5. With the playback tools displayed, take any of these actions:

- *Tap the Pause button to pause playback.*

- *Tap either Go to Previous Chapter or Go to Next Chapter to move to a different location in the video playback if the video supports chapters.*

- *Tap the circular button on the Volume slider and drag it left or right to decrease or increase the volume, respectively.*

6. To stop the video and return to the information screen, tap the Done button to the left of the Progress bar.

Watching non-iTunes videos

Are you limited to iTunes video content on your iPad or viewing all your downloaded content on the smaller screen? Not at all. You can connect iPad to your television, so you can watch videos on the more vision-friendly larger screen. To do this, you have to buy an Apple iPad Dock and a Component or Composite Adapter at the Apple Store. You also need any other appropriate cables for your TV to complete the connection.

Note that iPad supports only the following video formats: H.264 video up to 1080p, 30 frames per second; MPEG-4 video, up to 2.5 Mbps, 640 by 480 pixels, 30 frames per second; and Motion JPEG (M-JPEG), up to 35 Mbps, 1280 by 720 pixels, 30 frames per second. If you want to play AVI videos, you can use conversion software such as Mac AVI to iPad Video Converter to be able to convert, edit, and play AVI movies

on your iPad. You can also stream with Air Video Live Conversion, or use the free HandBrake app to convert to an iPad-friendly format.

In addition, you can rip Blu-ray video disc content to an iPad-compatible format and then transfer the content by syncing to your computer using iTunes. You can use the Blu-ray Ripper for Mac here: www.softdiggs.com/blu-ray-ripper-for-mac.php. You can use the free Windows Aiseesoft Blu-ray to iPad Ripper at www.softdiggs.com/blu-ray-ripper.php to handle the transfer.

Finally, check out the Air Video app from InMethod. Using this app, you can stream content to your iPad, convert content, or save content to iTunes, which you can then sync to your iPad.

You can set up widescreen viewing options in the Videos section of iPad Settings. For more about using Settings, see Book I, Chapter 8.

Note that if you've watched a video and stopped it partway through, the next time you open the video in iPad it opens, by default, at the last spot you were viewing. To start a video from the beginning, just as with most players, you simply tap and drag the circular button on the Progress bar all the way to the left. You can also change the default setting from start where you left off to start from the beginning in iPad's Settings under Video.

Turning on Closed-Captioning

If you have hearing challenges or are a fan of foreign flicks, you'll be glad to hear that iPad offers support for closed-captioning and subtitles. This feature requires that you have content that supports closed-captioning (not all shows or movies do) and that you use iPad Settings to turn on the feature. Look for the CC logo on media you download to use this feature; be aware that video you record using the iPad video camera won't have this capability.

Turn on the feature in iPad Settings by following these steps:

1. **Tap the Settings icon on the Home screen.**

2. **On the screen that appears (see Figure 3-4), scroll down and then tap Videos in the Settings pane.**

Tap Videos...   then tap to turn on Closed Captioning.

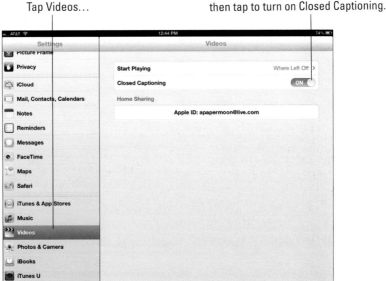

Figure 3-4: Use the Settings icon on your Home screen to access video settings.

3. **In the menu that displays on the right side of the screen (refer to Figure 3-4), tap the Closed Captioning On/Off button to turn on the feature.**

 Now when you play a movie with closed-captioning, you can click the Audio and Subtitles button to the left of the playback controls to manage these features.

Going to a Movie Chapter

You know that movies you view on a DVD or online are usually divided into *chapters,* so you can jump from one part to another quickly. Jumping to another chapter using the Videos app is a pretty simple procedure. Follow these steps:

1. **Tap the Videos app icon on the Home screen.**
2. **Tap the Movies tab if it isn't already displayed.**
3. **Tap the title of the movie you want to watch.**

   Information about the movie displays. (Refer to Figure 3-2.)

4. **Tap the Chapters tab.**

   A list of chapters displays, as shown in Figure 3-5.

Chapters tab

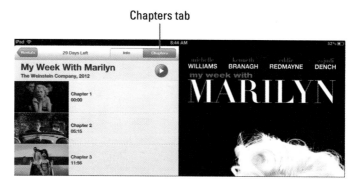

Figure 3-5: Click a chapter in this list to go to it.

5. **Tap a chapter to play it.**

You can also use the playback tools to go back one chapter or forward one chapter. For more information, see the "Playing Movies, Podcasts, or TV Shows" section, earlier in this chapter.

Deleting Video Content

Media files can, as you know, take up lots of space in a computing device. Even if you bought the iPad model with the largest amount of memory, its memory can fill up fast. When you've bought content on iTunes, you can always download it again, so if you're not planning on watching an item again soon, it's a good idea to delete it from your iPad and free up some space. If you want to delete content you didn't purchase from iTunes, be sure to back it up to your computer first, otherwise you can't get at it again once it's gone from your iPad.

Note that if you rent content and delete it before watching it, you can't get it back without paying for it once again.

To delete items, tap the Videos app icon on the Home screen. Locate the item you want to delete on the Movies, TV Shows, or Podcasts tab and then press and hold the item; a Delete button appears, as shown in Figure 3-6. Tap the Delete button, and the item is deleted. (To delete multiple items, tap the Edit key instead at this point.)

Tap the Movies or TV Shows tab

Figure 3-6: Click Delete, and your video is gone.

If you buy a video using iTunes, sync to download it to your iPad, and then delete it from iPad, you'll find it saved in your iTunes library. You can sync your computer and iPad again to download the video once more at no additional charge. However, rented movies, after being deleted, are gone with the wind.

Connecting iPad to high-definition devices

iPad 2 added the capability to connect the device, using an Apple Digital AV Adapter cable (a $39 accessory), to another device that supports Thunderbolt and HDMI connections. At this writing, you'll find lots of HDMI devices; however, there aren't many Thunderbolt devices actually out there, though many are being developed.

Thunderbolt is the latest and greatest high-speed input/output interface. Thunderbolt's major advantage is speed when working with high-resolution displays, and because of that speed, it may just become the new technology *du jour.*

Chapter 4: Getting the Most Out of iPad Cameras and FaceTime

In This Chapter

✒ **Looking good in photos**

✒ **Taking videos**

✒ **Working with your videos in iMovie**

✒ **Making video calls with FaceTime**

*W*ith its gorgeous screen, especially the third- and fourth-generation iPads with their Retina display, the iPad is a natural for viewing photos and videos. It supports most common photo formats, such as JPEG, TIFF, and PNG. You can shoot your photos and videos by using the built-in cameras in iPad.

If you have the third- or fourth-generation iPad, you have a built-in iSight camera for your rear-facing camera. This improvement on previous iPad cameras is a 5-megapixel beauty with an illumination sensor that adjusts for whatever lighting is available. Face detection balances focus across as many as ten faces in your pictures. The video camera option offers 1080p HD (high-definition video) with video stabilization that makes up for some shaking as you hold the device to take videos.

When you have photos to play with, the Photos app lets you organize photos from the Camera Roll and view photos in albums, one by one, or in a slideshow. You can also e-mail, message, post to Facebook, or tweet a photo to a friend; print it; or use your expensive gadget as an electronic picture frame. And if you like to play around with photo effects, you'll enjoy the photo-editing features as well as the preinstalled app, Photo Booth.

If video is more up your alley, in this chapter, you also discover how to use the video cameras in iPad and edit videos with the popular iMovie app. For those who want to share videos of themselves and their surroundings with others, I cover using the video cameras along with FaceTime to make video calls.

Working with Photos

iPads (except for the original iPad) come with cameras — two, to be exact. These cameras allow you to capture video and photos. And because one camera is front-facing and the other is rear-facing, you can switch between them to capture images of yourself holding the iPad or images of what you're looking at.

On an iPad, the front-facing camera captures high-definition video and photos at 800 x 600 resolution; the rear-facing camera captures high-definition video and photos at 1280 x 720 resolution.

When you capture photos, they appear in the Photos app's Camera Roll, where you can view them, e-mail them, and so on. (See Chapter 6 in this minibook for more about using the Photos app). The Photo Streams feature lets you share groups of photos with people using iCloud on an iOS 6 device or on a Mac computer with the Mountain Lion OS installed. (See Book V, Chapter 1 for more about sharing files using iCloud.)

The cameras in the iPad are just begging to be used, so get started!

Taking pictures with the iPad camera

When you use an iPad that has a camera, you can switch it between a standard camera and a video camera, and choose whether to use the front or rear camera. To work with the standard camera to take pictures, follow these steps:

1. **Tap the Camera app icon on the Home screen to open the app.**

   If the Camera/Video slider setting at the bottom-right corner of the screen (see Figure 4-1) is shifted to the right, slide it to the left to choose the still camera rather than video.

2. **Tap the Options button, tap the On/Off button for Grid, and then tap Done.**

   This turns on a grid that helps you position a subject within the grid and autofocus.

3. **Move the camera around until you find a pleasing image, and then you can do a couple of things at this point to help you take your photo:**

   • Tap the area of the grid where you want the camera to autofocus.

   • Pinch the screen to display a zoom control; drag the circle in the zoom bar to the right or left to zoom in or out on the image. Note that zooming doesn't change resolution and so can degrade the image.

Capture button

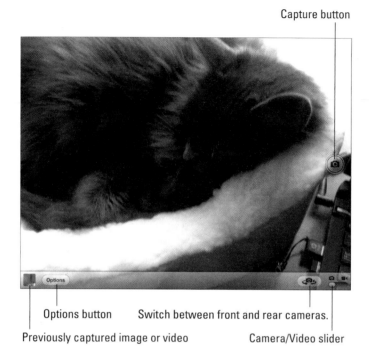

Options button   Switch between front and rear cameras.

Previously captured image or video   Camera/Video slider

Figure 4-1: The Camera app.

4. Tap the Capture button at the right side of the screen.

You've just taken a picture, and it's stored automatically in the Photos app.

5. Tap the icon in the bottom-right corner to switch between the front camera and rear camera.

You can now take pictures of yourself.

6. Tap the Capture button, hold and release it to take another picture.

Alternately you can use the volume rocker as a shutter release. Remember to smile!

7. To view the last photo taken, swipe to the left or tap the thumbnail of the latest image in the bottom-left corner of the screen.

The Photos app opens and displays the photo.

8. Tap the Menu button.

A menu appears, allowing you to e-mail, instant message, share with others using Photo Stream, post to Facebook or tweet the photo; assign it to a contact; use it as iPad wallpaper; print it; or copy it (as shown in Figure 4-2).

Figure 4-2: The simple set of controls for the Camera app.

9. **Tap the Delete button if you want to delete the photo.**

    The image is deleted.

10. **Tap the Home button to close Photos and return to the Home screen.**

Printing photos

If you have a wireless printer that's compatible with Apple AirPrint technology, you can print photos. As of this writing, most major manufacturers offer printers that have this capability, and you can bet that Apple's working with other manufacturers to provide more compatible choices. However, if you don't want to spring for one of these models, you can also use apps such as Printopia and AirPrint Activator 2 to provide this functionality to other printers on your network.

If you don't have access to this kind of wireless printer, when you plug iPad into your computer, you can sync them via iTunes or simply use Finder (Mac) or Windows Explorer (PC) to double-click a series of folders on your iPad until all photos are displayed, select the ones you want, and copy and paste the photos into your computer for printing.

To print a photo, do this:

1. **With Photos open, maximize the photo you want to print.**

2. **Tap the Menu button (refer to Figure 4-2) and then tap Print.**

   The Printer Options dialog appears. (See Figure 4-3.)

Tap this option.

Figure 4-3: The Printer Options dialog.

3. **Tap Select Printer.**

   iPad searches for a compatible wireless printer.

4. **Tap the plus or minus signs in the Copy field to set the number of copies to print.**

5. **Tap the Print button.**

   Your photo is on its way to your printer.

Playing around with Photo Booth

With each new iteration of its operating system, iPad tends to add an app or two that comes preinstalled. With iOS 4.3, Apple added Photo Booth, a photo-manipulation app that goes hand in hand with the still camera built into the iPad (except for the original iPad) hardware. You can use this app to capture photos using various fun effects, such as Kaleidoscope and X-Ray. You can then copy or e-mail photos from within Photo Booth.

Note that photos you take with Photo Booth open automatically and are saved to your Photos app's Camera Roll.

Here's how to take photos using Photo Booth effects:

1. **Tap the Photo Booth icon on the Home screen.**

   The different possible effects that can be used in the current view of the camera appear. (See Figure 4-4.)

Figure 4-4: Effects from mild to wild.

2. **Tap an effect.**

3. **Tap the Capture button.**

   An image using that effect is captured. (See Figure 4-5.)

   To return to the various effects, tap the Effects button in the bottom-left corner of the screen.

   The image appears along with a filmstrip of all the images you've captured using Photo Booth.

4. **If you want to delete a photo, tap the Menu button, tap a photo, tap the X that appears, and then tap Delete.**

5. **Tap the Home button.**

   You return to the Home screen, and your photos are available in the Camera Roll folder of the Photos app.

Figure 4-5: My calculator, twisted with a Photo Booth effect.

Exploring the iPad Video Camera and iMovie

Perhaps you have a bit of Steven Spielberg in you — you long to make your own movies and edit them into masterpieces. If so, the iPad video camera turns this really cool device into your dream machine.

You can capture video with the iPad and then use iMovie software to edit and combine video clips any way you like. You can also edit videos taken with an iPhone or iPod touch you've synced through iTunes or iCloud. In this section, you discover the ins and outs of making movies with iPad.

Capturing your own videos with the built-in cameras

In iPads (except for the original iPad), two video cameras that can capture video from either the front or rear of the device make it possible for you to take videos that you can then share with others or edit. (Find out more about video editing in the next section.)

To record a video, follow these steps:

1. **Tap the Camera app on the Home screen.**

   The Camera app opens.

2. **Use the Camera/Video slider to switch from the still camera to the video camera (as shown in Figure 4-6).**

Record button

Previously captured image or video

Switch between front and rear cameras.

Camera/Video slider

Figure 4-6: It takes one tap to move between camera and video.

3. **If you want to switch between the front and rear cameras, tap the icon near the bottom-right corner of the screen (as shown in Figure 4-6).**

4. **Tap the Record button to begin recording the video.**

   The Record button flashes when the camera is recording.

5. **To stop recording, tap the Record button again.**

   A thumbnail link to your new video displays in the bottom-left corner of the screen.

Before you start recording, make sure you know where the camera lens is (in the top-center portion of the device on the front and top-right side of the back when holding iPad in a portrait orientation) — while holding the iPad and panning, you can easily put your fingers directly over the lens!

Editing movies with the iMovie app

The iMovie app has been supplied with Mac computers for several years, and now a scaled down version is available for the iPad. After you capture a video, you can use iMovie to edit it. This task gives you a brief overview of what you can do with iMovie.

Now you should know, this one will cost you some cash. Start by purchasing iMovie from the App Store. (It costs $4.99.) For more about purchasing apps, see Book I, Chapter 5. After you install the app, you can edit movies by following these steps:

1. **Tap the iMovie app icon on the Home screen.**

   iMovie opens.

2. **On the screen that appears, tap the New button, as shown in Figure 4-7.**

   A new movie project opens. Any videos you've taken (see the preceding section) display as thumbnails in the top-left corner of the screen.

3. **Double-tap a video to open it (see Figure 4-8).**

New button

Figure 4-7: Starting a new iMovie project.

Thumbnails of media Toolbar Media preview Settings button Undo button

Camera button Storyboard Microphone button Music button Video Camera button

Figure 4-8: Open a video on your iPad.

4. **Tap the storyboard to scroll through your video frames.**

   Wherever the red line sits (refer to Figure 4-8) is where your next action, such as playing the video or adding a transition, begins.

5. **To add one video to the end of another, double-tap another clip in the list of media.**

   The clip appears to the right of the first one in the storyboard.

6. **If you want to add music to your videos, tap the Music button (refer to Figure 4-8).**

   The option of sound effects, music in your Music library, or theme music becomes available.

7. **Tap a music option to add it to the video, or drag the item to the time-line to make it a background track or associate it with a specific clip.**

   To undo any action, tap the Undo button. (Refer to Figure 4-8.)

8. **(Optional) Record an audio narration:**

a. *Scroll to the point in the movie where you want it to be heard and tap the Microphone button (refer to Figure 4-8).*

b. *Tap the Record button, wait for the countdown to complete, and then record.*

c. *When you're done recording, tap Stop (as shown in Figure 4-9).*

Tap this button.

Figure 4-9: Use the red button to start and stop recording.

d. *In the options shown in Figure 4-10, tap Review to hear your recording, tap Accept to save the recording, or tap Discard or Retake if you're not completely happy with it.*

If you accept the recording, it appears below the storyboard at the point in the movie where it will play back.

Figure 4-10: Choose options for recording your video.

You can do more things with iMovie, such as add transitions between clips or rearrange and cut segments out of clips. Play around with iMovie to see the possibilities, or check out *iLife '11 For Dummies,* by Tony Bove, or *iPhone Photography & Video For Dummies,* by Angelo Micheletti (both published by John Wiley & Sons, Inc.).

If you want to create a slideshow with still photos rather than video, tap the Camera button (shown in Figure 4-8), and your stored photos are listed instead.

To quickly return from iMovie to your camera, perhaps to capture more footage, tap the Video Camera button shown in Figure 4-8.

You can tap the Settings button (refer to Figure 4-8) to open a menu that lets you make settings for playing theme music, looping the music to play continuously, and using a special effect to fade your movie in or out at the beginning and end.

Getting Face to Face with FaceTime

FaceTime is an excellent video-calling app that's been available on the iPhone 4 since its release in mid-2010 and is now available on iPads (except for the original iPad). The app lets you call people who have FaceTime on their iOS 5 or later devices using a phone number. You and your friend or family member can see each other as you talk, which makes for a much more personal calling experience.

You can also show the person on the other end of the call your surroundings by using the rear iPad camera and panning around you. The possibilities are limitless: Show your husband the toy you're thinking of buying your son for his birthday, let your girlfriend see the new car you're thinking of buying while she's busy at work, or share your artwork or trip to the wine country with friends.

You can use your Apple ID and e-mail address to access FaceTime, so after you install it, it works pretty much out of the box. See Book I, Chapter 5 for more about getting an Apple ID.

If you're having trouble using FaceTime, make sure the feature is turned on. Tap Settings on the Home screen and then tap FaceTime. Tap the On/Off button to turn it on, if necessary. You can also select the e-mail account that can be used to make phone calls to you on this Settings page.

Who can use FaceTime

Here's a quick rundown of what device and what iOS you need for using FaceTime's various features:

- FaceTime is available on all iPads except the original iPad.
- You can call people who have iPhone 4 or later, iPad 2 or later, fourth-generation iPod touch, or Mac (running OS X 10.6.6 or later).
- You can use a phone number to connect with iPhone 4 or later.
- You can connect using an e-mail address with a Mac, iPod touch, or iPad.

Making a FaceTime call

You can make and receive calls with FaceTime using a phone number (iPhone 4/4S/5) or an e-mail account (iPad 2 or later, iPod touch, or Mac) and show the person on the other end what's going on around you.

If you have a Wi-Fi only iPad and use FaceTime over a Wi-Fi network that limits the places from which you can make or receive video calls to your home wireless network or a public hotspot. On the other hand, you avoid costly data usage over a 3G or 4G network with this setup even if you own a 3G/4G iPad model.

You have to use the appropriate method for placing a FaceTime call, depending on the kind of device the person you're calling has. If you're calling an iPhone 4 or later user, use a phone number the first time you call, and thereafter, you can use the phone number or e-mail address; if you're calling an iPad 2 or later, an iPod touch, or a FaceTime for Mac user, you have to make the call using that person's e-mail address.

You can't adjust audio volume from within the app or record a video call. Nevertheless, on the positive side, though its features are limited, this app is very straightforward to use.

Follow these steps to use FaceTime:

Book II
Chapter 4

1. **Connect to a Wi-Fi or cellular (with iOS 6) network.**

   See Book I, Chapter 5 for details on connecting.

2. **If you know that the person you're calling has FaceTime on an iPhone 4/4S/5, an iPad 2 or later, or a Mac, add the person to your iPad Contacts.**

   See Book V, Chapter 5 for how to do this if that person isn't already in Contacts.

3. **Tap the FaceTime app icon on the Home screen.**

   The FaceTime screen appears.

4. **Tap the Contacts button in the bottom-right corner of the screen.**

5. **Scroll to locate and tap a contact's name.**

   The contact's information displays (as shown in Figure 4-11).

Getting the Most Out of iPad Cameras and FaceTime

Figure 4-11: Information displayed in Contacts.

You can also place a FaceTime call using Siri. Just say something like "Make a FaceTime call to Joey", confirm Joey's contact information, and the call is placed.

6. **Tap the contact's stored phone number or e-mail address.**

   You've just placed a FaceTime call!

When you call somebody using an e-mail address, the person must be signed in to his Apple ID account and have verified that the address can be used for FaceTime calls. iPad 2 or later and iPod touch (fourth-generation and later) users can make this setting by tapping Settings and then FaceTime; FaceTime for Mac users make this setting by choosing FaceTime⬄Preferences.

When the person accepts the call, you see the person's image and a small, draggable box containing your image. (See Figure 4-12.)

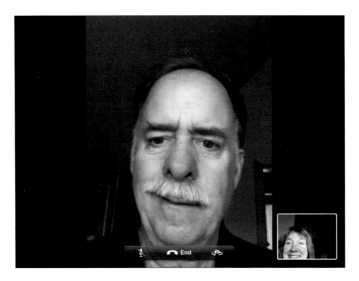

Figure 4-12: A FaceTime call in progress.

You can also simply go to the Contacts app, find a contact, and tap the FaceTime icon in that person's record and then tap her phone number or e-mail address in the pop-up menu that appears to make a FaceTime call.

To view recent calls, tap the Recents button in Step 4. Tap a recent call, and iPad displays that person's information. You can tap the contact's phone number or e-mail to call the person back.

Accepting or ending a FaceTime call

If you're on the receiving end of a FaceTime call, accepting the call is about as easy as it gets. When the call comes in, follow these steps:

1. **Tap the Accept button to take the call or tap the Decline button to reject it (see Figure 4-13).**

   Chat away with your friend, swapping video images.

Figure 4-13: You're it; accept or decline the call.

2. **When you're done talking, tap the End button (shown in Figure 4-14).**

   The call ends.

Mute button   End button   Switch Camera button

Figure 4-14: Ending a FaceTime call.

To mute sound during a call, tap the Mute button. (Refer to Figure 4-14.) Tap the button again to unmute your iPad or iPhone.

To add a caller to your Favorites list, with FaceTime open, tap the Favorites button and then tap the plus sign and select the person's name from the contact list to add the person to Favorites. You can then locate the person to make a call to her by tapping Favorites and choosing that person from a short list rather than scrolling through all your contacts.

Switching views

When you're on a FaceTime call, you might want to use iPad's built-in camera to show the person you're talking to what's going on around you. Tap the Switch Camera button (refer to Figure 4-14) to switch from the front-facing camera that's displaying your image to the rear-facing camera that captures whatever you're looking at (shown in Figure 4-15).

Figure 4-15: Show your friend what's in front of you.

Tap the Switch Camera button again. You switch back to the front camera, displaying your image.

Chapter 5: Getting Social with Twitter, Facebook, and iMessage

In This Chapter

✓ Using Twitter or Facebook on iPad

✓ Creating an iMessage account

✓ Utilizing iMessage to address, create, and send messages

✓ Deleting a conversation

*U*nless you've spent the last few years working in Antarctica without a radio, you know that Twitter is a social networking service referred to as a *microblog,* because it involves only short posted messages. Twitter support was incorporated into iOS 5, so you can tweet people from within the Safari, Photos, Camera, and Maps apps. With iOS 6 you simply activate Twitter in Settings and the app is installed, ready for you to use it to post tweets whenever you like.

The Facebook app can also be activated through iPad Settings. Facebook, the most popular social networking site, has become more integrated into iPad with the arrival of iOS 6. You can also post messages and items such as photos to your Facebook page right from within several apps.

iMessage is another feature that was new in iOS 5 (available through the preinstalled Messages app) for instant messaging (IM). IM involves sending a text message to somebody's iPhone (using his phone number) or iPod touch or iPad (using his e-mail address) to carry on an instant conversation. (Note that iMessage is also available on your Mac with the Mountain Lion version of the operating system.)

In this chapter, I introduce you to ways in which iPad makes use of Twitter, Facebook, and instant messaging to let you stay connected to the world.

Experiencing Twitter and Facebook on iPad

Twitter and Facebook are the darlings of the social networking world. Twitter, as a microblog, allows only short messages to be posted. Facebook is much more robust, allowing lengthy postings as well as photographs, videos, and various gifting schemes to woo Facebook friends. Each is integrated into iPad, typically via the Share feature in apps. When you tap Share you can tap either the Twitter or Facebook icon (see Figure 5-1).

Figure 5-1: Use app-sharing features to tweet or post to Facebook.

Tweeting to your heart's content

Twitter is a social networking service for *microblogging*, which involves posting very short messages (*tweets*; limited to 140 characters, and an attachment like a photo may limit this further) online so your friends can see what you're up to. Many readers already have a Twitter account and are hooked on tweeting. If you've never tweeted, you can go to www.twitter.com to sign up with the service; then activate Twitter in iPad Settings and use the Twitter for iPad app to manage your Twitter account. After you have an account, you can post tweets, have people follow your tweets, and follow the tweets that other people post.

With iOS 5 for iPad, the ability to tweet became integrated into several apps. You can post tweets using the Share button within Safari, Photos, Camera, and Maps. First, go to iPad Settings and tap Twitter. Then tap the Install button to install the app, and then add your account information.

Now, when you're using Safari, Photos, Camera, or Maps, you can choose Twitter from a Share menu. You see a Tweet form like the one shown in Figure 5-2. Just write your message in the form and then tap Send. Note that a number in the bottom-right corner lets you know how many characters you have left to use in your tweet.

See Book I, Chapter 6 or Chapters 3 and 6 in this minibook for more about tweeting in the Safari or Photos apps, respectively.

When you're filling in the tweet, tap Add Location to turn on Location Services, which allows Twitter to ascertain your location and share it with others. Be cautious about using this feature; if many people follow you on Twitter, they can use your location to track your movements and know where you live, where you go to school, where you socialize, and so on. This information can be used to commit a variety of online and offline crimes.

Enter your message here...   then tap Send.

Figure 5-2: Tweeting is a simple menu choice in several apps.

Connecting your iPad to Facebook

With iOS 6, more integration of Facebook came to iPad. When you're in an app such as Maps and you tap the Share button, you can post an item such as a map to your page.

Before trying this, you should install the Facebook app and enter information about your Facebook account. Follow these steps to do this.

1. **Tap Settings, and then tap Facebook.**

2. **In the resulting settings (see Figure 5-3) tap the Install button to install the app.**

3. **When prompted, enter your Apple ID and password.**

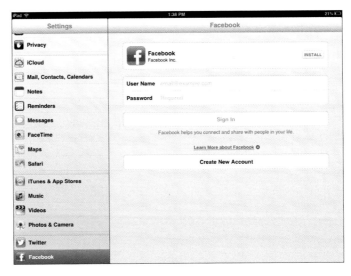

Figure 5-3: Tap the Install button and the Facebook app appears on one of your many Home screens.

4. **Enter your Facebook username and password and then tap Sign In.**

5. **On the confirming screen, tap the Sign In button.**

Note that signing into Facebook downloads all Facebook friends to your Contacts app, as well as downloading any Facebook events to your Calendar app on iPad. You can turn off individual apps that use your Facebook account one by one in the main Facebook settings.

Setting Up an iMessage Account

iMessage support was added in iOS 5 (available through the preinstalled Messages app) that allows you to send and receive instant messages (IMs) to others using an Apple iOS device (and on your Mac, if you have Mountain Lion). Instant messaging differs from e-mail or tweeting in an important way. Whereas you might e-mail somebody and wait days or weeks before that person responds, or you might post a tweet that could sit a while before anybody views it, instant messaging communication happens immediately. You send an IM, and it appears on somebody's Mac, iPhone, iPod touch, or iPad right away, and assuming the person wants to participate in a live conversation, it begins immediately, allowing a back-and-forth dialogue in real time.

To set up iMessage, follow these steps:

1. **Tap Settings on the Home screen.**

2. **Tap Messages.**

   The settings shown in Figure 5-4 display.

Make sure this is set to On.

Figure 5-4: Turn on iMessage in Settings.

3. **If iMessage isn't set to On, tap the On/Off button (shown in Figure 5-4) to turn it on.**

4. **Check the Send & Receive setting to be sure the e-mail account associated with your iPad is correct.**

   This should be set up automatically based on your Apple ID.

5. **To allow a notice to be sent when you've read somebody's messages, tap the On/Off button for Send Read Receipts.**

   You can also choose to show a subject field in your messages.

6. **If you want to include a subject field in messages, tap the On/Off button for the Show Subject Field option.**

7. **Tap the Home button to close Settings.**

To change the e-mail account that iMessage uses, tap the Send & Receive button, tap Add Another Email, and then follow the directions to add another e-mail account.

Using iMessage to Address, Create, and Send Messages

Now you're ready to use iMessage. This is a remarkably simple process that involves typing and sending a message, and then waiting while the other person types and sends a message back. This can go on for hours, so prepare a quick exit message ahead of time, just in case. (I have to walk my dog, the cat just exploded . . . you get the idea.) Follow these steps to use iMessage:

1. **From the Home screen, tap the Messages icon.**

2. **If this is the first time you're using iMessage, on the screen that appears (see Figure 5-5), tap the New Message button to begin a conversation.**

3. **You can address a message in a couple of ways:**

   • Begin to type an address in the To field or tap the iPad's Dictation key (not present on the original iPad or iPad 2) on the onscreen keyboard and speak the address, and a list of matching contacts appears.

     • Tap the plus icon to the right of the address field, and the All Contacts list displays, as shown in Figure 5-6.

You can also use Siri to send a message by simply pressing and holding the Home button and speaking your command, selecting the correct contact and method of messaging (phone or email).

New Message button   Address field

Camera button   Message field   Send button

Figure 5-5: Get the conversation going here.

Figure 5-6: You can choose somebody
to message from your Contacts list.

4. **Tap a contact on the list you chose to display in Step 3.**

   If the contact has both an e-mail address and phone number stored, the Info dialog appears, allowing you to tap one or the other, which addresses the message.

5. **To create a message, simply tap in the message field near the bottom of the screen and type or dictate your message.**

6. **To send the message, tap the Send button (refer to Figure 5-5).**

   When your recipient(s) responds, you see the conversation displayed on the right side of the screen, as shown in Figure 5-7.

The conversation is displayed here.   Share button

Figure 5-7: Follow the conversation as you and your friend text back and forth.

Note that you can modify your own profile with the Messages app. Just tap the tiny silhouette of a person in the upper-right corner, and an Info screen appears. Tap Edit, and a form displays where you can change your information, including your name, phone number, or e-mail, and add your photo to your messages.

If you want to include another photo or video with your message, tap the Camera button to the left of the message field. (Refer to Figure 5-5.) Tap Take Photo or Video or Choose Existing and then tap Use to attach a photo/video. When you send your message, the photo or video will go along with your text.

Here are some additional tips for using iMessage:

✓ **Talking with multiple people:** You can address a message to more than one person by simply choosing more recipients in Step 4 in the preceding steps list.

✔ **Canceling a message:** If you begin a conversation and change your mind before sending your message, tap the Cancel button near the top of the screen.

✔ **Viewing a conversation:** Your conversations are listed in the left pane of the Messages app. Tap one, and the various comments in it display, along with a note of the date and time of each comment.

Clearing a Conversation

When you're done chatting, you might want to clear a conversation to remove the clutter before you start a new one.

To clear a conversation, follow these steps:

1. **With Messages open, tap the Edit Menu button on the top right of the screen (refer to Figure 5-7).**

2. **Tap the Clear All button (see Figure 5-8).**

3. **Tap Clear Conversation.**

**Book II
Chapter 5**

**Getting Social with
Twitter, Facebook,
and iMessage**

Clear All button

Delete button   Forward button

Figure 5-8: Get rid of yesterday's IM with a tap.

You can also tap the Edit Menu button, tap the text of a particular conversation, and then tap the Delete or Forward button on the bottom of the screen (refer to Figure 5-8) to delete that one conversation or forward its contents to somebody. One final option is to tap on text and then tap the Edit button and tap the Delete button to the left of a comment to delete it.

Chapter 6: Playing with the Photos App

In This Chapter

✔ **Importing photos from iPhone or a digital camera**

✔ **Viewing an album or individual photos**

✔ **Editing photos**

✔ **Organizing photos in Camera Roll**

✔ **Sharing and deleting photos**

With its gorgeous screen, iPad is a natural for viewing photos. It supports most common photo formats, such as JPEG, TIFF, and PNG. With an iPad (except the original iPad), you can shoot your own photos using the built-in cameras (see Chapter 4 in this minibook for more about using them) or sync your photos from iCloud or your computer, iPhone, or digital camera. You can also save images you find online to your iPad or receive them by e-mail, iMessage, or tweet.

After you have photos to play with, the Photos app lets you organize photos from the Camera Roll (called Saved Photos on iPad 1), view them in albums, one by one, or in a slideshow. You can also e-mail, message, post to Facebook, tweet a photo to a friend, print it, or use your expensive gadget as an electronic picture frame. Finally, new with iOS 6, you can use the Photo Streams feature to share groups of photos with people using iCloud on an iOS 6 device or on a Mac with Mountain Lion OS, all of which you read about in this chapter.

Getting Photos into iPad

Before you can play around with photos, you have to take some with the iPad camera (except on the original iPad) covered in Chapter 4 in this minibook or get them into iPad from another source. There are a few different ways to get photos from elsewhere. You can buy an accessory to import them from your camera or iPhone; save a photo you find on the web or receive as an e-mail, message, or tweet attachment; or sync to iCloud or your computer to download photos you've saved there. The whole syncing process is discussed in Book I, Chapter 5. The two other methods are explained here.

Screenshots you take of your iPad screen are also saved to the Saved Photos/Camera Roll album. To take a screenshot, display what you want to shoot, press and hold the Home button, tap the Sleep/Wake button, and then release. You'll find your screenshot in Photos' Camera Roll album on an iPad (except the original iPad) or Saved Photos album on an original iPad.

Importing photos from an iPhone, iPod, or digital camera

Your iPad camera and a computer aren't the only sources of photos. You can import photos from a digital camera and photos or videos from your iPhone/iPod touch if you buy the iPad Camera Connection Kit from Apple, which will set you back about $29. The kit contains two adapters (see Figure 6-1): a USB Camera Connector to import photos from a digital camera or iPhone, and an SD Card Reader to import image files from an SD card.

If you have an iPhone 3G or earlier model or an iPhone 5, sad to say, it isn't supported by the Connection Kit.

USB Camera
Connector

SD Card
Reader

Figure 6-1: These two adapters are included in the Connection Kit.

You can find information in Book I, Chapter 5 about syncing iCloud content or your computer with your iPad to port over photos. You can also find out how to take and use photos from iPad's built-in camera in Chapter 4 of this minibook.

Follow these steps to import photos, after you have the Connection Kit in hand:

1. **Start the import process by putting your iPad to sleep using the switch on the top right.**

2. **Insert the USB Camera Connector into the Dock Connector slot of your iPad.**

3. **Connect the USB end of the cord that came with your digital camera or iPhone into the USB Camera Connector.**

4. **Connect the other end of the cord that came with your camera or iPhone into that device.**

5. **Wake your iPad.**

   The Photos app opens and displays the photos on the digital camera or iPhone.

6. **Tap Import All on your iPad; if you want to import only selected photos, tap individual photos, and then tap Import. Finally, tap Import rather than Import All.**

   The photos are saved to the Last Import album.

7. **Disconnect the cord and the adapter.**

   You're done!

You can also import photos stored on an *SD (secure digital)* memory card often used by digital cameras as a storage medium. Simply put the iPad to sleep, connect the SD Card Reader to the iPad, insert the SD card containing the photos, and then follow Steps 5–7 in the preceding list.

Though not promoted as a feature by Apple, people have discovered that you can also use the USB connector in the Connection Kit to connect some audio devices such as speakers or headphones, and to hook up some USB-connected keyboards that have lower power consumption. Some media readers will also allow you to get photos off compact flash drives, memory sticks, and SD and xD cards.

Saving photos from the web

The web offers a wealth of images that you can download to your Photos library on the iPad. The built-in Safari browser makes it simple to save any image you come across to your iPad. (Of course, you should be careful not to violate copyrights when using pictures you've grabbed online.)

Several search engines have advanced search features that allow you to search for only nonlicensed images, meaning, at least theoretically, you don't have to pay for the images. But it's always a good idea to get written permission to use an image, especially if you intend to use it to make money (as with a company brochure or online course).

Follow these steps to save images from the web:

1. **Open Safari and navigate to the web page containing the image you want.**

2. **Press and hold the image.**

   A menu appears, as shown in Figure 6-2.

Tap this option.

Figure 6-2: Use this menu to save an image to your iPad.

3. **Tap Save Image.**

   The image is saved to your Camera Roll album in the Photos app, as shown in Figure 6-3. Note that this album is called Saved Photos on the original iPad.

Camera Roll album

Figure 6-3: Photos you save from the Internet go into the Saved Photos/ Camera Roll album.

For more about how to use Safari to navigate to or search for web content, see Book I, Chapter 6.

Looking at Photos

Pictures were made to be looked at, so knowing how to view the albums and individual photos you manage to get into your iPad is a way to tap into the key strength of the Photos app. In this section, you get some tips for taking your viewing experience to the max.

If you want to do more than look at photos, check out a few of these photo-editing apps that were designed to work with iPad: iPhoto for iPad from Apple, Photogene for iPad, PhotoForge for iPad, and the free PhotoPad by ZAGG. All are available through the Apple App Store.

Viewing an album

The Photos app organizes your pictures into albums using such criteria as the folder on your computer from which you synced the photos or photos captured using the iPad. You may also have albums for images you synced from devices such as your iPhone or digital camera.

To view your albums, start by tapping the Photos app icon in the Dock on the Home screen. If the Photos tab is selected when the Photos app opens, tap the Albums tab shown in Figure 6-4. Now you can tap an album, and the photos in it display.

Tap this tab.

Figure 6-4: Switch between individual photos and albums using these tabs.

If you're a Mac user, use iPhoto to create new albums for organizing your iPad content before you sync to your iPad. If you're on a Windows machine, check out two products for managing and syncing photos to iPad: Lightroom from Adobe (www.adobe.com) or Adobe's Photoshop Elements (version 8 or later). You can also create picture subfolders in Windows Explorer and when you sync, each subfolder becomes an album on your iPad.

Viewing individual photos

After you figure out what album your images are in, you have several fun ways to interact with individual photos. The iPad touchscreen is the key to this very tactile experience.

Tap the Photos app icon on the Home screen and then tap the Photos tab (shown in Figure 6-5).

Now try these techniques:

Tap this tab.

Figure 6-5: Viewing thumbnails of individual photos.

- ✐ **Full-screen view:** To view a photo, either tap the photo thumbnail or pinch your fingers together, place them on the photo, and then spread your fingers apart. The picture expands, as shown in Figure 6-6.

- ✐ **Browsing an album:** Flick your finger to the left or right to scroll through the individual photos in that album.

- ✐ **Multiple photos:** To reduce the display size of an individual photo and return to the multipicture view, place two fingers on the photo and then pinch them together. You can also tap the Albums button (which may display the currently open album's name) to view the album's entire contents.

- ✐ **Twirling:** Place two fingers on a photo and spin them to the left or right. This maneuver, known as *grab and spin,* twirls the photo on the screen (and it's lots of fun to do).

Figure 6-6: An expanded photo.

Do you like to associate a face with a name? Doing so can help you keep your clients or other contacts straight. You can place a photo on a person's information page in the Contacts app on your iPad. For more about how to do this, see Book V, Chapter 5.

Editing Photos

The Photos app also lets you do some simple editing to your photos. This feature allows you to rotate images, enhance image quality, get rid of that pesky red-eye, or crop to exactly the area of the image that you want to display.

Follow these steps to edit photos:

1. **Tap the Photos app on the Home screen to open it.**
2. **Using methods previously described in this chapter, locate a photo you want to edit.**
3. **Tap the Edit button.**

   The Edit Photo screen, shown in Figure 6-7, appears.

Figure 6-7: With iOS 5 came the ability to edit photos.

4. **At this point, you can take four possible actions:**

   • *Rotate:* Tap the Rotate button to rotate the image 90 degrees at a time. Continue to tap the button to move another 90 degrees.

   • *Enhance:* Tap Enhance to turn Auto-Enhance on or off. This feature optimizes the crispness of the image.

   • *Red-Eye:* Tap Red-Eye if a person in a photo has that dreaded red-eye effect. When you activate this feature, simply tap each eye that needs clearing up.

   • *Crop:* To crop the photo to a portion of its original area, tap the Crop button. You can then tap any corner of the image and drag inward or outward to remove areas of the photo.

In each of the four editing features, you see Cancel, Undo, and Revert to Original buttons. If you don't like the changes you made, use these to stop making changes or undo the changes you've already made. Choosing Cancel will end the editing session, while Revert to Original leaves you in Editing mode.

Organizing Photos in Camera Roll

You can organize photos in albums so it's easier to locate them in the future. To do this, follow these steps:

1. **Display the Camera Roll album.**

   If you have the original iPad with no camera, this album is called Saved Photos.

2. **Tap the Edit button in the top-right corner and then tap individual photos to select them.**

   Small check marks appear on the selected photos. (See Figure 6-8.)

Figure 6-8: Select the photos you want to work with here.

Book II
Chapter 6

Playing with the Photos App

3. **Tap the Add To button and then tap Add to Existing Album (which appears only if you've previously created albums) or Add to New Album.**

4. **Tap an existing album or enter a name for a new album (depending on your previous selection) and tap Save.**

   If you created a new album, it appears in the Photos main screen with the albums displayed.

You can also tap the Copy or Delete button when you've selected photos in Step 2 of this task. This allows you to copy or delete multiple photos at a time.

Sharing Photos with Mail, Twitter, Message, and Facebook

Part of the fun of taking photos is sharing those images with others. It's easy to share photos stored on your iPad by posting them to Facebook, tweeting, sending with via iMessage, or sending them as e-mail attachments. Follow these steps to do just that:

1. **Tap the Photos app icon on the Home screen.**

2. **Tap the Photos tab and locate the photo you want to share.**

3. **Tap the photo to select it and then tap the Menu button (it looks like a box with an arrow jumping out of it).**

   The menu shown in Figure 6-9 appears.

Figure 6-9: The Menu offers different options.

4. **Tap the Mail, Twitter, Messages, or Facebook option.**

   Note that you must install the Twitter and Facebook apps and set up a Twitter or Facebook account in Settings before you can use this feature with these services.

5. **In the message form that appears, make any modifications you want in the To, Cc/Bcc, or Subject fields for e-mail, or enter your Facebook posting or tweet text.**

6. **Tap the Send button.**

   The message and photo go on their way.

You can also copy and paste a photo into documents, such as those created in the Pages word-processor app (available in the App Store for about $9.99).

To do this, press and hold a photo in Photos until the Copy command appears. Tap Copy, and then in the destination app, press and hold the screen and tap Paste.

Sharing Photos Using Photo Stream

 Photo Stream allows you to automatically send copies of any new photos to any iCloud devices, and to share photo streams with others. You can also subscribe to another person's photo stream if he or she shares it with you. First you should set up Photo Stream. Follow these steps to share your photos using Photo Stream:

1. **Tap Settings⇨Photos & Camera and tap the On button for My Photo Stream to share among your devices and Shared Photo Streams to share with others.**

2. **To share a photo stream with somebody else, return to the Home screen and tap Photos.**

3. **Locate a photo that you want to share, tap the Menu button, and then tap Photo Stream.**

4. **In the form that appears (see Figure 6-10), enter a recipient and photo stream name, and then if you like, click the On/Off button to allow anybody to view the photo stream on iCloud.com.**

5. **Tap Next and enter a comment in the following dialog if you want.**

6. **Click Post and the photo is posted.**

Figure 6-10: Fill out this form to post your photo.

Running a Slideshow

You can run a slideshow of your images in Photos and even play music and choose transition effects for the show. This is a great way to give a presentation to a client on your easy-to-carry iPad, or show your friends a slideshow of your last adventure travel vacation.

To use the slideshow feature, follow these steps:

1. **Tap the Photos app icon to open the application.**
2. **Tap the Photos tab.**
3. **Tap the Slideshow button to see the Slideshow Options menu, shown in Figure 6-11.**

Tap this button.

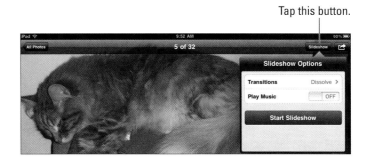

Figure 6-11: Use this menu to add transition effects and start the slideshow.

4. **If you want to play music along with the slideshow, tap the On/Off button in the Play Music field.**
5. **To choose music to play along with the slideshow, tap Music and, in the list that appears (see Figure 6-12), tap any selection from your Music library.**

Figure 6-12: Pick a song that matches your slideshow's mood.

6. **In the Slideshow Options dialog, tap the transition effect you want to use for your slideshow (refer to Figure 6-11).**

7. **Tap the Start Slideshow button.**

   The slideshow begins.

To run a slideshow that includes only the photos contained in a particular album, tap the Album tab in Step 2, tap an album to open it, and then tap the Slideshow button to make settings and run a slideshow.

Displaying Picture Frame

You can use the slideshow settings you create in the preceding section to run your slideshow while your iPad screen is locked so that you can view a continuous display of your pictures. This feature can help you make good use of the time when your iPad is recharging or subliminally flash images of your products again and again at your client while you make your sales pitch.

Here's how to use the Picture Frame feature:

1. **Tap the Sleep/Wake button to lock iPad and then tap the Home button to go to the Lock screen.**

   The bottom of this screen looks like Figure 6-13.

The Picture Frame button

slide to unlock

Figure 6-13: Picture Frame is a great feature for showing off your product line — or cool new car.

2. **Tap the Picture Frame button (refer to Figure 6-13).**

   The slideshow begins. (See Figure 6-14.)

3. **To end the show, tap the Home button.**

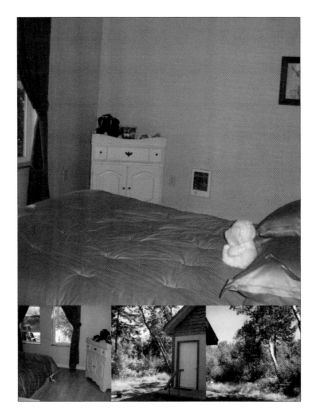

Figure 6-14: Use Picture Frame to show off several images at once.

If you don't like the effects used on the picture frame, go back to Photos and use the Slideshow button to change the slideshow's settings.

One iPad accessory you might look into is the iPad Frame Dock, which you can purchase at www.theipadframe.com. This item is a stand for your iPad that looks like a picture frame. You can even hang it and your iPad on a wall. That is, if you have nowhere else to place your several-hundred-dollar electronic device. Of course, the dock does allow you to charge your iPad while it's hanging around.

Deleting Photos

You might find that it's time to get rid of some of those old photos of the family reunion or the last project you worked on. If a photo wasn't transferred from your computer but instead was downloaded or captured as a screenshot on the iPad, you can delete it using this procedure:

1. **Tap the Photos app icon on the Home screen.**
2. **Tap the Albums or Photos tab and then tap an album to open it.**
3. **Tap the Menu button.**
4. **Tap each photo you want to get rid of (a blue check mark appears on each), and then tap the Delete button, as shown in Figure 6-15.**
5. **Tap the Delete Photo/Selected Photos button that appears to finish the deletion.**

Delete button   Check marks indicating selected photos

Figure 6-15: If you don't need it anymore, delete it!

Note in Step 4 that if you're using an album you created, you get a Remove button rather than a Delete button. That's because you may remove a photo from that album, but it remains in the Camera Roll.

Chapter 7: Using Your iPad as an E-reader

In This Chapter

- Discovering how iPad differs from other e-readers
- Finding and buying books at iBooks
- Navigating a book
- Working with bookmarks, highlights, and the dictionary
- Organizing books in collections
- Experience periodicals with Newsstand

*A*pple has touted iPad as a great e-reader, so though it isn't a traditional dedicated e-reader device like the Barnes & Noble Nook, you won't want to miss out on this cool functionality.

Apple's free, downloadable app that turns your iPad into an e-reader is called *iBooks,* an application that enables you to buy and download books from Apple's iBookstore and other e-book sources, as well as to read PDF files. You can also use several other free e-reader applications, such as Kindle, Stanza, or Nook, to download books to your iPad from a variety of online sources, such as Amazon and Google, so you can read to your heart's content.

A new app that arrived with iOS 5 is Newsstand, which has a similar look and feel to iBooks, but its focus is on subscribing to and reading magazines, newspapers, and other periodicals.

In this chapter, you discover the options available for reading material, and I tell you how to buy books and subscribe to periodicals. You also find out how to navigate a book, interactive textbook, or periodical and adjust the brightness and type, as well as how to search books and organize your iBooks and Newsstand libraries.

Discovering How iPad Differs from Other E-readers

An *e-reader* is any electronic device that enables you to download and read books, magazines, or newspapers, as well as documents such as manuals or reports. These devices are portable and typically dedicated only to reading electronic content. Most use E Ink technology to create a paper-like reading experience.

The iPad is a bit different: As you know, it isn't used for only reading books, and you have to download an app to enable it as an e-reader (though just about every e-reader app I've found is free). Also, iPad doesn't offer the paper-like reading experience — you read from a computer screen (though you can adjust the brightness of the screen and change its background color).

When you buy a book or magazine online (or get one of many free publications), it downloads to your iPad in a few seconds using your Wi-Fi or 3G/4G connection. After you have your e-reader app and some content, iPad offers several navigation tools to move around a book, all of which you explore in this chapter.

iBooks 2 introduced tools for reading and interacting with textbook content. You can even create and publish your own interactive textbooks using a Mac app called iBooks Author. Read more about this hot new feature in the later section, "Working with interactive textbooks."

Finding and Buying E-books

Before you can read books or other publications, you have to get your iPad's hands on them (so to speak). This involves downloading e-reader software, and then using it or online stores to buy publications. I start by introducing you to iBooks, a free e-reader that you can download from iTunes.

You can also buy content on your computer and sync your purchases to your iPad using iTunes or iCloud. See Book I, Chapter 5 for more about this topic.

Finding books at iBooks

In Book I, Chapter 5, I walk you through the process of downloading apps, so you should use those steps to download the iBooks app first, if you haven't already.

With iBooks downloaded, you can shop using iBooks by tapping the iBooks application icon to open it. (Note that it's probably on a secondary Home screen, so you may have to display another Home screen to locate it.)

If you become addicted to iBooks, consider placing it on the iPad Dock for quick access from any Home screen. To do this, press and hold the app 'til all apps jiggle, and then tap and drag the iBooks icon to the Dock. Tap the Home button, and the jiggling stops.

The iBooks Library opens. (See Figure 7-1.) At this point, you see a bookshelf with no books on it. (If you don't see the bookshelf, tap the Library button to go there or, if no Library button is displayed on the screen, tap the Bookshelf button in the top-right corner of the screen — it sports four small squares.) Note that any PDF documents you download don't appear on this bookshelf; you have to tap the PDF Collection to view them (more about Collections later).

For a cool effect, tap the Store button, and the shelf pivots 180 degrees to display the iBookstore.

Figure 7-1: Your virtual iBooks bookshelf.

In the iBookstore shown in Figure 7-2, featured titles are shown by default. Try any of the following methods to find a book:

- Tap the Search field and type a search word or phrase using the onscreen keyboard.

- Tap a category along the top of the screen or tap the More button to see a list of types of books, as shown in Figure 7-3. Tap a category to view those selections.

- Tap All to view all categories of titles.

- Tap the appropriate button at the bottom of the screen to view categories: Featured Books; *The New York Times* bestsellers list; books listed on Top Charts; Browse to see browse-worthy lists of authors, categories, or only paid or free items; or Purchases to review the titles you've already purchased on any Apple device connected to iCloud.

Library button   Browse categories   Search field

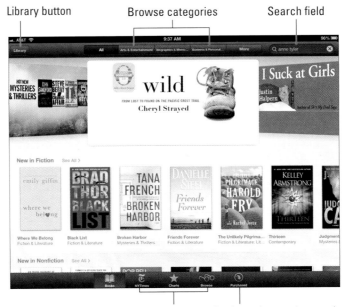

Browse lists.   Look at what you've purchased.

Figure 7-2: Use various links and tools to find the content you want.

If you go to an item by tapping a button at the bottom of the screen and you want to return to the original screen, just tap Books again.

↙ Tap a suggested selection or featured book to display more information about it.

To avoid buyer's remorse, you can download free samples before you buy. You get to read several pages of the book to see whether it appeals to you, and it doesn't cost you a dime! Look for the Get Sample button when you view details about a book to get your free preview.

Exploring other e-readers

Though iBooks can handle content from many ePub sources such as Google and Project Gutenberg, you may prefer to explore the tools offered by other e-readers. Your iPad is capable of using other e-reader apps to display book content from other bookstores, so you can get books from sources other than iBookstore. To do so, first download another e-reader application such as Kindle from Amazon or the Barnes & Noble Nook from the iPad App Store. (See Book I, Chapter 5 for how to download apps.) Then use that application's features to search for, purchase, and download content.

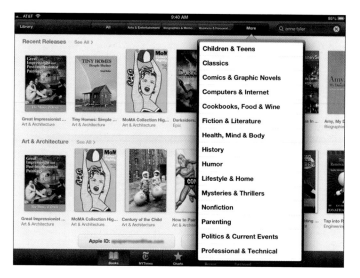

Figure 7-3: Find your publication using the Categories list.

The Kindle e-reader application is shown in Figure 7-4. Any content you have already bought from Amazon for the Kindle is archived online and can be placed on your Kindle home page on your iPad for you to read anytime you like. Tap the Device tab to see titles stored on iPad. To delete a book from this e-reader, just press the title with your finger, and the Remove from Device button appears.

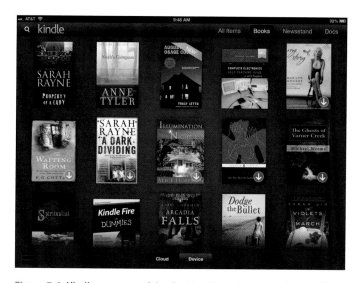

Figure 7-4: Kindle was one of the first to offer a free e-reader for iPad.

You can also get content from a variety of other sources: Project Gutenberg, Google, some publishers like Baen, and so on. Get the content using your computer if you want and then just add it to Books in iTunes and sync to your iPad.

You can also sync books you've downloaded to your computer to your iPad by syncing to the computer and your iTunes account. Using this method, you can find lots of free books from various sources online, as long as they're in the ePub or PDF format, and drag them into your iTunes Books Library; then simply sync them to your iPad. See Book I, Chapter 5 for more about syncing. You can also download books from the web and use an online file-sharing site such as Dropbox to make them available to iBooks via an Internet connection. To convert e-books in other formats such as Mobi or RTF to ePub, use an application such as Calibre.

Buying iBooks

If you have set up an account with iTunes, you can buy books at the iBookstore easily using the iBooks app. (See Book I, Chapter 5 for more about iTunes.) To buy a book, follow these steps:

1. **When you find a book in the iBookstore that you want to buy, tap it, and then tap its price button as shown in Figure 7-5.**

   The button changes to a Buy Book button. (If the book is free, these buttons are labeled Free and Get Book, respectively.)

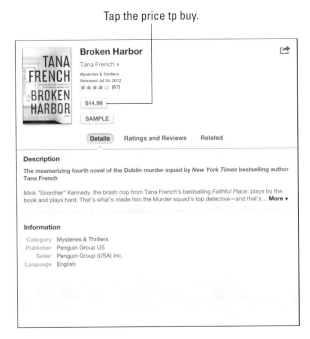

Figure 7-5: Click the price to buy the book.

2. **Tap the Buy Book or Get Book button.**

   If you haven't already signed in, the iTunes Password dialog shown in Figure 7-6 appears.

Figure 7-6: Enter your iTunes password to buy anything.

3. **Enter your password and tap OK.**

   The book appears on your bookshelf, and the cost is charged to whichever payment method you specified when you opened your iTunes account — or the cost is deducted from your store credit, if you have a balance.

If you have signed in, your purchase is accepted immediately — no returns are allowed, so tap carefully!

Experiencing E-reading

After you have an e-book in iBooks, put on some music, settle back in a comfortable chair, and read it. Luckily, reading an e-book isn't much harder than reading a paperback. Here's how to do it.

Navigating an e-book

Here are the simple steps involved in making your way around an e-book using the iBooks e-reader:

1. **Tap iBooks, and if your Library (the bookshelf) isn't already displayed, tap the Library button.**

2. **Tap an e-book to open it.**

   The book opens, as shown in Figure 7-7. (If you hold your iPad in portrait orientation, it shows one page; if it's in landscape orientation, it will show two.)

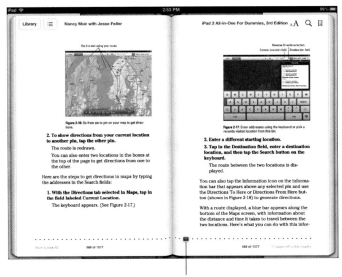

Slider to move to another page

Figure 7-7: Landscape orientation on iPad.

3. Take any of these actions to navigate the book:

- *To go to the book's Table of Contents:* Tap the Table of Contents button in the top-left corner of the page (it looks like a little bulleted list) to go to the book's Table of Contents (see Figure 7-8) and then tap the name of a chapter to go to it.

- *To turn to the next page:* Place your finger anywhere on the right edge of a page and flick to the left.

- *To turn to the preceding page:* Place your finger anywhere on the left edge of a page and flick to the right.

- *To move to another page in the book:* Tap and drag the slider at the bottom of the page to the right or left.

To return to the Library to view another book at any time, tap the Library button. If the button isn't visible, tap anywhere on the page, and the tools appear.

Tap any chapter to go to it

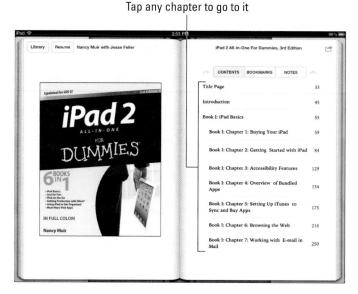

Figure 7-8: Use this virtual Table of Contents to go where you like in your e-book.

Working with interactive textbooks

With the introduction of iBooks 2 came the ability to purchase books that have interactive features. For example, you might be browsing through a textbook and find a small image of a map; click the map, and it enlarges to display the full map. Or, you might see an icon and a label indicating a movie clip. Click that icon, and the movie plays.

Interactivity goes beyond displaying or playing objects. Such books can also include quizzes, such as the one shown in Figure 7-9. You might be asked to click a picture to select the right match, or click a button to answer a multiple-choice question. At the end of the series of questions, your score for the number of correct answers in the quiz displays.

This feature in textbooks is bound to be a huge boon to students who will spend less money on the books and suffer less from the weight of carrying the books around campus or town. To explore some of these titles, get the iTunes U app.

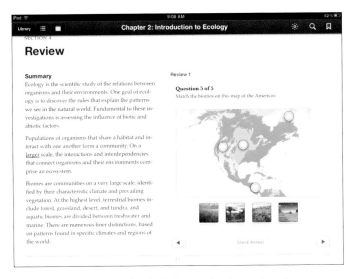

Figure 7-9: Quizzes in textbooks help you check your learning progress.

Creating your own books

iBooks Author is a free app you can download from the App Store to your Mac (with Lion 10.7.2 or later) and use to create your own interactive books. It's a pretty nifty app that makes it easy to flow Word or Pages documents and pictures into handy templates (see an example of a book design in Figure 7-10).

Figure 7-10: Easy-to-use templates make your book look professional.

You can build in interactive elements, such as pictures that expand when clicked and multiple-choice quizzes. When you're done, you can publish your e-book and offer it in the iBooks bookstore or another website.

For more about working with iBooks Author, check out *iBooks Author For Dummies, Portable Edition,* by Galen Gruman.

Adjusting brightness

iPad doesn't offer a simulated page surface as some dedicated e-readers like Kindle do, so it's important that you make the reading experience as comfortable on your eyes as possible by adjusting the brightness.

iBooks offers an adjustable brightness setting that you can use to make your book pages comfortable for you to read. Follow these steps to make an adjustment:

1. **With a book open, tap the Font button shown in Figure 7-11.**

   The Brightness slider appears.

Tap the Font button...

and adjust the screen brightness.

Figure 7-11: Adjusting brightness can ease eyestrain.

2. **Tap and drag the slider to the right to make the screen brighter, or to the left to dim it.**

3. **Tap anywhere in the book to close the Font dialog.**

Experiment with the brightness that works for you. It's commonly thought that bright white computer screens are hard on the eyes, so setting the brightness to halfway (default) or below is probably a good idea.

Try using the Themes button located in the Font dialog to choose Normal, Sepia tone, or Night (black background with white lettering), which is covered in the next task. Sepia mutes the background to a soft beige color that may work better for some.

Changing the font size and type

If the type on your screen is a bit small for your taste, you can change to a larger font size or choose a different font for readability. Follow these steps:

1. **With a book open, tap the Font button.**

   It sports a small letter *a* and a large capital *A*, as shown in Figure 7-12.

Tap the Font button to change font size and type.

Figure 7-12: Need larger type? Set that up here.

2. **In the Font dialog that appears (refer to Figure 7-12), tap the small letter *a* button on the left to use smaller text, or tap the button labeled with the capital *A* on the right to use larger text.**

3. **Tap the Fonts button.**

   The list of fonts, as shown in Figure 7-13, appears. This list may vary slightly if Apple adds more or you're using a language other than English on your iPad.

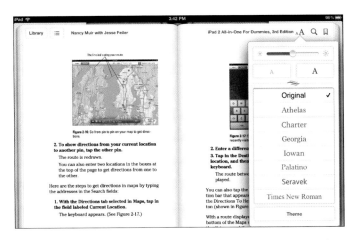

Figure 7-13: Though limited, a selection of fonts is available in iBooks.

4. **Tap a font name to select it.**

   The font changes on the book page.

5. **If you want a sepia tint on the pages, or to reverse black and white, which can be easier on the eyes, you can change from the default Normal setting to one of these. Tap the Theme button and then tap Sepia or Night, respectively, to choose the theme you want to display.**

6. **Tap outside the Font dialog to return to your book.**

Some fonts appear a bit larger on your screen than others because of their design. If you want the largest fonts, use Cochin or Verdana.

Searching in your book

You may want to find a certain sentence or reference in your book. To search for a word or phrase, follow these steps:

1. **With the book displayed, tap the Search button shown in Figure 7-14.**

   The onscreen keyboard appears.

2. **Enter a search term or tap the Dictation key and speak the search term; then tap the Search key on the keyboard.**

   iBooks searches for any matching entries.

Search button

Dictation key

Figure 7-14: Find the content you need using the iBooks Search feature.

3. **Use your finger to scroll down the entries (see Figure 7-15).**

4. **You can use either the Search Google or Search Wikipedia button at the bottom of the Search dialog if you want to search for information about the search term online.**

Scroll through the entries.

Figure 7-15: Find a spot in your e-book.

You can also search for other instances of a particular word while in the book pages by pressing your finger on the word and tapping Search on the toolbar that appears.

Using bookmarks and highlights

Bookmarks and highlights in your e-books are like favorites you save in your web browser: They enable you to revisit a favorite page or refresh your memory about a character or plot point. Note that iBooks can retain these bookmarks and highlights across iDevices such as iPad and iPhone.

To add and use bookmarks and highlights, follow these steps:

1. **With a book open to a page you want to bookmark, tap the Bookmark button in the upper-right corner, as shown in Figure 7-16.**

   A colored bookmark is placed on the page.

2. **To highlight a word or phrase, press the text.**

   The toolbar shown in Figure 7-17 appears.

Bookmark button

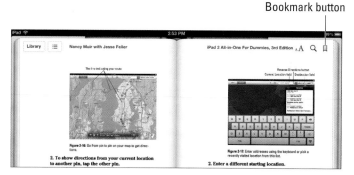

Figure 7-16: Assign a bookmark to a page.

Figure 7-17: Use these tools to perform a variety of actions.

3. **Tap the Highlight button.**

   A colored highlight is placed on the word.

4. **To change the color of the highlighted word, remove the highlight, or add a note, tap the highlighted word.**

   The toolbar shown in Figure 7-18 appears. Note that a shortcut for removing a bookmark is to simply tap the Bookmark button in the top-right corner of the page.

Figure 7-18: Choose the highlight color from this toolbar.

5. **Tap one of three items:**

   * *Colors:* Tap any colored circle to change the highlight color.

   * *Note:* Tap the Note icon to add a note to the item.

   * *Remove Highlight:* Tapping the white circle with a red line through it removes the highlight.

6. **Tap outside the highlighted word to close the toolbar.**

7. **To go to a list of bookmarks and highlights, tap the Table of Contents button on a book page.**

8. **In the Table of Contents, tap the Bookmarks or Notes tab.**

   As shown in Figure 7-19, all bookmarks or notes and highlights display on their respective tabs.

Bookmarks and Notes tabs

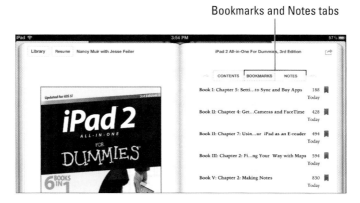

Figure 7-19: Tap the highlight or bookmark you want to display in this list.

9. **Tap a bookmark or highlight in this list to go there.**

iPad automatically bookmarks the page where you left off reading in a book, so you don't have to do it manually.

You can also highlight illustrations in a book. Display the page and press the image until the Highlight button appears above it. Tap the button, and the illustration is highlighted in yellow. As with highlighted text, you can tap a highlighted illustration to change the color or remove the highlight.

Using My Notes and Study Cards in textbooks

Interactive books work slightly differently from other books when it comes to saving notes, highlights, and bookmarks. When you're in a textbook, the toolbar across the top of the book includes an icon to the right of the Table of Contents icon on the left side of the screen. Tap this little white rectangle, and the My Notes pane appears (see Figure 7-20). This is where the list of notes, highlights, and bookmarks in the currently selected chapter display (rather than in the Table of Contents as with other types of books).

In interactive books, when you display the book in portrait orientation, scrolling moves down the entire document. In landscape orientation, your book looks like facing pages and you flip from one page spread to the next using your finger.

Tap the Study Cards button, and a stack of virtual index cards appears with notes you've made, as well as cards for built-in topics that the textbook publisher included, such as glossary terms with definitions located on the back of the cards. You can flip through the stack of cards with your finger, or reveal the back of a card by tapping those that sport two arrows in the bottom-right corner. You can customize study options for study cards. Tap the Study Options button in the top-left corner. Here you have three options:

Book II
Chapter 7

Using Your iPad as an E-reader

- ✔ Tap the arrow on the right of the Highlights and Notes option, and from the menu that appears, choose what you want included in the cards (all the highlights, only highlights of a certain color, or underlined items).

- ✔ To stop displaying Glossary Terms, tap that option in the Study Options menu.

- ✔ To randomly shuffle study cards rather than displaying the most recent on top, tap the Shuffle On/Off button.

When you're finished reviewing your study cards, tap the Done button to return to the My Notes pane.

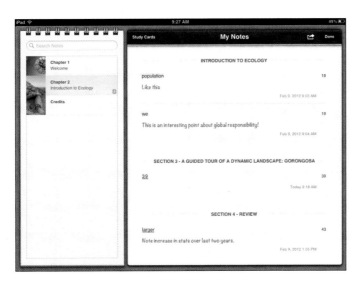

Figure 7-20: All your notes and highlights and notes display here.

Checking Words in the Dictionary

I know some people just skip over words they don't understand when reading, but being a writer, I like to know what every word means. If you do, too, you'll appreciate the iPad's built-in dictionary. As you read a book, if you come across unfamiliar words, don't skip over them — take the opportunity to learn a word! The built-in dictionary in iBooks even recognizes many proper names, such as historical figures and geographic locations.

Follow these steps to look up a word in the dictionary:

1. **With a book open, press your finger on a word and hold it until the toolbar shown in Figure 7-21 appears.**

Figure 7-21: Check a selected word in the built-in dictionary.

2. **Tap the Define button.**

   A definition dialog appears, as shown in Figure 7-22.

Figure 7-22: Find definitions for words, fast, using the dictionary.

3. **Tap the definition and scroll down to view more.**

4. **When you finish reviewing the definition, tap anywhere on the page.**

   The definition disappears.

Organizing Your Library

Your iBooks Library looks like a bookshelf with all downloaded books stored on it, with the most recently downloaded title in the top-left corner. You can drag titles around on this bookshelf, and you can view your library in a few other ways:

1. **With the bookshelf version of the library displayed, tap the List button shown in Figure 7-23.**

   Your books appear in a list, as shown in Figure 7-24.

Book II
Chapter 7

Using Your iPad as an E-reader

List button

Figure 7-23: Switch back and forth between Bookshelf and List view using these buttons.

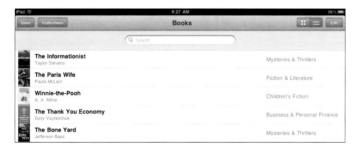

Figure 7-24: Organize your titles in various ways.

2. **To organize the list alphabetically by Titles, Authors, or Categories such as Series, tap the appropriate button on the bottom of the screen.**

   For example, if you tap Categories, your titles are divided by category titles such as Fiction, Mysteries & Thrillers, or Literary.

 3. **To return to Bookshelf view at any time, tap the Bookshelf view button.**

Tap the Bookshelf button at the bottom of the List view to remove categories and list the most recently added book first.

Use the Edit button in List view to display small circles to the left of all books in the list. Tap in any of the circles and tap the Delete button at the top of the page to delete books, and then tap the Done button to exit the Edit function.

Organizing Books in Collections

After you download lots of books (I know one woman who has 600), you may become organizationally challenged. iBooks lets you create collections of books to help you organize them by your own logic, such as Astronomy, Work-Related, and Cooking. You can place a book in only one collection at a time, however.

Here are the steps for creating and working with collections:

1. **To create a collection from the Library, tap Collections.**

2. **In the dialog that appears, tap New.**

3. **On the blank line that appears, type a name (see Figure 7-25) and tap Done.**

Enter a name for the collection...

then tap Done.

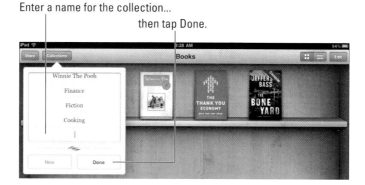

Figure 7-25: Name your collection.

4. **Tap Books.**

   The dialog closes, and you return to the Library.

5. **To add a book to a collection from the Library, tap Edit.**

6. **Tap one or more books and then tap the Move button that appears in the top-left corner of the screen.**

   A dialog appears. (See Figure 7-26.)

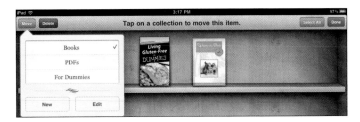

Figure 7-26: Move books into collections one by one or several at a time.

7. **Tap a collection to move the book to.**

   The item you tap becomes the active collection on the bookshelf.

8. **When you finish a book, with the collection displayed, tap Edit, tap the selection circle for the book, and then tap Delete.**

   The book is deleted from iPad.

Book II
Chapter 7

Using Your iPad as an E-reader

To delete a collection, with the Collections dialog displayed, tap Edit. Tap the minus sign to the left of any collection and then tap Delete to get rid of it. A message appears, asking you to tap Remove to remove the contents of the collection from your iPad or Don't Remove. Note that if you choose Don't Remove, all titles within a deleted collection return to their original collections in your Library.

Browsing the Newsstand

Newsstand is a feature, introduced with iOS 5, that focuses on subscribing to and reading magazines, newspapers, and other periodicals rather than books. Newsstand offers an interface to periodicals you subscribe to, and has a similar look and feel to iBooks.

Downloading magazine apps to Newsstand

Newsstand provides an interface for accessing periodicals has a similar look and feel to iBooks. When you download a free publication, you're actually downloading an app to Newsstand. You can then tap that app to buy individual issues, as covered in the next section. To download magazine apps to Newsstand, follow these steps:

1. **Tap the Newsstand icon on the Home screen to open Newsstand (see Figure 7-27).**

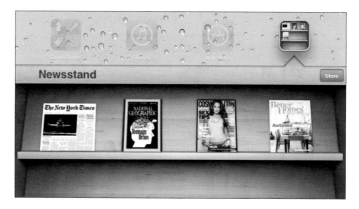

Figure 7-27: View all your subscriptions and publication issues in one place.

2. **Tap the Store button.**

   The store opens, offering Featured periodicals, Top Charts, and Genius recommendations, and along the top of the screen, Categories for your shopping pleasure (see Figure 7-28).

Figure 7-28: Browse for periodicals to your heart's content.

3. **Tap any of the items displayed, tap the arrow buttons to move to other choices, or tap in the Search field at the top and enter a search term to locate a publication you're interested in.**

If you tap other icons at the bottom of the screen, such as Top Charts or Purchased, you're taken to other types of content than periodicals. Also, if you tap Featured again after tapping one of these icons, you're taken to other kinds of apps than periodicals. Your best bet: Stay on the Store screen that displays when you tap the Store button in Newsstand.

4. **When you find an item, tap it to view a detailed description (see Figure 7-29).**

Figure 7-29: Get the lowdown on a particular publication by viewing details.

5. **Tap the Free button and then tap Install App.**

The app downloads to Newsstand.

Buying issues

To purchase issues of periodicals and magazines within Newsstand, follow these steps:

1. **Tap a periodical app in Newsstand.**

The message shown in Figure 7-30 appears, asking whether you want to be informed of new issues.

2. **Tap OK if you want to be informed, or tap Don't Allow if you don't want to be informed.**

Figure 7-30: If you want to know about upcoming editions, let iPad know here.

3. **Tap the Preview Issue button to take a look at a description of its content, or tap the Buy button.**

4. **In the purchase confirmation dialog that appears, tap Buy.**

   The issue is charged to your iTunes account.

Reading periodicals

To read issues of periodicals and magazines within Newsstand, follow these steps:

1. **If you buy a periodical or you have downloaded a free subscription preview, such as *The New York Times* Update shown in Figure 7-31, you can tap the publication in Newsstand to view it.**

Figure 7-31: Open any publication with a tap.

2. **In the publication that appears, use your finger to swipe left, right, up, or down to view more of the pages.**

   For many publications, you can tap the Sections button shown in Figure 7-32 to navigate to different sections of the publication.

Figure 7-32: Moving around publications may vary from one to the other.

3. **To subscribe to a publication when viewing a free sample, tap the Subscribe Now button (refer to Figure 7-32).**

Note that different publications offer different options for subscribing, buying issues, and organizing issues. Think of Newsstand as a central collection point for apps that allows you to preview and buy content in each publication's store.

Chapter 8: Playing Games

In This Chapter

- ✔ Appreciating iPad's gaming strengths
- ✔ Getting a grip on the accelerometer
- ✔ Finding games and accessories of all kinds
- ✔ Exploring iTunes Game Center
- ✔ Sharing high scores with friends

*i*Pad is, after all, a close relative of the iPhone, and no matter who tells you that he uses his iPhone to get work done, he's probably spending most of his time gaming. iPad outstrips iPhone as the ultimate portable gaming machine because of its beautiful screen (especially if you have a third- or fourth-generation iPad with Retina display) and the ability to rotate the larger screen as you play and track your motions. You can download game apps from the App Store and play them on your device. You can also use the preinstalled Game Center app to help you find and buy games, add friends to play against, and track and share scores.

In this chapter, you discover why iPad is such a great mobile gaming device, what kinds of games are out there, how to create a Game Center account and purchase and download games, how to play games against yourself and others, and what cool accessories you must get to be a completely awesome iPad gamer.

Let the games begin!

Appreciating iPad's Gaming Strengths

The iPhone is a fun gaming device, but the screen is too small. Your computer is a good gaming device, but it may lack some of the tactile input of a touchscreen. iPad may be just right as the ultimate gaming device for many reasons, including these:

- ✔ **iPad's fantastic screen:** If you have an original iPad or iPad 2 you have a few things going for you here. First, the high-resolution, 9.7-inch screen has a backlit LED display. As Apple describes it, it's "remarkably crisp and vivid." They're not lying. The in-plane switching or IPS technology means you can hold it at almost any angle (it has a 178-degree viewing angle) and still get good color and contrast. If you own a third- or fourth-generation iPad, things get even better. This version of iPad with its Retina display gives you four times as many pixels as earlier iPad models (3.1 million, to be exact). You get 2048 x 1536 resolution, greater color saturation, and a crisp image that rivals many HDTVs.

✓ **Faster processor:** The dual-core A6X chip in your fourth-gneration iPad is a super-fast processor that can run rings around your iPhone, making it a great device for gaming. The A6X chip in the fourth-generation iPad is very speedy and drives the Retina display without sacrificing the ten-hour battery life iPads are known for.

✓ **A built-in accelerometer and three-axis gyroscope:** Gamers will find these elements useful to shift around in a more versatile manner as they virtually move through games that involve motion. The built-in accelerometer and three-axis gyroscope let you grab your iPad and use it as a steering wheel or other game feature, so you really feel in the action. With iPad 2, the gyroscope, accelerometer, and compass were added to help apps like Maps pinpoint your location and movements as you stroll around town.

✓ **Playing games in full screen:** Rather than playing on a small iPhone screen, you can play most games designed for the iPad in full-screen mode on your iPad. Having a full screen brings the gaming experience to you in an even more engaging way than a small screen ever could.

✓ **Dragging elements around the screen:** The multi-touch screen in iPad may be based on the same technology as the iPhone, but it's been redone from the ground up for iPad. The iPad screen is responsive — and if you're about to be zapped by aliens in a fight-to-the-death computer game, that responsiveness counts.

✓ **The ten-hour battery life of an iPad:** This long battery life on every version of iPad means you can suck energy out of it playing games into the wee hours of the night.

✓ **Specialized game-playing features:** Some games are coming out with features that take advantage of iPad's capabilities. For example, Gameloft came out with a version of its N.O.V.A. game that includes a feature called *multiple-target acquisition,* which lets you target multiple bad guys in a single move to blow them out of the water with one shot. The Need for Speed racing games allow you to look in your rearview mirror to see what's coming up behind you, a feature made possible by iPad's large screen, compared to an iPhone.

✔ **Great sound:** The built-in speaker is a powerful little thing, but if you want things even more up-close and personal, you can plug in a head-phone, some speaker systems, or a microphone using the built-in jack.

Understanding the Accelerometer

iPad has a built-in motion sensor called an *accelerometer,* as well as a three-axis gyroscope. These allow those developing apps for iPad to have lots of fun as they use the automatically rotating screen to become part of the gaming experience. For example, they can build in a compass device that reorients itself automatically if you switch your iPad from landscape to portrait mode. Some racing games allow you to grab the iPad as if it were a steering wheel and rotate the device to simulate the driving experience.

Check out Firemint's Real Racing 2 HD app ($6.99) to try out the cool motion sensor feature. As you can see in Figures 8-1 and 8-2, this is a very fun gaming environment.

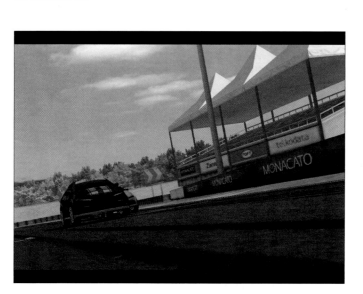

Figure 8-1: Move the iPad around to steer left or right.

Figure 8-2: Size up your competitors in this cool racing game that takes advantage of iPad's accelerometer.

Finding Some Very Cool Games

Now it's time to tell you about some of my favorite iPad games (the part of the book where you wonder why I get paid for what I do, 'cause reviewing games is so fun).

Check out some sites such as `http://ipadgames.org` and `www.tcgeeks.com` for cool downloadable, free iPad games.

Looking at what's out there

First, take a look at the gaming landscape. Several types of games are available (some ported over from iPhone and some customized for iPad), for example:

- **Arcade games** include apps such as Arcade Bowling Lite, Arcade SpinBall Lite, Foosball HD, and The Simpsons Arcade.

- **Kids' games** are sometimes educational, but almost always entertaining. These include Ace Kids Math Games, Addition UnderSea Adventures, and Word Monkey.

- **Card and board games,** such as Astraware Solitaire – 12 Games in 1 by Handmark, Inc., Mahjong Epic HD, and Payday Roulette.

- **Adventure games** like Animals vs. Zombies (see Figure 8-3), Everest: Hidden Expedition, AirAttack, Amazon: Hidden Expedition, and Carnivores: Dinosaur Hunter.

Figure 8-3: Animals vs. Zombies: May the best animal (thing?) win!

✔ **Sports games,** such as X Games SnoCross, Stick Golf, and Pool Bar – Online Hustle.

Exploring a half-dozen games

Narrowing down choices to just a few must-have games is hard because everyone likes different kinds of fun. To add to the choices, there are both iPhone- and iPad-engineered games you can use on your iPad, and more are coming out all the time. If you have a third- or fourth-generation iPad, you might want to look for games that are optimized for the new Retina display.

Still, the following list is a sampling of six recommended games for you to try that won't break the bank:

✔ **SCRABBLE for iPad ($4.99):** You remember SCRABBLE, that favorite old board game that can let you shine or put you to shame for your spelling and vocabulary skills? SCRABBLE is now available on iPad, and it's hot. (See Figure 8-4.) Shake your iPad to shuffle tiles. Use the drag-and-drop motion to play your letters. Want to share the fun? Reach out to your Facebook friends to take the game to the multiplayer level.

✔ **Broken Sword – The Smoking Mirror ($2.99):** This classic adventure game lets you virtually become the main character to experience all the game has to offer. Great art and animation distinguish this game, and the iPad version (see its description in the Game Center Store; Figure 8-5) has a handy hint system you'll appreciate.

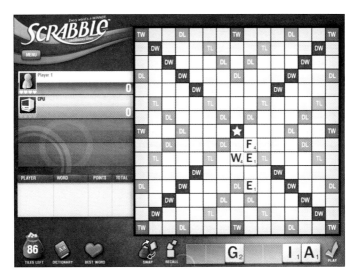

Figure 8-4: SCRABBLE is awesome on iPad.

Figure 8-5: Broken Sword is a classic game updated from its iPhone version for iPad.

✔ **Civilization Revolution for iPad ($6.99):** If you like a world-building type of game, you'll find Civilization Revolution right up your alley. It's been fine-tuned for iPad to be even better than the iPhone version. The game also offers a feature called Scenario Creator, which lets you create your own unique challenges, essentially allowing for unlimited variety in the game.

✔ **Flight Control HD ($4.99):** Ever wanted to be an airline pilot? This game gives you a taste of the experience. Create flight paths that ensure your plane lands safely. A favorite with iPhone gamers, this one translates well to iPad. This game has lots of multiplayer options, including the option of using a split screen to keep both players in the action.

✔ **Monkey Island 2 Special Edition: LeChuck's Revenge for iPad ($4.99):** A point-and-click adventure game classic on iPhone, in its iPad incarnation, Monkey Island has great graphics and sound, and an engaging story at its heart. If you like adventure games, don't miss this one.

✔ **Angry Birds HD ($.99):** This game has become a cult — you can even buy Angry Birds stuffed animals. Use little birds to attack pigs (see Figure 8-6) and smash them in a variety of intriguing and oddly satisfying ways. You have lots of levels to work your way through, but don't worry; if you get stuck, the Mighty Eagle is there to help you out!

Figure 8-6: Angry Birds can become addictive.

✔ **tChess Pro ($7.99):** This game is another app designed for iPhone that works just great on iPad. You can play against the computer or another player. You can modify the appearance of the chess pieces. It even sports features that help chess beginners learn the game painlessly, but more advanced players will enjoy it as well.

As well as costing money, games take up a lot of memory, so choose the games you buy wisely. If you no longer want to play a game, delete it from your iPad to save space, keeping a backup on iCloud or via iTunes on your Mac or PC in case you change your mind at a later date. If you play games over the Internet with other players, remember to quit these apps when not playing to save resources and battery power.

Special mention: ComicBookLover isn't a game, but it's a blast of an app that most gamers can appreciate. The iPad screen is perfect for those bright, crisp graphics, and iPad's navigation tools let you swipe your way through the panes in several interesting ways.

Getting Gaming Accessories

Some interesting accessories are coming out for iPad. No doubt more will appear over time, and Apple itself may add features or gaming accessories in a next-edition device. For example, for a future iPad Apple or somebody else might offer an external control accessory so you don't have to cover up your onscreen game to use onscreen control mechanisms, and Apple might add rumble to simulate gaming sounds.

For now, here are a few iPad gaming accessories in the works that caught my attention:

- ✏ **Incipio iPad Hive Honeycomb dermaShot Silicone Case ($19.99)** is a rugged case for serious gamers. The back sports molded grips that help you keep a good hold on your iPad while playing those action-packed games.

- ✏ **JoyStick-It (around $20)** from ThinkGeek is an arcade-style stick you attach to your iPad screen. The joystick won't harm your screen, and you can move it around at any time. It gives you that real arcade game feel for controlling games. It won't work with every game but does claim to work with thousands of them.

Game Center

The Game Center is an app that comes preinstalled with iPad (iOS 4.2 and later). If you're into gaming, you may enjoy the features it offers that allow you to invite friends to play games, buy games, and keep track of your games, friends, and achievements.

Of course, you can also download games from the App Store and other online game stores and play them on your iPad without having to use Game Center. What Game Center provides is a place where you can create a gaming profile, add a list of gaming friends, keep track of and share your scores and perks, and shop for games (and only games) in the App Store, along with listings of top-rated games and game categories to choose from.

Think of the Game Center as a kind of social networking site for gamers, where you can compare your scores and find players to go a few rounds with. The app can automatically match you with other players who have a similar ability. Say you need three other people to play a certain game; Game Center can find them for you. And the Achievements listing shows you your score history for all the games you play. Finally, Leaderboards allows you to compare your performance with your gaming friends.

Figure 8-7 shows you the Game Center interface with the following five choices along the bottom:

✔ **Me:** Contains your profile and summary of number of friends, games, and achievements.

✔ **Friends:** Tap to invite friends to play.

✔ **Games:** Takes you to iTunes to shop for games.

✔ **Challenges:** Friends can challenge their friends to do better than they did. Tap a friend's score in the Friends area of Game Center to challenge her.

✔ **Requests:** Shows you any requests from your friends for a game.

Figure 8-7: Game Center's opening screen shows an overview of your friends, games, and achievements.

Opening an account in Game Center

Using the Game Center app, you can search for and buy games, add friends with whom you can play those games, and keep records of your scores for posterity. In order to do this, however, you must first open a Game Center account by following these steps:

1. **From the Home screen, tap the Game Center icon.**

   If you've never used Game Center, you're asked whether to allow *push notifications:* If you want to receive these notices alerting you that your friends want to play a game with you, tap OK. You should, however, be aware that push notifications can drain your iPad's battery more quickly.

2. **On the Game Center opening screen (refer to Figure 8-7), if you haven't yet created an account, tap Create New Apple ID.**

3. **If the correct country isn't listed in the New Account dialog, tap the Location field and select another location; if the correct location is already showing, tap Next to confirm it.**

4. **In the next dialog you see, tap the Month, Day, and Year fields, enter your date of birth, and then tap Next.**

5. **In the Game Center Terms & Conditions dialog, swipe to scroll down (and read) the conditions, and then tap Agree if you want to continue creating your account.**

6. **In the confirmation dialog that appears, tap Agree once more to accept for real!**

7. **In the next dialog that opens, tap each field or the Next button at the top of the onscreen keyboard and enter your name, e-mail address, and password information.**

Tap the Question field to select a security question to identify yourself, and tap the Answer field and type an answer to the question. Be sure to scroll to the bottom of this dialog and choose to turn off the e-mail notification subscription if you don't want to have Game Center send you messages.

8. **Tap Next to proceed.**

See the next section to find out how you can create your Game Center profile in subsequent dialogs.

Creating a Game Center profile

When you reach the last dialog in Step 8 of the preceding section, you're ready to create your profile and specify some account settings. You can also make most of these settings after you've created your account, by tapping your Account name on the Game Center Home screen and then tapping View Account. To create your Game Center profile, follow these steps:

1. **In the Create Profile dialog that appears (see Figure 8-8), in the Nickname field, enter the "handle" you want to be known by when playing games.**

2. **If you don't want other players to be able to invite you to play games when Game Center is open, tap the Game Invites On/Off button to turn off the feature.**

3. **If you don't want other players to be able to see your real name, tap the Public Profile On/Off button to turn off this feature.**

4. **If you want your friends to be able to send you requests for playing games via e-mail, check to see whether the e-mail address listed in this dialog is the one you want them to use. If not, tap Add Another Email and enter another e-mail address.**

5. **Tap Done when you're finished with the settings.**

You return to the Game Center Home screen, already signed in to your account with information displayed about friends, games, and gaming achievements (all at zero initially).

Figure 8-8: When you're playing games with others, your handle identifies you.

6. **To add a picture to your profile, tap Change Photo.**

   You see a message that your photo will be shared with all other Game Center players.

7. **Tap OK.**

   The two options of Take Photo and Choose Photo appear (only the Choose Photo option appears for an original iPad).

8. **Tap Choose Photo to select a photo from your Camera Roll or a photo album.**

9. **Tap the album you want to use and scroll to locate the photo.**

10. **Tap the photo.**

    It appears in a Choose Photo dialog.

11. **Use your finger to move the photo around or scale it, and then tap Use.**

    The photo appears on your Game Center Home screen.

After you create an account and a profile, whenever you go to the Game Center, you log in by entering your e-mail address and password and then tapping Sign In.

You can change account settings from the Game Center Home screen: Tap your account name and then tap View Account, make changes to your settings, and then tap Done.

Adding friends

If you want to play Game Center games with others who have an Apple ID and an iPhone, iPod touch, Macs with Mountain Lion or later, or iPad, follow these steps to add them as friends so you can invite them to play:

1. **From the Game Center Home screen, tap the Friends button at the bottom of the screen.**

2. **On the Friends page, tap Add Friends.**

3. **Enter an e-mail address in the To field and edit the invitation, if you like.**

4. **Tap the Send button.**

   A confirmation message tells you that your invitation has been sent.

5. **In the confirmation message, tap OK.**

   After your friend accepts your invitation, his name is listed on the Friends screen.

 With iOS 5, Game Center gained a friend Recommendation feature. Tap the Friends tab, and then tap the A–Z button in the top-left corner. A Recommendations section appears above the list of your current friends. These are people who play the same or similar games, so if you like, try adding one or two as friends. You can also tap Use My Contacts to find recommendations of friends from your Contacts app and add them.

 You will probably also receive requests from friends who know you're on Game Center. When you get these e-mail invitations, be sure that you know the person sending it before you accept it — especially if you've allowed e-mail access in your account settings. If you don't double-check, you could be allowing a stranger into your gaming world.

Purchasing and downloading games

Time to get some games to play! Remember that you can buy any game app from the App Store and simply play it by tapping to open it on your iPad. But if you want to use Game Center to buy games, here are the steps involved:

1. **Open Game Center and sign in to your account.**

2. **Tap the Games button at the bottom of the screen, and then tap Find Game Center Games (see Figure 8-9).**

Tap here to find more games.

Figure 8-9: Game Center takes you right to a great world of games apps.

3. **In the list of games that appears, scroll through the list of featured games.**

   To view the most popular games, tap the Charts button at the bottom of the screen.

   REMEMBER

   Accessing apps from the Game Center displays only game apps, as opposed to accessing apps from the App Store, which shows you all categories of apps.

4. **To search for a particular title, tap the Search field at the bottom of the screen and enter the name by using the onscreen keyboard.**

5. **Tap a game title to view information about it.**

6. **To buy a game, tap the button labeled with either the word *Free* or the price, such as $1.99; tap the button again, which is now labeled Install App or Download App, if it's free.**

7. **Enter your Apple ID and password in the dialog that appears and then tap OK.**

   Another verification dialog appears, asking you to sign in.

8. **Follow the instructions on the next couple of screens to enter your password and verify your payment information if this is the first time you've signed in to your account from this device.**

9. **When the verification dialog appears, tap Buy.**

   The game downloads.

You may see buttons labeled Buy It Now or Available at the App Store while you're exploring game recommendations in the Games section of Game Center. Tapping these buttons takes you from Game Center directly to the App Store to buy the game.

If you've added friends to your account (see the preceding section), you can go to the Friends page and view games your friends have downloaded. To purchase one of these games, just tap it in your friend's list.

Playing against yourself

Many games allow you to play all on your own. Each game has different rules and goals, so you'll have to study a game's instructions and learn how to play it, but here's some general information about these types of games:

- Often a game can be played in two modes: with others or in a *solitaire* version, where you play yourself or the computer.

- Many games you may be familiar with in the offline world, such as Carcassonne or SCRABBLE, have online versions. For these, you already know the rules of play, so you simply need to figure out the execution. For example, in the online Carcassone solitaire game, you tap to place a tile on the board, tap the placed tile to rotate it, and tap the check mark to complete your turn and reveal another tile.

- All the games you play on your own record your scores in Game Center so you can track your progress.

Playing games with friends in Game Center

After you've added a friend and both of you have downloaded the same game, you're ready to play. The rules of play are different for each game, but here are the basic steps for getting a game going:

1. **Tap the Game Center app icon on the Home screen and sign in, if necessary.**

2. **Tap the Friends button on the bottom of the screen.**

   The Friends page shown in Figure 8-10 appears.

3. **Tap the name of the friend you want to play and then tap the name of a game you have in common.**

   At this point, some games offer you an invitation to send to the friend — if so, wait for your friend to respond, which he can do by tapping Accept or Decline on his device.

   The game appears on your screen.

4. **Tap Play to start playing according to whatever rules the game has, and your scores mount up as you play.**

Figure 8-10: Keep adding friends to widen your gaming universe.

5. **When you're done playing, tap either the Friends or Games button on the bottom of the Friends screen in Game Center to see your score and your friend's score listed.**

   Game Center tracks your achievements, including points and perks that you've earned along the way. You can also compare your gaming achievements to those of top-ranking players across the Internet — and check your friends' scores by displaying the Friends page with the Points portion showing. (Refer to Figure 8-10.)

If your friends aren't available, you can play a game by tapping its title on the Games page and then tapping Play. You can then compare your scores with others around the world who have also played the game recently.

Sharing high scores with friends

It's fun to share your best scores with friends, and as of iOS 6, you can. Try these steps to share scores using Game Center:

1. **Tap Game Center on the Home screen and then tap Me.**

2. **Tap a game score in the list on the left (see Figure 8-11) and then click Share.**

3. **In the dialog that appears (see Figure 8-12), tap Mail, Message, or Twitter, or tap the second dot at the bottom of the dialog to scroll over to other options and tap Facebook.**

4. **Depending on what method you chose for sharing, enter an e-mail address and message if sharing by Mail or enter your account information for services such as Twitter, and follow directions to forward your score.**

Figure 8-11: Choose the score to share.

Figure 8-12: Choose whether you want to share by Mail, Messages, Twitter, or Facebook.

Book III
iPad on the Go

The 5th Wave   By Rich Tennant

iPad

"In fact it does come with a compass."

1 t's lightweight, portable, and packed with features, so why shouldn't iPad be your go-to device when you're going on the road? In this part, you get all set up with your Wi-Fi and 3G and 4G settings for connecting to the Internet from just about anywhere. You get to play with the Maps app, a very cool way to swipe and flick your way to just about anyplace on the planet. Finally, in this part I address you road warriors out there — you know who you are. You are the iPad users who need to find the best hotels, airfares, travel guides, and restaurants in the next city or next country. You want to track expenses and keep in touch with the office. That's just what you find out about in the last chapter of this part.

Chapter 1: Configuring iPad to Connect Everywhere

This chapter is all about connecting, whether you're connecting to the Internet via Wi-Fi, 3G, or 4G (not available on the original iPad or iPad 2) or connecting to your company network. Apple has made an effort over the years with iPhone to support enterprises, meaning that you can use the phone to connect with your company network and vital work data. The iPad continues that tradition with support for Microsoft Exchange Server, virtual private networks (VPNs), and Lightweight Directory Access Protocol (LDAP) accounts.

Your best ally in setting up the more technical of these is your network administrator. In this chapter, I give you an overview of the capabilities of iPad to connect and some guidance in making the settings you need to make.

Making Wi-Fi and 3G/4G Settings

The way people with iPads can connect to the Internet, the grandmother of all networks, is via its Wi-Fi or 3G/4G capabilities (assuming they have a 3G or 4G model).

The original iPad and iPad 2 offered either Wi-Fi only or a Wi-Fi and 3G connection. The third- and fourth-generation iPad and the iPad mini offers Wi-Fi only or Wi-Fi and 4G, which gives you the ability to connect to a super fast 4G LTE network; if a 4G network isn't available (and they aren't yet in many areas), your 4G iPad can still access several types of 3G networks as well as GSM/UMTS networks around the world.

In this section, I go into the settings you can make to manage your Wi-Fi or 3G/4G connection.

Making Wi-Fi settings

Book I, Chapter 5 gives you the information you need to connect to a Wi-Fi network, a matter of simply signing in to the network, with a password if necessary. Now it's time to go over some of the finer points of your Wi-Fi connection.

A basic Wi-Fi setting tells iPad to automatically search for and join networks that are in range. If several networks are in range, using this setting, iPad joins the one that it used most recently.

After iPad has joined a network, a little Wi-Fi icon appears in the Status bar. The number of bars indicates the strength of the signal, just as you're used to seeing on your cellphone.

To get to Wi-Fi settings, tap Settings on your Home screen and then tap Wi-Fi. (See Figure 1-1.) Here's a rundown of the items you can work with in Settings for your Wi-Fi configuration:

- **Wi-Fi On/Off:** Simply tap this to On to turn on Wi-Fi. If you want it off, perhaps to save battery drain or because you're on an airplane and the pilot tells you to, set this to Off. (Note that iPads also have an Airplane Mode setting, which I discuss in the next section.)

- **Other:** If you want to join a network that doesn't appear on the list, tap Other under the Choose a Network section of these settings. In the dialog that appears, enter the network name and choose a type of security, such as WEP or WPA. When you choose a form of security and return to the dialog shown in Figure 1-2, a Password field appears. Some networks might need other information, such as a username or static IP address, to complete this dialog. Check with your administrator for any information you can't provide.

- **Ask to Join Networks:** iPad automatically connects to the previously joined network but doesn't look for other networks unless this setting is on. Tap this to the On position, and iPad displays all possible network connections in this dialog. If a network requires a password, it sports a padlock symbol. If no known networks are available, you're asked whether you want to join unknown networks. To forget a network so iPad doesn't join it automatically, tap the arrow on the right of the network name and then tap Forget This Network.

To adjust settings for individual Wi-Fi networks, tap the arrow icon to the right of a listed network.

Figure 1-1: Wi-Fi settings.

Figure 1-2: Accessing a closed network.

**Book III
Chapter 1**

Configuring iPad to
Connect Everywhere

After you set up your Wi-Fi and sign in to your home network, you can set up Home Sharing to share music and video content from your Mac or PC with your iPad. See Book V, Chapter 1 for more about Home Sharing.

Making 3G/4G settings

When you own a Wi-Fi and 3G/4G model of iPad, in addition to modifying Wi-Fi settings as covered in the preceding section, you can make changes to your cellular data in Settings. Cellular Data settings enable you to manage data roaming and your account information. (See Figure 1-3.) You can use this dialog to sign up for a data plan by entering your name, phone, and credit card information; when you submit this information, your account is set up with your provider with a unique phone number associated with the account. You need this phone number to speak to customer representatives about your account.

Figure 1-3: Cellular Data Account dialog.

You can find the following items under the Cellular Data category in Settings:

- ✔ **Cellular Data Network:** Turn 3G/4G on or off here.

- ✔ **Enable LTE:** To enable your iPad to search for and connect to LTE networks, turn on this setting. Data may load faster using LTE, but it may take a toll on your battery life.

- ✔ **Data Roaming:** Data Roaming is a feature of cellular networks that takes advantage of other carriers' networks, if you're out of range of your primary carrier's network. Using data roaming can result in additional charges, so you may want to turn it off when you don't need it.

- ✔ **View Account:** Tap this setting to view account information.

- ✔ **Add a SIM PIN:** If you want to protect the data on your SIM card from prying eyes, beyond setting a password to unlock your iPad, you can assign a PIN to your SIM card here. When you've assigned a PIN whenever you try to use a new SIM card or restart your Wi-Fi or 3G/4G iPad, you have to enter the password. Don't forget your PIN, though, or you can't unlock your SIM card.

If you change your cellular data carrier, you might need to remove the SIM card and replace it with another. To do this, you need to use a SIM eject tool to press and open the SIM tray located on the left side of 3G/4G-enabled iPads. (Don't have a SIM eject tool? Don't worry; Apple recommends using a very high-tech instrument — a paper clip.) Replace the SIM card and push the tray back in. That's it! You can also use a local SIM card to get a local connection when traveling.

With any Wi-Fi and 3G/4G model iPad with iOS 4.2 or later, you also have access to the Airplane Mode setting. This setting allows you to disable wireless features of your device as required by airline regulations when you're flying. With Airplane Mode turned on in Settings, you won't be able to browse, e-mail, sync, buy stuff online, or stream videos (which you would only be able to do with a 3G/4G model a few miles in the sky). Also, the GPS locator of Maps won't work, but you can play content you've downloaded, play games, and create documents in apps like Pages and Numbers unless the airline provides Wi-Fi. Just don't forget to turn off the Airplane Mode setting when you land!

Connecting with Personal Hotspot or iPhone Tethering

If you want to connect iPad to your smartphone to go online when out of range of a Wi-Fi network, you can tether it using Verizon's Personal Hotspot or AT&T's iPhone 3G/4G Tethering. *Tethering* with either service allows your iPad's Wi-Fi capability to tap into your phone's data connection to go online. You can get a connection anywhere your phone gets a connection — even if you have a Wi-Fi–only iPad model.

Tethering involves a few challenges. You don't go online instantly because you have to complete a few steps to do so, the connection speed might be a tad slow, and it can drain your phone battery quickly.

After you're comfortable with the trade-offs of the tethering option, you need to do two things:

1. **Add the tethering option for your carrier on the carrier's website by logging in to your account and adding the feature.**

   There is a cost; for example, AT&T offers two levels of tethering support at $45 and $60 at the time of this writing.

2. **Make the setting on your iPad to turn on the tethering service feature:**

   a. *Tap the Settings icon.*

   b. *Tap Wi-Fi.*

   c. *Tap the tethering service in the Choose a Network section and make settings specific to your carrier.*

Sprint, AT&T, and Verizon pricing and features are still in flux, and you need both a basic data plan and a tethering feature plan, which can add up. Still, if you often wander into areas that have no Wi-Fi and you don't have a 3G or 4G iPad, it may — or may not — be more cost-effective to use this feature.

Consider using the FaceTime app to make Wi-Fi calls. Using this app, you can make video calls to others who have FaceTime on their devices. See Book II, Chapter 4 for more about using FaceTime.

Connecting to an Enterprise Remotely

When previewed in early 2010, iPad had no support for Microsoft Exchange. Between that time and its release in April 2010, somebody got smart and added Exchange support. That opened possibilities for connecting with an enterprise network and its data remotely. If you work at a company using Microsoft Exchange and use an iPad, this is very good news.

Thanks to these enterprise features, here are some of the things you can do to connect to your organization's network and data.

Setting up a Microsoft Exchange account

Microsoft Exchange is a messaging standard that allows the exchange of information between networks. Many companies use Microsoft Exchange and a feature called ActiveSync to exchange its e-mail, contacts, and calendar information with devices. iPhone has supported Microsoft Exchange for a while now, and iPad carries on the tradition. You can use Microsoft Exchange to wirelessly sync that information to your iPad from your corporate network.

One benefit of a connection with Microsoft Exchange is that you can wipe the data and settings off a device remotely by using a command in Exchange if it's lost or stolen, keeping those confidential business contacts private. Another option for this is to use iCloud's Find My iPad feature, covered in more detail in Book I, Chapter 9.

With a configuration profile in place, you can set up a Microsoft Exchange account on your iPad. To do so, follow these steps:

1. **Tap Settings.**
2. **Tap Mail, Contacts, Calendars.**
3. **Tap Add Account.**
4. **Tap Microsoft Exchange.**

5. **Enter your account information in the dialog shown in Figure 1-4 (e-mail address, domain such as IT or Marketing, username, password, and a description) and then tap Next.**

   iPad then uses Microsoft's Autodiscover feature to verify your Exchange server.

Figure 1-4: The Exchange dialog box.

6. **If it can verify your information, tap Save, and you're all set.**

   If it can't, you may have to enter additional information yourself. Check with your network administrator to get what you need.

Book III Chapter 1

Configuring iPad to Connect Everywhere

When you're setting up a Microsoft Exchange account, you can choose which items you want to sync with, including e-mail, contacts, or calendar. You get choices for how existing data on your iPad is handled (merged, kept in a separate account, or overwritten).

Setting up a configuration profile

A *configuration profile* is a way for the network administrator at your enterprise to set up your iPad to use the systems in your company, via Microsoft Exchange or a VPN, which controls access to corporate e-mail or contacts.

Your administrator should check out the Enterprise Deployment Guide and iPad Configuration Utility from Apple (`www.apple.com/support/ipad/enterprise`) to get a configuration profile set up. After a configuration profile is in place, it can be e-mailed to you or placed on a secure web page. Also, your company's network administrator can install a configuration profile on your iPad.

If you receive a configuration profile, you can install it yourself by opening the message and tapping the file. Tap Install and enter any information that's requested, such as your password.

You can't change the settings in a configuration profile. To set up a different configuration profile, first remove the existing configuration profile, have the new profile sent to you, and then install it. To remove a profile, in Settings, choose General, then Profiles, and then select the configuration profile you want to get rid of and tap Remove.

Setting up an LDAP account

You can also set up an LDAP (Lightweight Directory Access Protocol) account. LDAP accounts allow you to search for contacts on an LDAP server, which many organizations use to store data, and access them through iPad Contacts.

Here's how to set up an LDAP account on your iPad:

1. **In Settings, tap Mail, Contacts, Calendars.**

2. **Tap Add Account.**

3. **Tap Other.**

4. **Tap Add LDAP Account.**

5. **Enter your LDAP account information (see Figure 1-5) and then tap Next to verify the account.**

6. **Tap Save.**

Figure 1-5: The LDAP dialog.

When you've set up this type of account, contacts imported from the account appear as a group in the iPad Contacts app. To see these contacts, your iPad has to be connected to the Internet because they aren't stored locally. If necessary, check with your company's network administrator for information about your network and LDAP requirements.

Setting up a virtual private network

If you want to be able to connect to your organization's network, you may be able to use a virtual private network, or VPN. VPN works over both Wi-Fi and 3G/4G cellular data connections. A VPN allows you to access data securely whether you're using your home network to access certain browsers or sites or accessing a public Wi-Fi connection. After a VPN is set up at your company, you can use Network Settings on your iPad to modify your VPN settings and connect to your network.

You might need to ask your network administrator for information on making settings for accessing a VPN. If you've set up VPN on your computer, you should be able to use the same VPN settings on your iPad. You might want to let your admin know that iPad can connect to VPNs that use the L2TP, PPTP, or Cisco IPSec protocol.

To add a new VPN configuration, go to iPad Settings. Tap General, tap VPN, and if necessary, tap to turn on VPN. The dialog shown in Figure 1-6 appears. Fill in the information requested and tap Save.

To delete a VPN configuration, tap the blue arrow to the right of the configuration name in the Network settings and then tap Delete VPN.

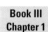
**Book III
Chapter 1**

Configuring iPad to
Connect Everywhere

Figure 1-6: The Add Configuration dialog.

Have your administrator check out third-party tools that help to enable the use of the corporate network by remote iPad users. Good for Enterprise helps a user manage and update smartphone-like standards if that person's company has no single standard. Array Networks provides the iPad app Desktop Direct – My Desktops that, along with Citrix Receiver software, helps users access their desktop from afar.

Status icons

In case you're wondering what the icons in the Status bar on top of the iPad screen mean relative to your connections, here's a rundown:

Icon	*Meaning*
✈	Airplane mode is on, and your Wi-Fi and 3G/4G connection capabilities are turned off.
3G	A 3G/4G network is available.
E	A carrier's EDGE network is available.
O	A GPRS network is available.
📶	Your iPad has a Wi-Fi Internet connection. The more bars you see, the stronger your connection.
☀	Network or another type of activity involving a third-party app is detected.
VPN	You're connected to a VPN network.

Chapter 2: Finding Your Way with Maps

In This Chapter

- ✓ Going to your current location
- ✓ Knowing where you've been
- ✓ Finding directions, info, and more
- ✓ Conveying location information beyond maps
- ✓ Getting turn-by-turn navigation help

*Y*ou may have used a maps app on a smartphone before. The big difference with iPad is its large screen, on which you can view all the beautiful map visuals, traffic flow, and maps in 3D as long as you have an Internet connection. You can also display the map and written directions simultaneously, or have Maps speak your directions, guiding you as you drive with your 3G/4G iPad.

You will find lots of great functions in the Maps app, including getting directions with suggested alternate routes from one place to another by foot, car, or public transportation. You can bookmark locations to return to them again. And the Maps app makes it possible to get information about locations, such as the phone numbers and web links to businesses. You can even add a location to your Contacts list, or share a location with your buddy using Mail, Message, Twitter, or Facebook.

Be prepared: This app is a fun app that will help you find your way.

Getting Where You're Going

The first duty of a map is to get you where you want to go. The Maps app can go directly to wherever you are or to any other location you wish to visit. You can also use tools that help you find different views of locales by displaying streets, terrain, or aerial views, or zooming in and out for various levels of detail. In this section, you find out how to use Maps to get around.

Going to your current location

iPad is pretty smart; it can figure out where you are at any point in time and display your current location using GPS technology (with a 3G/4G model) or a triangulation method (Wi-Fi model). You must have an Internet connection; your location can be pinpointed more exactly if you have a 3G or 4G iPad, but even Wi-Fi models do a pretty good job, and do even better when you're surrounded by hotspots.

To display your current location in Maps, follow these steps:

1. **From the Home screen, tap the Maps icon.**

2. **Tap the Current Location icon (the arrow in the lower-left corner; see Figure 2-1).**

   Your current location is displayed with a pin in it and a blue circle around it. (See Figure 2-1.) The circle indicates how accurate the location is — it could actually be anywhere within the area of the circle.

Your current location

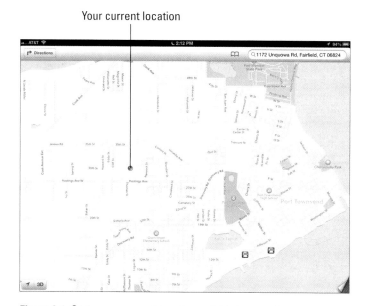

Figure 2-1: Go to your current location quickly to see where you are.

Having trouble getting Maps to work? That could be because if you turn off Location Services in iPad Settings, Maps can't find you. Go to Settings and make sure that Location Services is set to On.

3. **Double-tap the screen to zoom in on your location.**

   Additional methods of zooming in and out are covered in the "Zooming in and out" section, later in this chapter.

If you don't have a 3G/4G version of iPad, your current location is a rough estimate based on a triangulation method. Only 3G- and 4G-enabled iPads with GPS can really pinpoint your location. Still, if you type a starting location and an ending location to get directions, you can get pretty accurate results even with a Wi-Fi–only iPad.

Changing views

The Maps app offers three views: Standard, Satellite, and Hybrid. You view the Standard view by default the first time you open Maps. Here's what these views offer:

- **Standard:** Your basic street map you might find in any road atlas
- **Satellite:** An aerial view
- **Hybrid:** A satellite view with street names included

Another cool app for those who like their maps of the topographical variety is Topo Maps for iPad from Phil Endecott ($7.99). This app taps into the United States Geological Society (USGS) and Canadian topographical maps and is great for planning that next trek into the wilderness.

Follow these steps to switch among the views in Maps:

1. **To change views, with Maps open, swipe the bottom-right corner of the screen to the left to turn the "page" and reveal the Maps menu shown in Figure 2-2.**

Book III
Chapter 2

Finding Your Way
with Maps

Figure 2-2: The controls for Maps are tucked underneath the map display page.

2. **Tap the Satellite option.**

The Satellite view shown in Figure 2-3 appears.

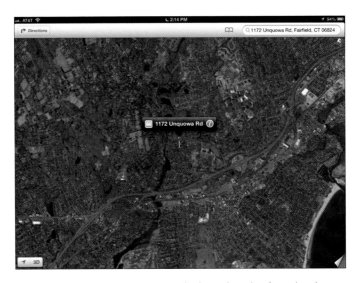

Figure 2-3: Using Satellite view, you look at a location from the sky.

3. **Swipe to reveal the menu again and tap Hybrid, as shown in Figure 2-4.**

Doing this displays a Satellite view with street names superimposed.

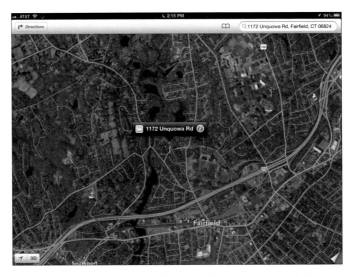

Figure 2-4: Street names and highway numbers appear in Hybrid view.

4. Tap the 3D button in the lower-left corner.

A 3D effect is applied to whatever view is displayed (see Figure 2-5).

Figure 2-5: 3D seems to rotate and slant the map before your eyes.

You can drop a pin to mark a location on a map that you can return to. See the "Dropping a pin" section, later in this chapter, for more about this feature.

You can also turn on a feature that displays an overlay on the Standard map to show current traffic conditions. (The Traffic setting is shown earlier in Figure 2-2.) This feature works best in major metropolitan areas and displays red dashes on roads indicating accidents or road closures to help you navigate your rush-hour commute or trip to the mall.

Tap the Print button on the Maps menu to print a displayed map with an AirPrint-compatible printer.

Zooming in and out

If you've used an online mapping program, you know that you frequently have to move to more or less detailed views of the map to find what you're looking for: The street detail doesn't show the nearest highway, and the region level doesn't let you see that all-important next turn. You'll appreciate the feature in the Maps app that allows you to zoom in and out to see more or less detailed maps and to move around a displayed map.

You can use the following methods on a displayed map to zoom in and out and move around a map:

✔ **Double-tap with a single finger** to zoom in (and reveal more detail), as shown in Figure 2-6.

Figure 2-6: Zoom in to see more detail.

✔ **Double-tap with two fingers** to zoom out (and reveal less detail), as shown in Figure 2-7.

✔ **Place two fingers together on the screen and move them apart** to zoom in.

✔ **Place two fingers apart on the screen and pinch them together** to zoom out.

✔ **Press your finger to the screen and drag the map in any direction** to move to an adjacent area.

It can take a few moments for the map to redraw itself when you enlarge, reduce, or move around it, so have a little patience. An area that's being redrawn will look like a blank grid but will fill in, in time. Also, if you're in Satellite or Hybrid view, zooming in may take some time; wait it out because the blurred image will resolve itself.

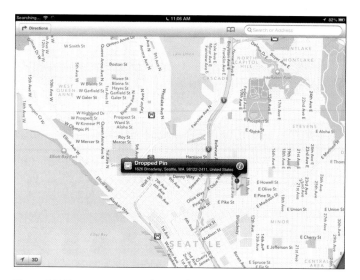

Figure 2-7: Zoom out to get a larger view of the region — with less detail.

Going to another location

If you're at Point A and want to get to Point B, Calcutta, Des Moines, or wherever, you need to know how to find any location other than your current location using Maps. Doing this involves entering as much information as you have about the location's address in the Search field.

Try going to another location using these steps:

1. **With Maps open, tap in the Search field.**

    If you don't see the Search field in the upper-right corner, you may have to tap the Clear button.

    The keyboard opens (as shown in Figure 2-8).

2. **Type a location, using a street address with city and state, a stored contact name, or a destination, such as *Empire State Building* or *Detroit airport*.**

    Maps may make suggestions as you type if it finds any logical matches.

Search field

Dictation key

Figure 2-8: You can use the onscreen keyboard to enter location information.

Tap the Dictation key (not available on the original iPad and iPad 2) on the onscreen keyboard (refer to Figure 2-8) and speak a location to iPad if you prefer. Tap in the Search field, and then tap the Dictation key and say the location; tap the Dictation key or in the Search field again and what you've spoken appears there.

Double-tap the Home button and ask Siri for a type of business or location by zip code. For example, if you crave something with pepperoni, say "Find pizza in **99208 zip code,**" the results typically display a small map that you can tap to open the Maps app to find your way there. See Book V, Chapter 6 for more about using Siri.

3. **Tap the Search button.**

The location appears with a red pin inserted in it and a label with the location and an Information icon (shown in Figure 2-9). Note that if several locations match your search term, you may see several pins displayed in a Suggestions list.

Street view   Information bar   Bookmark   Search field

Information icon

Figure 2-9: The more specific the address information you enter, the more likely you are to find just the right location.

4. **You can also tap the screen and drag in any direction to move to a nearby location.**

   See the upcoming "Dropping a pin" section to find out how to zero in on the location and get the label with links to additional information, like you see in Figure 2-9.

5. **Tap the Bookmark icon (the little book symbol to the left of the Search field; refer to Figure 2-9) and then tap the Recent tab to reveal recently visited sites.**

6. **Tap a bookmark to go there.**

As you discover later in this chapter in the "Adding and viewing a bookmark" section, you can also quickly go to any location you've previously visited and saved using the Bookmarks feature.

Add the city and state, if you know them, whenever you enter a destination. A search for *Bronx Zoo* landed me in the Woodland Park Zoo in Tacoma, Washington, because the search uses the individual words and the closest geographical location for a *Zoo* match to find results!

Remembering Where You've Been

Why reinvent the (mapping) wheel? One of the great capabilities of a mapping program is the ability to store locations you like to go to for future reference. In Maps, you can do this in a few ways. You can drop a pin on a map, which marks a beginning point for getting directions from one site to another. Or you can place a bookmark for a site you want to revisit often.

Dropping a pin

With iPad, pins act like the pins you might place on a paper map to note routes or favorite locations. With iPad, pins are also markers; a green pin marks a start location, red pins mark search results, a pin you drop yourself appears in a lovely purple, and a blue pin (referred to as the *blue marker*) marks your iPad's current location.

Use these steps to try the pin feature of iPad:

1. **Display a map that contains a spot where you want to drop a pin to help you get directions to or from that site.**

   If you need to, you can zoom in to a more detailed map to get a better view of the location you want to pin using the techniques I cover in the earlier "Zooming in and out" section.

2. **Press and hold your finger on the screen at the location where you want to place the pin.**

   The pin appears, together with an information bar (shown in Figure 2-10).

Figure 2-10: The information bar provides access to yet more Maps tools.

3. **Tap the Information icon (refer to Figure 2-10) on the information bar to display details about the pin location (shown in Figure 2-11).**

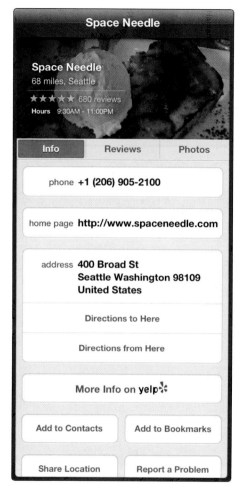

Figure 2-11: This very useful dialog gives you information and lets you share what you know.

Book III
Chapter 2

Finding Your Way
with Maps

TIP

If a site has associated reviews on Yelp, you can click the More Info on Yelp button in its Information dialog to install the Yelp app and read them. If you like the destination, add it to your contacts to find easily in future.

Adding and viewing a bookmark

Bookmarks are a tried-and-true way to save a destination so that you can display a map or directions to that spot quickly. You've probably used a bookmark feature in a web browser that works similarly. With Maps, you can save bookmarks and access those locations from a drop-down list.

Here's how to add a bookmark in Maps:

1. **Place a pin on a location, as described in the preceding section.**

2. **Tap the Information icon to display the Information dialog.**

3. **Tap the Add to Bookmarks button (refer to Figure 2-11).**

   The Add Bookmark dialog and keyboard appear (as shown in Figure 2-12). If you like, you can modify the name of the bookmark.

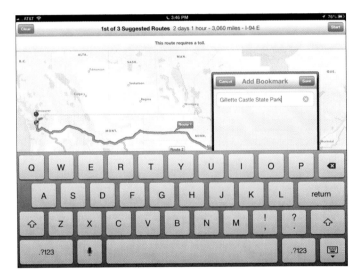

Figure 2-12: Name the bookmark.

4. **Tap Save.**

5. **To view your bookmarks, tap the Bookmark icon (it looks like a little open book; refer to Figure 2-9) at the top of the Maps screen.**

   Be sure the Bookmarks tab is selected; a list of bookmarks displays, as shown in Figure 2-13.

6. **Tap a bookmark to go to the location in Maps.**

You can also view recently viewed locations even if you haven't bookmarked them. Tap the Bookmark icon, and then, on the bottom of the Bookmarks dialog that appears, tap Recents. Locations you've visited recently are listed there. Tap a location to return to it.

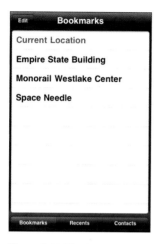

Figure 2-13: The list of saved bookmarks.

Deleting a bookmark

Eventually, a site you used to visit gets crossed off your A list. At that point, you might want to delete a bookmark, which you can easily do by following these steps:

1. **Tap the Bookmark icon and then tap the Bookmarks tab at the bottom of the dialog that appears.**

2. **Tap the Edit button.**

   A red minus icon appears to the left of your bookmarks, as shown in Figure 2-14.

Figure 2-14: Tap a bookmark's red icon to select it for deletion.

3. **Tap a red minus icon.**

4. **Tap Delete.**

The bookmark is removed.

You can also use a touchscreen shortcut after you've displayed the bookmarks in Step 1. Simply swipe across a bookmark and then tap the Delete button that appears.

You can also clear all recent locations stored by Maps to give yourself a clean slate. Tap the Bookmark icon and then tap the Recents tab. Tap Clear and then confirm by tapping Clear All Recents.

Getting Directions, Information, and More

Maps can provide all kinds of information, from directions from one location to another to the street address and phone number for a particular business or landmark.

Getting directions

You can get directions by using pins that you drop on a map for the starting and ending locations, or by entering an address or name of a place, such as an airport or shopping mall. The directions are shown in a blue line leading from one place to another. You can even choose directions by car, bus, or foot. Directions also give you an idea of the miles and hours it will take you to get to your destination. (It will take you 15 hours and 43 minutes, for example, to walk from the Bronx Zoo to the Empire State Building — in case you wondered.) Here are the steps to get directions to two different locations in Maps using pins:

1. **With at least one pin on your map (at your destination) in addition to your current location, tap the Directions button and then tap another location on the list that appears.**

   A line appears, showing the route between your current location and the closest pin. (See Figure 2-15.)

2. **To show directions from your current location to another pin, tap the other pin and in the dialog that appears tap Route.**

   The route is redrawn.

   You can also enter two locations in the boxes at the top of the page to get directions from one to the other.

Your route

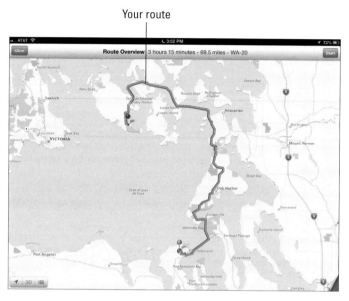

Figure 2-15: Go from pin to pin on your map to get directions.

Here are the steps to get directions in maps by typing the addresses in the Search fields:

1. **Tap the Directions button in Maps and then tap in the field labeled Start.**

   The keyboard appears. (See Figure 2-16.)

Figure 2-16: Enter addresses using the keyboard or Dictation key.

2. **Enter a different starting location.**

3. **Tap in the End field and enter a destination location. If you like, you can tap the Driving, Walking, or Public Transit button to select a category of information and then press the Route button on the keyboard.**

   The route between the two locations displays.

You can also tap the Information icon on the information bar that appears above any selected pin and use the Directions to Here or Directions from Here button (refer to Figure 2-11) to generate directions.

With a route displayed, an information bar appears along the top of the Maps screen, telling you about the distance and time it takes to travel between the two locations. Here's what you can do with this informational display:

- **Transportation mode:** Tap the Directions button (it's the last icon on the right of the toolbar in the lower-left corner) to display directions (see Figure 2-17).

- **Turn-by-turn directions:** Tap Start to begin turn-by-turn narrated directions. See the "Getting Turn-by-Turn Navigation Help" section, later in this chapter, for more about this feature.

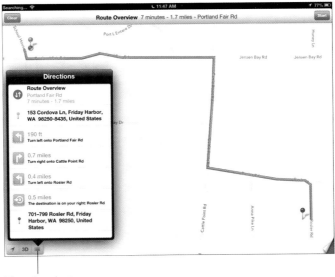

Directions button

Figure 2-17: Find out how long a trip you're in for.

✔ **Alternative route:** Maps notes, along the top of the informational display, the number of alternative routes it finds and adds the routes to the
map. Tap a route number to make it the active route, which displays in a
darker blue than the alternates, as shown in Figure 2-18.

Route 1

Route 3   Route 2

Figure 2-18: Select the active route or an alternative.

Book III
Chapter 2

Finding Your Way
with Maps

Getting information about a location

You've displayed the Information dialog for locations to add a bookmark or
get directions in previous sections of this chapter. It's time to focus on the
other useful information displayed there. Using the Information button for
any location, you can get the street address, phone number, and even the
URL for some businesses or landmarks.

To get to the Information dialog, go to a location and tap the pin. In the information bar that appears above the pinned location, tap the Information icon
(shown in Figure 2-19).

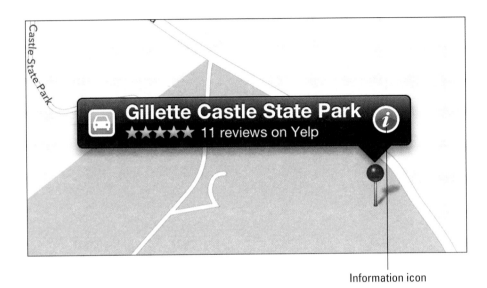

Information icon

Figure 2-19: Display the Information dialog.

In the Information dialog, you can tap the web address listed in the Home Page field to be taken to the location's web page, if it has one associated with it.

You can also press and hold the Phone or Address field (see Figure 2-20) and use the Copy button to copy the phone number, for example, so you can place it in a Notes document for future reference. When you have all the information you need, tap anywhere outside the Information dialog to close it.

Rather than copy and paste information, you can easily save all the information about a location in your Contacts address book. See the "Adding a location to a contact" section, later in this chapter, to find out how that's done.

Figure 2-20: Copy information from the Information dialog.

Sending Location Info beyond Maps

When you find a location you want to come back to or tell others about, you can use features of Maps that help you out. You can save a location to the Contacts app, which also saves the address, phone number, and URL, if any. You can also share a link to locations with friends via e-mail, Facebook, or Twitter. They can then access the location information by using Maps.

Adding a location to a contact

The beauty of this feature is that not only can you store valuable information such as phone numbers and street addresses in Contacts quickly and easily, but you can also use stored contacts to quickly find locations in Maps.

Here's how this works:

1. **Tap a pin to display the information bar.**

2. **Tap the Information icon.**

3. **In the Information dialog that appears (refer to Figure 2-20), tap Add to Contacts.**

4. **Tap Create New Contact.**

   The New Contact dialog appears (as shown in Figure 2-21). Whatever information was available about the location has been entered.

5. **Enter any additional information you need, such as name, phone, or e-mail.**

6. **Tap Done.**

   The information is stored in your Contacts address book.

You can choose a distinct ringtone or text tone for a new contact. Just tap the Ringtone or Text Tone field in the New Contact form to see a list of options. When that person calls via FaceTime or texts you via iMessage, you will recognize her from the type of tone that plays.

After you store information in Contacts, you can also share it with friends from there by tapping the Share button in the address record. See Book V, Chapter 5 for more about using Contacts.

Sharing location information

Have you found a fantastic restaurant or movie theater you absolutely have to share with a friend? From within Maps, you can use a simple procedure to e-mail a link to your friend. When your friend, who is connected to the Internet, taps the link, it opens the map to the location in Maps (a free service).

After you save a location in Contacts, take these steps to share a location:

1. **Tap a pin to display the information bar.**

2. **Tap the Information icon.**

Figure 2-21: Any available information can be stored to Contacts.

3. In the Information dialog that appears, tap Share Location.

In the dialog that appears (see Figure 2-22), you can choose to share via text message, Facebook posting, tweet, or e-mail.

4. Tap Mail to see how this option works.

5. In the e-mail form that appears, use the onscreen keyboard to enter a recipient's information as appropriate to the service you chose to share.

6. Tap Send.

A link to the location information in Maps is sent to your designated recipient(s).

If you tap Twitter or Facebook in Step 4, you have to have activated Twitter or Facebook and have the appropriate account set up using iPad Settings. Tapping Message in Step 4 displays a new message form; just enter an e-mail address or phone number in the To field, enter your text message, and then tap Send.

Figure 2-22: You have a variety of ways to share locations.

Use this feature to share your current location so a friend or emergency service can find you. However, beware of sharing your current information with strangers!

Getting Turn-by-Turn Navigation Help

When you've entered directions for a route and displayed that route, you can then, with a 3G/4G iPad model, get spoken instructions that can be helpful as you're driving. Follow these steps to get spoken navigation:

1. **Tap the Start button.**

2. **The narration begins and large text instructions are displayed, as shown in Figure 2-23.**

   Continue driving according to the route until the next instruction is spoken.

3. **For an overview of your route at any time, you can tap the screen to display and then tap the Overview button.**

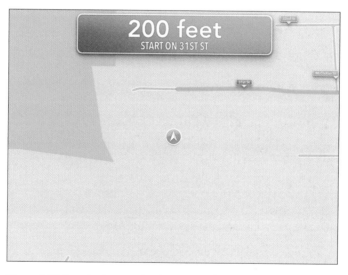

Figure 2-23: Turn-by-turn navigation may make your car's navigation system obsolete.

Book III
Chapter 2

Finding Your Way
with Maps

To adjust the volume of the spoken navigation aid, go to Settings⇨Maps and then adjust the Navigation Voice Volume settings to No Voice or Low, Normal, or Loud volume.

Chapter 3: Apps for Road Warriors

In This Chapter

- Arranging travel
- Finding the best hotels
- Locating restaurants
- Using maps and travel guides
- Tracking your expenses
- Staying connected

iPad is practically perfect for people who have to travel a lot for business or for pleasure. It's lightweight, slender, and stays powered up for about ten hours at a time. Depending on the model, you can connect around the world using 3G/4G or Wi-Fi (or both) to stay in touch or browse the Internet for whatever you need. You have an onscreen keyboard, so you don't have to tote around a physical keyboard. Robust business apps such as those in the iWork suite let you get work done as you travel. You may never drag a laptop on a trip again!

That's why, in this chapter, the focus is on how people on the road can use iPad. I start by pointing out the pre-installed apps that work for travelers and then provide some general advice and specific app suggestions for making travel arrangements, finding great hotels and restaurants, getting maps and travel guides, and keeping track of what you spend as you travel. I also provide a reminder about using Personal Hotspot to make phone calls where no Wi-Fi connection exists, and FaceTime, a great way to connect with others who are remote, face to face.

You can use Siri in iOS 6.0 with an iPad (except on the original iPad and iPad 2) to ask for answers and information about many of the things handled in the apps in this chapter, such as the time of the next flight to Dallas or the highest-rated hotel or restaurant in town. See Book V, Chapter 6 for more about Siri.

Starting with Built-in Apps

Before I get into the marvelous world of apps for travelers, consider the tools that come with iPad out of the box. You can find your way around the world quite nicely with these little gems, including the following:

✔ **Maps:** This app allows you to locate worldwide locations and get detailed street maps (see Figure 3-1), show directions from one point to another, and bookmark favorite locations. You can navigate as you drive, take public transportation, walk around using blow-by-blow navigation, and share location information with others by e-mail. (See Chapter 2 in this minibook for details about how to use Maps.)

Figure 3-1: If your rental car doesn't have a navigation feature, use iPad instead!

✔ **Contacts:** If you're going on the road to visit clients or friends and have their address information in Contacts, you can tap the address and be taken to it instantly in the Maps app. Keep phone numbers handy to get in touch when you hit town, and even use the Notes field in a Contacts entry to keep track of your business activities with that person or company. Remember that you can add fields to contact records, including job title, related people, department, and birthday using editing tools in Contacts. (See Book V, Chapter 5 for more about Contacts features.)

✔ **Safari browser:** Don't forget that if you have an Internet connection, you can use the Safari browser to get online and tap into all the travel-related information and sites on the web. Use sites such as Expedia.com, shown in Figure 3-2, or KAYAK.com to book travel, check flight information at airline websites, go to sites such as MapQuest to get directions and maps, and so on. (For more about using Safari, go to Book I, Chapter 6.)

Figure 3-2: Expedia offers travel booking services for flights, hotel, car rental, and more.

Book III
Chapter 3

Apps for Road Warriors

✔ **Mail:** This built-in e-mail client lets you keep in touch through any accounts you set up in iPad as long as you have an Internet connection. Find out more about setting up e-mail accounts in Book I, Chapter 7.

✔ **Notes:** Although there isn't a travel expense tracker in iPad, you can always use Notes to keep a record of what you spend or any other information about your trip you need to recall after you get home. You can even e-mail a note to yourself or your accountant so it's on your office computer when you get back.

Travel can get tedious with long waits in line or terminals. Don't forget that you have a built-in music player in Music and a built-in video player in the Videos app to keep you entertained.

Making Travel Arrangements

Now I move on to apps that don't reside on your iPad when you buy it. This chapter features just a few of the available apps — more are covered in Book VI, Chapter 2. Some are actually iPhone apps that work on iPad (so be sure to check out the iPhone apps category), and some were built specifically for iPad.

Start at the beginning, when you're planning your trip. You need to book flights or other modes of travel and check to see that your flight is on time. You may need a rental car when you arrive and perhaps maps of public transit to help you plan your route. All these are covered in this section.

Getting there by air

This list is a mixed bag of travel booking tools and apps that help you check on your seat assignment or flight status. Try these:

- ✔ **Travelocity for iPad:** This free, nicely designed app, shown in Figure 3-3, lets you book travel online, save itineraries, and get flight information. My favorite feature is the ability to explore destinations by great deals, upcoming events, or available travel guides. You can even check out hotels and sort the results by distance, price, or rating.

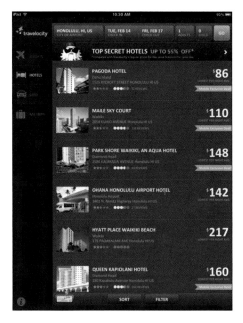

Figure 3-3: Travelocity is free and offers lots of travel booking options.

- ✔ **Airline Seat Guide:** You know how you always get on the plane thinking your seat will be fine only to find out you're three miles from the restroom or stuck in the middle of a seven-seat row on an international flight? By using Airline Seat Guide, which has data from over 100 airlines and 1,200 plane models, you get the advice you need to choose the best seat to make your travel more enjoyable. This one costs $1.99 but may be well worth it in terms of in-flight comfort.

- ✔ **AirportStatus:** Get information about flight status and delays all around the United States and parts of Canada with this 99-cent app. (See Figure 3-4.) You even get information about the cause of delays, such as weather and airport closures.

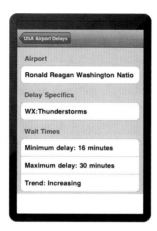

Figure 3-4: Check about delays before you leave home using AirportStatus.

Several airlines have their own mobile apps for booking or checking flight status (see Figure 3-5 for an example) and, in some cases, features for checking your standby status, checking in, and generating a boarding pass. These include

✔ American Airlines HD

✔ Southwest Airlines

✔ Alaska Airlines/Horizon Air Mobile

✔ British Airways

✔ Virgin Atlantic Flight Tracker

✔ United Airlines

If you're a frequent flier, check out the Air Milage Calculator app. (Make sure you exclude the first *e* in *mileage* when searching iTunes for this app.) For $1.99, you can get the mileage for travel between airports worldwide with up to three legs for each trip. You can also have the app calculate bonuses based on your frequent flyer status and the class of travel.

If packing is a challenge for you and you don't have a valet to help you out, try Packing Pro. Keep track of lists of what you need by trip, including your passport, clothing, and vital accessories such as an umbrella for that trip to Seattle. It costs you $2.99, but if you're organizationally challenged, it might save your neck as you prepare for business or family trips.

Figure 3-5: Enter information about your flight and getinformation back.

Renting a car

If you want to deal with your car rentals from your iPad, you'll be glad to hear that there are apps that help you do just that. Consider sites such as these that help you find the right rental deal:

✔ **Priceline Hotel & Car Negotiator:** Helps you find the best deal on airport car rentals, as you can see in Figure 3-6. If you're in a rush, you can book up to 30 minutes before you need your car using this app. And Priceline lets you bid on the best price to save you the most money on your rental car.

Figure 3-6: Priceline helps you get the best deal on your rental car.

✓ **Car Rentals — CarRentals.com:** This app, which you can download from the website, lets you search among 15,000 national and international car rental options. You can sort your options by their distance from you and book the car of your choice from major car rental companies.

You can also get individual apps for your favorite car rental companies, such as Avis Reservation App or Hertz Car Rental.

Road Trip Lite is a free utility that helps you track your mileage and fuel economy, which may help you estimate your costs if your rental car doesn't include unlimited miles. It sports a nice visual graph of fuel economy, and if you use your own car on the road, the feature that lets you track mileage and fuel cost by trip can be a neat way to sum up your travel expenses every month.

Finding your way around town

Before you set off on your trip to cities such as New York, San Francisco, or Chicago, you may want to download one of these apps to get local transit system maps, schedules, and more.

Transit Maps is free and comes with one transit map, but enables you to download transit maps as graphics files from the Internet using its own browser feature.

iTransitBuddy is a series of $1.99 apps for various metro areas designed for iPhone but usable on iPad. If you want lots of transit maps, you can subscribe to iTransitBuddy and get access to all its map apps. This app has a helpful feature for looking up free transfers and schedule updates. Maps are downloaded to your device, so you don't have to have an Internet connection to use them. This one is handy for commuters as well as those who travel to metro areas on business or for pleasure.

As you're exploring a new town, make sure you're dressed right for the weather. PocketWeather lets you get weather reports on the go.

Finding Just the Right Hotels

Hotel chains have begun to jump on the app bandwagon. Some chains, such as Holiday Inn, Marriott, Hilton, and Best Western, offer apps. Some only offer apps for individual hotels within the chain. Another option for finding hotels around the country or world is to depend on hotel booking apps for your hotel travel.

Here are a few free hotel-booking apps (be sure to check out Book VI, Chapter 2 for a few more) that can get you started on your iPad hotel search/booking experience. Most (including the Hotels for iPad app, shown

**Book III
Chapter 3**

**Apps for Road
Warriors**

in Figure 3-7) allow you to search for hotels and check ratings, price, and availability. You can also book your reservation and, in some cases, check local attractions.

✔ Hotels for iPad

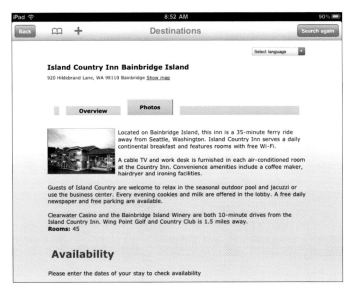

Figure 3-7: Details about hotels include a description, map, list of facilities, policies, and more.

✔ Hotels HD

✔ Booking.com

✔ Choice Hotels Locator

✔ HotelPal — Hotels & Hotel Room Reservations

✔ HotelsByMe — Hotels & Hotel Room Reservations

Some general travel sites, such as KAYAK.com and Travelocity.com, also have hotel searching and booking features. Check out Book VI, Chapter 2 for more about these.

Locating the Perfect Restaurant

What's a road warrior without his lunch? Hungry, that's what. So, why not use your iPad to find food? Here's a selection of some intriguing restaurant-listing apps for you to explore:

✔ **Vegetarian Restaurants:** Do you avoid meat in your diet? If so, check out the free Vegetarian Restaurants app (shown in Figure 3-8). Look for vegetarian restaurants worldwide as well as vegetarian recipes and information about the vegetarian lifestyle.

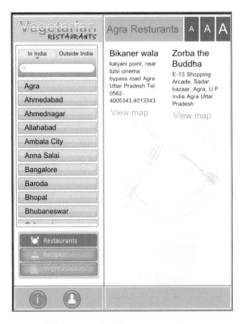

Figure 3-8: Vegetarian Restaurants helps you locate food without meat around the world.

Book III
Chapter 3

Apps for Road
Warriors

✔ **ZAGAT:** This one is a bit pricey at $9.99 but provides a wealth of information and ratings from a reliable source. You also get maps and menus from major restaurants and chains around the world.

✔ **Michelin Travel Guide:** For anywhere from $9.99 to $18.99, you can get the latest Michelin guide by country. Michelin is kind of the gold standard in restaurant rating systems, so if you're a serious world traveler and gourmand, you can appreciate its insights into the quality of food, specialties of the house, hours, and even the name of the chef.

✔ **Where to Eat? HD:** A poor man's Michelin Guide can be found in Where to Eat? HD, a $2.99 app that has been reworked for iPads. Search for the closest restaurants anywhere you are in the world, find the cuisine you're looking for, and customize searches.

If you want to find a restaurant with available Wi-Fi, you can find such locations using WiFi Get HD. This very handy app helps you spot hotspots even if you're not connected at the moment. This one costs $2.99.

If you're concerned about your waistline, here are a few more free and helpful food-oriented apps:

✐ **Fast Food Calories Hunter:** Can help you control how many calories you ingest along with your fast food meal for a mere 99 cents.

✐ **Restaurant Nutrition:** Shows you carbohydrates, calories, and fat for more than 80 chain restaurants, such as TGI Friday's and The Cheesecake Factory. (Well, forget what I said about watching your waist!)

Note that in the Maps app, you can enter the term *restaurants* in the Search field, search, and pins are dropped on the map indicating restaurants near your location.

Using Maps and Travel Guides

One important part of the road warrior experience is finding your way around and connecting with the local culture. For that, you can explore some mapping apps and travel guides. These will get you started:

✐ **Barefoot World Atlas:** With this $4.99 app, you get an interactive globe you can browse using your finger and touchscreen. The app is optimized for third- and fourth-generation iPads, so the visual experience is stunning.

✐ **cityscouter.com guides:** These handy little guides run about $3.99 per city and can be used offline. That's useful if you're on a plane, wandering around a foreign city nowhere near a hotspot, or out of range of your 3G provider's services. Find out about top attractions, take advantage of a currency converter, or find a wiki article, photos, or maps. (See Figure 3-9.) Many include up-to-date information about local public transportation as well.

✐ **Worldly — An Offline Travel Guide:** This guide costs $2.99 and acts as a browser for Wikitravel, an open source travel database. After you download it, you don't need an Internet connection to read all about your travel locations. This app supports full-screen iPad display, unlike some iPhone apps.

✐ **World Customs & Cultures:** Do you know whether it's appropriate to tip in Turkey? Or whether you should bring a gift to a dinner host in Japan? It's important to understand local customs to shine at international business interactions or to just appear polite. This free app covers more than 165 countries, giving you tips on common greetings, eye contact, acceptable (and unacceptable) gestures, and local laws, among other things.

Figure 3-9: The cityscouter.com guide to Copenhagen.

In addition to the preceding apps, check out popular travel guides and tools with an iPad presence, including

**Book III
Chapter 3**

Apps for Road Warriors

✓ Lonely Planet Travel Guides

✓ Frommer's Travel Tools

Tracking Your Expenses

My favorite part of any business trip is when I get that expense reimbursement check. Of course, to get that check I have to go through my receipt collection trying to figure out what I spent where and itemize it for my client.

To make your iPad travel experience easier, try these great apps that help you keep all your trip expenses in order:

✓ **JetSet Expenses and JetSet Expenses Lite:** These are identical, except that the Lite version is free and supported by advertising and the advertisement-free version costs $2.99. They allow you to track expenses in 15 expense categories and more than 100 subcategories. Use either app to track mileage, calculate business expense percentages, and generate a daily summary of expenses.

✔ **my Travel Assistant:** With a $2.99 price tag, this app designed for the iPhone is easy to use for tracking expenses and has some very nice tools for analyzing your expenditures as well. Plus, it supports 51 different languages.

✔ **Shoebox Receipt Tracker and Receipt Reader:** This handy and free iPhone app helps you make sense of all those receipts you collect as you travel. You can snap pictures of receipts and even create expense reports that you can send in from the road.

If you frequently travel out of the country, you may want to check out Book VI, Chapter 5 for apps that help you juggle currency exchange rates.

Don't forget that when you're in the privacy of your hotel you can use the Dictation feature to speak your expense entries into a Numbers or other dictation-compatible app. Hands-free expense reporting!

Staying Connected

When you're on the road, staying connected with your office or family is important. That's why you should be sure to take advantage of two cool features, FaceTime and Personal Hotspot. Here's what you can do with these two:

✔ **FaceTime:** This video-calling app (covered in detail in Book II, Chapter 4) allows you to take advantage of the video camera in iPad (except for the original iPad) to call others who have the FaceTime feature on their iPad, Mac, iPhone, or iPod touch. You can use the front camera to show the person you called your own bright smile, or switch to the rear camera to let that person see what you're looking at right now. Great way to make others jealous when you snagged that sales account in Hawaii!

✔ **Personal Hotspot:** Gives you the ability to use your iPhone's 3G/4G connection (for a fee to your service provider) to take your Wi-Fi model iPad online when Wi-Fi is out of reach. Personal Hotspot can, in fact, perform this service for up to five Wi-Fi devices on the Verizon, Sprint, and AT&T versions of iPhone. This is a very useful feature for driving road warriors who can't sit in an airport or hotel lobby to get online or make calls. (I cover Personal Hotspot in more detail in Chapter 1 of this minibook.)

Don't forget that by using the iCloud storage and sharing service, you can have all the content you buy on other Apple devices automatically synced to your iPad. If your spouse downloads some new music or a movie to her iPhone and you both use the same Apple ID, for example, you can access that movie on your iPad wherever you are! Of course, remember that if you're both reading the same e-book, iBooks syncs to the last automatic bookmark, so you may pick up where your spouse left off!

Book IV
Getting Productive
with iWork

The 5th Wave

By Rich Tennant

"Other than this little glitch with the landscape view, I really love my iPad."

You may not think of your iPad as a productivity tool (it's way too fun for that!), but it can be. One good place to start is to find out all about iWork, Apple's productivity suite of apps. The first chapter in this part gives you an overview of some of the common features of this suite of products. Then I dive into chapters about each of the three software products in the suite: Pages, Numbers, and Keynote. These word processing, spreadsheet, and presentation software programs provide some pretty robust tools and features that let you get your work done on your favorite new device, your iPad.

Chapter 1: Introducing the iWork for iOS Apps for iPad

In This Chapter

- ✔ Getting familiar with the iWork for iOS apps
- ✔ Discovering the basics of the iWork apps
- ✔ Improving documents by adding photos and images
- ✔ Managing your iWork documents

*W*ord-processing and spreadsheet applications are among the most widely used software products; presentation software is not far behind, along with programs such as graphics and database editors. Having started from scratch on the hardware side and then the operating system side, Apple employees started dreaming about what they could do if they were to start from scratch to write modern versions of word-processing, spreadsheet, and presentation programs. They knew they'd have to follow one of their advertising campaign themes: *Think Different*.

The result was the iWork suite of applications (a collection of applications that can work together) for the Mac — Keynote, Pages, and Numbers — that were developed one by one over a period of several years.

Today, iWork is a terrific suite of programs that have become a trio of dynamite apps for iPad.

In this chapter, you find an introduction to the three iWork for iOS apps, including how to use their common interface elements. You also find a summary of differences between iWork for iPad and iWork for Mac in those cases where it matters.

Apple's development tools now allow developers to easily develop a single app that runs on all the iOS devices — iPhone, iPod touch, and of course, iPad. Separate versions no longer exist because the code automatically adjusts to the device on which it's running (these apps are called *universal* for this reason). So do not look for Pages for iPhone or Numbers for iPad; look instead for Pages, Numbers, and Keynote for iOS. They are separate programs, each of which runs on all the iOS devices.

Presenting the iWork for iOS Apps

iWork provides applications that are office-oriented. The iWork office suite includes three applications that are similar to Microsoft Office applications (but way cooler, I think):

- **Pages:** A word-processing application (similar to Microsoft Word)
- **Numbers:** A spreadsheet application (similar to Microsoft Excel)
- **Keynote:** A presentation application (similar to Microsoft PowerPoint)

All three apps have been recently optimized for the third- and fourth-generation iPads' brilliant Retina display, as well as receiving some new templates you can base your presentation on.

On OS X, all three programs are sold at the Mac App Store. They also come preinstalled on some Macs as trial versions and can be configured as part of a build-to-order Mac. On iOS, each program is sold on its own for about $10 each, but each app runs on all your iOS devices. You can purchase the iWork for iOS apps from the App Store. (See Book I, Chapter 5, for more information.) Their features and integration are almost the same on both platforms.

In the following sections, you take a quick look at these three iWork for iOS apps.

Pages

For many people, word processing is the core of an office suite. In fact, many people don't get beyond it. Pages for Mac adds a big desktop publishing plus to word processing in that it also allows you to create page layout documents. These have the type of structure you see in newspapers and magazines — articles don't just flow one after the other. Instead, an article on Page 1 may be continued on Page 4, and another article on the first page may be continued on Page 8. Also, objects such as photos are often placed in specific positions on a page, and they don't move as text is added or deleted.

iWork provides you with a variety of sophisticated tools to create your Pages documents. These include advanced font handling, color, tables, and charts, as well as the ability to place QuickTime movies and hypertext links in your Pages documents. iWork applications also provide a variety of template options for your documents. Figure 1-1 shows some of the templates available with Pages for iOS.

Figure 1-1: Choose a Pages template as a starting point.

For more on the Pages app, see Chapter 2 in this minibook.

Numbers

Like all spreadsheet programs, Numbers enables you to enter data in rows and columns. One of the most useful features of spreadsheets is that they perform calculations by means of formulas. For example, if you have a column listing your grocery expenditures by week, the addition of another grocery bill will cause the program to recalculate the column's total. Spreadsheets are about data (usually numbers) and fast calculation updates, but they can also help you organize data such as address lists and even generate charts to show data trends.

Spreadsheets can go beyond the common grid interface, and Numbers excels at this approach. Take a look at the Numbers document shown in Figure 1-2, a Numbers document based on the Travel Planner template. A single document can have a number of *sheets* (like sheets in a Microsoft Excel workbook). On iPad, sheets appear as tabs, as shown in the figure.

Book IV
Chapter 1

Introducing the
iWork for iOS
Apps for iPad

A Numbers sheet can contain a variety of objects such as tables and charts, but it can also contain other iWork objects, such as graphics, text boxes, movies, and audio. In Figure 1-2, the sheet is shown with a table and five pictures above it.

For more on the Numbers app, see Chapter 3 in this minibook.

Sheets in a Numbers document

Figure 1-2: A typical Numbers spreadsheet.

Keynote

Call them lectures, classes, sermons, or sales pitches, but presentations are all much the same: Someone stands in front of a large or small group of people and explains, teaches, entertains, or informs them. In some cases, a presentation can run on its own or be run by the viewer. Today, a presentation often includes multimedia elements: slides of buildings in an architecture class, slides with music in a presentation about your community theater's latest musical production, and movies of good times on the beach in a talk about Uncle Charlie's summer vacation.

Keynote was the original iWork application. Built by Apple engineers for MacWorld and Worldwide Developers Conference keynote speeches delivered by Steve Jobs, Keynote has been refined over the years to become the powerful tool it is today. (See Figure 1-3.)

For more on the Keynote app, see Chapter 4 in this minibook.

Figure 1-3: Editing a Keynote presentation.

Starting Out with an iWork App and iCloud

If you're running iOS 5 (or later), you can use an iWork app with iCloud. The first time you run an iWork app, you're greeted by a Welcome screen. After the first time you open an app, you find yourself exactly where you were the last time you left it. Each iWork app has its own graphic; the first-time Welcome screen for Keynote is shown in Figure 1-4.

Figure 1-4: Keynote is launched for the first time on an iCloud-enabled iPad.

Book IV
Chapter 1

Introducing the
iWork for iOS
Apps for iPad

Click Continue, and you're given the option to use iCloud, as shown in Figure 1-5.

Figure 1-5: You can use iCloud . . . or not.

If you choose Later, you can turn iCloud on or off with Settings. All your apps that have settings are listed together at the bottom of the Settings list. Just tap your iWork app and turn iCloud on or off as you wish.

The next screen looks like Figure 1-6, although the details vary by the specific iWork app. You can choose a tutorial or just get started creating your own iWork document.

Figure 1-6: Get started or find out more.

Getting Familiar with the iWork Interface

You'll find that each of the iWork apps has a similar look and feel. One of the coolest advantages of iWork is that major features — not just small operations such as changing a font or selecting a color — are available using the same method in all its apps. You have only one set of features you must understand when you're using iWork, so I give you an overview of all that common functionality to get you started.

The iWork apps are updated periodically. If an update is available, you see the App Store on your iPad Home screen with a number indicating that downloads are available. It's generally a good idea to update your iWork apps when updates are available so that their interfaces remain in sync. You don't have to worry about massive changes: The apps are quite stable, and updates are few and far between. The latest update came with iOS 5.1 and included the addition of 3D charts in Numbers, a new animation and new transitions for Keynote, and optimization to take best advantage of the third- and fourth-generation iPads' Retina display. The iWork.com hooks to this online sharing service that existed in previous versions were also removed.

Book IV
Chapter 1

Introducing the
iWork for iOS
Apps for iPad

Creating a new document

You create a new document in the same way for each iWork app. Follow these steps:

1. **Tap any of the iWork app icons to launch the application.**

   The Documents screen appears. This screen is titled Pages in the Pages app (see Figure 1-7), Spreadsheets in Numbers, and Presentations in Keynote.

   Note that when you first open an iWork app, you see a single document that contains basic information and instructions for that app. After that, if you create and save any documents, they will also display on this screen.

   If you see Documents on the button in the top-left corner, you're not on the Documents screen; you're on the screen for working with an individual document, and tapping Documents (or Spreadsheets or Presentations) brings you to the Documents screen.

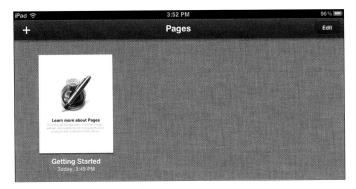

Figure 1-7: Create a new document from the Documents screen.

2. **Tap the plus sign (+) in the top-left corner of the Documents screen.**

   The popover shown in Figure 1-8 appears. You can create a new document with Create Document, or you can make a copy of a document from iTunes or a WebDAV server. The three copy options are described later in this chapter, in the section "Managing Your iWork Documents."

3. **Tap the Create Document (or Presentation or Spreadsheet, as appropriate to the app) button (refer to Figure 1-8).**

   The Choose a Template or Theme (Keynote) screen appears.

Tap this button.

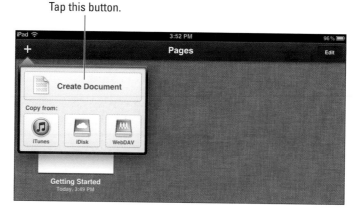

Figure 1-8: Select a template.

4. **Tap the template or theme you want to use as a starting point, or tap Blank (Pages and Numbers) or Black or White (Keynote) to start working with a completely clean document.**

   If you change your mind, you can tap Cancel (which replaces +) and you return to the Documents screen.

   The templates are different for each of the iWork apps, so I discuss them in the appropriate chapters in this minibook.

   Your new document opens on the screen.

Locating a document

Before long, you'll have created several documents, and chances are good that you'll want to go back and work on some of them or print them, e-mail them, or share them via iCloud. As with creating new documents, locating a document is done the same way in each of the iWork apps.

To locate a document, follow these steps:

1. **Tap any of the iWork app icons to launch the application.**

   The Documents screen appears. After you've created several documents, that screen looks like Figure 1-9.

2. **View the documents and find the one you want to work with.**

   Below each document, you see its title and the date you last worked on it.

3. **Tap the document you want to work with.**

   The document opens, and you can begin working in it.

**Book IV
Chapter 1**

Introducing the
iWork for iOS
Apps for iPad

Figure 1-9: Gradually, your Documents screen fills up.

Identifying other common iWork features

You've already seen the major iWork controls. Now you look at them more closely.

Using popovers

An important interface element in the Pages document shown in Figure 1-8 is the popover. Common to all iWork apps, the *popover* resembles the dialog in OS X and other operating systems but is redesigned for iPad. This list describes three actions you can take with a popover:

- ✔ **Recognize the purpose of the popover:** Each popover box includes an arrow that points to the object that opened it.

- ✔ **Dismiss the popover:** If you want to dismiss the popover (the equivalent of the Close or Cancel button on your Mac), tap anywhere outside the popover.

- ✔ **Make a selection on the popover:** When you tap a choice in a popover, it's carried out and the popover closes automatically.

Working with the Documents toolbar

Also visible in Figure 1-8 and most other figures in this chapter is the toolbar, which runs along the top of the screen. On a Documents screen, the toolbar displays the name of the app in the center and the Edit button at the right along with the + at the left.

Tap Edit, and your document icons start to jiggle — just as the icons do on the Home screen of your iPad. (And, just as on the Home screen, tap and hold a document icon and you enter Editing mode automatically.) While the icons are jiggling, you can drag one onto another to create a folder — just as on your iPhone and iPad Home screen.

Tap a folder to open it, as shown in Figure 1-10. From there, you can tap any document to open it.

Figure 1-10: Name your folders.

Tap the folder name, and the keyboard slides up so that you can rename the folder.

You can drag a document out of the folder and back to the Documents screen. When you remove the last document from a folder, the folder disappears.

When you're finished organizing your documents, tap Done to make them stop jiggling.

If you choose an action such as copying a document, the iWork app automatically ends the jiggle-editing without your having to tap Done.

Working with a toolbar for a single document

When you're working within a single document, you see a different toolbar, as you can see in Figure 1-11. (This is from Keynote.)

On the far-left side of the toolbar, the Documents button lets you see all your documents. Next to Documents is the Undo button. (It's the same as the Edit↔Undo command you may have on OS X for iWork and most other apps.) In the center of the window is the document's name.

Book IV
Chapter 1

Introducing the
iWork for iOS
Apps for iPad

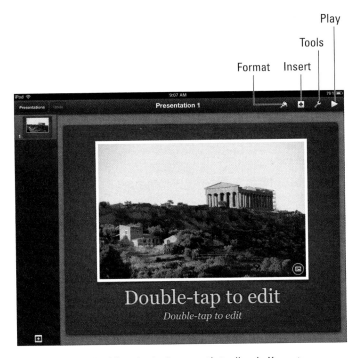

Figure 1-11: Work with a single document's toolbar in Keynote.

At the right of the iWork toolbar are three or four buttons:

- **Format:** Provides information and formatting choices about the current selection in the document. From here, you may choose a style, a list format, or a layout (alignment, columns, and line spacing) for a selected paragraph. If nothing is selected, this button is dimmed.

- **Insert:** Lets you insert images from your photo albums on iPad. If you want to insert a photo into your iWork document, add it to your album by taking the photo or synchronizing it in iTunes. (I tell you more about this button in the next section.)

- **Tools:** The wrench opens a popover containing tools that are based on the document as a whole rather than on the current selection within the document. Figure 1-12 shows the tools for a Pages document.

  Both Share and Print as well as Settings have disclosure triangles that let you drill down one more level. Figure 1-13 shows the Share and Print options. Note that though the figure shows sharing via iWork and iDisk options, tapping either of these currently displays a message that these options are discontinued. Print settings are described in Book V, Chapter 1.

You can use the left-pointing arrow in the popover to return to the tools.

The Settings submenu of the Tools menu is shown in Figure 1-14. Note that Word Count has been turned on; it appears at the bottom of the document.

Figure 1-12: Tools for a Pages document.

Figure 1-13: Sharing documents.

Figure 1-14: Adjusting settings.

Book IV
Chapter 1

Introducing the
iWork for iOS
Apps for iPad

Keynote also has a Play button to the right of the Tools button. (Refer to Figure 1-11.) Tapping the Play button begins playing your presentation.

The ruler that you may have seen in Pages is used by its word-processing features. Similar tools at the top of the screen are used in Numbers and Keynote depending on what you're trying to do. I discuss them in the relevant chapters in this minibook.

Another interface element that you encounter from time to time is known as a *Modal view.* Think of it as a dialog that appears on top of the screen (sometimes covering it all) with the background appearing to be slightly dimmed. Often, a button in the upper-right corner (usually with a blue background) lets you accept the information in the view. Sometimes, a Modal view presents you with a choice — buttons appear in both the upper-right and upper-left corners (they may be labeled Cancel, Edit, or Done in most cases). In these instances, tap the button that represents the action you want to take.

Working with Photos and Images

One important feature that distinguishes Apple software from many other products is how easily you can use graphics and video in the documents you create. It's probably not surprising for you to see Pages templates with photo placeholders in them, and it certainly makes sense that Keynote templates often include photos. In today's world, you expect images in word-processing documents and presentations. But spreadsheets? Take a look at the Numbers templates to see how the people at Apple are suggesting you rethink your understanding of spreadsheets.

Photos, images, and video can be added — easily and productively — to any iWork for iPad document. You have two ways to do this:

․ Tap the Insert button at the right end of the toolbar.

․ Select a template that includes a placeholder image.

Using a template with a placeholder image requires one more step than using the Insert button. Here's how this process works:

1. **Create a document based on a template that includes a placeholder image.**

    Figure 1-15 shows the Harmony template in Keynote. Some templates contain several placeholder images.

    Notice in the lower-right corner of the image is a button. This indicates that the image is a placeholder.

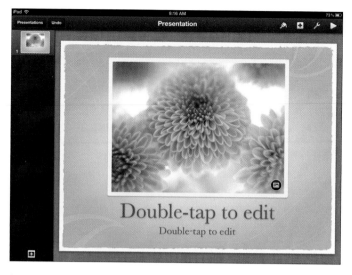

Figure 1-15: Create a document with placeholder images.

2. **Tap the placeholder button to open a list of your photo albums, as shown in Figure 1-16.**

   You can browse photos on your iPad as well as albums you have created in iPhoto or other programs such as Photoshop Elements and synchronized to your iPad.

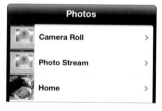

Figure 1-16: Choose a photo.

3. **Select the image you want to use instead of the placeholder.**

4. **Double-tap the image to show the masking control (see Figure 1-17), which lets you adjust the size of the image.**

5. **Adjust the slider to change the image mask.**

   The slider adjusts the size of the image. It starts with the image the same size as the frame, but if you move the slider toward the right, as you see in Figure 1-18, the image is shown dimly filling the entire screen. You can drag the image around so that the part you want is inside the frame. You

Book IV
Chapter 1

Introducing the
iWork for iOS
Apps for iPad

can also use the eight handles on the frame to change its size and shape. This is a hands-on way to handle tasks such as cropping images. Rest assured that the original image file is unchanged by these steps: You're only changing the image's appearance within the document.

Figure 1-17: Double-tap to mask the image.

Figure 1-18: Adjust the mask.

Managing Your iWork Documents

The data for your iWork documents is stored in files on your iPad, possibly on your Mac or PC, and also sometimes on shared WebDAV (Web-based Distributed Authoring and Versioning, used for collaboration and managing of files on the web) servers and, as you will see, on iCloud, if you choose.

You can store iWork files on a PC, but iWork runs on only iOS and OS X. As you'll see, you can easily convert your iWork files to the comparable Microsoft Office file types so that you can work on them on a PC in that format.

One feature that makes iWork for iOS successful is that the iWork team has made it easy for you to move documents around and work on them in whatever environment you want, from your desktop to a mobile device such as your iPad.

What matters is that you can get to your documents, read and write them, and share them with people. It's also critical that you can get to documents that other people share with you without either one of you having to jump through hoops.

Deep down inside the iPad operating system (iOS) are files and folders, but most of the time you manipulate them indirectly through apps. When it comes to apps, the files and folders are in a special area reserved only for that app (it's called a *sandbox*). Some apps such as the iWork apps can read files from servers such as WebDAV; if you select one of those files, as you can see later in this section, it's copied into the appropriate place on your iPad for you to work on it.

The storage areas for files on your iPad are kept separate for each app. If you install Pages and then remove it from your iPad, your Pages documents disappear along with the Pages app. Before uninstalling any app from your iPad, make certain that you have backed up any files you've created.

Copying a file into an iWork for iPad app

If you have a file on your Mac or on a WebDAV server, you can copy it into an iWork app to work on it there. Of course, the document needs to be saved as one of these compatible file types:

- **Numbers:** `.numbers`, `.xls`, `.xlsx`
- **Keynote:** `.key`, `.ppt`, `.pptx`
- **Pages:** `.pages`, `.doc`, `.docx`

Book IV
Chapter 1

Introducing the
iWork for iOS
Apps for iPad

These are the primary document types. You can import other files such as JPEG image files by adding them to your iPhoto library, music files in formats such as `.wav` in iTunes, and so forth.

Here's how to import a file from your Mac or server to your iPad:

1. **From your Documents (Spreadsheets or Presentations) screen, tap + at the left end of the toolbar, as described previously in the section "Creating a new document." Click the WebDAV icon.**

2. **Log in to your WebDAV server with your password.**

   You have no login for iTunes because your account ID is stored and your iPad is paired with only one computer.

3. **Select the file you want.**

   As you can see in Figure 1-19, you can navigate folders. Files that are dimmed out aren't compatible with the app you're running. In Figure 1-19, the only file that can be copied is a Keynote presentation because it's the Keynote for iOS app. The file will be copied into your documents (Presentations, Spreadsheets, or Documents).

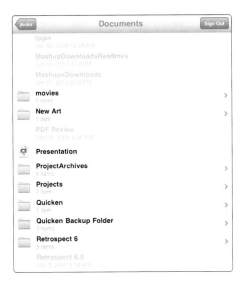

Figure 1-19: Select the file to copy.

You're warned if any errors occur, as you can see in Figure 1-20.

The most common errors are caused by opening a document created in another application or an earlier version of an app; these errors can include missing fonts, resizing of slides in Keynote, and the use of unsupported features. Wherever possible (almost always), the app works around these issues.

4. Correct any errors and then get to work.

Figure 1-20: Review any errors.

Copying a file from an iWork for iOS app

You've copied a file from another place onto your iPad, and now it's time to reverse the process. To share a file you've created in iWork on your iPad, follow these steps:

1. From the Documents screen, tap Edit at the right end of the toolbar.

2. Tap the document you want to copy.

As you see in Figure 1-21, the three buttons at the left of the toolbar are now enabled.

The one on the right lets you move the selected document to the trash. The one in the middle lets you make a duplicate of the document. The one at the far left is the one you want: It lets you copy the document to a new location.

3. Tap the Export button.

The popover shown in Figure 1-22 opens. Note that the iWork and iDisk options, though they display at the time of this writing, are discontinued.

You see that in addition to moving files to iTunes and WebDAV, you can e-mail a file.

When you e-mail a file, the recipient can work on the file or place it on a WebDAV server. Anyone with proper access (including you) can then copy it back into your or someone else's iWork for iPad app.

Export button
Duplicate button
Delete button

Figure 1-21: Copy a document.

Figure 1-22: Export a file.

4. Choose the export format.

In the case of a WebDAV server, you may be prompted to log in.
Figure 1-23 shows the export formats for Pages documents.

Tap a format and your document is on its way or, in the case of e-mail, a blank form appears at this point.

Figure 1-23: Choose a format.

Moving files with iTunes

You can move files to and from iTunes on your computer with a cable or, in iOS 5 and later, with a Wi-Fi connection.

You can also use utility programs such as Dropbox to manage files, which is sometimes simpler and avoids certain constraints imposed by Apple-centric iTunes.

Moving files to your computer from your iPad

Each iWork app has its own storage area for your files. You move files from your iPad to your computer using iTunes and these steps:

1. **Connect your iPad to the computer where you want to move the files.**

   Your computer can be a Mac or PC. It must have iTunes installed. If iTunes isn't installed, see Book I, Chapter 4, and then come back here.

   In iOS 5 and later, you can sync between your iPad and your computer using a Wi-Fi connection rather than a cable. On the iTunes Summary screen, select Sync with This iPad over Wi-Fi under Options. If you have that option turned off or do not want to use it, you can connect your iPad to your computer with a cable.

2. **When iTunes launches, find your iPad in the Devices section of the Source List (see Figure 1-24), and select it by clicking once.**

**Book IV
Chapter 1**

Introducing the
iWork for iOS
Apps for iPad

Locate your iPad here.

Figure 1-24: Connecting your iPad to iTunes on your Mac or PC.

3. **Select the Apps tab from the group of tabs running across the top of the pane.**

4. **Scroll down to the bottom of the pane and select the iWork app you're interested in.**

   The documents on your iPad for that app are shown.

5. **Select the document you want and click Save To.**

6. **Choose the folder and the name you want to use for the saved file.**

   The file is moved to your computer.

Moving files to your iPad from your computer

The process for moving files from your computer to your iPad is similar to the process described in the preceding section. To copy files from your computer to your iPad, follow these steps:

1. **Connect your iPad to the computer from which the files are to be moved.**

   You can use a cable or a Wi-Fi connection if you have selected that option.

   You can use a Mac or PC, but you must have installed iTunes on it.

2. **Find your iPad under the Devices section of the Source List (refer to Figure 1-24) and click it.**

3. **Select the Apps tab from the group of tabs running across the top of the pane.**

4. **Scroll down to the bottom of the pane and select the iWork app you're interested in.**

   The documents on your iPad for that app are listed.

5. **Click Add in the lower-right portion of the window.**

6. **When prompted, select the file on your computer's hard drive.**

   When you select a file, it moves to the list of files in iTunes and usually moves immediately to your iPad. If it doesn't move immediately, click Sync.

In Step 5 in the preceding list, you can also simply drag the document icon from the Finder or Windows Explorer window into the file list area.

To find out more about iWork, check out *iWork For Dummies,* 2nd Edition, by Jesse Feiler (published by John Wiley & Sons, Inc.).

Knowing the differences: iWork on the iPad versus iWork on a Mac

You can work happily and productively using only your iWork for iPad apps, but you may want to use your Mac for some additional work that iWork for Mac supports.

On iPad, you have a subset of the templates available on OS X. For example, the project proposal template on OS X has half a dozen sample pages (budget, schedule, and executive summary, for example); on iPad, only a couple are available. You can certainly add more if you want. Also, some of the large document features (track changes and automatic Table of Contents creation) are available only on OS X.

The range of document features available on iPad is amazing: spell-checking, fonts and styles (though you can't install additional fonts compared to full-blown Mac or Windows software), the ability to add and manipulate images, charts and tables (not just in Numbers!), columns and pagination, and much, much more. However, some features that tend to be used by large and complex documents aren't supported.

Don't make the mistake of thinking that iWork documents on iPad are small documents. Because of the way in which the iPad apps are designed, you have essentially no practical limits to document size except for the memory in your device. There's no reason to think that you can't write your 1,000-page novel on the Pages iPad app (but you'd better get busy).

**Book IV
Chapter 1**

Introducing the
iWork for iOS
Apps for iPad

Chapter 2: Pages Has a Way with Words

In This Chapter

- Making changes to a Pages document
- Toiling with text
- Focusing on formatting with the ruler
- Setting advanced formatting options with the Format button
- Formatting the document
- Using selection buttons

This chapter delves into the *Pages* app, which is the word-processing tool in the iWork suite of apps. Pages gives you powerful tools for creating documents of all kinds.

In this chapter, I tell you how to work with text and text boxes, format a document, and use the simplified Pages for iOS interface.

To find basic instructions for managing documents and sharing them via WebDAV, e-mail, or iTunes, see Chapter 1 in this minibook.

Editing a Pages Document

After you open a Pages document, you edit it in Document Editing view, shown in Figure 2-1.

To find out how to create a new Pages document, see Chapter 1 in this minibook.

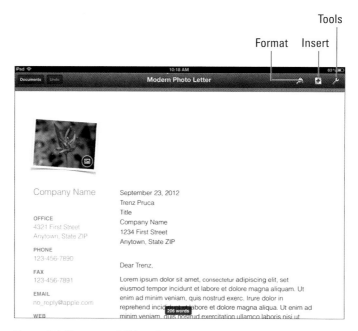

Figure 2-1: Document Editing view.

When you're editing a document, Document Editing view remains open until you move to another document, return to the Documents screen, or leave Pages. When you leave an iWork for iOS app and then return to it, remember that you return to the same location you left.

When you're in Document Editing view, the Documents button is visible at the left of the toolbar, at the top of the screen. When you're in Documents view, the button is labeled with the plus sign (+).

When working on a multipage document in the Document Editing view, you can quickly move through the document by swiping or flicking up or down.

In Pages, you can touch and hold your finger anywhere at the right side of a page to bring up the *navigator* (shown in Figure 2-2), which shows a thumbnail of a page; you can move very quickly through the document by dragging up or down on the screen. When you're on the page you want, just lift your finger off the screen. If you don't want to leave the page you started from, swipe to the right to make the navigator disappear.

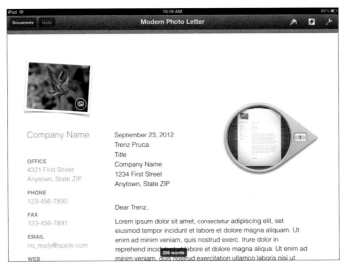

Figure 2-2: Using the navigator.

Working with Text in Pages

You can get a leg up on creating a document if you start from an iWork template (a template other than the Blank template, which is, well, blank). Even though you may see only a text placeholder in the template, the basic structure helps you get started.

After you open a document, entering the text is simple. You have four ways to start entering text:

- ✏ **Type text:** Tap the spot in the document where you want to enter text, and start typing. You can use the onscreen keyboard, a wireless keyboard, or the iPad Keyboard Dock.

- ✏ **Dictate text:** Tap the Dictation key (not available on the original iPad or iPad 2) on the onscreen keyboard and speak your text, including punctuation. Dictation also allows some simple commands such as "Next line."

- ✏ **Cut, copy, or paste text (or a combination):** Use the cut, copy, and paste tools to cut text in your Pages document and move it to another location, or to copy text in any iPad app (for example, from a website accessed by the Safari browser) and paste it into your Pages document.

✔ **Import text:** You can use iTunes or utilities such as Dropbox to move existing documents to your iPad. You can create the documents on your Mac or PC by using tools such as iWork, Microsoft Office, or Google Apps. When a large chunk of the document is ready, move it to your iPad as described in Chapter 1 of this minibook and continue working with the document using iWork for iPad.

After you have text in your Pages document, you can start to manage it.

Setting Basic Formatting by Using the Ruler

As is the case in most word-processing programs, a ruler at the top of a page in Document Editing view lets you set basic formatting. The ruler can be hidden (refer to Figure 2-1), but tapping in the document displays it, as shown in Figure 2-3. The small X-in-a-circle to the right of the ruler lets you hide the ruler when you no longer need it.

Figure 2-3: Displaying the ruler in Pages.

The ruler shows you the settings for whatever is selected in the document. Tap in the document, and the ruler is immediately enabled and reflects the settings for the selection (in this case, the location of the insertion point). Tapping in the document may also bring up selection buttons, as shown in Figure 2-4. You can use them to use features such as cut, copy, delete, and paste.

A single tap brings up the selection buttons, a double-tap selects the word at the insertion point, and a triple-tap selects the paragraph.

The ruler also provides basic formatting for the current selection. The tools on the ruler that can be used on the selection (from left to right in Figure 2-4) are described in this list:

✔ **Font:** In Figure 2-4, the font is Helvetica. Tap the font name to open a popover with a list of fonts to select from. Note that available fonts in Pages on iPad are fewer than in Mac or Windows programs and you can't add fonts as you can on a computer, so if a font isn't supported on iPad, another font is substituted, which could affect layout and appearance adversely.

✒ **Font Size:** Tap the large *A* on the right to enlarge selected text by one point; tap the smaller *A* on the left to decrease the text size. By using the tool in the middle, you can set the font size to an exact number.

✒ **Font Styles:** You can choose bold, italic, or underlining.

✒ **Alignment:** The selected paragraph can be aligned to the left, center, or right, or justified so that both margins are straight with no ragged edges. You don't have to select the paragraph with a triple-tap for alignment to work. If you have selected a word or an insertion point, the paragraph containing either item is the selected paragraph.

✒ **Indent:** Tap either of the Indent buttons to indent text in one level or out one level at a time.

Ruler settings for the selected text

Selection buttons

Figure 2-4: The ruler indicates settings for the current selection.

Feel free to experiment with the formatting within your Pages documents, and remember that the Undo button in the upper left is there to help you out if you change your mind about something you've done.

Most buttons on the ruler require you to simply tap them, but some (for example, the Fonts and Font Size buttons) open their own popovers for further selections; Figure 2-5 shows the Fonts popover.

Figure 2-5: Set fonts from the ruler.

You can also use the ruler to set the margins for paragraphs. Just slide the indicators along the ruler, as shown in Figure 2-6. Note that the top indicator for the left margin reflects the margin of the first line in a paragraph; the lower indicator is the left margin of all other lines in the paragraph. You can indent the first line of a paragraph, but you can also outdent it (or provide a hanging first line); an outdent works well in a list.

Figure 2-6: Set margins from the ruler.

Getting and Setting Info about the Selection

The Format button to the right of the toolbar opens a popover that provides settings in addition to those shown on the ruler. (See the preceding section.) When you select text and tap the Format button, you see a popover with three tabs along the top: Style, List, and Layout. Select a tab to access various formatting options, as I describe in the following three sections.

Setting character style: Font, size, and color

One setting you can adjust by using the Format button is Style. Tap the Format button, and the popover shown in Figure 2-7 opens. (The Style tab in the top-left corner of the popover is selected by default.)

The powerful Style popover has a wide range of functionality. The topmost section lets you set the character style for the selected text. The *character style* is simply the style applied to characters. The second section of the popover lets you set the paragraph style — the style for the entire paragraph in which the selection is set.

Figure 2-7: Use the Format button to set styles.

After selecting the characters you want to style, tap Format and then the current font setting in the popover. (It's 40-point Helvetica in Figure 2-7.) The popover shown in Figure 2-8 opens, and you can select another font, font size, or color for the font.

Figure 2-8: Adjust character styles.

Tap the color well (the swatch of color next to the word *Color*), and you can select a new color, as shown in Figure 2-9.

Figure 2-9: Change the font color.

Creating indents and list styles

After you select a paragraph, tap the Format button and then, in the pop-over, tap the List tab to experiment with indentation and lists. The options shown in Figure 2-10 include arrow buttons at the top of the view that let you move the left margin in *(indent)* or out *(outdent)*. You also can choose to make automatic numbering available by choosing a list format.

Figure 2-10: Handle indents and lists.

When you add an element to the list or delete an element from it, Pages automatically renumbers the list for you.

Establishing alignment, columns, and line spacing

The Layout tab in the top-right corner of the Format popover lets you set layout options, as shown in Figure 2-11. These include the options for creating columns and adjusting line spacing.

Figure 2-11: Adjust layout settings.

Formatting a Document

You can format the text in your document, but you should attend to one other type of formatting: formatting the document itself. It includes page headers and footers, page numbers, and backgrounds that appear on all pages. Here's how to proceed:

1. **Open a Pages document, and tap Tools.**

   The Tools popover appears, as shown in Figure 2-12.

Figure 2-12: Set up your document.

2. **Tap the Document Setup option.**

   You see a blueprint-like section that's markedly different from the view you see when you edit an individual page.

3. **Tap a header or footer to customize it.**

   You can use the three sections to insert the author's name, a title, the version number, or the page number, for example.

4. **Type some text in the section you want to customize.**

5. **To add page numbers to your document, tap in the header or footer section you want to use for the page number. Then tap the Page Numbers button in the toolbar that appears.**

   This toolbar is shown only when you select a header or footer.

   You can choose the format of the page numbers, as shown in Figure 2-13.

6. **Tap the style you prefer.**

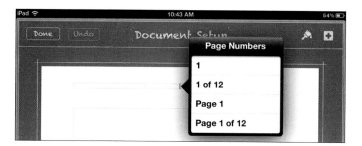

Figure 2-13: Insert page numbers.

7. Set the outer limits of the area for the page content (as well as for header and footer) by dragging the lines, as shown in Figure 2-14.

These settings determine the printable area of your document on the page. Margins you set using the ruler define this area.

Figure 2-14: Set the print margins.

8. Tap the bottom-right corner of the page (the corner that appears slightly curled) in the blueprint and select a predefined paper size, as shown in Figure 2-15.

Tap US Letter to print on 8½-x-11-inch paper or A4 to print on standard international letter paper.

9. Tap Done.

After your page is set up, you're ready to finish entering text in your document and print it when it's done.

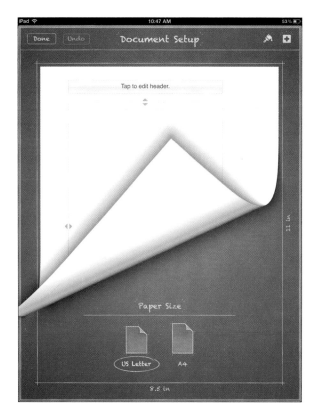

Figure 2-15: Select a paper size.

Working with Selection Buttons

When you read this chapter from start to finish, you see various sets of selection buttons shown on the black bar that appears whenever you double-tap in a document — and often shown with selected text. The command that's shown on a selection button varies depending on which element is selected. Some selection buttons may look familiar to you from other apps you may have used on the iPad and the Mac (as well as on other types of computers), including the Cut, Copy, and Paste commands.

When you select a chunk of text, you may also see these options:

- **Replace:** Look up words you might want to use in place of the selected word, such as synonyms or simple typing mistakes.
- **Define:** View the definition of a word.
- **Style:** Use special Copy and Paste commands. You can copy and paste a style so that it picks up the formatting from a word and applies it to other text that's selected elsewhere in the document.

Chapter 3: Counting on Numbers

In This Chapter

- ✓ **Getting to know Numbers**
- ✓ **Working with a template**
- ✓ **Using tabs and sheets**
- ✓ **Using tables, cells, and forms**
- ✓ **Creating new tables**

*N*umbers is a different approach to the concept of spreadsheets. It brings to spreadsheets not only a different kind of structure, but also data formats you may never have seen. In addition to being able to use numbers and text in your spreadsheets, you can use on-off check boxes and star ratings as part of your data. Think of an inventory spreadsheet with check boxes for in-stock items and star ratings based on reviews or user feedback. What you may have thought of as just a bunch of numbers can now provide true meaning and context to users.

First launched as part of iWork '08, Numbers joins the other iWork apps on iPad. Tables and charts are built into Keynote and Pages, but Numbers is the main number-crunching tool on iPad.

In this chapter, you discover how Numbers helps organize data into manageable units. After you enter your data, you can display it in charts and graphs.

Introducing Numbers

When you create a Numbers document, you work with these three items:

- ✓ **A Numbers document:** A container for all elements, including worksheets (sheets) and their data; similar to a Microsoft Excel workbook.

- ✓ **One or more sheets:** One or more spreadsheets called simply *sheets.*

- ✓ **Tables:** The subspreadsheets or tables created in other spreadsheet programs exist in Numbers as formal, structured tables rather than as a range of cells within a spreadsheet. Numbers gives them a specific name: *tables*. (And yes, a Numbers document can have no tables but must have at least one sheet.)

The simple idea of making tables into an actual part of the Numbers application rather than letting people create them any which way leads to a major change in the way you can use Numbers when compared to other spreadsheet programs. Because a table is an entity of its own and not a range of cells, you don't break the tables you've organized in a spreadsheet when you reformat another part of the spreadsheet. You can work within any table, and you can reorganize tables within a sheet, but you can't break tables by simply adding a row or column to your spreadsheet.

Figure 3-1 shows a Numbers for Mac template (Team Organization).

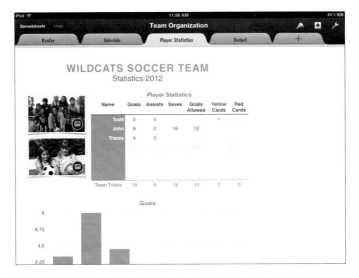

Figure 3-1: The Team Organization template in Numbers for Mac.

Figure 3-1 is a single document with four sheets visible at the left in the *Sheets pane:*

- Roster
- Schedule
- Player Statistics
- Budget

Some sheets contain tables or charts, and you see them listed in the Sheets pane under their corresponding documents. For example, the Roster sheet contains the Team Roster and Admin Info tables. At the bottom, the Budget sheet contains two tables (Cost Breakdown and Cost per Player) as well as a chart (Team Costs). The idea that a single sheet can contain defined charts and tables that don't depend on ranges of cells is the biggest difference between Numbers and almost every other spreadsheet program.

As you can see in Figure 3-1, sheets can also contain images and other graphics; they aren't parts of the structure of charts and tables. You simply insert these elements the same way you insert any other objects in iWork documents.

In Figure 3-1, the Player Statistics table on the Player Statistics sheet is selected. Notice in Figure 3-1 that a selected table has a frame with its column and row titles as well as other controls. Note also that each table within a sheet has its own row and column numbers (you can also name them, if you want) and that each table you deal with starts with cell A1. (The first row is 1, and the first column is A.)

Apple's iWork team moved the Numbers concepts elegantly to iPad. Figure 3-2 shows the comparable template on iPad. Each sheet is a tab. When you tap a table on iPad, you see a frame that lets you manipulate the table just as on Numbers for Mac. (See the section "Using Tables," later in this chapter, for more information.)

Figure 3-2: The Numbers Team Organization template on iPad.

Numbers for iOS lets you insert charts along with tables on your sheets, as you see in Figure 3-3. (Remember that you can also insert graphics and other objects on your sheet.)

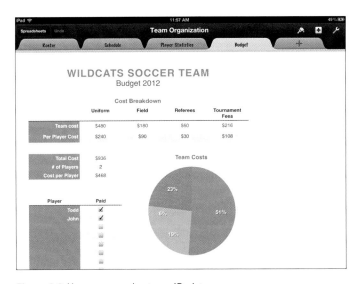

Figure 3-3: You can use charts on iPad, too.

Numbers for iOS also includes the ability to create *forms,* which simplify data entry. When you create a form, you select a table and you're taken to a tab that displays each column heading with a text entry box next to it. You can then focus on entering data for one row at a time and eliminate the possibility of accidentally tapping and entering data in the wrong row. You can find more about forms in the "Using Forms Efficiently" section, later in this chapter.

Using the Team Organization Template

This chapter uses the Numbers Team Organization template to demonstrate Numbers features. You can create your own copy of the template so that you can follow along on your iPad, if you want. Sample data is part of the template, so you have data to work with, but you can add any other data you want. After you've experimented with Team Organization, you can pick another template, including the Blank template, and customize it for your own data.

To create your own copy of the Team Organization template, follow these steps:

1. **Launch Numbers on iPad.**

2. **Go to the Numbers screen.**

   If you had a spreadsheet open when you were last using Numbers, you return to that spreadsheet. Simply tap Spreadsheets at the top left to go to Spreadsheets, and then tap the plus sign (+). If you need a refresher on creating a new spreadsheet, see Chapter 1 in this minibook.

3. **Tap Create Spreadsheet.**

4. **Tap Team Organization.**

   Your new spreadsheet opens. Any changes you make are saved automatically.

Working with Tabs and Sheets

Every tab displays a sheet, which can have one or more tables or charts (or both) on it. Tabs help you organize your Numbers documents. In this section, I tell you what you need to know about setting up tabs in a document.

Adding a new tab

As with all iWork apps, starting a new Numbers document involves choosing a template. Each template has its own, predefined tabs. (The Blank template has only one tab, cleverly titled Sheet 1.) You can add more tabs by using the + tab on the rightmost end of the tabs. (See Figure 3-4.)

Tap here to add a new tab.

Figure 3-4: The + tab always appears to the right.

Tap the + tab, and Numbers asks whether you want to add a new sheet or a new form. (See Figure 3-5.) Tap New Sheet, and Numbers creates for the sheet a new tab that contains one table. The sheet is labeled Sheet #, where # is the next number in the internal list of unnamed sheets you have created. See the section "Changing a tab's name," later in this chapter, if you want to rename the tab. (If you're interested in forms, I tell you about that topic later in this chapter, in the "Using Forms Efficiently" section.)

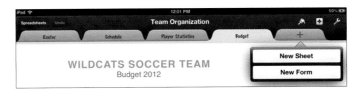

Figure 3-5: Add a new sheet or form.

Deleting or duplicating a tab

If you add a tab by mistake, Numbers allows you to remove it. Also, if you want to reuse a tab for a new tab, Numbers allows you to duplicate it. To perform either of these actions, tap the tab you want to delete or duplicate, and selection buttons appear below it. (See Figure 3-6.) All you have to do now is tap the option (Duplicate or Delete) for the action you want to take.

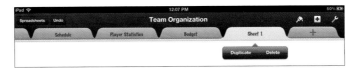

Figure 3-6: Duplicate or delete a tab.

Remember that a double-tap starts editing. A single tap brings up the selection buttons, if they're available for the object you've tapped.

Rearranging tabs

If you don't like the order of your tabs, tap and hold a tab to rearrange the tab order. You simply drag the tab to the right or left in the row of tabs and then remove your finger when the tab is in the position you want. (See Figure 3-7.)

Figure 3-7: Rearrange tabs.

Navigating tabs

If you have more tabs than can be shown on the screen, just flick right or left to slide along the tabs. Remember to flick in the row of tabs. Flicking the body of the sheet scrolls over to the right or left of the content on that sheet.

If you're holding iPad in portrait orientation, turn it to landscape orientation to allow more tabs to display on the screen.

Changing a tab's name

Double-tapping text anywhere on iPad allows you to edit the text. The same statement applies to tabs, too. Double-tap the name of a tab to begin editing it. (See Figure 3-8.) The onscreen keyboard appears and you can delete the current name and enter a new one.

Figure 3-8: Edit a tab's name.

Using Tables

Tables are at the heart of Numbers — they're where you enter your data. This section shows you how to work with a table as a whole; the later section "Working with Cells" shows you how to work with individual cells within a table.

Selecting a table

To be able to work on a table, you need to select it. If the table isn't visible in the current tab, just tap the tab it's in first. To select a table in Numbers, tap it.

If you need to find an entry within a table, it's easy to do. Tap the wrench in the top-right corner to open the Tools popover. Tap Find to search the entire Numbers document for a word or phrase that may be in the table you're looking for.

When a table is selected, its appearance changes. (See Figure 3-9.) A selected table is framed with gray bars above (the column frame) and to its left (the row frame). To the left of the column frame, a button with concentric circles lets you move the table. To the right of the column frame as well as beneath the row frame are buttons, each with four small squares (looking a bit like table cells). These Cells buttons let you add rows, columns, or cells and manipulate the cells in the table. (See the later section "Working with Cells.")

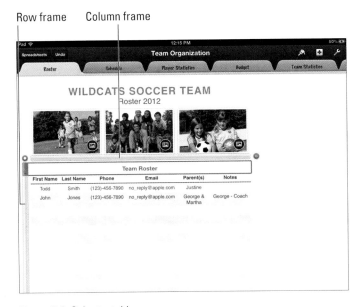

Row frame   Column frame

Figure 3-9: Select a table.

Select a table by tapping it once; the location of your tap is important:

- **If you tap in a cell, the table and that cell are selected.**

- **If you tap inside the table bounds but outside the cells, the table itself is selected.** For example, if you tap the table's title or the blank space to the left or right of the title, the table itself is selected. (Refer to Figure 3-9.)

Moving a table

You can move a table around on its sheet. Select the table and tap the round button to the left of the column frame. Then drag the table where you want it. As you can see in Figure 3-10, Numbers shows you the absolute coordinates of the location you're dragging to. Light-colored lines called *guides* help you align the table to other objects on the sheet. These lines appear and disappear as the table is aligned with the edges or centers of other objects.

Figure 3-10: Relocate the table.

TIP

You can select several objects at the same time. Tap the first object to select it, and then, while still holding your finger down, tap with another finger the other objects you want to add to the selection. After that, they move or resize together. (You may need two hands for this task.)

Cutting and pasting a table

You can select a table and then drag it around on a sheet by using the round button at the top left of the column frame; you can resize the table as described in the "Resizing a table" section, later in this chapter. But what if you want to place the table on a different sheet? To copy and paste a table onto a different sheet, follow these steps:

1. **Select the table by tapping the round button at the top left.**

   You see the Cut, Copy, and Delete buttons, as shown in Figure 3-11.

2. **Tap Cut from the selection buttons that appear above the table.**

3. **Tap the tab of the sheet you want to add the table to.**

4. **Tap in the sheet (but not in an existing table).**

   This step brings up new selection buttons.

5. **Tap Paste.**

6. **Move and resize the table as you want.**

Tap here to select the table.

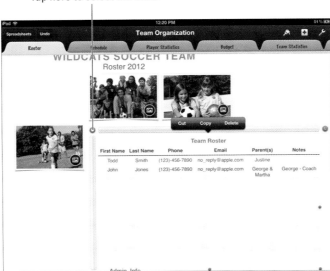

Figure 3-11: Select an entire table.

Adjusting columns or rows

If you've ever used a spreadsheet program, you know that data you enter doesn't always fit into preset columns and rows. In Numbers, you can select the columns or rows you want to work on and then rearrange or resize them.

Especially with spreadsheets that have lots of rows and columns, resizing can be easier using a stylus.

Selecting a row or column

Tap in the row frame to select the corresponding row, as shown in Figure 3-12.

Tap in the column frame to select the corresponding column.

After you select a row or column, you can adjust the selection by dragging the handles (the round buttons) at the top and bottom (or left and right for columns), as shown in Figure 3-13.

Tap in this bar to select a row.

Figure 3-12: Select a row.

Use the handles to adjust the selection.

**Book IV
Chapter 3**

Counting on
Numbers

Figure 3-13: Adjust a selection.

The selection buttons (Cut, Copy, Paste, Delete, Fill, Merge, and Create Chart) appear above a selected column or row. Select an object. Figure 3-14 shows several cells selected within a column.

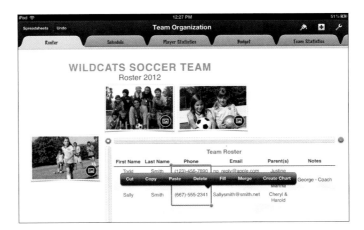

Figure 3-14: Select a few cells in a column.

The selection button you tap affects the selected column or cell.

For example, use the selection button to merge selected cells in a column (or row).

Resizing a row or column

The two vertical lines (known as the Cells button) in the top-right corner of the column frame (refer to Figure 3-14) and the bottom-left corner of the row frame (refer to Figure 3-12) let you resize the selected columns or rows. You always resize a column to its right and a row to its bottom, whether you're making it larger or smaller. The contents are automatically adjusted, and the adjoining rows or columns are moved aside.

Moving a row or column

Sometimes, you want to rearrange the rows or columns in a sheet. With one or more rows or columns selected, drag it (or them) to a new position. All selected rows or columns move as a unit, and the other rows or columns move aside.

Resizing a table

You can resize a table in two ways: add or remove rows or columns to or from the table, or leave the number of rows and columns the same and change the overall size of the table. You may even want to do both.

Adding or removing rows and columns at the right or bottom

Tap the Cells button in the top-right corner of the column frame to add a new column at the right of the table. To add a new row at the bottom, tap the Cells button in the bottom-left corner of the row frame, and a new row is added to the bottom of the table.

To remove a blank column or row at the right side or bottom of a table, drag the appropriate Cells button to the left or to the top of the frame — the extra rows or columns disappear.

Adding or removing rows and columns inside the table

Select the row or column below or to the right of the new row or column. From the selection buttons, tap Insert to add a new row above the selected row or a new column to the left of the selected column.

Changing a table's size

Select the table so that the handles (small blue dots) are visible at the right side and bottom. These handles work like any other resizing handles in Numbers: Simply drag them horizontally or vertically to change the table's size. The content of the table automatically resizes to fit the new table size. The numbers of rows and columns remain unchanged, but their sizes may be adjusted.

You can select the table by tapping the round button at the top left of a table. (Refer to Figure 3-11.)

Read more about formatting tables in the "Working with New Tables" section, later in this chapter.

Working with Cells

You double-tap a cell if you want to add or edit data. A blue outline appears around the cell, and the keyboard appears so that you can begin entering data.

Single-tap if you want to select a cell. The cell is outlined, and the table-selection elements (the column and row frames, the Cells button, the round button to the left of the column frame, and the button to the right of the column frame as well as beneath the row frame) appear.

A double-tap makes the cell available for editing. Figure 3-15 shows how, after a double-tap in a cell, the keyboard appears.

After you set up your spreadsheet, most of your work consists of entering and editing data of all types. That's what you find out about in the next section.

Book IV
Chapter 3

Formula bar

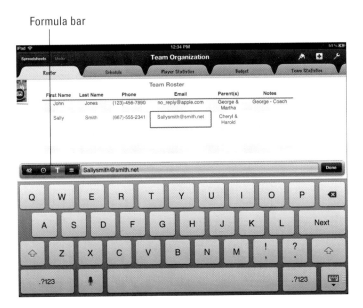

Figure 3-15: Start to edit a cell's data.

Entering and editing data

The keyboard for entering data into a Numbers cell is a powerful and flexible tool — it's four keyboards in one. Above the keyboard, the Formula bar lets you quickly and easily enter formulas. (Refer to Figure 3-15.) On the left of the Formula bar are four buttons that let you switch from one keyboard to another. You can choose these keyboards, starting from the left:

- **42:** The first button lets you use the numeric keyboard.
- **Clock:** The second button lets you enter dates and times.
- **Text:** The letter *T* displays the standard text keyboard.
- **Formulas:** The equal sign (=) opens the formula-editing keyboard.

Whichever keyboard you're using, you see the characters you're typing in the Formula bar above the keyboard. To the right of the oblong area is a button labeled Done (or a check mark, depending on which keyboard you're using) that moves your typing into the selected cell and then hides the keyboard.

The Dictation feature on iPad (not available on the original iPad or iPad 2) works in Numbers and the other iWork apps. Tap the Dictation key on the onscreen keyboard and speak your text; tap the key again to insert the text in your document.

You can bring up the keyboard when you double-tap a cell or another text field (such as a tab name). That means the cell is selected and that the keyboard knows where the data should go when you tap OK or Done.

Note that many of these features are unavailable on a Bluetooth keyboard, which may or may not have a number pad and special symbols used in entering formulas.

To the right of the keyboard in the 42 and Clock keyboards are three large keys:

✔ **Delete:** This is the standard keyboard Delete key.

✔ **Next (adjacent):** The Next key with the right-pointing arrow inserts the typed data into the selected cell and moves to the next cell to the right.

✔ **Next (next line):** The Next key with the hooked arrow pointing left and up inserts the typed data and moves to the next line and to the leftmost cell in the section of cells you're entering. For example, if you start in the third column of the fourth row, the Next (next line) key moves you to the third column of the fifth row, not the first column.

Entering numeric data

The numeric keyboard (accessed by tapping the 42 button) has a typical numeric keypad along with four large buttons on the left. These four buttons let you choose the formatting for the cell you're editing. If you need a symbol (such as stars for ratings or a currency symbol), it's added before or after the numeric value as is appropriate. Your formatting options, from top to bottom, are described in this list:

✔ **Currency:** This option adds the appropriate currency symbol, such as $ or €.

✔ **Percentage:** The percent symbol follows the value.

✔ **Stars (rating):** This option lets you display a number from 1 to 45 as a star rating. Numbers greater than 5 display with five stars. Figure 3-16 shows how to edit stars. To change the number of stars, type a new number or tap the star display in the cell or in the display above the keyboard. You can use stars in a spreadsheet and then sort the column of stars so that the ratings are ordered from highest to lowest, or vice versa.

Figure 3-16: Stars can be used for ratings.

✔ **Check box:** A check box is either selected or not. Check boxes are selected and deselected by a user or as the result of a calculation.

Customizing check boxes

A check box can indicate, for example, that an item is in stock or out of stock (yes/no or true/false). However, you can also use it to represent numeric data. Computers and programs often represent yes/no or true/false values. That's one way you can use check boxes to track inventory. If you have the number of in-stock items in a cell, you can use a check box to indicate that none is in stock (a deselected check box) or items are in stock (a selected check box). Numbers handles the conversion for you.

Here's how check box customization can work:

1. **Double-tap a cell to start editing it; tap 42 and then tap the Checkbox button when the keyboard opens.**

   You see a check box in the selected cell; in the area above the keyboard, you see the word *false* in a green outline, as shown in Figure 3-17. The green outline distinguishes the word *false* from text you type in. It has the value *false* because, before you type anything, its numeric value is zero.

Figure 3-17: A check box starts as off and false.

2. **Type a nonzero value.**

   This value can represent the number of items in stock, for example.

3. **Tap the Checkbox button again.**

   You see that the value you typed changes to *true* (see Figure 3-18) and that the check box is selected in the table.

   Because the formatting is separate from the data value, you can sometimes display the in-stock inventory count as a number and sometimes as the check box. Customers are likely to care only about the check box, but the inventory manager cares about the number.

Figure 3-18: A nonzero value is on and true.

Everything in Numbers is linked, so you don't have to worry about a sequence for doing most things. If you've followed these steps, you've seen how to enter a number and have it control a check box, but that's only one of at least three ways of working with a check box.

With a cell selected and the Checkbox formatting button selected, you see the true/false value above the keyboard and the check box itself in the table cell. Tap the check box in the table cell: The true/false value is reversed, as is the check box itself.

Likewise, if you tap the word *true* or *false* in the display above the keyboard, the check box flips its value and true/false reverses.

When you tap a formatting button, it turns blue and formats the number in the selected cell (or cells). You can tap another formatting button to switch to another format (from stars to a percentage, for example). Tapping a highlighted formatting button turns it off without selecting another.

Entering date/time data

Tap the clock to enter date/time or duration data, as shown in Figure 3-19. The Date & Time button lets you specify a specific moment, and the Duration button lets you specify (or calculate) a length of time.

Figure 3-19: Enter date or duration data.

Above the keyboard, the units of a date or duration display. To enter or edit a date or time (both), tap Month in the Formula bar and use the keypad to select the month. (The keys have both the month name abbreviations and the month numbers on them.) Similarly, tap any other component and enter a value. As you do so, the display changes to show the value. (Tapping AM or PM toggles the value — you don't need to type anything.)

Entering text data

When you tap T to enter text data, the QWERTY keyboard appears, as shown in Figure 3-20.

As with most onscreen keyboards, you can switch among letters, numbers, and special characters. (If you need a refresher on how to do it, see Book I, Chapter 2.) Everything you type or dictate is inserted into the selected cell until you tap the Done button, to the right of the display above the

**Book IV
Chapter 3**

**Counting on
Numbers**

keyboard. If you enter a Return character, it's part of the text in the cell. The cell automatically expands vertically to accommodate the text you type, and you can resize the column so that the cell is the appropriate size. Remember, these specialized features are not available on Bluetooth keyboards, so it's often preferable to use the onscreen keyboard when using Numbers.

Figure 3-20: Enter text.

Entering formulas

Tapping the equal-sign (=) button lets you enter a formula, which automatically computes values based on the data you type. The result of the formula can display in a cell in any of the usual formats, and that value can be used in a chart.

When you're entering a formula, the four buttons controlling the date-and-time, text, and numeric keyboards disappear. In their place, a button with three dots appears. Tapping this button returns you to the display that gives you access to the other three keyboards. It's just a matter of Numbers saving space.

Formulas are accompanied by good news and bad news. The good news is that you don't have to type many common formulas: Almost all spreadsheets have the same built-in list of formulas. The bad news is that the list of formulas is quite long.

Formulas can consist of numbers, text, dates, durations, and true/false values. They can also include the results of formulas and the values of individual cells.

The example in this section, which presents the basics of creating a simple formula in Numbers, adds a number to the value of an existing cell and then displays the result in the cell that contains the formula. In this example, I use the Team Organization template that you see in the figures throughout this chapter.

The formula adds 2½ hours to the starting time of a game and displays the estimated completion time in a new column. Follow these steps:

1. **Rename the Time column** Start.

2. **Add a column to its right and name it** End.

3. **Select the cell in which you want to insert the formula by double-tapping it.**

   I selected the End column cell next to Start, as you can see in Figure 3-21.

Figure 3-21: Select the cell that will contain the formula.

4. **Tap the equal-sign (=) button at the top-left side of the keyboard.**

   The keyboard changes to the formula keyboard, as shown in Figure 3-22.

   The table's column and row frames now contain row and column identifiers. The columns are labeled A, B, C, and so on; the rows are labeled 1, 2, 3, and so on. Every cell can be identified by its coordinates (such as A1 for the top-left cell).

   Also note that, at the right of the keyboard, is a different set of buttons than on the text, date, and number keyboards. On the right side of the keypad, you'll find four buttons that represent the following:

   - *Functions:* Brings up a list of functions for use in formulas. (Refer to Step 3.)

   - *abc:* Displays the text keyboard. You can type text and tap Done, and the text is added to the formula you're constructing. You return to the formula keyboard.

   - *Date/Time:* Takes you to the date keyboard. The date or duration you enter uses the same interface shown in Figure 3-19. When you tap Done, the date or duration is added to the formula, and you return to the formula keyboard.

**Book IV
Chapter 3**

Counting on
Numbers

- *True/False:* Uses the same interface as check boxes; the result is added to the formula you're constructing, and you return to the formula keyboard.

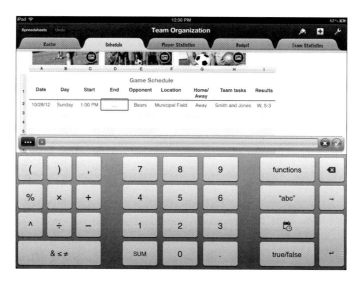

Figure 3-22: Begin to create a formula.

5. Add the game starting time to the formula.

Just tap the cell containing the game start time. The formula reflects the name of the table and the referenced cell. In this case, that reference is

C2

This references column C, row 2 in the Game Schedule table. You don't have to type a thing — just tap, and the correct cell is referenced.

You now need the formula to add 2½ hours to the starting time.

6. Tap + from the operators on the left side of the keyboard.

7. Tap the Date/Time button on the right side of the keyboard and then tap the Duration button at the left.

8. On the Formula bar, tap Hours and enter 2.

9. Tap Minutes and enter 30.

Figure 3-23 shows what the screen looks like now.

10. Tap Done.

You're done entering the duration. You return to the formula keyboard.

Figure 3-23: Enter the formula.

11. **Finish the formula by tapping the button with a check mark on it.**

Figure 3-24 shows the formula as it is now. Note that rather than seeing the Done button, as with other keyboards, you see a button with a check mark and a button with an X at the right. The X cancels the formula, and the check mark completes it. If you want to modify the formula with the keys (including Delete) on the keyboard, feel free.

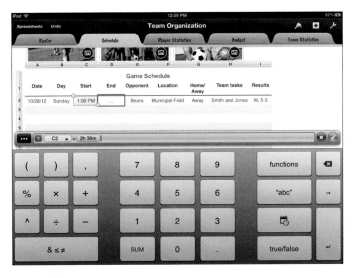

Figure 3-24: Tap the check mark to accept the formula.

Changing a cell's formatting

Your end time may include the date, which is probably not what you want. Here's how to change the formatting of a cell:

1. **Select the cell by making a single tap.**

   You can also select a cell and drag the highlighted selection to include more than one cell. Your reformatting affects all selected cells.

2. **Tap the Format button at the top of the screen.**

3. **In the Format popover, tap the arrow to the right of Date & Time.**

4. **Tap the format you want to use in the selected cell or cells, or tap the arrow at the right of the format name to customize the format.**

   Not all formats have customizations.

To properly format the end time cell, you may want to remove the date. Tap Date & Time Options and set the date option for None and the time option for the hour, as shown in Figure 3-25.

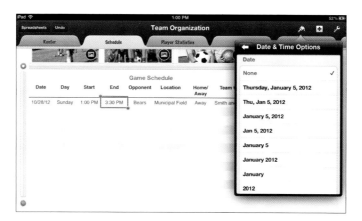

Figure 3-25: Format the result.

Using Forms Efficiently

A *form* is a user-friendly way to provide input to a single row of a spreadsheet. Because a form interacts with a table, you must create a table in your spreadsheet before you can create an associated form.

To create a form, tap the + tab on the rightmost end of the row of tabs. You're asked whether you want to create a new sheet or a form. (Refer to Figure 3-5.) Tap New Form, and you see a screen similar to the one shown in Figure 3-26 using the Team Organization template for the example.

You see a list of all the sheets and all the tables on them. Choose the one that the form will be used with. In this case, I'm using my Admin Info table.

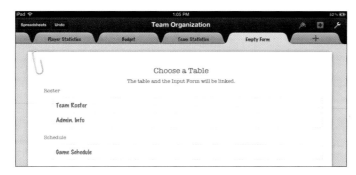

Figure 3-26: Start to create a form.

Every form is associated with only one table, and every table can be associated with only one form (though it doesn't have to be associated with any forms).

The form is then created automatically, as shown in Figure 3-27.

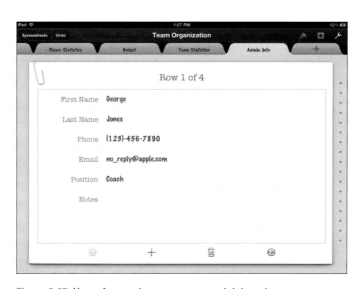

Figure 3-27: Use a form to browse, enter, and delete data.

The labels for the columns on the form are drawn from the labels of the columns on the tables. You don't have to label the columns on your tables, but it makes creating forms and calculations much easier if you do.

You can use the tab to go to the form and enter data or browse it. The four buttons at the bottom of a form let you (from left to right) go to the previous record (row), add a new row, delete the current row, or go to the next row.

You can delete a form by tapping the form's tab and then tapping Delete, but you can't duplicate a form as you can duplicate a sheet tab.

Working with New Tables

Tables contain the data for your spreadsheets and charts, so it may be a bit surprising if you've reached the end of the chapter without creating a single table. That's because you have numerous templates to work with. You don't have to start from the beginning; instead, you can start from further along in the development process.

Tables can be relatively small and focused. You can use formulas to link them, and that's a much better strategy than putting every single piece of data into an enormous spreadsheet.

Tables aren't simply repositories of data; they also drive charts. When you're organizing data in a table, you may want to consider how to transform it to create the kind of charts you want.

As you're planning the structure of your tables and sheets, pay attention to the moments when you realize you have to add more data to a table. Ask whether you truly need more data in that table or need a table that can be linked to the first table by a calculation.

A table often has a *header row* above its data rows; the header row usually contains titles but may also contain calculations such as sums or averages. Numbers tables can have several header rows. A column to the left of the table also has the same functionality — it's a *header column*. People often believe that a header appears only at the top, but in this usage, it appears on whichever side is appropriate.

Creating a new table

Follow these basic steps to create a new table:

1. **Go to the sheet you want the table to be on.**

   It can be an existing sheet from a template or a new sheet you create just for the table. Remember that tables can be cut and pasted, so you have a second (and third and fourth . . .) chance to determine the sheet for your table.

2. **Tap the Insert button (the one with the +) on the right side of the toolbar at the top of the window.**

   The Insert popover opens.

3. **Tap the Tables tab.**

4. **Swipe from one page to another to find the table layout you like.**

   Though you can change any element in the table layout, start with one close to what you want.

   There are six pages of templates — each of the six pages has the same layouts but with different color schemes. This list describes them from the upper-left corner, as shown in Figure 3-28:

   - *Header row and a header column at the left:* This is one of the most common table layouts.

   - *Header row at the top:* This one works well for a list such as students in a class.

   - *No header row or header column:* Before choosing this blank spreadsheet, reconsider. Headers and titles for the tables make your spreadsheet more usable. You can add (or delete) them later and change them, but take a few moments to identify the table along with its rows and columns as soon as you create it.

   - *Header and footer rows and a label column:* This one works well for titles at the top and left and for sums or other calculations at the bottom.

   - *Check boxes in the left column:* This option makes a great list of things to do.

5. **Tap the table layout you like.**

   It's placed on the sheet you have open.

Figure 3-28: Create a new table.

Changing a table's look

Whether you recently created a new table or created it long ago, you might want to change its appearance. Here's how:

1. **Select the table you want to format (to select the table, tap inside the table bounds but outside the cells) and tap the Format button in the toolbar.**

   The Format popover opens, as shown in Figure 3-29. You can change the basic color scheme and layout by tapping the design you want to use.

Figure 3-29: Use Format to reformat a table.

2. **Tap Table Options and fine-tune the table with a title, border, and shading (see Figure 3-30).**

Figure 3-30: Set table options.

Every table has a name. (It starts as Table #, with the next sequence number for all your tables.) The Table option simply controls whether the title is shown. Change the name to something meaningful that you can use in referencing it in formulas. Likewise, each table is a certain size. The Table Border option determines whether a thin line is applied as the table's border. In the Alternating Rows option, every other row is shaded with a contrasting color.

For large tables, alternating the shading of the rows can make it easier for users to follow the data.

3. **Tap Grid Options to show or hide the cell dividers.**

   Many people think that showing the lines in the main table and hiding them in the headers looks best. Experiment. As you tap Yes or No, the display changes so that you can see the effect.

4. **Tap Text Size and Table Font to format the text in the table.**

5. **Tap Headers to modify headers for rows and columns.**

   You can set the number of header rows or columns. (You have either zero footer rows or one footer row.) These elements are created using the existing color scheme. To change the scheme, tap Table in the pop-over and choose a new one.

   Freezing rows and columns keeps the header rows and columns on each page. As you scroll the data, the data itself moves, but the headers never scroll out of sight. This option is often the best one unless the table's content is self-explanatory.

6. **When you're finished, tap anywhere outside the popover to close it.**

Chapter 4: Presenting Keynote

In This Chapter

🖛 **Considering important issues before you create a presentation**

🖛 **Working with Keynote**

🖛 **Animating a presentation with transitions and builds**

🖛 **Preparing to present**

🖛 **Playing a presentation**

Keynote, the first component created for iWork, was originally written for Steve Jobs to use in presentations at conferences and trade shows, including Apple's Worldwide Developers Conference and IDG Worldwide's Macworld conferences. After these "trials by fire," Keynote was joined by Pages to become the first two components of iWork.

Presentation software is a different type of product, compared to the other two iWork applications. It typically consists of content presented by a speaker (whether in person or in absentia) to an audience.

Now, with the Keynote for iOS app in hand, you have new presentation possibilities. Small-group or one-on-one presentations using iPads are made possible in a new way because you can easily present short but impressive presentations almost anywhere. In addition, you can connect the iPad Dock Connector to a VGA adapter or connect using the Apple Digital AV Adapter and present to larger groups from a smaller machine. On iPad (except for the original iPad), you can also use the video mirroring feature AirPlay. If you choose to display a presentation to a single person or small group on the iPad itself and you have a third- or fourth-generation iPad, you'll find the Retina display a dazzling way to wow your audience.

In this chapter, you find out how to prepare and stage a presentation using Keynote. After adding text to slides and using animated transitions, you'll soon have a sophisticated and useful presentation.

Concepts to Consider before You Create a Presentation

A presentation is meant to be viewed. A person (usually you, but sometimes the viewer) controls the pace of the presentation. Follow these tips when building a presentation:

- ✔ **Weigh small-group versus large-group presentations.** You have options on iPad in addition to the traditional model of presenting to a group. This model offers an opportunity for one-on-one presentations that you can give in almost any setting, such as a sales call in a client's office. If you're working on a small-group or one-on-one presentation, the text and graphics don't have to reach across a ballroom to the viewer's eye, so size elements on the slide accordingly.

- ✔ **Make use of existing content.** Keynote for iOS helps you easily transfer presentations between your iPad and your Mac. Sometimes, that's the right thing to do. You can reuse the slides and rearrange them (possibly splitting a large presentation into many). Restructuring and rearranging an existing Keynote presentation that's going to be presented to a small group rather than to a larger audience can be a good idea.

- ✔ **Consider your canvas.** When working on a presentation, you're using a small canvas. A slide has much less space to hold information than does a piece of paper (or a spreadsheet page). No matter how large your audience, never overcrowd your slides.

- ✔ **Avoid too much variety.** Using too many graphical object styles (such as illustrations, photos, and line drawings) or too many font styles (such as bold and underline) can make for a choppy-looking presentation. Luckily, Keynote themes help you provide a cohesive and clean look for your presentation. Even though you may make small changes to text and add graphics, try to maintain an overall look and feel.

- ✔ **Adding movement to slides.** You have options for movement (see the "Using Transitions and Builds" section, later in this chapter) that you don't have with printed documents. You can add effects to transition from one slide to another. Experiment with the Keynote transitions, and use them to help people understand your progress in the presentation. For example, you can use a transition to introduce a new topic.

Getting Started with Keynote on iPad

You get started with the Keynote app the same way you do with Numbers or Pages: Create a new document, or open an existing one. The basic windows are the same, but Keynote has some minor differences. This section is your guide.

Navigating the Keynote screen

When you open (or create) a Keynote document, the basic Keynote screen appears, as shown in Figure 4-1. The name of the document is centered on the toolbar at the top. At the left, the Presentations button returns you to the Presentations screen — small images represent the first page of each of your saved files.

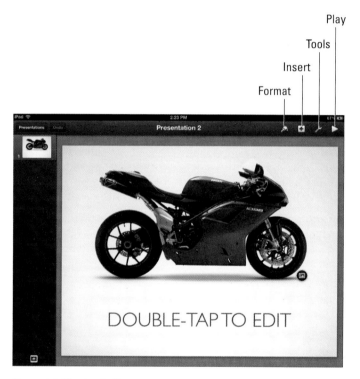

Figure 4-1: The basic Keynote screen.

On the right side of the toolbar (refer to Figure 4-1) are the usual buttons. The buttons, from left to right, are described in this list:

✔ **Format:** As always, this button lets you modify the selected object or objects. Your choices depend on which type of object is selected. (If nothing on the slide is selected, the button is grayed out.)

✔ **Insert:** Lets you insert media such as photos, tables, charts, and shapes, as shown in Figure 4-2.

Figure 4-2: Insert objects into slides.

✔ **Tools:** Shows you the popover you see in Figure 4-3. You can tap Find to search the Keynote document, go to Help for assistance with using the application, type presenter notes (even if they're directed to yourself), and get help.

Figure 4-3: Use the Keynote tools.

Tap Advanced on the Tools menu to access the following tools (see Figure 4-4):

- *Slide Numbers:* This option lets you turn slide numbers on and off. Just as with pages of a Pages document, you should let the app handle the numbering so that the slide (or page) numbers are correct even if you move elements around, delete slides, or add slides.

- *Guides:* The Guides option on the Advanced menu makes a setting available to display guidelines that appear as you move an object toward the center of the slide or other objects, at the edges of the slide, or in 10 percent increments horizontally and vertically along the slide. You can turn automatic slide numbering on and off.

Figure 4-4: Use the advanced tools in Keynote.

- *Interactive Hyperlinks:* Tap this selection and then tap an object and a Link menu appears. You can insert a link that takes you from the object to any slide in your presentation or to cause you to exit the presentation.

- *Presentation Type:* Tap this option to set a presentation to loop or to autoplay (see Figure 4-5) or set up a self-playing presentation.

  You don't need a special spell-checking option because it's built into the iOS.

Figure 4-5: Set the presentation type.

- *Remote:* Remote settings lets you enable a remote device to control the presentation. The remote device (such as an iPhone) communicates wirelessly with your iPad, which then plays your presentation as though you were tapping the screen. This setting means that you can put your iPad next to a projector and avoid a tangle of wires while you speak from the front of a room.

- ✔ **Play:** Use this button to play your presentation; if you have an external display adapter, the slides appear on the display while the iPad screen shows the controls.

One difference between Keynote and the other iWork apps is that it always appears in landscape (horizontal) orientation; as you rotate the iPad, the image doesn't rotate, because the slides are all designed to be shown

**Book IV
Chapter 4**

Presenting Keynote

horizontally. It isn't a Keynote limitation as much as a nod to the realities of projectors and displays.

On the left side of the screen, in the navigator, are thumbnail views of the slides in your presentation. To go to any slide in your presentation, just tap its thumbnail.

Creating your first Keynote slide and adding text

The templates in all iWork apps provide you with useful starting points. In Keynote, you're almost certain to find prebuilt slides you can use, so it's only a matter of organizing your own data.

1. **To begin a new presentation, tap Keynote on the Home screen.**

2. **On the Presentations screen, tap the plus sign (+) to create your new presentation from a template or from another presentation, as described in Chapter 1 of this minibook.**

3. **On the Choose a Theme screen, tap a theme for your presentation.**

   Note that the themes determine the background color and font to be used. The presentation appears with one slide in it.

4. **Double-tap a text placeholder on the slide to edit it.**

   The text placeholder opens for editing, and the onscreen keyboard appears.

5. **Enter any text you want and then tap the slide itself or the Hide Keyboard key to close the keyboard when you're done.**

Formatting text

With Keynote — perhaps more than with the other iWork apps — it's more fill-in-the-blanks than fuss around with formatting. You can get right to work. The font is determined by the theme you choose, but you can modify its size and add effects such as bold and italic. Here's how:

1. **Double-tap text to select the type you want to change.**

2. **Tap the Format button, and from the various tabs of the Format popover, choose a text style option (Title or Subtitle, for example), and tap any of the formatting choices (Bold, Italic, Underline, or Strikethrough) to apply them to the selected text.**

3. **Tap anywhere else on the screen to hide the Format popover.**

Adding a new slide

To add a new slide, tap + in the lower-left corner (see Figure 4-6) and choose the style of slide from the gallery that appears. Want to add a bulleted list? Just choose a slide style with a bulleted list already on it.

Figure 4-6: Add a new slide.

You can choose the layout for the slide you're adding from the thumbnails shown in the popover. As Figure 4-7 demonstrates, the layouts for new slides vary from template to template.

Figure 4-7: Slides vary by template.

Adding media

Themes provide some slide layouts with image placeholders in them. To change a placeholder image, simply double-tap it. A dialog opens, showing media sources, such as your Photo Albums. Locate an item and tap to insert it.

If you want to add an image outside a placeholder, make sure no placeholder is selected and then tap the Insert button. Tap any of the four tabs: Media, Tables, Charts, or Shapes. Choose the item you want to insert, and it appears on your slide.

You can now move the object around with your finger. You select an object on a slide with a single tap (the same as in Numbers and Pages). You can drag the object around; Keynote provides the coordinates for precise positioning and also provides you guidelines as you align the object with the center of the screen or the edge of another object. To resize an object, drag a corner handle until it's the size you want and then let it go.

Managing slides

Tap a slide in the navigator to select it. Then tap the slide again to bring up the selection buttons shown in Figure 4-8. You can now take an action; for example, tap Delete, and the slide is gone. (Remember, if it's a mistake, just tap Undo at the top left of the screen.) The Transition button brings up a selection of transition effects to apply (see the next section for more about this).

Figure 4-8: Delete a slide.

You can also use the selection buttons to cut, copy, and paste slides. After you have cut or copied a slide (tap it and tap Cut or Copy), tap the slide after which you want it to appear, and then tap Paste. (You always paste the contents of the clipboard after the slide you select.)

Another option appears in the selection buttons: Skip. It collapses the selected slide in the navigator into a thin line. When you play the presentation, the slide is skipped over. The thin line in the navigator is big enough for you to tap it to bring up its selection buttons: It now has a Don't Skip button, which lets you bring it back to full size and include it in the presentation as it plays.

Select the slide from the navigator. If you tap the slide itself, the selection buttons act on the selected object within the slide.

Using Transitions and Builds

You can enliven a presentation and make it a better communication tool by using Keynote animations to animate the transition from one slide to another. You can also use animations to build a slide. *Building* refers to the process of animating the appearance of each bullet or another object within a single slide. The process of creating transitions and builds is much the same, and I cover them in this section.

A little animation is a good thing. Feel free to try all the options, but then decide which one — or maybe two — you want for your presentation. Too many animations are distracting and compete with the content you're presenting, unintentionally becoming the focus of your presentation.

Working with transitions

Tap a slide and then tap Transition from the toolbar that appears (refer to Figure 4-8) to begin setting a transition. When you tap the button, you move to the transition editor. Notice the Done button in the top-right corner of the screen — until you tap the Done button, you're working on a transition.

Transitions can work on slides as a whole or work on parts of slides; when they work on parts of slides, they're often called *builds.* Note that a transition consists of two parts:

- ✏ **Effect:** This is the visual effect that's displayed.

- ✏ **Options:** Options include the direction in which the animation moves as well as whether it starts in response to a tap or after a previous transition is finished. Options also include the duration of the transition.

Though a transition may appear to happen *between* two slides, it happens *after* you tap a slide to go to the next one. The transition is attached to the from, or first, slide in the sequence of two adjacent slides.

Here's how to build a transition:

1. **In the navigator on the left side of the screen, tap the slide for which you want to build a transition and tap Transition on the toolbar that appears.**

    The list of transition effects appears in a popover, as shown in Figure 4-9. A number of transition effects are available; swipe up and down to see them all. (The list of transitions is controlled by the Effects button at the bottom-left corner of the popover.)

Figure 4-9: Choose an effect.

2. **When you find a transition effect that interests you, tap the name to select it and see a preview.**

3. **Tap the Options button in the bottom-right corner of the popover (refer to Figure 4-9) to set the effect options, as shown in Figure 4-10.**

4. **Set the duration and when the effect starts.**

Figure 4-10: Set the duration and start.

5. **Continue to change the effects and options until you're satisfied.**

   You'll probably want to try the combinations with the triangle in the upper-right side of the popover several times.

   After you apply a transition effect to a slide, it appears whenever you select that slide in the navigator while using Transitions, as shown in Figure 4-11.

Figure 4-11: The effect is shown on the slide in the navigator.

Working with builds

Builds are much like transitions except that they work within a single slide and control how elements such as bullets are displayed. Here's how to set a build:

1. **In the display portion of the screen, tap the object you want to build.**

   Each object can have two sets of builds: effects to build it *into* the slide (when the slide is shown) and effects to build it *out* of the slide (when the slide is closed).

2. **Tap the Tools button and then tap Transitions and Builds.**

3. **Tap to choose the type of build you want to apply — either a build-in or a build-out as shown in Figure 4-12.**

Figure 4-12: Set builds for an object.

4. **Select the build effect you want to use, as shown in Figure 4-13.**

   As with slide-to-slide transitions, as soon as you select an effect, it pre-views for you.

Figure 4-13: Select the build effect.

5. **Tap the Options button at the bottom of the popover to set options, as shown in Figure 4-14.**

You can begin the build when you tap or after the previous transition is complete. You can also set a delay in seconds before the transition begins. Note that a number in a yellow circle is created on the object you're applying the build to; you can tap the number later to go back and change the effect or options.

Figure 4-14: Choose an option.

6. **Tap the Delivery button at the bottom of the popover to select whether the build happens all at one time or with the addition of each component, as shown in Figure 4-15.**

Depending on what the selected object is, this step can build each item in a bulleted list separately or each wedge in a pie chart in sequence. (Delivery options may not be available if they don't apply.)

Figure 4-15: Set the delivery options.

Managing multiple builds on a single slide

As you create builds, each one is numbered. The numbers appear in small, yellow circles as soon as you have chosen an effect. You can manage the sequence of these builds. To do so, follow these steps:

1. **Select the appropriate slide, tap the Tools button, and then tap Transitions and Builds.**

   You see the yellow circles around the numbers of the builds on that slide.

2. **Tap any build to edit it using the techniques you used to create the build.**

   See the previous section.

   The yellow circle for a build is shown in Figure 4-16. You can see two transitions for the selected object. In this case, transition 2 is the build-in, and transition 1 is the build-out. (That happens to be the order they were created in, but they don't have to be in that order.) Thus, you can separately tap either transition number to change its settings or even delete it if you've gone transition-crazy.

3. **To reorder the builds, tap the Order button in the bottom-right corner of the popover (refer to Figure 4-15).**

   Using the horizontal bars at the right of each build (see Figure 4-17), drag them to the order you want them to be executed. The numbers automatically change. Keynote picks up identifying text, such as the title, so that you can keep them straight.

Figure 4-16: Edit an existing build.

Figure 4-17: Set the build order.

4. **When you're finished, tap Options again to review the reordered builds.**

   You can use the arrow in the top-right corner of the popover to test the builds.

5. **When you're satisfied, tap Done.**

Preparing to Present

After you've dotted every *i* and crossed every *t* in your presentation, added all the great ideas you've been storing in your brain, and tweaked the animations, you're happy with what you have. Now you need to prepare for a captivating presentation.

Using a projector

The cable known as the Apple iPad Dock Connector to VGA Adapter ($29 from the Apple Store at the time of this writing) connects your iPad to any VGA device, such as a projector. With it, you can use Keynote to give your presentation.

The Digital AV Adapter cable accessory is available for $39. You can use it to connect to devices enabled with Thunderbolt high-definition media technology or to devices such as HDTVs that have HDMI connectors.

When you connect a projector (or any other type of display) to your iPad with the iPad Dock Connector to VGA Adapter, the Keynote app can sense that it has a second display. It uses this display when you start a slideshow in the Keynote app. (See the "Playing Your Presentation" section, later in this chapter.) While it's sending the presentation to the external display, it lets you control it from your iPad. Figure 4-18 shows what you see on the iPad as it plays a presentation on an external display.

Figure 4-18: Control a presentation on an external display.

The slides display on the external display, but you can control the presentation using your iPad. On the left side of the screen, a navigator shows thumbnail images of your slides. Being able to see the next slide helps you transition to it elegantly without shuffling papers and distracting your audience and yourself. You can tap the arrows in the center of the iPad screen to move forward and backward among slides.

Using nanopresentations

iPad is a game-changer in many ways. Its size (and therefore its portability) and its remarkably clear screen (especially on a third- or fourth-generation iPad with its Retina display) are only two of its features that open great new opportunities. Keynote for iPad can help you take advantage of a new opportunity — *nanopresentations* (presentations you make one-on-one or to a small group of people).

Whether you're used to presentations as a presenter or an audience member, you'll probably be pleasantly surprised at how well presentations to small groups can work. Perhaps the most interesting difference is the simplest one: Because the speaker can sit down and join the audience around a table or in a circle or in a group of chairs, the speaker/audience or teacher/student paradigm of many presentations is immediately broken — and can be a breath of fresh air. It certainly seems to make discussions and audience questions livelier.

For presentations to large (or even medium-size) groups, your iPad and a projector work well. But for a smaller group, a projector is often a bit of overkill. You can use your iPad for a presentation to a few people seated around a table or — to be more iPad-like — seated or standing anywhere they want. This characteristic isn't one that most people have considered much because the mechanics of a presentation have been bulky; you wouldn't normally think of offering short presentations of a few minutes to informal groups who may not even be seated for a formal presentation.

Think about the possibilities. If you're selling something that's not easy to carry around, a photo album on your iPad is a helpful way to show prospective customers what you're talking about. But a Keynote presentation — even a handful of slides — can be much more effective and impressive than a photo album.

Are you canvassing door to door for a politician or a cause? Again, a Keynote presentation of perhaps half a dozen slides can present the issue with pictures, text, and diagrams. You can fill in the gaps and answer questions, but it's certainly more effective than knocking on a door and asking whether you can come in and set up a computer and a projector.

One great advantage of nanopresentations is that you don't talk to a large group that's sitting in the dark when you're presenting to a few people around a table or sitting on a sofa with you. People generally don't have enough time to doze off or become distracted.

Here are a few final presentation pointers:

✐ **Avoid the dark.** If you're using a projector, use the least possible amount of room-darkening for your presentation. Make certain you can see your audience.

✐ **Use question-and-answer sections.** Use frequent, short Q&A sections in your presentations to involve your audience as much as possible.

✐ **Use a road map.** Let people know where they're going in your presentation and where they are at any moment. When you're reading a book, the heft of the unread pages gives you an idea of how far you've come. With a presentation, one slide after another can come out of the dark with no clue to how each one fits into the presentation.

✐ **Use big font sizes.** Have you ever looked closely at the presentations given by the late Steve Jobs and others at Apple? Consider using 60 points for the font size. Whether you're creating your Keynote presentation on a Mac or an iPad, you're probably close to the screen. Your audience will be far away (even if you're just sitting across a table from them). In addition, you may have become accustomed to using font sizes that print well. Those font sizes are smaller than sizes that appear well on a screen. Go big.

✐ **Buy a Dock or cover for your iPad that acts as a stand.** Several iPad cover options let you prop up your iPad display so that somebody sitting across from you can get a good view of its screen. Check out the Apple iPad accessories section in the online store, or search for *iPad covers* at a search engine and find one that appeals to you.

Playing Your Presentation

After you prepare all the elements in your presentation, little remains to do when you want to play it. Tap the Play button at the right side of the toolbar to begin playing. The transitions and builds happen automatically.

Tap to advance to the next slide. If you're using an external monitor, tap the Next and Previous buttons. (Refer to Figure 4-18.)

If your presentation contains hyperlinks, simply tap to open them in Safari on iPad. (Keynote automatically detects hyperlinks by the presence of an Internet schema, such as `http://`.)

The Keynote app has a built-in laser pointer, so to speak: Tap and hold the iPad screen, and a red pointer appears on the display. (If you're using an external display or projector, it appears on that display as well.) You can then emphasize parts of the slide to the audience. One advantage of this method is that you can continue to face your audience while pointing out details on the slides. The alternative is to walk over to the slide, turn your back on the audience, and point — not an outstanding idea. (Audience members sometimes sneak out the moment you turn your back.)

Book V
Using iPad to Get Organized

The 5th Wave — By Rich Tennant

©RICHTENNANT

"What I'm doing should clear your sinuses, take away your headache, and charge your iPad."

*T*his is one of my favorite parts of this book because it's where you use so many wonderful bundled apps to keep your life in line. You discover how to manage files on iPad and print out those hard copies we all — let's face it — still need now and then. You explore the Notes app, a simple note-taking feature you can use for anything from writing to-do lists to creating the outline of your next novel. In addition to Notes, in this part I show you all the wonderful features of the Calendar and Contacts apps. These are the apps that will keep you on schedule and in touch with all those important people in your life. You also discover how the Reminders app and Notifications allow you to stay on track and alert to everything coming at you. Finally, the last chapter in this part introduces you to your new personal assistant, Siri. Siri allows you to speak questions about anything under the sun, and the feature searches databases and websites to provide text and spoken answers.

Chapter 1: Managing Files and Printing

In This Chapter

✔ Understanding how iPad stores files

✔ Sharing files by e-mailing or through the cloud

✔ Setting up Home Sharing

✔ Printing wirelessly from iPad

✔ Using third-party printing services

*O*kay, I'm going to be very upfront about this: Apple has not used a traditional paradigm for moving files to and from your iPad or managing files on the device. In essence, this is partially a chapter about the following:

✔ What iPad does differently from how traditional file management is handled by OS interfaces such as OS X's Finder or Windows Explorer (Windows Version 7 and earlier) or File Explorer (Windows 8). (For brevity, I just refer to this feature using the Windows 8 nomenclature, File Explorer, in the rest of this chapter).

✔ How you can get things in and out of the device without a USB port or DVD drive

One exciting development that arrived with iOS 5 is *iCloud,* which allows you to back up and store content online, and I discuss that in this chapter as well as in Book I, Chapter 5.

The other topic in this chapter is printing, and there are two options here: Use iPad's native printing capability with a compatible wireless printer, or use a third-party printing app.

Finding Your Files

iPad stores files locally by app, or if you use iCloud, iPad automatically stores and shares files among iOS devices and with your Mac or PC. Here's how this works.

How iPad stores files

Though there's no Mac Finder or Windows File Explorer on iPad where you can view all your stored files in one place, iPad does store files. Open the Photos app, for example, and you see lots of photos, each one contained in a separate file. The Music app contains audio files, Videos contains movie files, iBooks contains e-book files, and if you own Pages, it contains word-processing documents (as shown in Figure 1-1), and so on.

Though there's no Windows File Explorer feature on iPad, when you connect iPad to a PC, you can use the Windows File Explorer feature on your computer to move files around on iPad.

Figure 1-1: Documents stored by Pages.

How did those files get there? You may have created them in iPad (as with the Notes or Numbers apps); you may have downloaded them from the Internet, as with music or video purchases from iTunes; or you may have synced them from your computer or had them pushed to all your iOS devices from iCloud, as with music files or photos. Perhaps you grabbed a document from a website, or from an online storage service such as Dropbox.

Depending on the app you open, you may see a Documents button to display thumbnails of documents, as shown in Figure 1-1; libraries of photos as in Photos; albums of music or individual song files as in Music (see Figure 1-2); or bookshelves or lists of e-books as in iBooks. Each app offers a slightly different way to find whatever you've created on, downloaded to, or synced to your iPad.

If you go to iTunes on your computer with your iPad connected, you can see your iPad file structure organized by app. But however the files got in there and however you find them when you open an app, getting them out of your iPad is the focus of this chapter.

Figure 1-2: Music shows you files by album, song, composer, artist, and more.

See Book II, Chapter 1, for information about buying and downloading content, and Book I, Chapter 5, for information about syncing to your computer and buying apps. Book IV, Chapter 1, gives some details about moving files around for use with iWork products.

Going with iCloud

iCloud isn't so much a place as it is a storage service. If you choose to back up or share files by using iCloud, you can't go to a website and organize those files. Rather, they're automatically backed up from your devices, and new files created or downloaded to one device are automatically pushed to your other devices. In essence, this process is invisible to you. You still access these files by opening the associated app.

The one thing you can do at iCloud (at www.iCloud.com) is use the Find My iPad feature, which allows you to send a sound or message to your lost device, remotely lock it, or wipe data from it. See Book I, Chapter 9, for more about this feature.

Sharing Files

As mentioned in the previous section, iPad doesn't let you get at files the way your computer does with a series of folders and files. You open files in individual apps, such as Photos and Videos. You can't save files to a storage medium, such as a flash drive that you can remove and place in another computing device. Therefore, managing and sharing your files with other devices or other people works a bit differently on your iPad.

You have a few options for getting files out of your iPad: Sync them via iCloud, which automatically pushes them to other iOS devices; e-mail them; sync with a computer to share things like calendar events, contact records, music, or photos, which is covered in Book I, Chapter 5; share them over a network; or use the Safari browser and a third-party service, such as Dropbox, to upload and view files *in the cloud* (collectively, the places on the Internet where data or apps can be stored and accessed using a browser). Also consider using wireless devices from manufacturers such as Kingston and Maxell for external storage, or use third-party apps such as PhoneView that allow you to move and manage files.

Relying on good old e-mail

You can use tools in individual applications to e-mail files to yourself or others. E-mailing files to yourself can be useful if you've worked on a document on your iPad and then want to get a copy of it on your computer. You can't exactly save a copy because (remember) no removable storage medium exists on your iPad, so you e-mail the file and save the e-mail attachment to your computer hard drive or other storage.

Here's an example of e-mailing from an app, in this case, Photos:

1. **Open Photos and locate a picture you want to e-mail.**

2. **Tap the picture to open it and then tap the Menu button shown in Figure 1-3.**

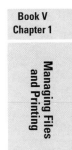

Figure 1-3: Tap the Menu button.

3. **Tap Mail.**

   The e-mail form shown in Figure 1-4 appears.

4. **Fill out the e-mail form and tap Send to get the e-mail on its way to yourself or somebody else.**

Figure 1-4: The e-mail form and onscreen keyboard appear together.

Going through the cloud

iCloud is a storage and sharing service from Apple that allows you 5GB of free storage or additional purchased storage for your content. This storage allowance doesn't include apps, contents shared via Photo Stream, any content shared via iTunes Match, or content you've purchased from the iTunes Store. However, you should know that backing up files to iCloud is an all or nothing proposition: You don't have the ability to pick and choose what you store there. Book I, Chapter 5, provides details on setting up an iCloud account and making settings to choose what to back up and share via iCloud.

You have, in addition to iCloud, other cloud-based options for sharing files. Apps such Dropbox, DropCopy Lite, and FileFly — Easy Wi-Fi Sharing and Viewing (a wireless file-sharing app) allow you to upload files to an online site and, using an app you download to your iPad, access and view those files. Some of these options provide more flexibility for managing your files than iCloud does.

Take a look at how this works with Dropbox, which is a good, free file-sharing app that provides one of the easiest ways to get any and all files to and from your iPad to any and all other computers and devices.

Dropbox is a cloud-based service that allows you to store your files on its servers and access them on any device that's connected to the Internet. (Figure 1-5 shows you what the Dropbox interface looks like if you surf there on your computer.) It directly supports (in the form of dedicated software) OS X, Windows, Linux, Android, BlackBerry, and of course iOS.

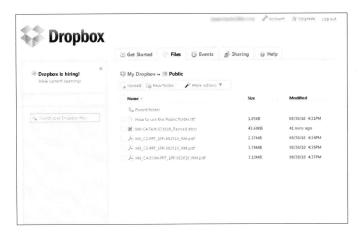

Figure 1-5: Dropbox with files stored in its Public folder.

When you're on a computer, Dropbox works like any other folder on your hard drive. When you open it with your browser, you have instant access to all your files. When you drop something into your folder, it's copied to the company's servers, and then pushed out to anywhere you've set up with your Dropbox account, including your iPad or others you're sharing folders with.

After you download the Dropbox app, you can open a file on iPad and view but not edit it, unless you choose the option of opening the document with an app you have on your iPad that would be a logical fit. For example, Figure 1-6 shows the Sharing button, and iPad suggests an app to use to open this Word document, where you may be able to edit it, or PrintCentral, a printing app I cover in the later section "Printing with third-party apps."

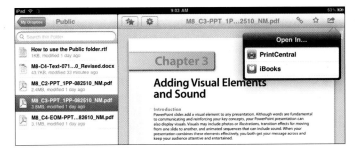

Figure 1-6: Choosing an app to open your document in.

Dropbox folders can be selectively shared with other Dropbox users, making it a great tool for any sort of collaborative project.

In addition to the Dropbox app, iOS app developers can add Dropbox functionality directly to their apps, just as the QuickOffice folks did. This functionality makes working with your files in those apps easier.

Setting Up Home Sharing

With Home Sharing, you can stream content from any Mac or PC to your iPad directly. You simply set up Home Sharing on your iPad, turn on the feature in iTunes on your computer, and you're good to go.

Here are the steps for setting up Home Sharing when you're connected to a Wi-Fi network:

1. **On your computer, open iTunes.**

2. **Click the Advanced menu and choose Turn On Home Sharing.**

   The Home Sharing dialog appears.

3. **Enter your Apple ID and password and then click Create Home Share.**

   A message appears, telling you to use the same account you just signed in to on devices you want to share with.

4. **Click Done.**

5. **On your iPad, tap Settings and then tap Music.**

6. **In the Home Sharing section, shown in Figure 1-7, enter your Apple ID and password for the same account you used in iTunes on your computer.**

Figure 1-7: The Home Sharing settings for Music.

7. **Tap the Home button and then tap Music.**

   Music opens, displaying a Library button.

8. **Tap More and then Shared, and then tap a shared library to display a catalog of what's available in it.**

   You can now play any content in that folder from your iPad. To view shared videos, open the Videos app.

Printing from iPad

If you need to print from your iPad, you can use its built-in wireless printing capability or a third-party app, which is likely to give you a few more printing controls.

Native printing from iPad

As of iOS version 4.2, native printing capability is part of iPad's bag of tricks. This capability requires a wireless-enabled printer that supports the AirPrint protocol. All the major printer manufacturers offer AirPrint-compatible printers, including HP, Epson, Canon, Brother, and Lexmark. The only control you have over your printing is to set the number of copies to be printed (though no doubt Apple will add more robust features to this in future iOS releases). You can also use an app such as Printopia or AirPrint Activator 2 to print from iPad to shared and networked printers, whether wireless or wired.

You can print photos, e-mail messages, web pages, and documents from iWork apps such as Pages. Tap the Menu button with an arrow on it (available in the Safari, Mail, and Photos apps) to display a menu including the Print command. When you tap that command, you see the Printer Options dialog. Follow these steps to print:

1. **In the Printer Options dialog, shown in Figure 1-8 (if you haven't yet used this feature with your printer), tap Select Printer.**

   iPad searches for any available wireless printers.

Figure 1-8: Choose your printer and the number of copies and print away!

2. **Tap your printer to select it.**

3. **Tap Printer Options to return to the Printer Options dialog and tap the + or – buttons in the Copies field to adjust the number of copies.**

4. **Tap Print.**

   Your print job goes on its way.

When you have print jobs going to your printer, you can access a Print Summary dialog that shows the name of the document that's printing, the printer it's printing to, the number of copies, when the print job started, and its status (for example, Printing 1 of 3). You access this summary by double-tapping the Home button and scrolling in the list of apps to locate the Print Center app. Tap it, and the summary displays.

Printing with third-party apps

You can choose from several third-party apps: PrintCentral, Print n Share for Advanced Printing, and PrintBureau, to name a few.

One of the best of these is PrintCentral Pro for iPad, available for $9.99. This app has a file browser and an e-mail reader that allows you to access anything on your iPad, and it also allows you to print to a network printer across your Wi-Fi network. If you install a free print server called WePrint, provided by EuroSmartz, on your Mac or PC, you can even print to your printer remotely through a 3G or 4G connection on the iPad model that includes Wi-Fi and 3G or 4G. (I recommend installing the print server anyway because it gives you more printing options.)

The Printopia and AirPrint Activator 2 (on a Mac) apps make any shared or network printer on your home network visible to your iPad. Printopia has more features but is more expensive, whereas AirPrint Activator is free.

After you purchase and download PrintCentral to your iPad, follow these steps to print:

1. **Download WePrint to your computer.**

   Both Mac and Windows versions are available at `http://mobile.eurosmartz.com/print/download.html`.

2. **Plug the Lightning end of your Lightning to USB Cable into your iPad and the USB end into one of your computer's USB ports.**

   For non–fourth-generation iPads, plug the Dock Connector end of your Dock Connector to USB Cable into your iPad and the USB end into one of your computer's USB ports.

3. **Open WePrint.**

   You see your server address, as shown in Figure 1-9.

Figure 1-9: The WePrint app on your computer.

4. **Open PrintCentral on iPad.**

5. **Tap the Getting Started file listed there to test your printer.**

6. **Tap the Print icon in the top-right corner.**

   The Print dialog shown in Figure 1-10 appears.

Figure 1-10: PrintCentral's Print dialog.

7. **Tap the Choose button and enter the server address you found in WePrint into the dialog that appears.**

   PrintCentral connects and displays all possible printers (see Figure 1-11).

8. **Tap the printer you want to use and then tap the Print button in the Print dialog.**

   The test document prints.

Figure 1-11: PrintCentral's possible printers dialog.

After you have PrintCentral working, you can use the Menu button from within apps to open a document in PrintCentral and print it. In other apps, you can make a copy of a file that places the copy on your Clipboard and then open the Clip archive in PrintCentral (see Figure 1-12), choose the file you want to print, and print the file.

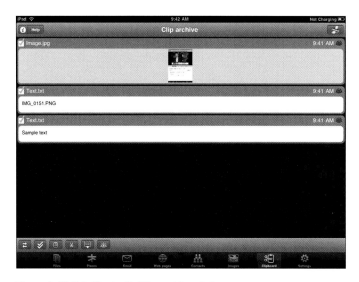

Figure 1-12: PrintCentral's Clip archive dialog.

Chapter 2: Making Notes

In This Chapter

✏ **Opening a blank note and entering text**

✏ **Creating a new note**

✏ **Finding, e-mailing, and deleting a note**

✏ **Displaying the Notes List**

✏ **Printing a note**

*N*otes is a preinstalled application you can use to do everything from jotting down notes at meetings to maintaining to-do lists. It isn't a robust word processor like Apple Pages or Microsoft Word by any means, but for taking notes on the fly or dictating a few pages of your novel-in-progress using the Dictation feature (not available on the original iPad or iPad 2) while you sit and sip a cup of tea on your deck, it's a great option.

In this chapter, you discover how to enter and edit text in Notes and manage notes by navigating among them, searching for content, or e-mailing, deleting, and printing them.

Making Notes

Notes are pretty simple to create — kind of like grabbing a sticky notepad, jotting down your thoughts, pulling off the note and sticking it somewhere, and starting to write the next one. You can even use Siri to create a note and the Dictation feature to speak your note contents. You can use the included editing tools to select, cut, copy, and paste. Notes are saved for you in a list of notes so you can easily find the one you need (covered in the "Finding Notes" section later in this chapter), and they can be synced across iOS devices and your Mac.

Opening a blank note and entering text

If you have no stored notes, Notes opens with a new, blank note displayed. (If you have used Notes before, it opens to the last note you were working on. If that's the case, you might want to jump to the next section to create a new blank note.)

If you have no stored notes and open Notes to a blank document, follow these steps:

1. **Tap the Notes app icon on the Home screen.**

   Depending on how you have your iPad oriented, you see the view in Figure 2-1 (portrait) or Figure 2-2 (landscape).

Figure 2-1: This yellow-lined pad format should look familiar.

2. **Tap the blank page.**

   The onscreen keyboard, shown in Figure 2-3, appears.

3. **Tap keys on the keyboard to enter text (or, if you're using third- or fourth-generation iPad or an iPad mini, tap the Dictation key to speak your text; refer to Figure 2-3) and speak your text using iPad's speech recognition feature.**

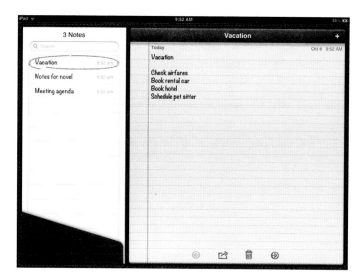

Figure 2-2: Landscape orientation shows you the current note and a list of saved notes on the left.

Dictation key

Figure 2-3: Use the onscreen keyboard or your Keyboard Dock or Bluetooth keyboard, if you have one.

If this Dictation key isn't available on your third- or fourth-generation iPad or your iPad mini, go to Settings⬦General⬦Keyboard and tap Dictation to turn it on.

If you use the Dictation feature, everything you say is sent to Apple to be changed into text. If you're not comfortable with that, you may want to disable the Dictation feature. For more about Dictation, see Book I, Chapter 3.

Here are some tips while working with the virtual keyboard:

✔ **Enter numbers or symbols:** Tap either of the keys labeled .?123 on the keyboard. The numeric keyboard, shown in Figure 2-4, appears. When you want to return to the regular keyboard, tap either of the keys labeled ABC.

Figure 2-4: Use this alternative keyboard for numbers and many common symbols.

✔ **Capitalize a letter:** Tap the Shift key and then tap the letter.

If you enable the Enable Caps Lock feature in Settings, you can also turn on Caps Lock by double-tapping the Shift key; tap the Shift key once to turn off the feature.

✔ **Start a new paragraph or the next item in a list:** Tap the Return key.

✔ **Edit text:** Tap to the right of the text you want to edit and tap the Delete key to delete text to the left of the cursor or enter new text.

✔ Change the default font: Go to the Notes Settings.

✔ **Find more symbols:** Tap either of the keys labeled #+= to access more symbols, such as the percentage sign, the euro symbol, and additional bracket styles. Pressing and holding some of these keys displays alternative characters. This also works on some keys on the alphabetic and numeric keyboards. (For example, pressing and holding N gives you foreign language options such as the Spanish ñ, and pressing and holding the exclamation key on the numeric keyboard offers the upside-down exclamation point used in some languages.)

No need to save a note — it's automatically kept until you delete it.

Creating a new note

If you have stored notes, when you open Notes, the most recently used note displays. If you then want to create a new note, it's a simple procedure. To create a new note, tap the New Note button (the one with the + symbol on it) in the top-right corner. A new, blank note appears (refer to Figures 2-1 and 2-2). Enter and edit text as described in the preceding section.

If your iPad is in portrait orientation and you want to display the list of saved notes beside the current note, switch to landscape orientation on your iPad or tap the Notes button at the top left.

Using copy and paste

After you enter content into a note, you may want to modify it. The Notes app includes essential editing tools you're familiar with from other word processors: Select, Copy, and Paste. You can use these to duplicate content, or to cut and paste it from one part of a note to another.

To use the Copy and Paste tools, follow these steps:

1. **With a note displayed, press and hold your finger on a word.**

   The selection toolbar, shown in Figure 2-5, appears.

Press and hold on a word to display this toolbar.

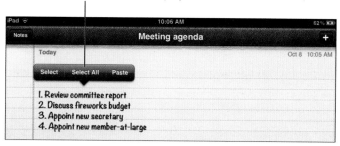

Figure 2-5: This toolbar provides selection and pasting tools.

2. **Tap the Select button.**

   The toolbar shown in Figure 2-6 appears.

Figure 2-6: After you select text, you can access the Copy command.

3. **If you want to modify the selection, you can tap either blue endpoint dot and drag it to the left or right.**

4. **Tap the Copy button.**

5. **Press and hold your finger in the document where you want to place the copied text.**

6. **On the toolbar that appears (see Figure 2-7), tap the Paste button.**

   The copied text appears.

Tap this button.

Figure 2-7: Use the press-and-hold method again to display the editing toolbar.

If you want to select all text in a note to either delete or copy it, tap the Select All button in the toolbar shown in Figure 2-5. All text is selected and the toolbar shown in Figure 2-6 appears again. Click a button to cut or copy the selected text.

To delete text, you can use the Select or Select All command and then press the Delete key on the onscreen keyboard.

Finding Notes

After you create a note, you'll need to find it if you want to view or edit it. You can scan the Notes List to find a note or use the Search tool. You can also use the Next and Previous buttons on the Notes pad to move among notes. The following sections help you find and move among notes you've created.

Displaying the Notes List

The Notes List contains all your notes listed chronologically by the last date/time you modified the note. This list isn't always available in every orientation, but it's the list you need in order to see the notes you have stored. If you're using landscape orientation, a list of notes appears by default on the left side of the screen. (Refer to Figure 2-2.)

If you're using portrait orientation, you can display this list by tapping the Notes button in the top-left corner of the screen; the Notes List appears, as shown in Figure 2-8. Tap any note in the list to display it.

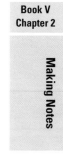

Tap this button...

to display the list of notes.

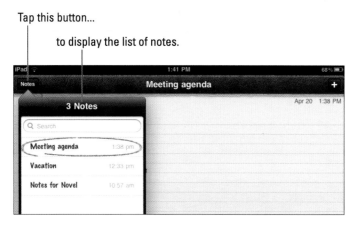

Figure 2-8: Tap the Notes button to display a list of saved notes.

Moving among notes

You have a couple of ways to move among notes you've created, and they're both simple:

1. **Tap the Notes app icon on the Home screen to open it.**

2. **With the Notes List displayed, tap a note to open it.**

   You can display the Notes List by either turning iPad to landscape orientation or tapping the Notes button in portrait orientation; see the preceding section for more on viewing the Notes List.

3. **Tap the Next button (the right-facing arrow) or Previous button (the left-facing arrow) on the bottom of the Notes pad, shown in Figure 2-9, to move among notes.**

Tap either of these buttons

Figure 2-9: The familiar Next and Previous buttons you've used in browsers make navigation easy.

Notes isn't a file-management pro; it allows you to enter multiple notes with the same title, which can cause confusion. Be advised, and name your notes uniquely!

Remember that Notes names your note using the first line of text. If you want to rename a note, first display the note, tap at the end of the first line of text, and then tap the Delete key on your onscreen keyboard to delete the old title. Enter a new title; it's reflected as the name of your note in the Notes List.

Searching notes

If you're not sure which note contains that very important item, you can search to locate a note that contains certain text. The Search feature lists only notes that contain your search criteria, however; it doesn't highlight and show you every instance of the word or words that you enter in a note.

The Spotlight Search feature in iPad also locates notes that match any search term you enter there, along with many other types of content. See Book I, Chapter 2, for more about the Search feature.

Follow this procedure to use the Notes Search feature:

1. **Tap the Notes app icon on the Home screen to open it.**

2. **Either hold the iPad in landscape orientation or tap the Notes button in portrait orientation to display the Notes List, as shown in Figure 2-10.**

Tap this button...

to display the list of notes.

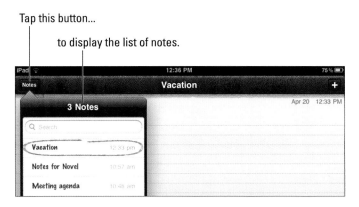

Figure 2-10: The Search feature is located on the Notes List.

3. **Tap in the Search field at the top of the Notes List (see Figure 2-11).**

The onscreen keyboard appears.

Tap here to display the onscreen keyboard.

Figure 2-11: Enter search terms using the onscreen keyboard or Keyboard Dock.

4. Begin to enter the search term.

All notes that contain matching words appear on the list, as shown in Figure 2-12.

Figure 2-12: The Search feature narrows the results by words that match your entry.

5. Tap a note to display it and then locate the instance of the matching word the old-fashioned way — by scanning through it.

If you want to look for a note based on how long ago you created or last modified it, it might help you to know that notes are stored with the most recently created or modified notes at the top of the Notes List. Older notes fall toward the bottom of the list. The day you last modified a note is also listed in the Notes List to help you out.

E-Mailing a Note

Today, it's all about sharing content. If you want to share what you wrote with a friend or colleague, or even access your note on your main computer to move it over into a word-processing program and flesh it out, you can easily e-mail the contents of a note by following these steps:

1. **With a note displayed, tap the Menu button on the bottom of the screen (see Figure 2-13).**

Tap this button.

Figure 2-13: Share your scribblings with others by e-mail.

2. **In the pop-up menu that appears, tap Mail.**

3. **In the e-mail form that appears (see Figure 2-14), type one or more e-mail addresses in the appropriate fields.**

   At least one e-mail address must appear in the To, Cc, or Bcc field.

Enter e-mail addresses here.

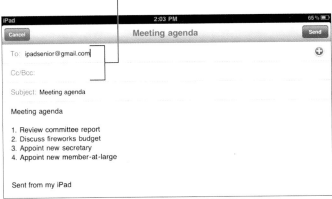

Figure 2-14: Enter addressees; use Bcc if you don't want that recipient to be visible to others.

4. **If you need to make changes to the subject or message, tap in either area and make the changes by using either the onscreen keyboard or the Dictation key (not available on the original iPad or iPad 2) to speak your changes.**

5. **Tap the Send button.**

   Your e-mail goes on its way.

You can tap the button with a plus sign (+) on it in the top-right corner of the e-mail message form to display your contacts list and choose recipients from there. This tip works only with contacts for which you've entered e-mail addresses. See Chapter 5 in this minibook for more about using the Contacts app.

 If you want to print a note in Step 2, tap Print rather than Mail. Complete the Printer Options dialog by designating an AirPrint-enabled wireless printer (or a shared printer on a network that you can access using AirPrint) and indicating how many copies to print; then tap Print.

To cancel an e-mail message and return to Notes without sending it, tap the Cancel button in the e-mail form and then tap Delete Draft on the menu that appears. To leave a message but save a draft so that you can finish and send it later, tap Cancel and then tap Save Draft. The next time you tap the Mail button with the same note displayed in Notes, your draft appears.

Deleting Notes

Over time, notes can accumulate, making it harder to find the note you need in the long list that displays. There's no sense in letting your Notes List get cluttered, or leaving old content around to confuse you. When you're done with a note, delete it. Follow these steps:

1. **Tap the Notes app icon on the Home screen to open it.**

2. **With the iPad in landscape orientation, tap a note in the Notes List to open it.**

3. **Tap the Trash Can button, shown in Figure 2-15.**

Tap this button.

Figure 2-15: With a note displayed, tap the Trash Can button to delete it.

4. **Tap the Delete Note button that appears (see Figure 2-16).**

The note is deleted.

Tap this button.

Figure 2-16: Go ahead; delete whatever you don't need with a tap of this button.

Notes is a nice little application, but it's limited. It offers no formatting tools, although you can change among three font options in Settings⇨Notes. You can't paste pictures into it. (Actually, you can, but what appears is the file-name, not the image.) So if you've made some notes and want to graduate to building a more robust document in a word processor, you have a couple of options. One way is to buy the Pages word-processor application for iPad, which costs $9.99, and copy your note (using the Copy and Paste feature discussed earlier in this chapter). Alternatively, you can send the note to yourself in an e-mail. Open the e-mail and copy and paste the text into a full-fledged word processor, and you're good to go.

If you want to move beyond Notes and use a note-taking app that lets you write with a stylus, check out PaperDesk for iPad ($3.99) or Penultimate ($.99) in the App Store. Both make drawing and writing handwritten notes easy and fun. Pogo Sketch and Pogo Stylus are two good stylus tools to check out (at www.tenonedesign.com).

Chapter 3: Keeping On Schedule with the Calendar and Clock Apps

In This Chapter

✔ Viewing your calendar

✔ Adding and repeating calendar events

✔ Working with, searching, and sharing calendars

✔ Deleting events

✔ Sharing calendars with other devices

✔ Using the Clock app

Most people have busy lives full of activities that aren't always easy to keep straight. You may need a way to keep on top of all those work-related and personal activities and appointments. The Calendar app on the iPad is a simple, elegant, electronic daybook that helps you do just that.

In addition to being able to enter events and view them by the day, week, month, or year, you can set up Calendar to provide alerts to remind you of your obligations, and you can search for events by keyword. You can also set up repeating events, such as the weekly staff meeting, a regular social get-together, or monthly flea treatments for your cat. And, given that you probably have calendars on your computer and mobile phone, you'll be happy to hear that you can sync your iPad calendar with them using iTunes or iCloud.

A preinstalled app that is new with iOS 6 is Clock. Though simple to use, Clock helps you view the time in multiple locations, set alarms, and use a timer and stopwatch.

In this chapter, I show you how to master simple procedures for getting around in your calendar, entering and editing events, setting up alerts, syncing, and searching. You also discover the simple ins and outs of using Clock.

Taking a Look at Your Calendar

You've probably used calendar apps in a slew of settings — in your e-mail client, on your cellphone, and even in robust contact management programs. The Calendar app on iPad is more robust than some and less robust than others, but it's quite a nicely designed and simple-to-use program that saves you the cost of buying one more app and it syncs with your computer and iCloud calendar. Calendar offers several ways to view your schedule, so the first step in mastering Calendar is to understand how to navigate those various views.

You get started by tapping the Calendar app icon on the Home screen to open it. Then tap one of the top buttons to change the view. The choices are described in this list:

✔ **Day:** This view, shown landscape orientation in Figure 3-1, displays your daily appointments and a small monthly calendar on the left page, along with an hourly breakdown of the day on the right page. In portrait orientation, the two pages are narrower.

Calendar for the month

List of today's appointments   Hourly breakdown of the day

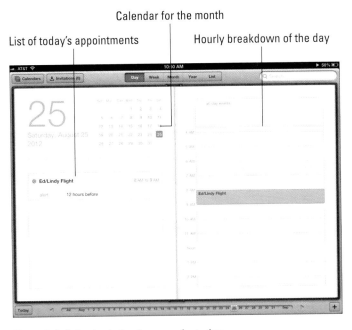

Figure 3-1: Calendar in landscape orientation.

- ✔ **Week:** Use Week view to see all your events for the current week, as shown in Figure 3-2. In this view, appointments appear in their scheduled time slots on the grid.

Week button

Figure 3-2: Tap another week in the row beneath the weekly calendar to jump there.

- ✔ **Month:** See one month at a time and switch among months in Month view. (See Figure 3-3.) In this view, you see the name and timing of each event. In this view, days that have scheduled events display the color of the calendar associated with the event.
- ✔ **Year:** Tap the Year button to see an entire year of commitments, as shown in Figure 3-4.

Month button

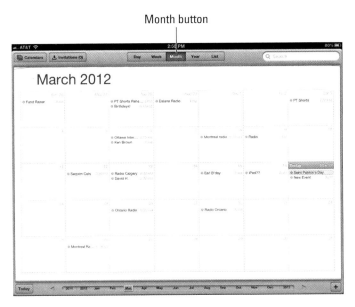

Figure 3-3: Tap a month name along the bottom of the screen to jump to another month.

Year button

Figure 3-4: If you want an overview of your year, this is the view for you.

✔ **List:** List view displays your daily calendar with a list of all commitments for the month to the left of it, as shown in Figure 3-5.

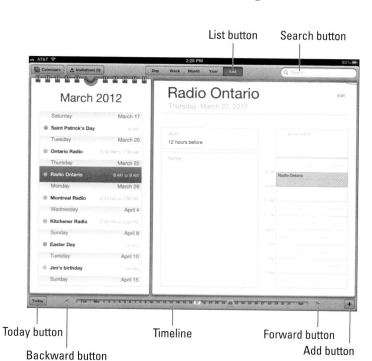

List button   Search button

Today button   Timeline   Forward button

Backward button   Add button

Figure 3-5: List view shows today and all the days containing events in the month ahead.

To move from one day, week, month, or year to another, use the *Timeline,* displayed along the bottom of every view. Tap a day to move to it, or tap the Forward or Backward button to move forward or backward one increment at a time: a day at a time in Day view, a week at a time in Week view, to the next scheduled event in List view, and so on.

To jump back to today, tap the Today button in the bottom-left corner of Calendar. And now you know the basics about views in Calendar!

For the feel of a paper calendar book, rotate the screen to landscape orientation in the Calendar app. This orientation provides a nice, booklike experience, especially in Day view.

If you're looking for a more robust scheduling app, consider buying Pocket Informant HD for $14.99. This app is easy to use and has helpful scheduling tools for your tasks. You can also sync information you save in the app by using Google Calendar. Also, if you want to use a calendar program for business, check out Shifty, a work-shift management app that has tools that can be quite useful to managers and supervisors.

Adding Calendar Events

Events in your life might range from business meetings to karaoke dates, but whatever the nature of your appointments, Calendar can help you keep them all straight. You can enter single events or repeating events and include alerts to remind you that they're coming up.

Adding one event at a time

If you've used other calendar programs, you know that adding events is usually a simple procedure. You can easily add events to iPad's Calendar app, but if you haven't used a touchscreen computer or smartphone, it's worth a walk-through.

Follow these steps to add an event to your calendar:

1. **With Calendar open in any view, tap the Add button to add an event.**

   The Add Event dialog, shown in Figure 3-6, appears.

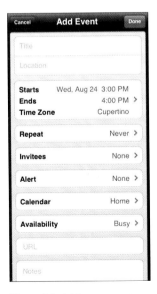

Figure 3-6: Add your event details in this dialog.

2. **Enter a title for the event and, if you want, a location.**

3. **Tap the Starts/Ends field.**

   The Start & End dialog, shown in Figure 3-7, displays.

Figure 3-7: Use this cool slot machine–like interface to set up event timing details.

4. **Place your finger on the date, hour, minute, or AM/PM column, and flick your finger to scroll up or down.**

5. **(Optional) To change the time zone, tap that field, begin to enter a new location, and then tap the location in the suggestions that appear.**

   Note that, if the event lasts all day, you can simply tap the All-day On/Off button and forget setting starting and ending times.

6. **(Optional) To add notes, use your finger to scroll down in the Add Event dialog and tap in the Notes field.**

7. **After all items are set correctly, tap Done.**

Note that you can edit any event at any time by simply tapping it in any view of your calendar. The Edit dialog appears, offering the same settings as the Add Event dialog (refer to Figure 3-6). Just tap the Done button in this dialog to save your changes.

Adding events with Siri

Siri, the personal assistant feature available on the third- and fourth-generation iPad and iPad mini with iOS 6.0, offers a hands-free way to schedule events. You have several variables to how you can schedule an event with Siri, because the feature is pretty flexible. For example, you can say, "Create event" and then Siri asks you first for a date and then for a time. Or you can say, "I have a meeting with John on April 1st" and Siri might respond by saying, "I don't find a meeting with John on April 1st; shall I create it?" Then you can say, "Yes" to have Siri create it, asking you for more details like the time and place.

Follow these steps to have Siri schedule an event for you:

1. **Press and hold the Home button.**

2. **Say "Create meeting October 3rd at 2:30 p.m."**

3. **When Siri asks you whether you are ready to schedule the event, say "Yes."**

You can also use Siri to delete events, change details about an event, or remind you about an event. Siri recognizes holidays so that you can say, "Schedule a family dinner on Christmas" and she'll know what you mean. Play around with Siri; it's a lot of fun!

Creating repeating events

Many events in your life probably happen regularly: that Tuesday evening book club, the monthly sales meeting, or your company's yearly audit, for example. You can use the Repeating Events feature of the Calendar app to set repeating events.

Follow these steps to create a repeating event:

1. **With any view displayed in the Calendar app, tap the Add button to add an event.**

   The Add Event dialog (refer to Figure 3-6) appears.

2. **Enter a title and location for the event, and set the start and end dates and times (see the preceding section).**

3. **Tap the Repeat field.**

   The Repeat Event dialog, shown in Figure 3-8, appears.

4. **Tap a preset time interval: Every Day, Week, 2 Weeks, Month, or Year.**

Figure 3-8: You have to use preset intervals, but you can choose from several.

5. **Tap Done.**

   You return to the Add Event dialog.

6. **Tap Done again to save your repeating event.**

Other calendar programs might give you more control over repeating events; for example, you might be able to make a setting to repeat an event every Tuesday or the first and third Sunday of the month. If you want a more robust calendar feature, consider setting up your appointments in iCal or Outlook and syncing them to iPad. But, if you want to create a simple repeating event in iPad's Calendar app, simply add the first event on a Tuesday and make it repeat every week.

If you have an iCloud or Gmail account, your iPad recognizes and supports all calendars you've compiled there as well as those you've synced and the iPad calendar.

Adding alerts

Once upon a time, helpful assistants placed printed paper schedules of the day's activities in front of their bosses to remind them of scheduled commitments. Today, I'm not sure anybody but the highest-paid CEOs get this type of service. Instead, most people set up alerts in calendar programs to remind them where to be, and when.

Luckily, in the iPad Calendar app, you can easily set up alerts by following these steps:

1. **Tap the Settings icon on the Home screen, tap General, and then tap Sounds.**

2. **Tap Calendar Alerts and then tap any alert tone, which plays the tone for you.**

3. **After you choose a tone, tap Sounds to return to the Sounds settings.**

4. **Tap the Home button and then tap Calendar.**

5. **Create an event in your calendar or open an existing one for editing (see the preceding sections).**

6. **In the Add Event dialog or Edit dialog for an existing event (refer to Figure 3-6), tap the Alert field.**

   The Event Alert dialog appears, as shown in Figure 3-9. Note that if you want two alerts — say, one per day before and one an hour before — you can repeat this procedure using Second Alert instead.

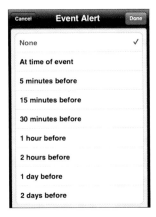

Figure 3-9: Use these preset
intervals to set up alerts.

7. **Tap any preset interval, from 5 Minutes Before to 2 Days Before or at the time of an event.**

   Remember that you can scroll down in the dialog to see more options.

8. **Tap Done to save the alert and then tap Done in the Add Event dialog to save all settings.**

9. **Tap the Day button to display the date of your event in Day view.**

   Note that the alert and time frame are listed under the event in that view, as shown in Figure 3-10.

If you're on the road and change time zones, iPad may not recognize the local time, which can cause your alerts to become useless. To avoid this problem, you can adjust the time of your iPad manually by using the Date & Time feature in the General category in Settings.

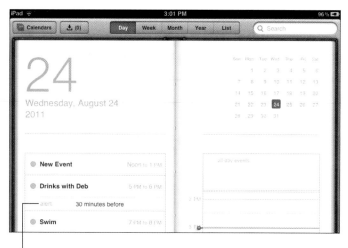

An event's alert and timeframe

Figure 3-10: An alert is noted along with the appointment in your calendar.

If you work for an organization that uses a Microsoft Exchange account, you can set up your iPad to receive and respond to invitations from colleagues. When somebody sends an invitation that you accept, it appears on your calendar. Check with your company network administrator (who will jump at the chance to get her hands on your iPad) or the *iPad User Guide* to set up this feature if having this capability sounds useful to you. Alternatively, you can check into iCloud, which does much the same thing, minus the IT person.

Working with Your Events

After you have entered some events in Calendar, you can use features to search for events, sync your events with other calendars on other devices, or delete events that have been canceled.

In this section, you work with the various events on your calendar to keep things up to date and organized.

Searching calendars

Displaying events by day or week and scrolling the pages is one way to look for appointments, but if you need to view a particular event and can't remember its time frame, you can use the Calendar Search feature to find it.

Don't forget that you can also search for events in your calendar by speaking a command to Siri or searching with the Spotlight Search feature.

Follow these steps to search for events in Calendar:

1. **With Calendar open in any view, tap the Search field (refer to Figure 3-5) in the top-right corner.**

   The onscreen keyboard appears.

2. **Type a word or words to search by and then tap the Search key on the onscreen keyboard.**

   As you type, the Results dialog appears, as shown in Figure 3-11.

Figure 3-11: Every instance of an event that includes your search term displays.

3. **Tap any result to display it in the view you were in when you started the search.**

   The Edit dialog appears, and you can edit the event, if you want.

Working with multiple calendars

You can choose a calendar — for example, Business, Personal, Parties, Classes, and Volunteering — for every event. If you're synchronizing your calendars with your Mac or PC or by using iCloud, Google, Microsoft Outlook, or AOL, each source can have its own calendar. On your iPad, tap Calendars at the top-left of the screen in the Calendar app. Every calendar's events appear in a different color.

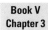

You can choose to display the events from several calendars at one time, including your iPad calendar and calendars you sync with from your PC or Mac, only your PC calendars, only your Mac calendar, or only your iPad calendar. With the Calendar app open, tap the Calendars button, and in the Calendars dialog, tap to select or deselect the calendars you want to display: All from My <Account>, Birthday Calendar, My Calendar, or US Holidays. If you have synced to calendars from other sources, you can choose them by tapping them to select or deselect them; for example, tap All iCloud to show all your iCloud-synced calendars. Tap Done, and your chosen calendar displays. When you add a new event, use the Calendar field to choose the calendar you want to add the event to.

If you've created lots of events, you might want to tap Hide All Calendars in the Calendar app and then tap the one or two calendars you need to see now so that you can quickly find their events.

Subscribing To and Sharing Calendars

If you use a calendar available from an online service, such as Yahoo! or Google, you can subscribe to that calendar to read events that are saved in it on your iPad. Note that you can only read, not edit, these events. To subscribe, follow these steps:

1. **Tap the Settings icon on the Home screen.**

2. **Tap the Mail, Contacts, Calendars option on the left.**

3. **Tap Add Account.**

   The Add Account options, shown in Figure 3-12, appear.

Figure 3-12: Choose accounts with calendars to copy to iPad.

4. **Tap an e-mail choice, such as Gmail or Yahoo!.**

5. **In the dialog that appears (see Figure 3-13), enter your name, e-mail address, and e-mail account password.**

Name	Helen Marks
Address	ipadsenior@gmail.com
Password	●●●●●●●●
Description	ipadsenior@gmail.com

Figure 3-13: Enter your calendar account information.

6. **Tap Save.**

   iPad verifies your address.

7. **Your iPad retrieves data from your calendar at the interval you have specified, so to review these settings, tap the Fetch New Data option in the Mail, Contacts, Calendars pane.**

8. **In the Fetch New Data pane that appears (see Figure 3-14), be sure that the Push option's On/Off button reads *On* and then choose the frequency option you prefer your iPad to use for querying the server for new data.**

   More frequent pushing of data can use battery power and incur data charges on a 3G/4G connection.

If you store your contacts' birthdays in the Contacts app, the Calendar app displays each one when the day arrives so that you don't forget to pass on your congratulations!

You can also have calendar events shared with your iPad if you use a push service such as iCloud. The service can sync calendars from multiple e-mail accounts with your iPad calendar. Keep in mind that if you choose to have data pushed to your iPad, your battery may drain faster.

Make sure this is set to On.

Figure 3-14: Choose how often you want data pushed to your iPad.

Deleting Events

Face it: Things change. When that scheduled luncheon or meeting is canceled, you may want to delete the appointment in Calendar. Here's how:

1. **With Calendar open, tap an event.**

   The information bar appears. (See Figure 3-15.)

Tap this button.

Figure 3-15: Tap an event, and use the Edit button to make changes to it.

2. **Tap the Edit button.**

3. **In the Edit dialog, tap the Delete Event button, shown in Figure 3-16.**

   Confirming options appear.

4. **If this is a repeating event, you can delete either this instance of the event or this and all future instances of the event (see Figure 3-17). Tap the button of the option you prefer.**

   The event is deleted, and you return to Calendar view.

Tap this button.

Figure 3-16: Get rid of an event you no longer need by tapping Delete Event.

If an event is moved but not canceled, you don't have to delete the existing one and create a new one; simply edit the event to change the date and time in the Edit dialog.

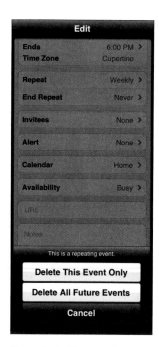

Figure 3-17: Choose whether to delete one instance or all instances of a repeating event.

Syncing with Calendars on Other Devices

Many people now have several computing devices they use to keep track of events. Now that you have an iPad as well, you don't want to have to enter and edit events one by one on it, your mobile phone, your desktop computer, and your laptop computer, right? That's where syncing comes in handy.

If you use a calendar, such as Microsoft Outlook or Apple Calendar or iCal (depending upon your version of OS X), on your main computer, you can sync that calendar to your iPad calendar via iCloud or iTunes. To use iTunes, change the iPad settings in iTunes to manage sync settings when your iPad is connected via the Lightning to USB Cable (Dock Connector to USB Cable for non–fourth-generation iPads) or wirelessly using the iTunes Wi-Fi Sync setting.

To make calendars in your other accounts available to your iPad, you subscribe to and share the calendars first. If you haven't done this, see the "Subscribing To and Sharing Calendars" section, earlier in this chapter, before proceeding.

Time to sync your calendars. Follow these steps to sync Calendar information using iTunes:

1. **Open iTunes and sign in.**

2. **Connect your iPad using the Lightning to USB Cable (Dock Connector
   to USB Cable for non–fourth-generation iPads), or choose
   Settings⇨General⇨iTunes Wi-Fi Sync and tap Sync.**

3. **When your iPad appears in the Source List on the left side of the
   screen, click it.**

4. **Click the Info tab, shown in Figure 3-18, and select the Sync iCal
   Calendars check box.**

Select this check box·

Figure 3-18: The iTunes Info tab.

5. **To sync all calendars, click the All Calendars option.**

   If you don't want older appointments to be synced, select the Do Not
   Sync Events Older Than *XX* Days check box and set the number of days.
   (It's 30 days by default.)

6. **To sync only selected calendars, click the Selected Calendars option
   and choose the calendars with which you want to sync.**

7. **Click Apply.**

8. **Click the Sync button.**

   Your Calendar settings are shared between your computer and iPad (in both directions).

Find out more about working with iTunes to manage your iPad content in Book I, Chapter 5.

iCloud syncs your calendars automatically on all your devices without your having to place the devices in Docks and sync them using a computer. For more about iCloud, see Book I, Chapter 5.

Using Clock

With iOS 6 comes the Clock app on the iPad. Using Clock, you can view the time anywhere in the world, set up alarms for certain times, and even use the timer and stopwatch features of Clock to keep track of the timing of events.

Displaying Clock

Tap the Clock app to open it. Preset clocks are displayed along the top, and the location of these clocks on the world map are displayed below. To see more views in Clock, follow these steps:

1. **Tap a clock along the top of the screen to display it full screen (see Figure 3-19).**

2. **Tap World Clock to return to the Clock World Clock screen.**

   If the World Clock button isn't visible, tap the screen once and it appears.

Figure 3-19: Clock lets you enlarge the display.

Cities that are in time zones currently in nighttime are displayed in black. Clock for cities that are currently in daytime are displayed in white.

Adding or deleting a clock

You can add a clock for many locations around the world (but not everywhere). You can also get rid of a clock when you no longer need it (especially useful for those who travel around different time zones frequently).

To add a clock, follow these steps:

1. **With Clock displayed, tap Add on the clock on the far right.**

2. **Tap a city on the list, or tap a letter on the right side to display locations that begin with that letter.**

   The clock appears in the last slot on the right, and the location is displayed on the world map.

To delete a clock, follow these steps:

1. **To remove a location, tap the Edit button in the upper-left corner of the World Clock screen.**

2. **Tap the minus symbol next to a location and then tap Delete; see Figure 3-20.**

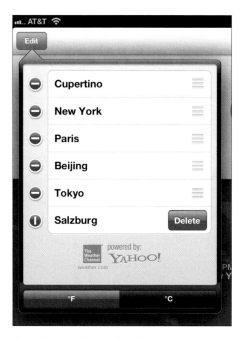

Figure 3-20: Delete a city when you no longer need to know its time.

Setting an alarm

Want to make sure that you're on time for that big meeting or date? Use the Alarm feature in the Clock app and make sure that you have your iPad near at hand.

Follow these steps to set an alarm:

1. **With the Clock app displayed, tap the Alarm tab.**

2. **Tap the Add button.**

3. **In the Add Alarm dialog, shown in Figure 3-21, take any of the following actions, tapping Back after you make each setting to return to the Add Alarm dialog:**

   - Tap *Repeat* if you want the alarm to repeat at a regular interval such as every Monday or every Sunday.

   - Tap *Sound* to choose the tone the alarm will play.

   - Tap the *On/Off button* for Snooze if you want to use the Snooze feature.

   - Tap *Label* if you want to give the alarm a name such as "Take Pill" or "Call Mom."

Figure 3-21: Alarms keep you from missing important events.

To delete an alarm, tap the Alarm tab and tap Edit. All alarms appear. Tap the red circle with a minus in it, and then tap the Delete button.

Using Stopwatch and Timer

Sometimes life seems like a countdown or a ticking clock counting up the minutes you've spent on a certain activity. You can use the Stopwatch tab of the Clock app to time the length of an activity such as a walk. Use the Timer feature to do a countdown to a specific time such as the moment when your chocolate chip cookies are done baking.

These two work very similarly: Tap the Stopwatch or Timer tab and tap the Start button. When you set the Timer, iPad uses a sound to notify you when time's up. When you start the Stopwatch, you have to tap the Stop button when the activity is done (see Figure 3-22).

Note that you can use the Lap feature with Stopwatch to time a quick series of events within a larger event, such as timing each of ten laps in a swimming race and getting a total time at the end of the race. Just tap the lap button while recording time to tally one lap and move on to the other. Tap Stop when all laps are complete.

Figure 3-22: Time your next walk to work using the Stopwatch feature.

Chapter 4: Working with Reminders and Notifications

In This Chapter

✔ Adding a new task in Reminders

✔ Editing a task

✔ Scheduling a reminder

✔ Displaying reminders in a list or by date

✔ Making a new list

✔ Syncing with other devices and calendars

✔ Completing or deleting a reminder

✔ Setting notification types

✔ Reviewing alerts and reminders in Notification Center

✔ Jumping from Notification Center to an app

✔ Getting rid of old notifications

✔ Using Do Not Disturb

*W*ith the arrival of iOS 5, the Reminders app and the Notification Center feature appeared, warming the hearts of iPad owners who need help remembering the details of their lives.

Reminders is a kind of to-do list that lets you create tasks and set reminders so that you don't forget them. Notifications let you review all elements you should be aware of in one place, such as new mail messages, text messages, calendar appointments, reminders, and alerts.

If you occasionally need to escape all your obligations, try the Do Not Disturb feature, new with iOS 6. Turn this feature on and you won't be bothered with alerts till you turn it off again.

In this chapter, I tell you how to set up and view tasks in Reminders, and I explain how Notification Center can centralize all your alerts in one easy-to-find place.

Creating a Task in Reminders

Reminders help you stay on schedule, avoid embarrassing missed appointments, and stay on track of your hundreds of errands each and every day. Creating a task in Reminders is pretty darn simple.

Note that when you first begin to use Reminders, you'll have only the Reminders list to add tasks to. However, you can create your own categories of reminder lists; see the "Creating a List" section later in this chapter to find out how to do this.

To create a reminder, follow these steps:

1. **Tap Reminders on the Home screen.**

2. **On the screen that appears (see Figure 4-1), tap the plus sign (+) to add a task.**

   The onscreen keyboard appears.

Tap to create a new task.

Reminders

	!! Radio program
	3/20/12, 11:00 AM
	Dentist
	3/26/12, 1:00 PM
	Vet with Mindy
	3/22/12, 11:20 AM
	Lunch with Ed
	3/20/12, 11:05 AM
	Call Earl
	7/22/12, 3:00 PM
	Appointment with John

Figure 4-1: Tap to add reminder tasks.

3. **Enter a task name or description using the onscreen keyboard and tap the Return button.**

   The new task is added to the Reminders list.

You can create reminders using Siri. Just press and hold the Home button till Siri asks what you need to do, and then say something like "Create a reminder to call Mom this Thursday at noon." Siri displays the reminder and asks you to confirm if you want to create it. Just say "Yes" and it's done.

You can't add details about a task when you create it, only a descriptive name. To add details about timing and so forth, see the next task.

Editing Task Details

What's a task without the details? For example, try to remember the task *Pick up Grammy Award* without having a few notes to specify when and where and what you should wear. Reminder tasks get you where you need to be when you need to be there.

To edit a task and add details, follow these steps:

1. **Tap a task to open the Details dialog.**

2. **To see all available options, tap Show More to display the choices shown in Figure 4-2.**

   I describe reminder settings in the next section.

Figure 4-2: Add the information you need about a particular event in this dialog.

3. **Tap Priority.**

4. **Choose None, Low, Medium, or High from the choices that appear.**

5. **Tap Done.**

6. **Tap List and then, from the options that display (see Figure 4-3), select a list to put your task on.**

7. **Tap Done.**

8. **Tap Notes.**

9. **Using the onscreen keyboard, enter a note about the task.**

10. **Tap Done when you're finished entering details.**

Figure 4-3: Your event can be viewed in either Calendar or the Reminders app.

As of this writing, the Notes priority settings don't do much of anything, such as set a flag of any kind on a task in a list or reorder tasks to show priority tasks first. You can see the priority of a task only by displaying its details.

Scheduling a Reminder

A major feature of Reminders, given its name, is to remind you of upcoming tasks. After you've saved a task, you can set a reminder for it.

To set a reminder, follow these steps:

1. **Tap a task.**

2. **In the dialog that appears, tap Remind Me on a Day to turn the feature on.**

   Another dialog appears.

3. **Tap the On/Off field for the On a Day field to turn it on.**

4. **Tap the date that appears below this setting to display the date and time, as shown in Figure 4-4.**

5. **Tap and flick the Day, Hour, and Minutes fields to scroll to the date and time for the reminder.**

6. **Tap the Done button.**

   The settings for the reminder are saved.

If you want a task to repeat with associated reminders, tap the Repeat field, and from the Details dialog that appears, tap Every Day, Week, 2 Weeks, Month, or Year (for annual meetings or fun-filled holiday get-togethers with the gang). Tap Done twice to save the setting.

Figure 4-4: Scroll to set the date and the time of your event.

If you want a reminder sent not on a particular day but when you arrive at a particular location, you can choose At a Location in Step 2 and then choose a location and either When I Leave or When I Arrive. This feature is available only with 3G/4G models of iPad, and you have to have an iCloud account set up and Reminders turned on in the iCloud Settings of iPad.

You can scroll the monthly calendar display to show months in the past or future by tapping the forward or backward arrows, and tap any date to show its tasks in the daily list on the right.

Creating a List

You can create your own lists of tasks to help you organize different parts of your life. To do so, follow these steps:

1. **Tap Reminders on the Home screen.**

   Reminders opens.

2. **Tap Create New List (see Figure 4-5) and enter the name of the list using the onscreen keyboard.**

3. **Tap Done on the keyboard.**

   You return to the Edit dialog.

If you tap the list name in List view now, a new, blank sheet appears on the right with the title you entered in Step 2. Tap the plus sign (+) to add new tasks to the list, as shown in Figure 4-6.

Tap to create a new list

Figure 4-5: Lists might include reminders for personal or work-related events.

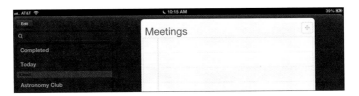

Figure 4-6: Keep creating tasks using the + button.

Syncing with Other Devices and Calendars

You can determine which tasks are transferred or pushed to your device from other devices or calendars such as Outlook in Windows or Calendar/ iCal on a Mac. To make all the settings in this task work correctly, first set up your default calendar and then set up your iCloud account under Accounts in the Mail, Contacts, Calendar settings.

After you've made these settings, follow these steps to sync with other devices and calendars:

1. **Tap the Settings button on the Home screen.**

2. **Tap iCloud.**

3. **Be sure that in the right pane Reminders is set to On.**

4. **Make sure that Calendars is also set to On in the right pane (see Figure 4-7).**

5. **Tap Mail, Contacts, Calendars in the Settings pane and scroll down to the Calendars category of settings.**

6. **Tap the Sync field and then choose how far back to sync reminders (see Figure 4-8).**

Make sure these are set to On.

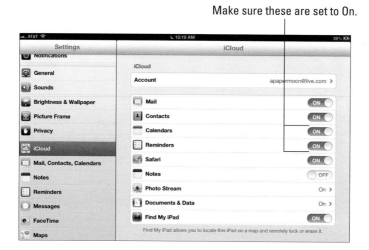

Figure 4-7: Make settings to control what information is shared with your iPad via iCloud.

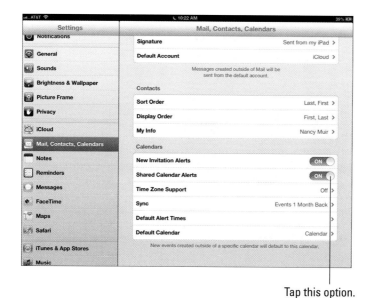

Tap this option.

Figure 4-8: If you don't need all reminders, sync to a specific period.

Marking as Complete or Deleting a Reminder

Are you making progress in checking tasks off your list? You may want to mark a task as completed, or delete it entirely so you don't continue to get notifications about it or to give yourself a feeling of accomplishment. Here's how:

1. **With Reminders open, tap a task.**

   The Details dialog, shown in Figure 4-9, displays.

2. **Tap Delete.**

   You're asked to confirm the deletion.

3. **Tap Delete again.**

4. **To mark a task as complete, tap in the check box to the left of the task in List view and then tap the Completed category.**

   The task moves to Completed and is removed from its previous category.

Figure 4-9: The Details dialog contains a handy Delete button to get rid of a reminder.

Setting Notification Types

Notification Center is a list of various alerts and appointments you can display by swiping down from the top of any iPad screen. Notification Center is on by default, but you can change certain settings to control which types of notifications are displayed.

Follow these steps to set notification types:

1. **Tap Settings.**

2. **Tap Notifications.**

   In the settings that appear (see Figure 4-10), you see a list of items included in Notification Center and a list of items not included. For example, Messages and Reminders may be included, but alerts in game apps may not.

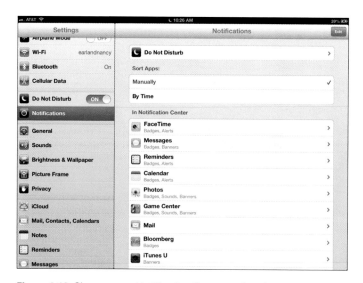

Figure 4-10: Choose your Notification Center options here.

3. **Tap any item.**

   Notification settings appear for that app, as shown in Figure 4-11.

4. **Tap the On/Off button to include or exclude that item from Notification Center.**

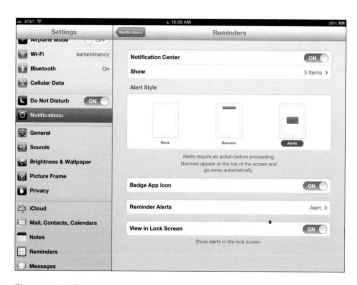

Figure 4-11: Control each item you want to include in Notification Center in this pane.

5. **Choose how to be notified:**

- *Alert Style:* No alert or banner appears.

- *Banners:* A banner appears and then disappears automatically.

- *Alerts:* You have to take an action to dismiss the alert when it appears.

- *Badge App Icon:* Places a red circle and a number on icons on your Home screens to represent alerts associated with those apps.

- *View in Lock Screen:* Turn on this setting if you want to be able to view alerts when the Lock Screen is displayed.

6. **When you've finished making settings for an individual app, tap the Notifications button to return to the Notifications settings or tap the Home button.**

Viewing Notification Center

After you specify which alerts and reminders should appear in Notification Center, you can review them regularly to keep yourself on track.

To view notifications, follow these steps:

1. **From any screen, tap the black Status bar on top and drag down to display Notification Center (see Figure 4-12).**

Note that items are divided into lists by type, such as reminders, Calendar items, and Mail.

Figure 4-12: Notification Center is a convenient one-stop location for all your commitments and reminders.

2. To close Notification Center, tap the three lines in the bottom-center of Notification Center and drag up, toward the Status bar.

To determine which alerts and reminders display in Notification Center, see the preceding task.

Going to an App from Notification Center

To jump easily from Notification Center to any app that causes an alert or reminder to be displayed, follow these steps:

1. Tap the Status bar and drag down.

Notification Center displays.

2. Tap any item.

The item opens in its originating app.

If you've tapped an e-mail message, you can reply to the message by using the procedures described in Book I, Chapter 7.

Clearing Notifications

Who needs notifications of past events? To get rid of old notifications for an app, follow these steps:

1. Tap the Status bar and drag down to display Notification Center.

2. Tap the pale gray X to the right of a category of notifications, such as Mail.

The button changes to read *Clear* (see Figure 4-13).

3. Tap the Clear button.

All items for that category are removed.

Tap this option.

Figure 4-13: Wipe your notification slate clean periodically!

If you change your mind about clearing all items in a group after you tap the Clear button, just close Notification Center. Remember that any new reminders from then on will populate your Notification Center again. To stop notifications entirely, go to Settings, tap Notifications, and then tap and turn off any app you don't want to get notifications from, such as Messages or Reminders.

Get Some Rest with Do Not Disturb

 Do Not Disturb is a simple but useful setting you can use to stop any alerts and FaceTime calls from making a sound or being displayed. You can make settings to allow calls from certain people to get through, or to allow several repeat calls from the same person in a short time period to come through. (Apple has assumed in designing this app that such repeat calls may signal an emergency situation or urgent need to get through to you.)

To set up Do Not Disturb, follow these steps:

1. **Tap Settings.**

2. **Tap Do Not Disturb to turn the feature on.**

3. **Tap Notifications and then tap Do Not Disturb.**

4. **In the settings shown in Figure 4-14, do any of the following:**

   • *Tap Scheduled* to allow alerts you scheduled using the Reminder app to be displayed.

   • *Tap Allow Calls From* and then select Everyone, No One, Favorites, or All Contacts from the next screen.

   • *Tap Repeated Calls* to allow a second call over FaceTime in a three-minute time period to come through.

5. **Tap the Home button to return to the Home screen.**

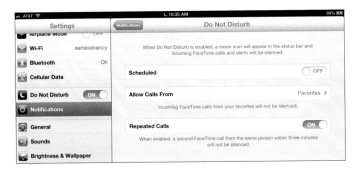

Figure 4-14: Manage how Do Not Disturb operates from here.

Chapter 5: Managing Contacts

In This Chapter

- ✔ Adding contacts
- ✔ Syncing contacts with iCloud
- ✔ Adding social media info
- ✔ Specifying related people
- ✔ Adding a ringtone and photo to a contact
- ✔ Sharing contacts
- ✔ Using Maps to view a contact's location
- ✔ Deleting a contact

*C*ontacts is the iPad equivalent of the address book on your cellphone. In fact, if you own an iPhone, it's similar to your Contacts app. The Contacts app on iPad is simple to set up and use, and it has some powerful little features beyond simply storing names, addresses, and phone numbers.

For example, you can pinpoint a contact's address in the iPad Maps application. You can use your contacts to quickly address e-mails, messages, and tweets. If you store a contact record that includes a website, you can use a link in Contacts to view that website instantly. And, of course, you can easily search for a contact by a variety of criteria, including people related to you by family ties or mutual friends.

In this chapter, you discover the various features of Contacts, including how to save yourself time by syncing your e-mail contacts lists to your iPad instantly.

Populating Your Contacts with Information

The Contacts app's sole purpose is to store contact information and make it available to you, but first you have to make that information available to it. You can do it by manually adding records one at a time or by syncing via iTunes or pushing your contacts to other devices via iCloud to transfer your contacts instantly.

Adding contacts

You can, of course, enter your contacts the old-fashioned way, by typing their names, addresses, phone numbers, and other information in a contact form.

Follow these steps to create a new contact record:

1. **Tap the Contacts app icon on the Home screen to open the application.**

   If you haven't yet entered a contact, you see a blank address book with the Add button at the bottom, as shown in Figure 5-1.

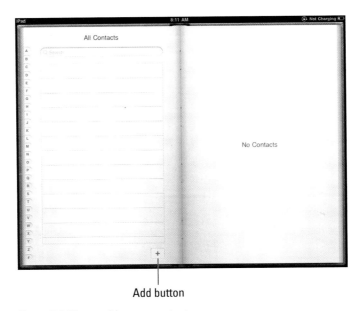

Add button

Figure 5-1: Tap to add a new contact.

2. **Tap the Add button (the button with a small plus sign on it).**

   A blank Info page opens, and the onscreen keyboard displays, as you can see in Figure 5-2.

3. **Enter some contact information.**

   Enter a first name in the First field, for example. To create a contact, only a first name, last name, or company name is required.

Figure 5-2: Enter as much information about your contact as you want.

To scroll down the contact page and see more fields, flick up on the page with your finger.

If you're entering a phone number that requires a pause, such as when you access an outside line from your workplace, insert a comma into the number at the spot where the pause must occur. If you sync this contact information to your phone via iTunes, it's then set up to dial correctly.

4. **(Optional) To add a mailing or street address, tap Add New Address, which opens additional entry fields.**

5. **(Optional) To add another information field such as Nickname or Job Title, tap Add Field. In the Add Field dialog that appears (see Figure 5-3), choose a field to add.**

You may have to flick your finger upward to view all available fields.

If your contact's name is difficult for you to pronounce, add the Phonetic First Name (or Phonetic Last Name) field to that person's record.

6. **Tap the Done button when you finish making entries.**

The new contact appears in your address book. Figure 5-4 shows an address book with several entries added.

If you've set up a *Lightweight Directory Access Protocol* (LDAP) account on iPad to connect with your organization's directory service, you may able to access its directories via Contacts. See Book III, Chapter 1, for more about setting up an LDAP account.

Figure 5-3: Round out a contact's information by adding information fields.

Figure 5-4: A list of contacts, arranged alphabetically.

Syncing contacts with iCloud

You can use your iCloud account to sync contacts from your iPad to iCloud to back them up. These also become available to your iCloud e-mail account, if you set one up. Follow these steps to sync your contacts:

1. **Tap Settings on the Home screen and then tap iCloud.**

2. **In the iCloud settings shown in Figure 5-5, tap Contacts to sync contacts.**

Figure 5-5: Choose what to sync through iCloud here.

3. **Tap Merge (see Figure 5-6) to merge your iPad Contacts contents with iCloud.**

Figure 5-6: Merge your iPad Contacts contents with iCloud.

You can use iTunes to automatically sync contacts among all your Apple devices and even a Windows PC. See Book I, Chapter 5, for more about making iTunes settings to specify how your contacts are synced in iTunes.

Assigning a Photo to a Contact

It's always helpful to associate a face with a name. In Contacts, you can do just that by adding a person's photo to his contact record. You can add photos from various sources, such as

- ✓ The Photos app albums you have saved from websites
- ✓ Digital cameras
- ✓ E-mail attachments
- ✓ iPad's camera
- ✓ Photo collections stored on your computer or in iCloud (see Book II, Chapter 6, for more about working with the Photos app)

Follow these steps to add a stored photo to a contact record:

1. **With Contacts open, tap the contact to whose record you want to add a photo.**

2. **Tap the Edit button.**

3. **On the Info page that appears (see Figure 5-7), tap Add Photo.**

Tap here...   then select a photo option.

Figure 5-7: Choose the location of the photo you want to include.

4. **Tap Choose Photo.**

5. **In the Photo Albums dialog that appears, tap Camera Roll (Saved Photos on the original iPad) or Photo Stream, Photo library, or any photo album you might have created yourself, depending on where the photo is stored.**

   You can also choose Take Photo to take that contact's photo on the spot, if you have iPad 2 or later.

A *saved* photo is one that you've downloaded to your iPad or taken using the Screen Capture feature or an iPad 2 or later camera; the Photo library contains photos synced from your computer.

6. **In the photo album that appears, tap a photo to select it.**

   The Choose Photo dialog, shown in Figure 5-8, appears. If you want to modify the photo, move the image around in the frame with your finger, or shrink or expand it by pinching your fingers inward or outward, respectively.

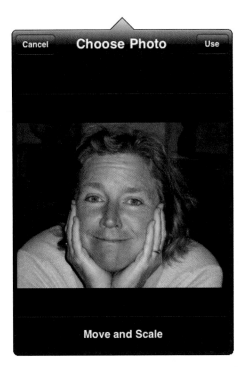

Figure 5-8: Select or edit the photo you want to include.

7. **Tap the Use button to use the photo for this contact.**

   The photo appears on the contact's Info page, as shown in Figure 5-9.

8. **Tap Done to save changes to the contact.**

To edit a photo you've added to a contact record, simply display the contact information and tap it. Choose Edit Photo from the menu that appears, and then, in the dialog that appears (refer to Figure 5-8), use the described gestures for moving and scaling the image with your fingers. Tap Use when you're done to save the changed figure.

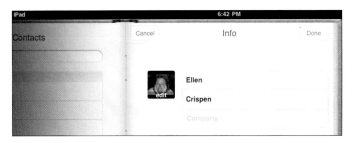

Figure 5-9: A photo displayed with a contact in iPad.

If you want a more powerful contact-management app, check out Contacts Journal – iPad Edition. It syncs with your Contacts app content and can also sync with a computer contact-management program such as Outlook. The most helpful aspect of Contact Journals for road warriors is that it maintains a record of whom you've visited and when you've e-mailed them.

Adding Twitter or Facebook Information

You can add Twitter and Facebook information to a contact so you can quickly *tweet* (send a short message) to others using Twitter or post a message to your contact's Facebook account.

To specify Facebook or Twitter account information for a contact, first be sure you've activated and set up User Name and Password for your Facebook and/or Twitter accounts are set up under Settings, and then follow these steps:

1. **With Contacts open, tap a contact.**

2. **Tap the Edit button.**

3. **Scroll down and tap Add Fields.**

4. **In the list that appears (refer to Figure 5-3), tap Twitter.**

   A Twitter field opens (see Figure 5-10). If you want to create a different social networking field, tap the Twitter label and a list of other options appears, including Sina Weibo (a Chinese social networking site), Facebook, Flickr, LinkedIn, and Myspace. You can also tap Add Custom Service to enter another service's information.

5. **Tap in the field and enter the contact's username information for an account.**

Twitter field

Figure 5-10: Choose Twitter to begin composing a tweet.

6. **Tap Done.**

The information is saved.

The account now displays whenever you select the contact. You can send a tweet, Facebook, or other message by simply tapping the username for a service and choosing the appropriate command (such as Tweet, as shown in Figure 5-11).

Figure 5-11: Your contact is now associated with the appropriate social network.

Designating Related People

You can quickly designate a relation — such as your mother, assistant, friend, or manager — in a contact record if the person is saved to Contacts. To add a relationship to a contact, follow these steps:

1. **Tap a contact and then tap Edit.**

2. **Scroll down the record and tap Add Field.**

3. **Tap Related People (see Figure 5-12).**

   A new field, labeled Mother, appears.

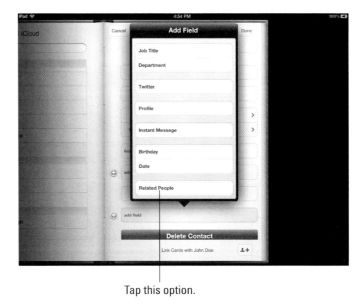

Tap this option.

Figure 5-12: How sweet; this field defaults to Mother!

4. **Tap the label Mother, and a list of other possible relations appears.**

5. **Tap one to change the label, if you want.**

6. **Tap the blue arrow in the field.**

   Your contacts list appears.

7. **Tap a person's name.**

   It appears in the field.

   A new, blank field also appears (see Figure 5-13).

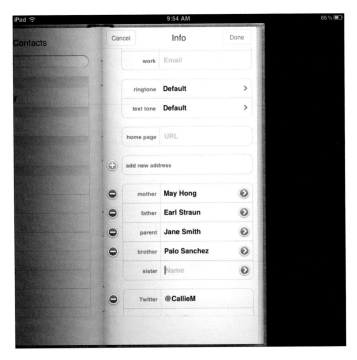

Figure 5-13: You can make someone a friend, an assistant, and a spouse, if you want!

After you add a relation to a contact record, whenever you select the person on the Contacts main screen, all related people for that contact are listed.

Setting Ringtones and Text Tones

If you want to hear a unique tone whenever you receive a FaceTime call or a text from a particular contact, you can set up this feature in Contacts. For example, if you want to be sure that you know instantly when your spouse, a sick friend, or your boss is calling, set a unique tone for that person by following these steps:

1. **Tap to add a new contact or select a contact from the list of contacts, and tap Edit.**

2. **Tap the Ringtone field.**

   If you want to assign Text Tones, make that choice in this step. A list of tones appears (see Figure 5-14). You can also tap Buy More Tones to buy additional ringtones from Apple or a variety of third-party sites, or even create your own.

Figure 5-14: Choose from these available ringtones.

3. **Tap a tone to preview it.**

4. **When you hear a tone you like, tap Save.**

5. **Tap Done to close the contact form.**

If your Apple devices are synced via iCloud, setting a unique ringtone for an iPad contact also sets it for your iPhone. See Book I, Chapter 5, for more about iCloud.

You can set a custom tone for FaceTime calls and text messages through Settings⇨Sounds. You can also create your own custom ring/text tones in GarageBand on a Mac, with any of several ringtone-maker apps, or by using the contents of your iTunes Library on either a Mac or PC.

Finding Contacts

You can use the Spotlight Search feature to find a contact in the Contacts app by looking for that person's first or last name or a company name. This feature on the iPad is much like every search feature you've ever used. It's somewhat simple in comparison to others because you can search only for names and because no advanced search techniques are available.

You can also use Siri or the Spotlight Search feature to locate contacts that match specified search criteria. The Spotlight screen is the leftmost Home screen when you scroll the screens.

Follow these steps to search for a contact:

1. **With Contacts open, tap in the Search field at the top of the left page (see Figure 5-15).**

   The onscreen keyboard opens.

Tap in the Search field.

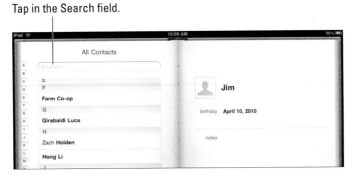

Figure 5-15: Easily search for contacts.

2. **Type the first letter of either the first or last name or company name.**

   All matching results appear, as shown in Figure 5-16. In the example, typing **N** displays Nancy Boysen, Nellie Dillon, and Space Needle in the results, which all have *N* as the first letter in either their first or last name.

Search results

Figure 5-16: Search results narrow as you type.

3. **Tap a contact's name in the results to display that person's information on the page on the right (refer to Figure 5-16).**

You can't search by address, phone number, or website in Contacts (at the time this book was written), though you can search by these criteria using Spotlight Search (the Search function for iPad described in Book I, Chapter 2).

You can use the alphabetical listing to locate a contact: Tap and drag to scroll the list of contacts on the All Contacts page on the left. You can also tap any tabbed letter along the left side of the page to scroll quickly to entries starting with that letter (refer to Figure 5-15).

Using Contacts beyond the Contacts App

Contacts isn't simply a static database of names and addresses. After you've entered contact information into the app, you can use the information to reach out to people in several useful ways. You can jump to a contact's website to see what she, or her company, is up to online; use a contact's e-mail information to quickly send an e-mail message; share the contact information with somebody else; or find the physical address of the contact by using the iPad Maps app.

Visiting a contact's website

Everybody (well, almost everybody) now has a website, so whether your contact is a person or an international conglomerate, you're likely to find an associated website that you might want to access now and then. You can access it from your iPad by using the Contacts app.

If you entered information in the Home Page field of a contact record, the text you entered automatically becomes a link to that person's website. With Contacts open, tap a contact to display the person's contact information on the page at the right and then tap the link in the Home Page field, as shown in Figure 5-17.

Tap this link.

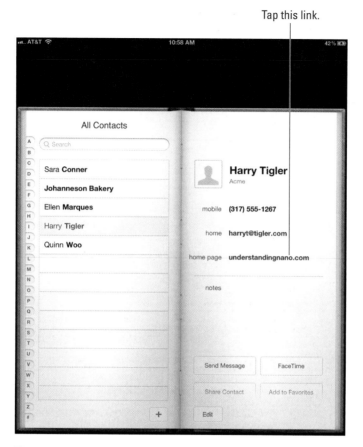

Figure 5-17: Tap to go to a web page related to a contact.

The Safari browser opens with the web page displayed, as shown in Figure 5-18.

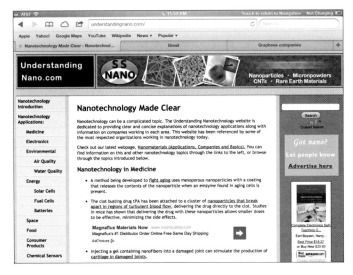

Figure 5-18: Visit contacts' websites to check on their latest information.

You can't return directly to Contacts after you follow a link to a website. You have to tap the Home button and then tap the Contacts app icon again to reenter the application. Or, you can use the multitasking feature to get back to Contacts by double-tapping the Home button and choosing Contacts from the icons that appear along the bottom of the screen. However, if you have gesture support turned on in General Settings, you can do the four-finger swipe to the left to return to the app you just left and keep swiping to go to the apps on the multitasking bar in sequence.

Addressing e-mails using contacts

If you've entered an e-mail address for a contact, the address automatically converts to a link in the record that allows you to open an e-mail form and send a message. This shortcut is handy for getting in touch.

First, be sure that you've entered an e-mail address in the contact's record and then follow these steps:

1. **Tap the Contacts app icon on the Home screen to open Contacts.**

2. **Tap a contact's name to display her contact information on the page on the right, and then tap the e-mail address link labeled Home, as in the example shown in Figure 5-19.**

   The New Message dialog appears, as shown in Figure 5-20. The title bar of this dialog initially reads *New Message* but changes, as you type on the Subject line, to the specific title, as shown in the figure.

Tap this link.

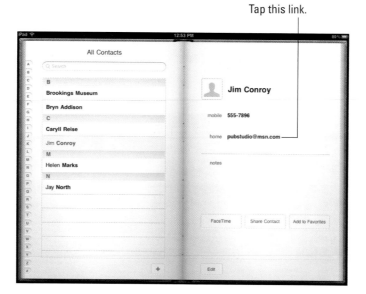

Figure 5-19: Tap to open a new e-mail message.

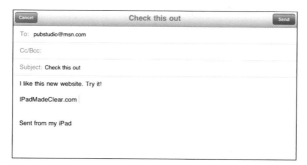

Figure 5-20: A new e-mail message form.

3. **Use the onscreen keyboard to enter a subject and a message.**

4. **Tap the Send button.**

   The message goes on its way!

Sharing contacts

After you've entered contact information, you can share it with others in an e-mail message. Sharing is especially handy when you store locations in Contacts, such as your favorite restaurant or movie theater.

Here's how to share your contacts' information:

1. **With Contacts open, tap a contact name to display its information.**

2. **On the information page, tap the Share Contact button, as shown in Figure 5-21.**

3. **In the dialog that appears, tap either Email or Message.**

   The New Message form appears.

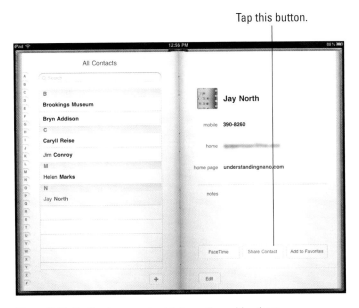

Figure 5-21: Easily share contact information with others.

4. **On the e-mail New Message form, shown in Figure 5-22, use the onscreen keyboard to enter the recipient's e-mail address.**

   Note: If the person is saved in Contacts, just type his or her name here. If you are sending a message, you'd enter an iMessage contact's info in the To line along with a message.

5. **Enter information in the Subject field.**

6. **If you like, enter a message and then tap the Send button.**

   The message goes to your recipient with the contact information attached as a .vcf file (in the *vCard* format, commonly used to transmit contact information).

Figure 5-22: If you like, enter a subject and a message.

Someone who receives a vCard containing contact information simply clicks the attached file to open it. At that point, the recipient can perform various actions (depending on the recipient's e-mail or contact-management program) to save the content. Other iPhone or iPad users can easily import `.vcf` records into their own Contacts apps.

Viewing a Contact's Location in Maps

If you've entered a person's street address in Contacts, you have a shortcut for viewing that person's location in the Maps app. Once again, this is useful for places you need to visit for the first time, such as several clients' offices on that next business trip.

Follow these steps to pinpoint your contacts in the iPad Maps app:

1. **To open the Contacts app, tap its icon on the Home screen.**

2. **Tap the contact you want to view to display her information.**

3. **Tap the address.**

   Maps opens and displays a map of the address, as shown in Figure 5-23.

You can use information stored in Contacts to access more than your friends' addresses. You can also save information about your favorite restaurant or movie theater or any other location and then use Contacts to jump to the associated website in the Safari browser or to the address in Maps.

After you jump to a contact's location in Maps, you may want to use the features of Maps to display different views, determine the condition of traffic on that route, or calculate the route between two locations. For more about using the Maps application, see Book III, Chapter 2.

Figure 5-23: Tap the information bar to view more details in the Maps app.

Deleting Contacts

Remember that iPad's memory is limited compared to your typical computer. Though a contact record is tiny compared to a TV show, there's no sense keeping lots of old records around when you no longer need them. When you need to remove a name or two from your Contacts, doing so is easy.

To make a wholesale update of your contacts, sync with iTunes, where you can choose to sync your Mac Contacts, Google, Outlook, Windows, or Yahoo! contacts to your iPad or coordinate contacts across devices using iCloud.

Follow these steps to delete contacts on your iPad:

1. **With Contacts open, tap the contact you want to delete.**

2. **On the information page on the right, tap the Edit button.**

3. **On the Info page that displays, drag your finger upward to scroll down (if necessary) and then tap the Delete Contact button at the bottom, as shown in Figure 5-24.**

   The confirmation dialog shown in Figure 5-25 appears.

4. **Tap the Delete button to confirm the deletion.**

During this process, if you change your mind before you tap Delete, tap the Cancel button in Step 4. But be careful because after you tap Delete, the only way to put it back is to resync with your computer, assuming you haven't deleted it there, or enter it manually!

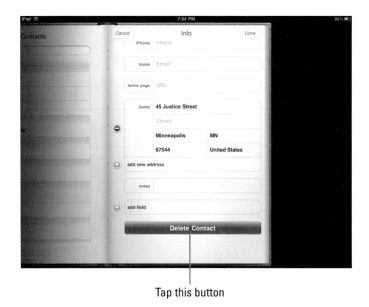

Tap this button

Figure 5-24: Tap this red bar, and your contact record is gone forever.

Tap this button.

Figure 5-25: Tap the Delete button to confirm.

Chapter 6: Talking to Your iPad with Siri

In This Chapter

✔ Activating Siri and understanding all that Siri can do

✔ Calling people or creating reminders and alerts

✔ Adding tasks to your Calendar

✔ Playing music, getting directions, and asking for facts

✔ Using Siri to search the web or send e-mail or messages

✔ Getting helpful Siri tips

*O*ne of the biggest changes in iOS 6 for iPad is Siri, a personal assistant feature that responds to spoken commands using a third- or fourth-generation iPad or an iPad mini. Siri first appeared with iPhone 4S, and now with Siri on your iPad, you can ask for nearby restaurants and a list appears. You can dictate your e-mail messages rather than typing them. Calling your mother is as simple as saying, "Call Mom." Want to know the capital of Rhode Island? Just ask. Siri checks an online database to answer questions ranging from the result of a mathematical calculation to the size of Jupiter.

Activating Siri

When you first go through the process of setting up your third- or fourth-generation iPad or iPad mini, making settings for your location, using iCloud, and so on, at one point, you see the screen shown in Figure 6-1. To activate Siri at this point, just tap Use Siri and then tap Next. When you first set up your iPad, iPad reminds you about using Siri by displaying a message.

Figure 6-1: Activate Siri now or later, but definitely give it a try!

If you didn't activate Siri during the registration process, you can use Settings to turn Siri on by following these steps:

1. **Tap the Settings icon on the Home screen.**

2. **Tap General, and then tap Siri (see Figure 6-2).**

Figure 6-2: Siri offers a few simple settings.

3. **In the dialog in Figure 6-3, tap the On/Off button to turn Siri on.**

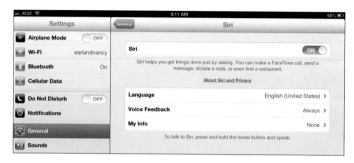

Figure 6-3: Get Siri going here.

4. **If you wish to change the language Siri uses, tap Language and choose a different language in the list that appears.**

5. **Tap My Info and select your own contact information in the Contacts list that appears.**

   Siri now knows your name, phone number, website, contacts who are related to you and the relationship, and so on, so it can respond to requests that require that information.

You can make a setting that allows Siri to be used when the Lock Screen is displayed, but Siri can then bypass any passcode you've required. If somebody else gets his hands on your iPad and you have this set to On, it could compromise your data security. To change this setting under General settings, tap Passcode Lock. When the lock is set to on, you can use the Siri field to turn access via Siri on or off.

Siri is only available on the iPad when you have Internet access and cellular data charges could apply if you're using a 4G model. In addition, Apple warns that available features may vary by area.

Now to use Siri, press and hold the Home button until Siri opens displaying a dialog with the phrase "What can I help you with" and a small microphone icon (see Figure 6-4). Remember this only works with third- and fourth-generation iPads and iPad minis with iOS 6 installed.

Figure 6-4: Siri awaits your command.

Understanding All That Siri Can Do

Siri allows you to interact with many apps on your iPad by voice. You can pose questions or ask to do something like make a FaceTime call or add an appointment to your calendar, for example. Siri can also search the Internet or use an informational database called Wolfram Alpha to provide information on just about any topic. You don't have to be in an app to make a request involving another app.

Siri is the technology behind the iPad Dictation feature. When you have the onscreen keyboard open, note that it contains a microphone key you can tap to begin dictation, and tap to end dictation. This works in any app that uses the onscreen keyboard.

Siri requires no preset structure for your questions; you can phrase things in several ways. For example, you might say, "Where am I?" to see a map of your current location, or you could say, "What is my current location?" or "What address is this?" and get the same results. Also, Siri gets better at responding to your requests the more you use it, as it learns more about you from your browsing habits and requests.

Siri responds to you both verbally and with text information, in a form as with e-mail (see Figure 6-5) or in a graphic display for some items such as maps. When a result appears, you can tap it to make a choice or open a related app.

Siri works with FaceTime, Music, Messages, Reminders, Calendar, Maps, Mail, Clock, Contacts, Notes, and Safari. In the following tasks, I provide a quick guide to some of the most useful ways you can use Siri.

Figure 6-5: If you ask to send an e-mail, Siri provides the e-mail form.

Staying in Touch and Staying on Schedule with Siri

When you're on the run, Siri can be a wonderful ally. You can ask Siri to make calls for you, set up reminders and alerts, and even add appointments to your calendar, all by speaking your requests.

Calling contacts via FaceTime

First make sure that the people you call are entered in your Contacts app and include their phone numbers in their records. If you want to call somebody by stating your relationship to her, such as "Call sister," be sure to enter that relationship in the related field in her contact record and make sure that the settings for Siri (refer to Figure 6-3) include your contact name in the My Info field. (See Chapter 5 in this minibook for more about creating contact records.)

1. **Press and hold the Home button until Siri appears.**

2. **Speak a command such as "Make a FaceTime call to Earl" or "FaceTime Mom."**

   If two contacts exist who might match a spoken name, Siri responds with a list of possible matches (see Figure 6-6).

3. **Tap one of the contacts in the list or state the correct contact's name to proceed.**

   The call is placed.

Figure 6-6: If two similar contacts exist, Siri asks you to choose.

4. **To end the call before it completes, tap the Home button and then tap End.**

To cancel any spoken request, you have four options: You can say, "Cancel," tap the Microphone button on the Siri screen, tap the Home button, or tap anywhere on the screen outside the Siri panel.

Creating reminders and alerts

You can also use Siri with the Reminders app. For example, you might want to set a reminder to meet a friend for lunch next Tuesday. Rather than opening the Reminder app and adding a new reminder and settings for it, you can tell Siri to do it for you.

To create a reminder using Siri, follow these steps:

1. **Press and hold the Home key and then speak a command, such as "Remind me to call Dad on Thursday at 10 a.m." or "Wake me up tomorrow at 7 a.m."**

    A preview of the reminder is displayed (see Figure 6-7), and Siri asks you whether it should create the reminder.

2. **Tap or say Confirm to create it or tap or say Cancel.**

Figure 6-7: Siri presents the reminder as she understood it for you to confirm.

3. **If you want a reminder ahead of the event you created, activate Siri and speak a command, such as "Remind me tonight about the play on Thursday at 8 p.m."**

    A second reminder is created, which you can confirm or cancel.

Adding tasks to your Calendar

If you live by your Calendar appointments, you'll be happy to hear that Siri can also set up events on your Calendar for you. Siri not only records the event on your Calendar, but it also alerts you if a conflict exists.

Follow these steps to set up an event using Siri:

1. **Press and hold the Home button and then speak a phrase, such as "Set up meeting at 10 a.m. on October 12th."**

   A sample calendar entry appears, and Siri asks whether you want to confirm it.

2. **If a conflict exists with the appointment, Siri tells you that you already have an appointment at that time (see Figure 6-8) and asks whether you still want to set up the new appointment.**

3. **Say Yes or Cancel or tap the Yes or Cancel button.**

Figure 6-8: Double-booked? Siri lets you know.

Playing Music

How many times do you find that you don't have the time or free hands to unlock the iPad screen, open Music, search for music, and tap to play it? Well, you'll find worse problems in the world, but if this is one that nags at you, just press and hold the Home button and tell Siri to play your favorite tune.

To play music using Siri, follow these steps:

1. **Press and hold the Home button until Siri appears.**

2. **To play music, speak a command, such as "Play music" or "Play 'As Time Goes By'" to play a specific song or album.**

3. **When the music is playing, use commands such as "Pause music," "Next track," or "Stop music" to control playback.**

One of the beauties of Siri is that you don't have to follow a specific command format as you do with some other voice command apps. You could say "Play the next track" or "Next track" or "Jump to the next track on this album" and Siri gets your meaning.

Letting Siri Put You in the Know

You're late for an appointment and need help. You can call on Siri. From getting you directions to your next appointment to calling up your customer's website to check her product catalog or checking facts on the price of the client's stock today, Siri can find it all.

Getting directions

You can use the Maps app and Siri to find your current location, find nearby businesses such as restaurants or a bank, or get a map of another location.

Here are some of the commands you can try to get directions or a list of nearby businesses:

✔ **"Where am I?"**

Displays a map of your current location. If you have a Wi-Fi–only iPad, this location may be approximate.

✔ **"Where is Apache Junction, Arizona?"**

Displays a map of that city.

✔ **"Find restaurants."**

Displays a list of restaurants near your current location as shown in Figure 6-9; tap one to display a map of its location.

✔ **"Find Bank of America."**

Displays a map with the location of that business (or in some cases, several nearby locations, such as a bank branch and all ATMs) indicated.

When a location is displayed in a map, tap the Information button on the location's label to view its address, phone number, and website address, if available.

Figure 6-9: If you're hungry, Siri could be your new best friend.

Note that all your requests to Siri are routed through Apple servers. If you are, say, a spy and you don't want your movements and potentially activities stored on somebody else's server, avoid using Siri for directions or reminders!

Asking for the facts

Wolfram Alpha is a self-professed online computational knowledge engine. That means it's more than a search engine because it provides specific information about a search term rather than multiple search results. If you want facts without having to spend time browsing websites to find those facts, Wolfram Alpha is a very good resource.

Siri uses Wolfram Alpha to look up facts in response to questions such as "What is the capital of Kansas?," "What is the square root of 2003?," or "How large is Mars?" Just press and hold the Home button and ask your question; Siri consults Wolfram Alpha and returns a set of relevant facts.

You can also get information about the weather, stocks, or the time. Just say a phrase like one of these to get what you need:

✔ **"What is the weather?"**

This shows the weather report for your current location. If you want weather in another location, just specify the location in your question.

✔ **"What is the price of Apple stock?"**

Siri tells you the current price of the stock or the price of the stock when the stock market last closed. (Let's hope you own some).

✏ **"What time is it?"**

Siri tells you the time in your time zone and displays a clock (see Figure 6-10).

Figure 6-10: Stay on schedule with Siri's help.

Searching the web

While Siri can use Wolfram Alpha to respond to specific requests such as "Who is the Queen of England?," for more general requests Siri searches the web.

For example, if you speak a phrase, such as "Find a website about birds" or "Find information about the World Series," Siri can respond in a couple of ways. The app can simply display a list of search results using the default search engine specified in your settings for Safari or suggesting, "If you like, I can search the web for such-and-such." In the first instance, just tap a result to go to that website. In the second instance, you can confirm that you want to search the web or cancel.

Sending E-Mail or Messages

You can create an e-mail or an instant message using Siri. For example, if you say, "E-mail Jack Wilkes," a form opens already addressed to that contact.

Siri asks you the subject and what to say in the message; speak your message and then say, "Send" to speed your message on its way.

Siri also works with the iMessage feature. Tap Siri and say Message Sarah. Siri creates a message and asks what you want to say. Say "Tell Sarah I'll call soon" and Siri creates a message for you to approve and send.

 It's hard to stump Siri. For example, at this point in time, Siri can't tweet unless you download and set up the Twitter app. But if you try to speak a tweet, she gives you a link to tap to install the app!

Getting Helpful Tips

I know you're going to have a wonderful time learning the ins and outs of Siri, but before I close this chapter, here are some tips to get you going:

- **If Siri doesn't understand you:** When you speak a command and Siri displays what she thought you said, if she misses the mark, you have a few options. To correct a request you've made, you can tap the bubble containing the command Siri heard and edit it by typing or tapping the Microphone key on the onscreen keyboard and dictating the correct information. If a word is underlined in blue, it's a possible error. Tap the word and then tap an alternative that Siri suggests. You can also simply speak to Siri and say something like, "I meant Sri Lanka" or "No, send it to Sally." If even corrections aren't working, you may need to restart your iPad to reset the software.

- **Headsets and earphones:** If you're using iPhone EarPods or a Bluetooth headset to activate Siri, instead of pressing the Home button, press and hold the center button (the little button on the headset that starts and stops a call).

- **Using Find My Friends:** You can download a free app from the App Store called Find My Friends that allows you to ask Siri to locate your friends geographically, if they are carrying a device with GPS turned on and location tracking allowed.

- **Getting help with Siri:** To get help with Siri features, just press and hold the Home button and ask Siri, "What can you do?"

Book VI
Must-Have iPad Apps

The 5th Wave — By Rich Tennant

"Hold on Barbara. I'm pretty sure there's an app for this."

*O*kay, you probably roamed around earlier parts of this book and picked up some useful information and advice. Now it's time to just play around with the wonderful world of apps out there, and let's face it, you can find an app for just about everything. The first two chapters in this part cover apps that help you conduct business or arrange your next trip. Chapter 3 gets you thinking about the possibilities of social web apps to stay in touch with all your online friends through Facebook, Twitter, blogs, and more. Chapter 4 covers news, sports, and weather, so you'll always be in the know and dry. Chapter 5 provides information on apps that help with your finances, while Chapter 6 is pure entertainment. Note that apps do come and go, change from free to at a cost, and even change names or disappear. However, the apps I suggest are current as of this writing and are likely to be as I describe them.

Chapter 1: Business Apps

In This Chapter

*O*ne compelling strength of all Apple iOS devices is the App Store — and its hundreds of thousands of apps you can download and then use to do just about anything you might want to do. (*iOS* is the name of the operating system that runs the iPad, iPhone, and iPod touch.) In this chapter, I show you some of the best apps for business, including some useful productivity apps. I tell you the qualities that make the app stand out and describe things you can do with it so that you can decide whether you need it on your iPad.

Some of the apps I describe in this chapter were written specifically for the iPad; others, however, were written by their developers to run as native apps on both the iPad and iPhone (or iPod touch) — the plus-sign (+) symbol appears next to the prices in the App Store for these *hybrid* apps (see Book I, Chapter 5, for more about buying apps). You can buy a hybrid app and then use it on whatever iOS devices you own.

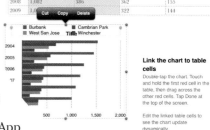

For the latest iPad updates, be sure to check out my website at www.ipad madeclear.com.

iWork

by Apple, Inc.

$9.99 per application

What you can do with it: *Pages:* Write letters and reports. *Numbers:* Create and manage spreadsheets. *Keynote:* Make gorgeous, professional-looking presentations.

iWork is Apple's productivity suite, made up of Pages, Numbers, and Keynote. Book IV covers the basics of using these apps. This chapter helps you decide whether they're right for you.

 Pages is Apple's advanced word-processor and page layout program for the Mac, and now for the iPad. It's one of the best apps available to demonstrate on the iPad how the touchscreen interface can be used to get things done.

Pages for iPad was built from the ground up to create letters, résumés, thank-you notes and cards, newsletters, proposals, reports, term papers, and even posters and flyers. It's a pretty darn good page layout app, as well.

Everything in the iWork suite of apps was designed to be accomplished by making *gestures* (pinch, zoom, tap, and swipe) and using the onscreen keyboard, including layout and formatting and placing graphics such as photos, charts, and graphs. The Pages app comes supplied with 16 templates and a library of tables, customizable charts, and shapes. You can also add photos from your photo libraries, as I did in Figure 1-1, including any images you may have created in another iPad app and saved to your Photos library.

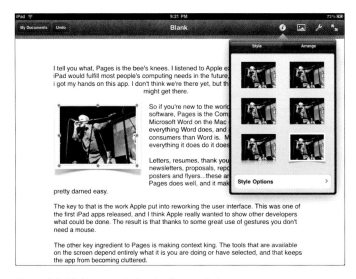

Figure 1-1: Picking a style for the inserted photo.

One cool characteristic of Pages is the way objects work. After you drop, say, a photo into your document, you can move the photo, resize it, change its presentation style, or even rotate it — and the text simply autoflows around it in real time. The app makes layout and design so easy on your iPad that you may have to try it to truly appreciate it.

For more on the Pages app, see Book IV, Chapter 2.

The Numbers spreadsheet app is useful for working with small-business and home-office spreadsheets, maintaining budgets and logs, and organizing teams and other group competitions. It's an even better app for turning your spreadsheets and data into gorgeous charts and graphs that you can use to make your reports, presentations, and other documents look great.

As in Pages, all tasks in Numbers were designed to be done by making gestures. Filling in data in a spreadsheet, changing colors, adding a chart or graph, resizing documents — all these tasks can be completed quickly and easily on your iPad. You can see a sample chart and data set in Figure 1-2. Some tasks are even easier and faster to complete using this app on the iPad than performing them on your desktop computer using a full-blown spreadsheet application.

**Book VI
Chapter 1**

Business Apps

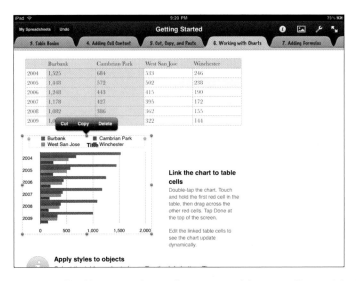

Figure 1-2: Double-tap an element in your spreadsheet to pull up resizing handles and the Cut/Copy/Delete selection buttons.

Numbers comes supplied with 16 templates (checklists, budgets, invoices, schedules, and rosters, for example), and the library of charts and graphs contains nine different varieties for you to use. All nine types feature several different color palette choices that can then be further edited. The same statement applies to the included shapes: You can edit the color, style, and other attributes in just a few taps.

For more on the Numbers app, see Book IV, Chapter 3.

Keynote on the iPad makes great-looking presentations and is just about as feature-rich as Keynote on a Mac, which makes it better than PowerPoint for Mac or Windows. Keynote is perfect for anyone wanting to work on a presentation on the go.

All 16 terrific-looking Keynote templates include several premade slides that comport to a different theme (such as Modern Portfolio, Showroom, Chalkboard, or Photo Portfolio, which you can see in Figure 1-3). You can create your own presentation without a template, of course, but if you want to start with a style all laid out for you, try using a template.

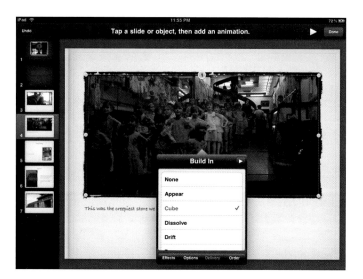

Figure 1-3: Choosing a transition in a Keynote presentation.

Most of the time, a presentation displays on a projector or another type of large display; if you have a small group, however (say, a couple of customers or your boss), you can simply create a presentation in Keynote and display it directly on your iPad!

After you're working on a presentation, you have access to awesome transitions and effects, each of which has options and controls that are a breeze to understand and use. You can add photos and images from your Photos library, and the app has the same charts, graphs, and shapes that come with

Pages and Numbers. Creating new slides is easy, and editing them is even easier.

For more on the Keynote app, see Book IV, Chapter 4.

Quickoffice Pro

by Quickoffice, Inc.

$14.99

What you can do with it: Create and edit word-processing and spreadsheet documents in the Microsoft Word and Excel formats. You can also view PowerPoint files, but you can't edit them.

This app is intended for people who are more comfortable using Microsoft Word and Excel than Apple's iWork approach. Quickoffice Pro for iPad is built on the same paradigms as Word and Excel — in fact, its *raison d'être* is to view, create, and edit files in Microsoft Office file formats. You can switch among your Mac, PC, and iPad with Word and Excel files (you can only view PowerPoint files with Quickoffice, as of this writing), as long as you use DOC, DOCX, DOT, DOTX, TXT, XLS, XLSX, XLT, and XLTX file formats. Unless and until Microsoft brings the real deal to iOS, Quickoffice is the best way to work on your Office files on the iPad in an Office-y kind of way.

Another useful aspect of Quickoffice is that it has Dropbox support built into it. The excellent Dropbox utility gives you access to files on a variety of devices, including iPad. (I talk about Dropbox in more detail in the next section.) With Dropbox support in Quickoffice, you can create a Word document on your PC at work and put it in your Dropbox. Then, when you're at the coffee shop that afternoon and you need to edit it, simply open it from your Dropbox in Quickoffice on your iPad. When you get home to your Mac, you can open the file from Dropbox there, too! If for some bizarre reason Dropbox doesn't float your boat, Quickoffice also supports Google Docs and Box (www.box.net).

The Quickoffice Pro app offers a nifty navigation tool, too: Press and hold the right margin in a multipage document to see the thumbnail view of all pages in your document, as shown in Figure 1-4. Just slide your finger down the page until you see the thumbnail of the page you want to jump to, and you're there. It's a nifty feature.

Quickoffice doesn't have a lot of fancy formatting tricks, like Pages and Numbers do, but it's the best app to use if you have to, or are accustomed to, working with Microsoft Office, OpenOffice, or another Office-like productivity suite.

Figure 1-4: Using the cool thumbnail-navigation feature to go to another page.

Dropbox

by Dropbox

Free — Hybrid

What you can do with it: Access important files on your iPad anywhere you have an Internet connection.

 If you're doing serious work on your iPad, whether it's for business or another type of task, Dropbox is the easiest and best way to move files from your iPad to any other computer or device, or from another device to your iPad.

Let me back up a bit. The Dropbox *cloud-based service* lets you store your files on the provider's servers and access those files from any device that's connected to the Internet. Dropbox directly supports (in the form of dedicated software) OS X, Windows, Linux, Android, BlackBerry — and, of course, iOS. Even if you're using another operating system (such as webOS, Windows Mobile, or Sun Solaris), or if you don't have Dropbox installed on the device you're using now, you can access your files by using a web browser.

When you're using a computer, Dropbox works like any other folder on your hard drive. You open Dropbox and see all your files, for instantaneous access. An item you drop into a folder is copied to the company's servers and then pushed to any location where you've set up a Dropbox account, including on the iPad.

A Dropbox folder can be selectively shared with other Dropbox users, making it a helpful tool for any sort of collaborative project.

Apple has provided iCloud to share documents among Apple devices, and you might use apps that support Apple iTunes File Sharing. Still, as a power user, you need a solution like Dropbox to share all your content among Apple and non-Apple devices.

Dropbox works on your iPad in two ways. First, you download this free app from the App Store and find all your Dropbox files and folders. Second, using the iOS Open In feature, you can tap a file to select it and then tap the Sharing icon in the upper-right corner, as shown in Figure 1-5, to choose which supporting app to send your file to for editing or another task.

Figure 1-5: Using the Open In feature in iOS to open a Pages document in My Dropbox with the Pages app.

The Dropbox file preview feature shows you the contents of the file you have highlighted (refer to Figure 1-5). The file preview, which supports many major file formats, lets you easily pick the app you want to work with on your iPad. Note that some formats, such as Kindle and iBooks, are recognized but no preview displays.

iOS app developers can add Dropbox functionality directly to their apps, like the Quickoffice folks did in the Quickoffice Pro app (discussed in the preceding section). You can work with your files even more easily in these apps. I hope to see more apps take advantage of the services that Dropbox can provide.

If you want to easily move files on and off your iPad assuming the app developer has integrated Dropbox support, Dropbox is currently the best way to do so. However, note that Dropbox currently doesn't work for audio or video files.

Dragon Dictation

by Dragon Naturally Speaking

Free — Hybrid

What you can do with it: Input words by speaking them instead of keying them. Edit and share text.

If you prefer to speak to your iPad rather than tap it and you want a more robust speech recognition option that includes more features such as extensive language support than Dictation, consider getting Dragon Dictation. The mobile version of the Dragon Naturally Speaking speech recognition software is darn simple for anyone to use, but if you're a busy professional who breaks a wrist playing handball or suffers another mishap that limits your typing ability, it might even save your hide.

With Dragon, you speak and then the app turns your speech into text typed on the screen. To be honest, recognition is the name of the game for any speech recognition program, and none of these apps are perfect. After you record yourself speaking, you will find that certain words don't sound quite right. (The word *darling* somehow worked its way into a paragraph from a review at the Macworld site — and I don't even know the author of the article.)

Don't worry: Part of the tool set in Dragon includes the ability to easily edit text to make corrections. (See Figure 1-6.) When the text matches exactly what you said, you can then easily cut or copy the text and paste it into a word processor or send it by e-mail. You can even find tools for posting the text you speak on your Twitter or Facebook account.

Settings allow you to choose which language to use, including the usual language suspects: English, French, German, Italian, and Spanish. Dragon is quite handy for taking trips abroad when you can speak in English and your waiter can read what you say in his own language. (Just hope that no *darling* glitches work their way in.)

One interesting feature of Dragon is its ability to import all your contacts into its database to help it recognize the names you speak.

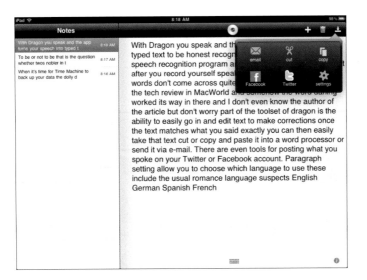

Figure 1-6: Tools allow you to work with the text generated from your speech.

Dragon is free, so why not install it and give it a whirl? It's fun to watch what you say being preserved in print!

Quick Hits

This section describes several apps you should check out.

OmniGraffle

by The Omni Group

$49.99

OmniGraffle is a somewhat expensive iPad app, but it's worth the cost if you need to make flowcharts or diagrams. The app is as intuitive as the apps in Apple's iWork suite, and it's a breeze to work with. OmniGraffle comes supplied with a wide array of customizable tools that let you make anything from basic flowcharts to complex drawings, such as the full espresso machine that The Omni Group includes in a sample chart in the app. Anyone who considers flowcharts, process charts, floor plans, diagrams, and other types of charts important will find that OmniGraffle on the iPad makes them rethink what they can do on a tablet device.

You can open on your iPad any OmniGraffle apps that were created in the Mac version of the software — or vice versa!

iThoughtsHD

by Craig Scott

$9.99

When you engage in *mind mapping,* you use a diagram to show the structure of an idea or plan and highlight the relationships between different aspects of that idea or plan. Many mind-mapping apps are available for Mac and Windows, but only a few (so far) are on the iPad. The dedicated iThoughtsHD mind-mapping app is the best one I've found, and it has easy-to-use tools for quickly developing your own maps. This area is one that's ideally suited to the tablet-in-your-lap form factor.

iAnnotate PDF

by Aji, LLC

$9.99

If you simply want to be able to view PDF files on your iPad, check out GoodReader for iPad. This useful app costs only 99 cents. If you need to be able to annotate or mark up PDF files on your iPad, check out iAnnotate PDF instead. It lets you quickly and easily highlight text, add notes, draw lines, strike out or underline text, or even doodle in the margins, if that's your thing. Workers in certain professions need to be able to annotate PDF files, and this app makes doing so on your iPad so easy that you might want to move all those tasks from your computer to your iPad. The latest version of this app added support for AirPrint, so you can also print what you mark up easily.

PowerME HD

by AppTime, LLC

$29.99

If you manage projects, consider buying PowerME HD. This handy (though not cheap) app helps you organize your workflow, collaborate with team members, and sync all your plans in the cloud. If you're a mobile professional, these tools come in handy for keeping track of your work and your team's activities. Create and manage projects, juggle deadlines, and organize tasks in your PowerME inbox. Check out the Drawing feature, which can quickly change the old way of creating preliminary plans, by jotting them down on napkins in hotel coffee shops. The latest version added integration with Google Docs and Dropbox, as well as the ability to record and play back movies.

Go To Meeting

by Citrix Online, LLC

Free — Hybrid

If you attend meetings remotely, you'll enjoy this app you can use to join meetings, view presentations, and take a look at any content a presenter shares with attendees. Tap a link in an e-mailed invitation and you can instantly join a meeting with others using Go To Meeting via Wi-Fi or 3G/4G. You can also enter a meeting phone number, your name and e-mail, and join. After joining, you can hear, see, and participate in meetings.

Agendas

by Jennifer Landefeld

Free

If your company has made iPad a standard, Agendas is going to ratchet your next meeting experience up a few notches. All iPad users on a single network, like everybody in your office, can not only create and send agendas to each other, but as the meeting progresses, you can post questions which others can vote on to push the question most people have in mind to the top of the list. With a set meeting schedule, you can use a timer bar to make sure each topic or speaker stays on that schedule. The person running the meeting can create polls on the fly, with everybody in the meeting responding and responses being automatically tallied. Everybody in the meeting is also given a notes feature to jot down thoughts during the meeting for later reference.

Prompster and Teleprompt+ for iPad

by Dante Varnado Moore and Gene Whitaker (respectively)

$9.99 and $14.99

In addition to all the other things your iPad can do, it can serve as a portable teleprompter, useful for giving speeches and other presentations. I recommend Prompster and Teleprompt+ for iPad. Prompster lets you record your speech right there on your iPad as you're giving it, and it has great onscreen controls. Teleprompt+ for iPad has more and better options for controlling your speech, and version 2.3.2 added a recorder function.

Chapter 2: Travel Apps

In This Chapter

- ✓ **KAYAK HD — Flights, Hotels, Explore**
- ✓ **Wikihood Plus for iPad**
- ✓ **Urbanspoon for iPad**
- ✓ **ZAGAT TO GO**
- ✓ **FlightTrack Pro – Live Flight Status Tracker by Mobiata**
- ✓ **TripIt**
- ✓ **INRIX Traffic! and INRIX Traffic! Pro**
- ✓ **Priceline Hotel & Car Negotiator**
- ✓ **iTranslate**
- ✓ **World Atlas HD**
- ✓ **WiFi Get HD**

I love to travel, but I'll be the first to tell you that I'm not very organized before or during (or after!) my outings. Fortunately, a lot of iPad apps can help me — and you — with that. You find apps for booking travel and accommodations, apps to show you where to go, apps for tracking flights, and even apps for helping you find local services and other information. In this chapter, I show you some of these apps so you can use your iPad to make your trips more fun, more efficient, and maybe even hassle-free. (But don't hold me to that last one!)

Many of the apps I talk about in this chapter are apps that were written for the iPad. Some apps, however, have been written by the developer to run as native apps on both the iPad and iPhone (or iPod touch). These are called *hybrid* apps, and you'll find a little + sign next to the price in the App Store for those apps. Hybrid apps have the advantage of allowing you to buy once and use on whatever iOS device you have.

Don't forget that with the addition of Siri as a feature of iOS 6 available to third- and fourth-generation iPads and iPad minis, you can get much of the information provided by these apps by simply double-clicking your Home button and asking Siri a question!

KAYAK HD — Flights, Hotels, Explore

by KAYAK Software Group

Free

What you can do with it: Find flights, rental cars, and hotels, or use the Explore feature to find destinations you might not even realize you want to visit.

You may be familiar with KAYAK as an online travel service. Or you may have used the company's iPhone apps, but either way, you should check out KAYAK HD — Flights, Hotels, Explore. This free app offers the standard flight search features, but it also has some cool features like Explore that may help you have a little fun, too.

KAYAK claims to offer the fastest flight search in the world. I can't speak to the claim of fast*est,* but it's definitely fast. The interface is straightforward and easy to use and understand. Plug in your From and To airports, your Departure and Return dates, number of passengers, class of flight (Economy, Business, First), and whether you prefer nonstop flights, and then tap Search. On the left side of Figure 2-1, you can see that I was looking for some flights from San Francisco to New York City in September, and in the Search History pane, you can see past searches. That's very handy if you're comparing prices between different date ranges and/or locations. You'll also see a map of my route. (In landscape mode, you also get a separate pane for recommended hotel deals.)

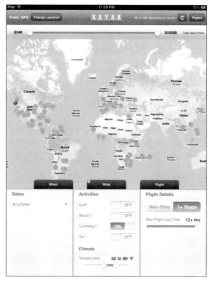

Figure 2-1: Search results for a cross-country flight (left) and the Explore interface for finding flights to destinations around the world (right).

You'll also find a pane called Hot Searches from *Your Departure City* that shows some great deals to random cities from the departure city you entered. These are deals that other KAYAK users found, and you never know when you might see a destination or killer price that strikes your fancy.

When you perform a search, you get a list of all the flights from the major airlines that service that route. A progress bar lets you know the status of your search. You can order the search results by Price, Airline, Stops, Duration, and Class. (Some search results may include a mix of classes, even though you specified a particular class.) You can also toggle any particular airline (or other factors) on or off from a list on the right side of the screen.

Under the Filter pane, tap the Price tab to get a slider that limits your search results from the cheapest flight in the list to a maximum price. This can limit the amount of scrolling you need to do.

I like this interface for searching and filtering my results, and I bet you will, too. You can also search for cars and hotels, and there's a Deals section that includes various vacation packages and other travel deals to and from different cities around the world. The Deals section is really a web page being served up through an in-app browser, and these pages include sponsored links to vacation packages and flights. Those sponsored links were not generated by the KAYAK engine, so be careful about what you tap in the Deals page if you want to limit yourself to KAYAK-searched results.

Next consider that fun Explore feature I mentioned. With Explore, you can choose your departure city and quickly get flight destinations to cities all over the world. It works like this: Set your city, and you'll get a map of the planet with orange dots all over it, as shown on the right side of Figure 2-1. Each of those dots represents a flight. Pinch and zoom in far enough, and those dots become red rectangles with prices in them. Tap a rectangle (or a dot), and you get a pop-up window with the name of the destination city and a date range that the price represents. Tap that square, and you're taken to the Flights search page so you can see all flights to that city.

But it gets even cooler because you find three tabs at the bottom of the screen, as you can see on the right side of the figure. The When tab lets you specify a date range; the What tab lets you specify activities (Golf, Beach, Gambling, Skiing) and a temperature range (how cool is that?); and the Flight tab lets you specify whether you want nonstop flights and a maximum travel time. Tweak these as you want, and the dots (or rectangles) filter accordingly!

I realize that this isn't a great feature for planning a business trip, but how about for planning a vacation or a get-away-from-it-all trip? I think it's just great for finding a place to visit that you might not otherwise have considered.

Under the Settings menu, you can specify the currency you want to see your prices in. It defaults to U.S. dollars, but you have a dozen currencies to choose from.

You can sign in with your KAYAK account login, but you don't have to do so to use the flight search and other features of the app.

Lots of travel sites and services are available, but KAYAK is one of the best apps on the iPad for finding a flight. It's also one of the only apps that will help you if you don't know where you want to go!

Wikihood Plus for iPad

by Dr. Stephan Gillmeier

$6.99

What you can do with it: Find nearby sights, landmarks, buildings, and shopping destinations, all with links to their Wikipedia entries for in-depth information.

I'm not that great of a tourist. No, seriously, when I travel I want to hang out with friends in local (nonchain) restaurants and coffee shops. If sidewalk seating is available, all the better! I don't want to rush around ogling every tourist trap and monument that I could squeeze into the four hours I allotted to this city or that village. I don't rush around, and I don't get up early, unless I have a very compelling reason to do so. On the one hand, I enjoy traveling this way. On the other, I don't get around to seeing a lot of stuff even when I do want to take the time to sightsee, in part because I often don't even know it's there. Wikihood Plus for iPad is the kind of app that might solve this issue for me, and it might even change the way I travel.

Wikihood Plus for iPad is an app that taps into that vast reservoir of (mostly accurate) information known as Wikipedia. Using either your current location or a location you pick, Wikihood Plus tells you what's nearby, based on the millions of entries in Wikipedia. The creator said his app "intelligently organizes Wikipedia information for any place in the world using advanced semantic data mining." In other words, the app digs into Wikipedia for you and uses algorithms to sift through that data to show you what's near you, what's significant, and how to get there. Building further on the wiki theme, you find thousands of in-app user ratings, too.

A *wiki* is a website that can be edited by its users, which usually means anyone and everyone. Some wikis have no oversight, whereas others have professional editors or moderators. Wikipedia is an encyclopedia that is comprised of information supplied by its users, and it boasts hundreds of thousands of contributors around the world! It's far more often than not accurate info, though that's certainly not always the case. In recent years, however, the organization behind the project has increased the amount of oversight that entries and edits are given. But if you have any questions, you should probably check with another source just to be sure.

Say I am visiting New York City and am ready to leave from hanging out in Central Park. If I open Wikihood Plus and let it use my current location (you'll need an Internet connection for that!), it shows me that the Museum of Natural History's subway stop is right next to me (and the museum itself is close, too), and a really cool apartment building (if you like looking at architecture) and the Hayden Planetarium are nearby, as you can see on the left side of Figure 2-2. If I scroll farther down, I find more museums, galleries, theaters, historical societies, and schools than I could shake a stick at, even if I had a really big stick!

Book VI
Chapter 2

If I tap the Hayden Planetarium entry, I'm taken to a new page, as you can see on the right side of the figure. That page has more entries that relate to the planetarium, and I can drill down for more information. For instance, when I tap the top entry for the planetarium, I get the full Wikipedia entry for the page, all laid out nice and pretty for my iPad.

Travel Apps

In the image on the right in Figure 2-2, you see a star icon at the top of the screen. Tap the star to rate the main place described in the main entry — in this case, the Hayden Planetarium.

Figure 2-2: Search results for locations near me (left) and info on the Hayden Planetarium, including other Wikipedia entries relating to it (right).

Additional tabs appear on the bottom of the screen, too, that allow you to filter the entries you see relating to a particular location. When you have drilled down to the entry on a specific location, those icons include a link to directions (which takes you to the iPad's Maps app).

I love this app, and although I intend to use it for traveling, I've even learned things about my neighborhood and city that I hadn't known before. If you're the type of traveler who's curious about what's near, you need this app.

Urbanspoon for iPad

by Wanderspot, LLC

Free

What you can do with it: Find nearby restaurants based on your location, or based on the city or neighborhood you choose. The app has a great random search feature that gives you as much, or as little, control over your results as you want.

I think a lot of people consider Urbanspoon an app that solves the "I don't know; where do you want to eat?" eternal quandary, but to me, it has a lot of value as a travel companion, especially when you're visiting an unfamiliar place where you don't have any friends (or a good concierge) to give you advice.

The basic premise of the app is to let you find restaurants by randomly choosing from various cuisines, price points, and different neighborhoods on three slot machine reels. Shake your iPad (or tap the Shake button) and you get a random suggestion for where to eat. If you don't like the result, shake it again. If you want to limit your options, say to a particular neighborhood or a type of food, you can lock one, two, or even all three reels to try to find a particular kind of restaurant.

When you get a restaurant you like, just tap its name and you see a screen with its address, phone number, kind of restaurant, Urbanspoon user rating, cost rating (connoted by one, two, or three dollar signs), and reviews of the place (where applicable).

Tap various items on the screen to reveal details such as hours, a menu (sometimes), more about the restaurant's user rating (such as how many people voted), the opportunity to submit your own rating, suggestions of other restaurants you might like, an advertisement (it's an ad-supported app), and directions in Google Maps, as you can see on the right side of Figure 2-3.

If you really like (or hate) a place, take the time to contribute to the user ratings, and make sure you leave a written review. More importantly, think about the kinds of reviews that you find helpful and include similar information in yours. ("This place rocks" isn't any more helpful than "This place stinks.")

Figure 2-3: All about Joe The Art of Coffee (left) and locking in my search for a coffee shop in the West Village, in the $10-or-less range (right).

Because I'm talking about Urbanspoon as a travel app, I should also note that a map feature is embedded right in the app. When you view the app in Map mode, all the results come up on the map that dominates two-thirds of your screen, as shown on the right side of the figure. When you shake for a restaurant, the map zooms to that location's neighborhood, with the selected restaurant and other restaurants nearby represented by pins in the map. This makes it easy to quickly look at what other options you have in that neighborhood.

The more popular a restaurant is with Urbanspoon's users, the darker its pin will be. If you tap the Show Popular button in the upper-left corner of the map, all the light blue pins go away. Also, the restaurant that is currently selected is denoted by a bright red pin, as you can see on the right side of Figure 2-3.

Using the map to display the results this way cuts a couple of steps out of the process of using Urbanspoon for iPad, and being a visual learner, I really like it. You find a List mode, as well, but it shows only the most popular restaurants in the city you're looking at.

This is some of my favorite advice to give to people who have even an ounce of adventure in them: Instead of spinning and spinning until you get a result that's familiar to you, try limiting yourself to one shake and sticking to whatever comes up. Oh yeah, it could be awful, but it might also be great! This is a must-have app if you're going to be traveling and don't have every second of every day already planned. With Urbanspoon, finding a restaurant is only a shake away.

Yelp is another great app for this sort of crowd-sourced finding of nearby restaurants, and I recommend both it and Urbanspoon for the traveler.

ZAGAT TO GO

by Handmark, Inc.

$9.99 — Hybrid

What you can do with it: Find nearby restaurants that have been reviewed and rated by ZAGAT. You can get directions, hours of operation, features of the restaurant, contact information, and the menu, and many restaurants have links to their websites.

While I'm talking about finding good restaurants while traveling, I should mention ZAGAT TO GO, which represents a different approach for a restaurant guide. There's a time and place for crowd sourcing, but ZAGAT TO GO offers reviews compiled by professional editors based on customer surveys, and in an age where budget-constrained newspapers are cutting back on local coverage like restaurant reviews, ZAGAT is the kind of resource that will only become more valuable as time goes on, especially with iOS devices.

ZAGAT is one of the most comprehensive restaurant guides on the planet, and this hybrid iPhone, iPod touch, and iPad app gives you access to thousands of restaurant reviews, a GPS-enabled restaurant locator, the ability to search for restaurants according to multiple criteria, and more. This is definitely a must-have app for foodies, and unlike the print version (after you buy it), the app is constantly updated with new reviews.

Because ZAGAT is not a crowd-sourced guide, its reviews are limited to major metropolitan areas. That means you should check to make sure the areas where you're intending to use it are actually covered.

ZAGAT TO GO allows you to pick a city or use your iPad's Location Services to determine your current location. The interface itself is almost entirely dominated by a map display of the area, with ZAGAT-reviewed restaurants highlighted with Z pins. Tap a pin, and you get a pane at the top of the screen with basic information about the place, including its name; its food, decor, and service ratings on a scale of 0–30, along with the average cost of a meal (including one drink and a tip). You'll also find the beginning of the ZAGAT review, which is often enough to let you know whether you want to eat there.

In Figure 2-4, I'm looking at restaurants in Brooklyn, where I found The Grocery, which has a stunning 27 rating for its food, though it's what I'd call pricey, at $60 per meal.

Figure 2-4: The Grocery is a very highly rated restaurant in Brooklyn.

If that isn't enough information for me, however, I can tap the pane to get a full-screen workup on the restaurant. This includes the hours of operation, features of the restaurant, address and phone number, an e-mail link, and the ability to drop the contact information directly to your iPad's Address Book! I really like that feature, and I hope to see it make its way to more apps in the future.

What's with all those quotes in a ZAGAT review? The company's editors compile their reviews from customer surveys, and they use (very) short quotes from those surveys throughout their reviews.

There's also a Star icon for adding the restaurant to your Favorites, and a little *i* (for *information*) icon you can tap to see an explanation of ZAGAT's review system. ZAGAT uses a 30-point scale, and if you're not familiar with just what those numbers mean, this is a very handy explanation that's just a tap away.

If you don't want to browse restaurants from a map, tap the icon that looks like six little boxes at the bottom of the screen to browse local restaurants in list form. You can sort by food, decor, and service ratings; by cost; or alphabetically. Just swipe the screen to go to the next page, and tap any of the eight listings on each page to get the full-screen workup I mentioned previously.

Note that you need a connection to the Internet to make the most use of this app, as it pulls reviews from the company's servers. This ensures you have the very latest information and most up-to-date reviews. You can, however, view reviews in your History and Favorites without a connection.

ZAGAT TO GO is the app for foodies or anyone who is interested in getting a more formal, organized, and edited approach in a restaurant guide. Whether you're traveling for business or pleasure, if you care about where you eat, take ZAGAT TO GO with you.

FlightTrack Pro — Live Flight Status Tracker by Mobiata

by Ben Kazez

$9.99 — Hybrid

What you can do with it: Track flights all over the globe. With integrated TripIt support, entering your flight information is super easy.

Ignore the long name and call this app what everyone else calls it, FlightTrack Pro. This app is great for when you're traveling, but it's also a good app to have when you're expecting friends, family, or business associates who are traveling to you! With it, you can track flights all over the world on a map, and you can do it in real time, too. In addition, it has integrated support for TripIt (see the next section), which makes tracking those flights super easy.

I don't have any upcoming flights of my own to show you, but FlightTrack Pro has a fun little feature that allows you to shake your iPad to find a random flight. To be honest, this fun feature is easier to use on the iPhone, but it's still a great way to show off the app to your friends. You can also add flights by hand if you know the flight number, or search for them by route if you don't.

You can also make an in-app purchase for $3.99 to add the ability to search for flights according to the departing airport. Except for those who live in metro areas with two or three airports servicing travelers, most users aren't likely to need that ability, but if you're a flight junkie — and flight junkies are out there, let me tell you — you won't want to miss it.

On the left side of Figure 2-5, I've picked several random flights in the United States. The pop-up window lists all the flights I'm tracking, and I can remove any individual flight by tapping the little eyeball icon underneath the date. You can see take-off and landing times, status (the top flight is en route), and I can delete a flight by tapping the Edit button.

Now, on the map you see green and red squares, and an airplane icon and line representing each of the routes. The red squares are destinations, and the green ones are departure cities. If you tap those squares, you get a pop-up window with information and any warnings regarding that specific airport.

Figure 2-5: Monitoring several flights in the continental United States (left) and a push notification about a flight I was monitoring (right).

Tap a jet, and you find additional information about that flight. The pop-up window includes take-off and landing times and on-time status, and if I scroll down, I get total air time, elapsed time, the remaining time for the flight, a weather forecast, and other information.

The mapping service is provided by Google, and it includes an overlay of live weather information, as you can see on both sides of the figure.

Most people aren't going to fire up this app just to watch random flights. Its main use is to monitor flights you actually care about. Two key features make this app very convenient for this use. The first is support for TripIt, a third-party service that monitors your flights for you. You can use TripIt to get e-mail notifications of status updates for your flight, and with support for the service in this app, you can use it to make entering your flight information easy. TripIt, which is free (FlightTrack Pro currently doesn't support a paid Pro level), allows you to simply forward your itinerary to the company, and then it automagically grabs all your flight (and other data) for you. When you enter your TripIt account information in FlightTrack Pro, it automatically looks to TripIt for any flights you're taking and presents them to you on a silver platter. No muss, no fuss!

The other key feature is the way the app uses Push Notification Service to send you any updates on the flights you're tracking. On the right side of Figure 2-5, you see a Push notification for a new arrival time for one of my flights. These Push notifications appear even if you don't have the app open, meaning you get those status updates without having to go look for them! And because this app is a hybrid app that works on your iPhone and iPod touch, you're a lot more likely to find out when your wife is landing early or when your boss's flight has been canceled. Believe me, this is a great feature, especially if you have to travel frequently or work with people who do.

You can e-mail flight information directly from the app, too. You'll appreciate this when you get a Push update that a flight has been delayed and need to send it to your coworker or family member so they can meet the flight.

FlightTrack Pro is gorgeous, and tracking a flight is fun (to me) even if I'm not involved with it. To me, it's a must-have app for anyone involved with any sort of semiregular travel. It's more convenient on your iPhone when you're in the car, but it looks so great and is so much easier to use on your iPad that you'll use it there whenever you can.

Quick Hits

In addition to the apps discussed up to this point, here are some quick reviews of other apps worthy of your inspection.

TripIt

by Concur Technologies

Free

If you travel at all, definitely get TripIt. You can set up trips and share your itineraries with anybody in your life from business associates to your BFF. TripIt pushes notifications to you of flight delays or gate changes. You can keep track of hotel and even restaurant reservations in one convenient place. In addition, if a better price comes along before you set off on your trip, you might be able to get a refund, all courtesy of TripIt's notifications about the best available fares. You also find features that help you track your frequent traveler points and get a few perks such as rental car VIP memberships.

INRIX Traffic! and INRIX Traffic! Pro

by INRIX, Inc.

Free; $9.99 per year or $24.99 for life

The preinstalled Maps app on your iPad is a new app with iOS 6 and Apple has acknowledged it is flawed, so if you travel a lot by car and need accurate traffic updates you might consider a third-party app. When you're traveling to another city, one thing you're not likely to have much knowledge of is local traffic. Of course, if you have to commute for 45 minutes each way just to get to work, you might consider that "travel," too. Whatever the case, INRIX Traffic! and its Pro counterpart can provide you with the kind of real-time traffic data that could be the difference in getting to that wedding, business meeting, dinner reservation, or maybe just your job, on time. The free version works well enough for most people, and it displays real-time conditions on maps in a straightforward and easy-to-follow way. (It shows green lines for normal traffic, orange for slow, and red for heavy traffic.) The Pro version, which costs $9.99 per year or $24.99 for a lifetime subscription, offers you fastest-route information, expected travel time (and ETA), directions, the best time to leave, traffic cameras, and the ability to save frequent destinations. Try out the free one, and if you like it, you'll probably want the Pro version.

Priceline Hotel & Car Negotiator

by Priceline

Free

Whatever you may think about Captain Kirk, aka William Shatner, the spokesperson for Priceline, the concept of the service could just save you money on your next trip. Called the "ultimate booking machine," Priceline offers a handy map interface to find accommodations near you, if you let the app use your location information, and provides the most current, best rates. You can also enter any location in the world and get a list of hotels with guest rankings and the best price per night. For extra savings, you can choose the level of hotel you want and place a bid. You can also find car rental deals and reap Priceline's promoted savings.

iTranslate

by Sonico GmBH

Free or $1.99 without ads

If you travel internationally and don't happen to have mastered seven languages like James Bond, iTranslate might just be a great app to have on your iPad. It has an easy-to-use interface; just type a word in the top pane set to a language such as English, and then tap the setting for the second language and scroll to find the one you need, such as Italian. Want to hear the pronunciation? Just tap the little speaker icon in the second language, and the word is pronounced correctly. If you purchase an add-on voice recognition package, you can speak words to the translator. Tap an icon to mark a word or phrase, such as "I'll have a glass of wine" as a favorite and you can look it up easily anytime you need it. You can even slow down a pronunciation and choose to hear either a male or female voice.

World Atlas HD

by The National Geographic Society

$1.99

Admittedly, this app is probably of more use to you before you travel than when you're traveling, but it's so cool that I'll take any excuse to talk about it. World Atlas HD is produced by The National Geographic Society, so you know it has quality maps and information about countries around the world. It comes with a global map that you can pinch and zoom around to look at whatever part of the planet you care to check out. It features an Executive map, a Political Map, and a Satellite map. The first two are really just different styles for displaying countries, whereas the Satellite map shows pictures of the areas as they appear from satellites orbiting the globe. With these maps, you can tap and hold a country to get some information about that country. You can tap the + button to bookmark that country, and that also places a pin on the map, which is handy for seeing which countries you have and haven't read about. All these maps are available for online browsing, but you can also download them for offline (and faster) viewing, which I recommend.

WiFi Get HD

by WiTagg, Inc.

$2.99

If you're traveling with an iPad, you should probably know where you can get a Wi-Fi hotspot. WiFi Get HD can tell you. It comes with 150,000 known free hotspots preinstalled, which means you can browse them even when you don't have a connection. If you have a connection but need to find a different hotspot, or you're planning ahead, you can access the company's online database of more than 200,000 free or paid hotspots. The app allows users to add hotspots they find (hopefully it's not the poor schmuck living near the coffee shop who didn't protect his network), or update known hotspots if their status changed. Wi-Fi is becoming more and more common, but it isn't yet ubiquitous. If you're traveling to a place you don't know well and plan to use your iPad, you should probably take this app with you.

Chapter 3: Social Web Apps

In This Chapter

Apps for social interaction online range from clients for gathering all your Facebook- or Twitter-type postings in one environment to collections of pictures you can use when instant messaging and online content readers to follow your favorite blogs.

In this chapter, I give you an idea of some social-type apps you might want to explore. The good news: Just about every one of them is free from the App Store.

Remember that with iOS 6, the ability to post content to Facebook and Twitter is built into many apps such as Photos and Music.

Friendly for Facebook

by Oecoway, Inc.

Free

What you can do with it: Do everything you usually do on Facebook with a simpler, friendlier interface.

Are you spending way more than the daily recommended allowance of time on Facebook? If so, you'll appreciate Friendly for Facebook. This app was specifically designed for iPad, which makes your Facebook experience — well — friendlier. One of its strengths is filtering your content in logical ways, so you can view things by updates, photos, videos, links, friends, or notes.

Other features are more subtle, enhancing the original Facebook experience in small but useful ways. For example, a full-screen photo viewer lets you see more of your Facebook photos on the iPad screen.

When you're viewing the dizzying amount of constant social content coming at you, speed is also a factor. With Friendly for Facebook, your photos upload faster, you log in faster, and your chats move along with noticeable speed. Of course, the touchscreen experience on iPad adds an interesting dimension as you swipe your way through feeds and photos, truly getting in touch with your friends. Some customizing features in Friendly for Facebook are also appealing, including the ability to set up colors and fonts the way you want them.

If you have more than one Facebook account (and who doesn't?), you can switch among them on the fly. And if you want your friends to constantly know where you are, use the Share Where You Are with Your Friends feature that takes advantage of iPad's location technology.

Do be a bit cautious about using any location feature. If you've befriended friends of friends, who are essentially strangers, letting them know your every move might not be in your best interest. Want people to know when you're away from home so they can rip you off? Want your boss to see you're at the mall when you're supposed to be at a client's office? I'm just saying . . .

So how do Facebook and Friendly for Facebook really differ? Here I compare Home pages. On Facebook, you see categories like News Feed, Messages, Events, and Friends along the left side like a sort of navigation bar. On the right are suggestions of friends and sponsored links (ads). In Friendly for Facebook (Figure 3-1 shows a typical event page), tabs replace the navigation bar in many cases. If you tap the Friends button at the top of the screen, you get another tabbed interface with Friends, Phonebook, and Pages (web pages) dividing information into simple sets.

iPad provides some interesting functionality in this environment. For example, if you go to the Phonebook tab on the Friends page, you can just tap a phone number to place a call (assuming you're within range of Wi-Fi or have a 3G/4G model and a phone app such as Skype set up). The Friendly menu gives you quick access for sharing Friendly for Facebook with friends, uploading photos, editing your profile, customizing Friendly, switching to another Facebook account, and more.

Bottom line, Friendly for Facebook provides a simple-to-use interface for Facebook customized for the iPad user. Some perks may be subtle, but collectively, they make for a smooth iPad Facebook environment.

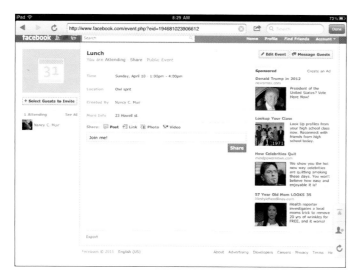

Figure 3-1: A Friendly for Facebook's event page.

Blogshelf

by gdiplus

99 cents

What you can do with it: Subscribe to and read blogs and news feeds. E-mail, tweet, or post content to Facebook. Save images to an album in Photos.

Blogshelf is touted as "the iPad reader for the rest of us." It makes it possible to view lots of blogs (which is why I've put it in the social web category) and news feeds in one place, avoiding the native environment of these sites until or unless you want to visit them. The plus here is that you get to the content without weeding through the other stuff. If you want to jump to the originating site, you can, and then you can read or post comments to your heart's content.

Pick the blogs and news feeds (up to 90) that appeal to you most, and Blogshelf goes out and gathers content for you. One strength of this app is how easy it is to read blogs with it. It has an attractive magazine-like layout that's easy to navigate. (See Figure 3-2.) The layout gets rid of all the surrounding web page banners and ads you see on the original blog or news page just like the Reader feature in Safari, which is a very nice feature. And swiping through blog content or moving from one blog to the next with iPad's touchscreen feels effortless.

If you're intrigued by exploring blogs from other lands, you'll appreciate the feature for translating foreign languages into your own.

You can browse the blogs and feeds that come set up in Blogshelf or look for more content to subscribe to. Tap the Subscribe button to see a lot of featured blogs and news sites. If you prefer to view a blog in Safari, use the View in Safari or View Original Article links to go to the blog post online. At that point, you can leave replies to express your own ideas on the topic.

Figure 3-2: You can find a variety of blogs on special interests to subscribe to.

If you find something you like, you can e-mail it, tweet it, or publish it to Facebook. You can even save images from a blog or news story to an album in Photos. Don't like one of the presubscribed blogs? Tap the Edit button to delete it.

Another nice feature of this app is the ability to modify the screen brightness, font size, font color, and font style you use to read text. Your blogs are arranged neatly on a bookcase very reminiscent of the iBooks reader library bookshelf.

If you want an e-reader that focuses on blogs and news feeds, this might be one for you to check out.

Flipboard

by Flipboard, Inc.

Free — Hybrid

What you can do with it: Access Facebook and Twitter postings from a centralized location, as well as news content on topics such as Tech and Style. Add your own sections of news categories to follow.

 One of the challenges in today's world is to keep up with all the information that's coming at you through a variety of sites and sources. Flipboard provides a visual way to organize and view all that content.

Now I have to admit, I'm a sucker for good design, and Flipboard is quite simply a nicely designed, graphical, magazine-style interface for accessing blogs, postings, and news in one place. Each item you're following displays in a section on the Flipboard home page (as shown in Figure 3-3).

Figure 3-3: Flipboard's interface is neat, clean, and graphical.

Sign in to your Facebook or Twitter account and add a Flipboard section on a person to follow in the news as well as view his or her online postings. For example, you'd be amazed how active the Dalai Lama is online (see Figure 3-4); you find pictures of his latest activities in the news as well as his comments. ("As human beings, we are all the same, there is no need to build some kind of artificial barrier between us," he posted at 2:36 a.m. one fine morning in April.)

Figure 3-4: The Dalai Lama in words and pictures.

You can add sections from the home page by tapping a blank block sporting the words *Add a Section.* You can also tap the Featured tab, tap some featured content to open that page, and then tap the Add to Contents button to add it as a section in Flipboard Contents.

In adding sections for Flipboard (you're limited to nine items on a page, but you can use your finger to flip to the next page to add more sections), you can choose a persona, list, or blog from Twitter for easy access to that content. You also find categories of news and blogs provided by Flipboard such as News, Business & Finance, and Tech & Science.

I'm particularly fond of the Cool Curators category, where you can follow folks like film critic Roger Ebert, New Yorker Writers, or Big Think, a very interesting blog on current events and politics. If you just can't decide what to view, tap the Featured tab on the Flipboard home page and choose a recommendation from there to view.

To delete a section that doesn't interest you anymore, tap the Edit button and use the Delete buttons that appear on each section to delete one or more.

In short, if you want a very clean graphical way to get to news, blogs, and postings, Flipboard is highly recommended.

Quick Hits

Here are several more apps you should check out.

SocialSeek

by Sensidea

Free

This app is like a police-channel scanner for social content. Scan through blogs, tweets, videos, and events by topic. You can look through categories of topics focused on entertainment, sports, and more to get the hottest news and opinions. One cool feature of this app is the ability to make your own SocialSeek site. Imagine all the videos, photos, tweets, and other content that interests you most all in one place and you get what SocialSeek is all about.

TextPics+

by Mangoo

Free — Hybrid

If using the shorthand language of texting is limiting for you, consider adding some visual zing to your messages. These pictures are made up of text and font images, but they take these to an art form. The Happy Birthday message is formed of little i's representing a row of candles and layers of asterisks forming a birthday cake. Snoopy at a typewriter is drawn with hyphens and punctuation symbols.

You find many categories of images here, from Animals and Celebrations to Scenery and Vehicles. Find an image you like and tap it to display a menu that gives you several options. You can make an image a Favorite so you can access it quickly, copy it and paste it into a text message, or e-mail it to your-self or others, for example.

Try using an IM client such as IM+, covered next, to access popular IM services such as AIM and MSN.

IM+

by SHAPE Services

Free — Hybrid

This instant messaging app works with Google Talk, Yahoo! Messenger, MSN/Windows Live Messenger, AIM/Messages, ICQ, Myspace, Twitter, Facebook, and Jabber. You can share text, photos, voice, and video, and organize your various IM messages easily. You can choose from several really attractive backgrounds to customize your IM environment, making chats an appealing visual experience. You can also see at a glance which of your contacts is online at any moment.

IM+ is free, but you get advertisements. If you want the advertisement-free version, fork over $9.99 for IM+ Pro, which also adds a handy conversation history feature and Skype chat.

Bebo Mobile

by Bebo.com

Free — Hybrid

If you really love social networking, you probably want to get the Bebo app. Bebo is considered one of the safer social networks in terms of privacy and use of your data. This app allows you to all the usual things — upload photos, stay connected to friends, post and edit your profile — all from your iPad.

This is a hybrid app, meaning it works on iPhone, iPad, and iPod touch, but it seems like it works just fine on your iPad.

ooVoo Video Chat

by ooVoo, LLC

Free — Hybrid

Finally, I just assume you have a Facebook account along with just about everybody else on the planet. If you do, getting this free app allows you to text and chat with you Facebook friends who also have ooVoo accounts (you can chat with up to 12 at one time). You can enjoy the group chat feature, and even get notifications of incoming video chats and messages.

Chapter 4: News, Sports, and Weather Apps

In This Chapter

- ✔ Pulse News for iPad
- ✔ Instapaper
- ✔ NPR for iPad
- ✔ BBC News
- ✔ The Weather Channel Max for iPad
- ✔ Newsy for iPad
- ✔ LIFE for iPad
- ✔ Watch ESPN
- ✔ Reuters NewsPro for iPad
- ✔ Wall Street Journal

From all the anecdotal evidence I see at my local coffee shops, I have surmised that reading on the iPad is one of the most popular activities for iPad users, especially when it comes to catching up on the news. Of course iPad includes Newsstand, a gathering place for publications and subscriptions, but you might want to explore a news aggregator or want to get a particular publication app for its unique features. You can find a lot of different newspapers, magazines, sports rundowns, and RSS news readers in the App Store; however, and in this chapter, I show you some of the best of them. To keep you out of the rain, I also throw in some cool weather apps, just for good measure.

Many of the apps I talk about in this chapter are apps that were written for the iPad. Some apps, however, have been written by the developer to run as native apps on both the iPad and iPhone (or iPod touch). These are called *hybrid* apps, and you'll find a + sign next to the price in the App Store for those apps. Hybrid apps have the advantage of allowing you to buy once and use on whatever iOS device you have.

Pulse News for iPad

by Alphonso Labs, Inc.

Free

What you can do with it: Follow up to 20 RSS feeds, or create your own Pulses for others to follow. Because each article in a feed is displayed along with any images in the feed, it offers a more graphically intense way of viewing your news.

Alphonso Labs' Pulse News reader is one of the most interesting apps to come out of the iPad ecosystem yet. Pulse is an *RSS news reader,* but rather than presenting those feeds as straightforward lists, Pulse presents them as graphically rich blocks that look almost like a filmstrip, as you can see in Figure 4-1. If the RSS feeds you're following include images with them, those images display by the text, making it a lot easier to get the gist of each article, and it certainly makes scrolling through your feeds more interesting. The Smart Dock is a nice feature that recommends sources based on the items that you read.

RSS stands for *Really Simple Syndication,* and it's another way for a website to serve up new articles, stories, or other forms of content, usually with a headline link to the full article, a teaser, and sometimes an image. An *RSS news reader* is an app that displays RSS feeds from one or more sites. It's just another way to read a website.

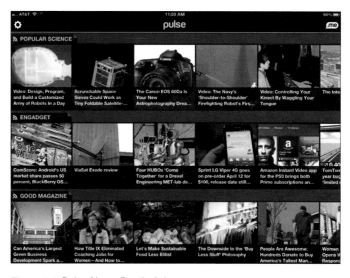

Figure 4-1: Pulse News Reader's home screen.

If you follow a lot of RSS feeds (more than 20), Pulse may not be the best news reader for you. As of this writing, it's limited to 20 RSS feeds and five custom feeds called Pulses that you or your friends create (for 25 total feeds). If you're a news junkie with more than that, you'll want to look at NetNewsWire, Reeder, or some other RSS news reader.

Each of your feeds is featured as a horizontal strip, with the newest article to the left. You can swipe up and down to see more of your feeds, and you can swipe from side to side to scroll the articles in a given feed. It's pretty simple. When you see an article you want to read, just tap its box (articles you haven't read yet are brighter than articles you have already read), and it's pulled in its own pane. If your feed offers entire articles, you get the whole thing right there. Most RSS feeds (in my experience) offer teasers, though, and for those you'll get the title, the teaser, and any images included. Tap the title, and you're taken to the full web page via the in-app browser.

You can also tap the Web button in the upper-right corner of the screen and automatically open the full article every time you tap a block! To go back to reading just the RSS feed, tap the Text button.

One of my favorite things about this app is a real help to a lot of users. RSS readers allow you to add feeds by adding the direct URL of that feed. That's great on a computer where you have a mouse, can cut and paste, and can have two apps open side by side. On iPad, however, it's a little harder. You can copy a URL to your Clipboard in one app and then go back to Pulse and paste it, or you can memorize it and type it by hand. Or — and this is that cool feature I mentioned — you can enter a search term, say *The Mac Observer,* and Pulse gives you a list of links it believes contains an RSS feed for that term. Choose the one you want, and boom! It's added! It's a great feature, and I won't be surprised if it makes its way to other news readers sooner rather than later.

Lastly, you'll find a social networking component in Pulse. When you see an article you like, you can tap the Heart icon and add it to your own Pulse. This is basically an RSS feed that you create that has only those articles you pick. You can have up to five Pulses, and your friends can follow them. I'd personally trade these Pulses for more standard feeds, but that's just me.

Pulse is a really cool news reader for casual RSS users, and it offers a much more aesthetically pleasing way of viewing your feeds than any other reader out there.

Instapaper

by Marco Arment

$2.99

What you can do with it: Browse RSS feeds, get articles and other web pages from within other apps, save favorite articles, share articles with others through your Starred list, and view articles offline.

 Instapaper has been . . . dare I say it? An insta-hit! This app taps into one of the fundamental side effects of the information blitz that makes up a big part of your digital life today, and that's managing all the cool things you see but don't ever get around to actually reading. Instapaper allows you to tag articles, websites, Flickr pics, and just about everything else on the web for viewing later when you have a moment to spare. You can even view your tagged content offline, when you're not connected to the web. You can do it from within the Instapaper app, but currently several dozen iOS apps have added support for Instapaper, too!

To help you understand how cool this is, let me paint a scenario for you. You're catching up on tweets from your friends. One friend links to a hilarious picture of her kitten that can't figure out how to get out of a box, and then another friend has a link to an article with tips on how to get the most out of your iPad. And then you see an editorial over at *The Mac Observer* about how Apple's strategy in the tablet market has thrown Amazon for a loop. And then . . . well, you probably know just what I mean. You see all these things when you're reading tweets, looking at RSS feeds, or sometimes just reading your e-mail, and you usually don't get around to reading very much of it.

But back up a little bit and look at the app itself. As you can see in Figure 4-2, the app allows you to browse RSS feeds, each with its own folder. When browsing your feeds, you can either read the articles right then and there or save them to your Read Later folder.

 You can also Star articles as favorites. Tapping the star saves the article, but Instapaper also allows you to follow the Starred folders of your friends. (You have to do this on the service's website.)

If you're in one of those other apps that supports Instapaper — say Twitter for iOS — when you're finding all those cool things that I mentioned previously, you can add items to your Read Later folder from within those apps. This is handy for offline viewing, but it's especially great if you're going through a lot of tweets and want to be able to gather everything together at one time, and then read it later.

 Check out the Editor's Picks folder for some interesting articles you might not have otherwise found!

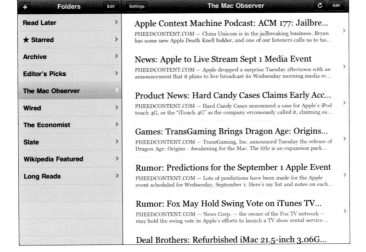

Figure 4-2: On the left are the RSS feeds I've added to Instapaper. On the right are the articles found in *The Mac Observer*'s RSS feed.

Each article in Instapaper has a link to the original posting on the web, allowing users to view the article with its original formatting and layout, including any ads that paid for it.

Instapaper is a capable RSS news reader, but most users like it for its offline capabilities and the ability to gather lots of material from browsers and other apps for reading all at one time.

I don't want to leave out mention of The Daily, a much-touted news aggregation app and winner of the App Store Rewind 2011 Best in Newsstand award. This service touts itself as having a mission to "provide the best news experience by combining world-class storytelling with the unique interactive capabilities of the iPad." You can only get this app for your iPad, and it comes with a free two-week subscription — after that, it will cost you $0.99 for a weekly subscription or $39.99 for a yearly subscription.

NPR for iPad

by NPR

Free

What you can do with it: Read articles and listen to news reports from NPR's news arm, find and stream public radio stations, and listen to many of the organization's entertainment radio programs.

NPR (that stands for *National Public Radio*) for iPad is one of those best-in-class iPad apps in terms of its user interface. More importantly, it offers you access to just about everything NPR produces, including written stories, radio news stories, and a broad selection of the entertainment and informational radio shows.

You can browse NPR's content in several ways. The home screen features three scrollable timelines, one each for News, Arts & Life, and Music, as you can see in Figure 4-3. These three streams are all stories and articles produced by the NPR news organization — the different radio programs are offered separately. You can swipe through these three streams from left to right, and when you tap a story that interests you, it takes over the screen, with the category stream at the bottom.

Figure 4-3: The home screen for NPR for iPad.

Some of these articles are offered in text only, but most of them have an accompanying radio report embedded right there. You can listen to the audio report from the home screen by tapping the Speaker button in the teaser, or by tapping the Listen Now button in the full article. Better yet, you can queue up stories in a Playlist for later listening. It's a great way to make sure you're hearing all the articles you want to listen to.

Most of these articles have pictures in them. Tap a pic for a full-screen version.

NPR for iPad also offers about 20 of its radio programs, from *All Things Considered,* to *Fresh Air,* to *Science Friday,* to *On the Media.* If you tap the Programs button at the bottom of the screen, you get a pop-up window with each program listed. Tap a show and you get a list of current and recent episodes you can play or add to a playlist. If it has a podcast version on iTunes, you'll find a button for getting it there, too!

Any show currently being aired somewhere in the world has an On Air label. You can tap into these shows live.

Lastly, the app lets you find local public radio stations that offer NPR content, and you can stream that station's broadcast directly to your iPad! This is a great way to listen to your local station, or to listen to what used to be your local station before you had to move. If you're in one of those few places without a public radio station, this makes it easier than ever before to find and listen to a station.

NPR for iPad is a must-have app for any fan of NPR's awesome news and entertainment shows. It looks great, and it's so easy to use that you may find yourself using it more than your radio.

BBC News

by BBC Worldwide, Ltd.

Free — Hybrid

What you can do with it: The BBC News app offers you news content from all over the world, as well as one-tap access to BBC Radio.

The BBC is one of the most respected news organizations in the world, and it's also one of the largest. The BBC News app for iPad brings that news to you, including written news reports and BBC radio, too. Some articles even have video additions that include background interviews for added color, broadcast TV reports, and more.

One of the coolest things about the BBC News app is that it's highly customizable. The home screen of the app shows several rows of news articles, with each row representing a different category of news. You can swipe up and down to scroll through these categories, or from right to left to scroll through the individual stories in a category.

The app defaults to featuring Top Stories, Americas, Technology, and Features and Analysis, as you can see in Figure 4-4, but many more categories are available, including Science & Environment, Europe, U.K., and several other global regions. The featured categories are expanded to show individual stories, and although you can tap any other category to expand it, you can also define which categories are featured by tapping the Edit button at the top of the screen. This is great for expats who want to start off with news from home, or anyone who's interested in a particular category of news. In addition to being able to decide what is featured, you can also reorder the categories as you see fit.

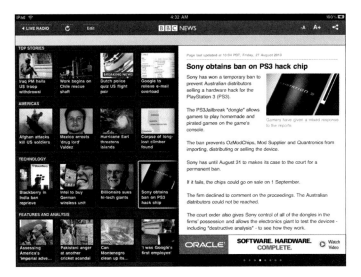

Figure 4-4: The BBC News app.

 BBC News even offers news in several languages other than English, including Mundo, Brasil, Chinese (Traditional), Chinese (Simple), Russian, Arabic, Persian, and Urdu. You can find the stories offered in those languages at the bottom of the category list.

The other great thing about this app is that it offers one-tap access to the BBC's great radio news coverage. Just tap the Live Radio button at the top of the screen (make sure to wait a moment while the app buffers the stream), and you have whatever is being streamed by BBC Radio delivered straight to your iPad. You can use other apps while BBC Radio streams in the background, too.

Just about every single story has an accompanying photograph or other image, but some stories come with a video component instead, as I mentioned previously. You'll know which is which because the videos have a big label that reads Tap to Play. Follow those directions, and a video player takes over your screen. I've found those videos to be of high quality — they aren't full HD quality, but they look good on your iPad. Note that because they are high quality, you'll want a good connection to the Internet to watch them without interruption. If your connection is slow, let them load before playing.

I want to mention one more cool feature of this app: When you're in a story, you can swipe from left to right to navigate to other stories in the same category.

The biggest advantage this app has over some of the other news apps is the BBC's focus on global news. It's well designed, and the developers made great use of the iPad's screen real estate in creating this app. If you have an interest in what's happening outside the borders of the United States, try BBC News on your iPad.

The Weather Channel Max for iPad

by The Weather Channel

Free

What you can do with it: View several weather maps, get local conditions and forecasts, watch The Weather Channel (TWC) video content, read severe weather alerts, and follow TWC-related Twitter accounts.

I'm a bit of an information junkie, and I regularly check the weather forecast with Apple's Weather app on my iPhone. No default weather app is available on the iPad, for some mysterious reason unknown to me, but (or maybe because of this) some great options are available for you to choose from in the App Store. Now, I point out right up front that weather apps are one of those things that people take pretty seriously, and what works for me may not work for you. But for my money (okay, it's a free app), The Weather Channel Max for iPad is one of the best of the bunch.

The Weather Channel Max for iPad is basically like having a big slice of The Weather Channel itself. It has forecasts, weather maps, warnings, and even some of the TV station's video reports. It also has ads . . . a lot of them. This turns off some people, but you're getting a lot of content that is otherwise free. And it's those ads that pay for all that content.

That out of the way, look at the app! When you first launch it, it asks whether it can use your current location (assuming you have your iPad set to ask for that permission). If you tap OK, you see a Google Maps display of your local area and six buttons for you to choose different features of the apps: Maps, Local, Video, Severe, Social, and On TV.

I think the way The Weather Channel — I call it TWC from here on, okay? — offers up maps is very cool. Some of the other weather apps give you different views (radar, satellite, temperature, and so on), but TWC's app gives you an overlay with all eight types of maps it offers, including Radar, Clouds, Radar & Clouds, Temperature, Feels Like, UV Index, 24 Hr Rain, and 24 Hr Snow. This overlay has example map slices, as you can see in Figure 4-5, which helps you quickly understand what you're picking and what it's going to show you. I like this feature.

Figure 4-5: The Weather Channel Max for iPad app.

Some of the map views can play through the observed weather for the last two hours or the forecast for the next four hours. I'm enough of an information junkie to think that's super cool.

The Local pane is what most people use the most, I think. In one view, it offers current weather conditions and the forecast for the next ten days. (Swipe sideways to scroll through all ten days.) With a tap, you can also get an hourly forecast through the next 24 hours, along with four-hour forecasts for the 12 hours after that, and then daily forecasts for the next eight days. There are also mini-panes for the other major features (swipe to scroll through them), as well as a pane for ads. Other apps do a better job of displaying just current conditions or a forecast, but enough is here to satisfy most weather junkies.

The Video pane offers local weatherperson forecasts, regional forecasts, national forecasts, travel forecasts, storm watch videos, weather-related news stories, and other content from TWC's TV network. And you can display these videos full screen, though it's not HD quality. You have a lot here to watch, and I'd call it a premier feature of the app.

Now scoot over to the Severe pane, where you can get local and national severe weather warnings. If you live in a place where severe weather can occur, you'll find this a great resource for keeping abreast of these warnings.

The Social pane offers you direct access to TWC-related Twitter feeds, for what that's worth, and the On TV pane is just a one-touch way to get to the video feature stories I mentioned previously.

A lot of material is here for the weather junkie, including lots of video content, great map views, and a passable local weather display. If you want a simple display of current conditions and the forecast, look to one of the apps I highlight in the next sections, but if you want to dig around in detailed weather information, try this free app.

Quick Hits

Here are several more apps you should check out.

Newsy for iPad: Multisource Video News Analysis

by Media Convergence Group, Inc.

Free

TechCrunch called this a "must download" app, and it's not surprising. If you like to be updated on world events in small video snippets, choose from categories such as World, U.S., Politics, Business, Entertainment, and Technology to download the video stories that interest you to watch offline. You can download in either standard quality or HD, read a transcript of each video, look up the source of the story, comment on it, or share it via e-mail, Facebook, or Twitter. You can also create playlists of stories and watch them online.

And yes, for you sports fans out there, you can use the Sports category to look for video coverage of all the big games and accompanying blow-by-blow analyses.

Newsy requires that you have iOS 4.3 or later with AirPlay.

LIFE for iPad

by TI Media Solutions, Inc.

Free

LIFE Magazine has always cornered the market on outstanding photos of world events, places, and people. Download this free app to put *LIFE*'s amazing photo collection at your fingertips. A cool feature figures out where you are and presents relevant photos to you. Follow the You May Also Like link to see other photos that are likely to engage you, and definitely use the Skip This Ad button to breeze past the sales pitches.

The photos in this collection are high definition and look great on the iPad screen. You can use the Email, Facebook, and Twitter buttons to spread the word about your favorite photos. Whether you're interested in current events or historical events, this huge collection has it all. And, it's free!

Watch ESPN

by ESPN, Inc.

Free — Hybrid

This free app lets you get live video streaming of all manner of sports from the several ESPN channels. From regular season games to those playoffs that support the entire hot wing and pizza industries, you can watch football, tennis, soccer — you name it. You'll also find sports news programs and all the usual commentary made up of personal opinion and insightful hindsight, as well as all the sports facts you crave.

Reuters NewsPro for iPad

by Thomson Reuters

Free

Reuters is one of the oldest providers of news from around the world, and its app for iPad continues its tradition of news for businesspeople and professionals. If you take your news seriously, you'll enjoy the well-written articles on everything from news events to entertainment and the stock market. I like that you can load your content offline to read when you can't get a connection.

Wall Street Journal

by Wall Street Journal

Free (subscription required)

News Corp. has brought *The Wall Street Journal* to the iPad, and in a big way. CEO Rupert Murdoch has talked about the future of newspapers being on devices like the iPad, and the company was among the first to invest major resources in developing a dedicated app for the device before it was even released. What you get is a sort of print newspaper look on your iPad display. Swipe and scroll, tap, pinch, and zoom, and you can navigate through individual stories and different sections of this business publication. It's not the best iPad app out there, but it's really good. And I personally think *The Journal*'s business coverage is top-notch. One thing about pricing: News Corp. has been experimenting with how to monetize this property online. As of this writing, the iPad app is free with an online subscription, which is where I imagine it will stay, but you should check before you download it.

Chapter 5: Financial Apps

In This Chapter

- ✔ StockWatch – iPad Edition
- ✔ Bloomberg for iPad
- ✔ SplashMoney for iPad
- ✔ PowerOne Financial Calculator
- ✔ Daily Stocks
- ✔ Pocket Expense Lite
- ✔ iSlick
- ✔ Quick Sale for iPad
- ✔ Pageonce – Money & Bills
- ✔ E*TRADE Mobile Pro for iPad

The term "financial app" can conjure up different things. You find apps to balance your checkbook or home budget, apps to buy stocks, banking apps, invoicing and billing apps, apps to read up on financial news, and even a few combinations of all those features. In this chapter, I show you some of the best of them so that you don't waste your finances having to try them all!

Many of the apps I talk about in this chapter are apps that were written for the iPad. Some apps, however, have been written by the developer to run as native apps on both the iPad and iPhone (or iPod touch). These are called *hybrid* apps, and you find a + sign next to the price in the App Store for those apps. Hybrid apps have the advantage of allowing you to buy once and use on whatever iOS device you have.

StockWatch – iPad Edition

by Todd Barnes

$4.99

What you can do with it: Monitor one or more stock portfolios, set up stock watchlists, and access financial news relating to specific stocks or the broader markets. You can also sync your portfolios and watchlists with other devices running StockWatch.

 I start the look at financial apps with an all-around stock app called StockWatch – iPad Edition. This is a great app for people who want to monitor one or more stock portfolios and follow news pertaining to those stocks or the broader markets. It can be particularly handy for those with investments across multiple brokerage firms.

One of the things I like most about this app is something I'm a little persnickety about: the fact that it's a good-looking app with a good interface. Okay, fine — I'm a lot persnickety about those kinds of things; it's true. It has a color scheme that's muted and easy on the eye; navigation is intuitive; and the app works in both portrait and landscape modes, though I prefer landscape mode. It also has all the features you need to monitor your portfolios, making it a one-stop shop for most users.

You find two main tabs in this app, Watchlist and Portfolios. As the name suggests, Watchlist is for setting up a list of individual stocks you want to watch. This is useful for individual companies you want to monitor from your portfolio, or for watching a company you're considering adding to your portfolio. This tab offers a snapshot of the current status for each of the stocks you're watching, and it includes the name of the company (or index), its ticker symbol, the last trade, and the change that trade represents (green for up and red for down). The middle pane offers you details about the stock in the list you have selected, as well as a chart for the stock. The third pane offers you a list of recent news articles pertaining to the stock or index you have selected in your list.

 Tap the chart to get a larger version, along with different viewing options from which to choose. These include the type of chart (line, bar, candlestick), the time frame (from one day to five years), and the different values you want to see in the chart.

The other main tab is the one labeled Portfolios. On this tab, you can set up one or more portfolios and monitor both their individual and collective performance. This is useful if you have a broad portfolio and want to be able to monitor it by sector (or whatever other breakdown you fancy) or if you have your investments spread among multiple brokerages. In Figure 5-1, you can see that the view for this tab includes a pane that shows the value of all your portfolios, another pane for the portfolio you have selected, and a third pane for the individual stocks in that portfolio. The middle of the screen shows detailed information on the day's trade and a chart, just like the Watchlist tab has. The third pane is for news relating to the individual stock you have selected.

There are a lot of preference options in StockWatch, and they're useful options. You can choose from three date formats, the ability to set your default tab, preferences for setting your default chart range, and more. Poke around in the Settings tab to see everything you can tweak.

TIP

You can set an app-specific passcode if you wish to prevent other users of your iPad from accessing the information in this app. You can find this on the Settings tab.

You see another tab in Figure 5-1, called Sync Data, that allows you to sync your data between your iPad and iPhone. Set up your Portfolios and Watchlist once, and then manage them on whatever device is convenient at the moment.

E*TRADE customers should use that company's iPad app (and I tell you about it later in this chapter), as I think it is even better than StockWatch, but StockWatch is a must-have app for anyone else looking to monitor her portfolios or set up stock watchlists. Its great design, awesome features, and intuitive interface make it a pleasure to use.

Book VI
Chapter 5

Financial Apps

Figure 5-1: Viewing a sample portfolio.

Bloomberg for iPad

by Bloomberg, LP

Free

What you can do with it: Monitor your stocks, as well as all the world's major equity indices, global currency markets, commodities, futures, and bonds. You also get all of Bloomberg's extensive financial news and several of the company's financial podcasts.

I'm a big fan of Bloomberg's financial news coverage, and I'm a bigger fan of this app. For one thing, it offers instant access to all that great news coverage, and it provides stock and index data like you'd expect. It also provides currency, commodities, and bond data — one of the few iPad apps I've seen that does so. For some icing on this cake of financial goodness, it offers direct access to a number of Bloomberg-produced podcasts that will be invaluable to traders and investors wanting to find out more about the markets as well as related video content.

Start with the home screen (accessed by a button simply labeled Bloomberg when you're in another tab). In Figure 5-2, you see that it offers you all the top financial news of the day and snapshots of the major global indices (DOW JONES, S&P 500, FTSE 100, and NIKKEI 225), two of the stocks in a watchlist you set up, current data on the U.S. dollar, and tappable links to the different tabs in the app.

Figure 5-2: Top News in the app, along with snapshots of the major indices.

TIP

Like many other iPad apps I talk about, Bloomberg works in both landscape and portrait mode, but I think it looks best in landscape mode. For instance, in the figure, the buttons at the bottom of the screen are laid out nicely in landscape mode, but in portrait mode, they take up one-third of the screen because they're stacked three deep.

The best thing about this app to me is all the Bloomberg news articles which, in the latest update, you can set up to read offline. In the News tab, you get all of Bloomberg's news coverage divided into many categories over seven swipeable pages. The first page has panes for Worldwide news, the Most Read stories of the day, Bonds, Commodities, and the company's Exclusive content. Swipe to the left, and you get a new page of news categories, such as Currencies, Economy, and Commodities. Another swipe, and you get five more categories, and so on. You can edit the order of all these categories, making this a convenient place to catch up on the news that's important to you.

The Equity Indices, Currency, and My Stocks sections all contain simple, scrollable lists of those markets. You can't customize them; but these are finite lists to begin with, so that's not a big deal to me. Having quick and easy access to them is what I think is important.

The other big feature of this app is all the Bloomberg podcasts you listen to on your iPad. Yeah, you can get these podcasts from iTunes, but Bloomberg for iPad gives you easy access to the lot of them without you having to monitor and manage podcast subscriptions. You find podcasts for News, Economics, Politics, and the Markets. You can also listen to them as you are messing around in other parts of the app.

Lastly, I'd be remiss in my duties if I didn't point out that some people are put off by the black background with orange or white text theme of this app, but I personally like it. I think it makes for easy reading.

You can find better apps (like StockWatch, covered earlier in the chapter) if you just want to monitor your stocks, but Bloomberg is the app if you want to monitor the markets as a whole. The company's financial news coverage is among the best, and access to all the markets outside of the usual stock markets is convenient.

Book VI
Chapter 5

Financial Apps

SplashMoney for iPad

by SplashData, Inc.

$4.99

What you can do with it: Manage your household budget, download your banking transactions, track your spending, and get charts and reports showing you where your money goes.

Most people need help when it comes to managing budgets, and the reality is that different things work for different people. I know people who know how much they have in their checking accounts to the penny but have never recorded a check in the ledgers or balanced their checkbooks, not even once. On the other end of the spectrum, I know people who spend lots of time and effort in planning their budgets, balancing their checkbooks, and trying hard to be on top of their spending, yet nothing seems to work for them despite their best efforts. Most fall between those two extremes and just need a little extra help in watching what's spent and where. If that's you, SplashMoney for iPad might be the app for you.

SplashMoney HD is a money-management app for the iPad that allows you to monitor credit cards and online banking accounts (checking, savings, and so on), create budgets, and track your actual spending. You can sync data between the iPad app and the Mac or Windows version of the company's software, too, which is very handy. You can also directly download online banking information from a list of a couple of hundred banks and online banking services, including most of the major banks. The app is designed well, is colorful, and provides attractive and informative graphs to help you visualize what you're doing with your money. It also includes an app-specific password option for additional security.

Setting up this app takes some work, but after you perform that initial setup, it's pretty easy to work with on a day-to-day basis. The key is to simply make sure you keep up with it. It comes with a few default accounts, including Checking, Savings, and three credit card accounts. In Figure 5-3, I added a couple of other accounts and then added a bunch of (fake) transactions under my (fictional) checking account. When I set up each account, I named it, picked an icon, and established a beginning balance. Then when I make payments, write checks, buy things with my debit card, or make deposits, I just enter each one as I go. I can assign categories, the payee, and the date, and assign it as either a personal transaction or a business transaction.

After you enter a transaction assigned to a particular payee, the next time you select that payee for a new transaction, the category, payment type, and other things you selected are autofilled from the preceding transaction. This is a handy timesaver, especially for those transactions you conduct frequently, such as buying gas or groceries. You can also set up recurring transactions with reminders, and who doesn't need that kind of help?

If you're like me, I wouldn't worry about trying to backdate a bunch of transactions when you first start using the app. Instead, just set your starting balances properly and focus on entering new transactions going forward!

Figure 5-3: Viewing a sample checking account with recent checking activity on the right.

After you set up all the proper accounts and have some transactions under your belt, you get reports that show you where your money is going. You can view these reports in list form or as a pie chart, and doing both might really change the way you think about how you spend your money. For instance, it turns out that I spend a lot of money on books and games like *World of Warcraft.* Who knew?

If you're really ambitious, you can even establish budgets for each and every category you want to track. Need to cut back on how much you spend on movies, or maybe coffee? Establish a budget and monitor it throughout the month. SplashMoney will show you what your budget is, what you've actually spent, and the difference. I think a lot of people will appreciate that feature, and most should probably use it!

This app offers a lot, and it's up to you how much you take advantage of all these features. I think that people who are comfortable with (or need to be more comfortable with) maintaining detailed financial records to manage their budgets are going to like this app. It's not what I would call a perfect app, but it's very good, and it's getting better with each update.

One more note: PocketMoney from Cantamount Software ($4.99) is another great entry in this category of personal finance apps.

PowerOne Financial Calculator

by Infinity Softworks, Inc.

$4.99 — Hybrid

What you can do with it: You can perform a variety of complex calculations with it, and it includes many easy-to-use templates for commonly used equations in the world(s) of finance.

Do you remember the days when the math and engineer guys proudly walked around with their calculators from TI and HP? Uhhh . . . yeah, me neither . . . Okay, I admit it: I had one back in the 1970s, but I had no idea how to use it, which might help explain why I like PowerOne Financial Calculator so much. This app does super-complex finance-related calculations for you, but with the included templates, you don't have to really know what you're doing to get the right answers for a lot of things — I call that a score.

For instance, when you're shopping for a car, it's sometimes hard to get a straight answer out of the salesperson regarding how much your car is going to cost. Many dealerships like to try to sell you a car based on the car payment, and that can make it hard to understand how much you're really paying! At the same time, if you're price-shopping for a car and know the total price, you do still need to know what your monthly payment is going to be. PowerOne has a template called Auto Loan that will get you the information you need. As shown in Figure 5-4, you enter the price, sales tax, any fees you might need to pay, the interest rate on your loan, down payment, and the number of months you intend to carry the loan, and you can get your monthly payment with a simple tap.

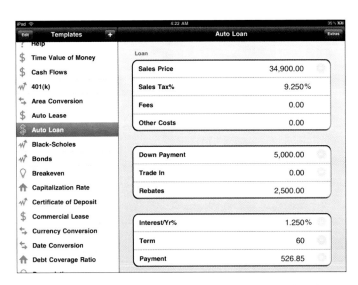

Figure 5-4: Figuring out the specifics of a car loan with the Auto Loan template.

You can work backward, too: Say you want to change what you want your payment to be. If you enter that, you can tap the equal sign next to any of the other categories and get that figure. For instance, if you want to pay a certain amount per month, you can see how many months you'd need to carry the loan to hit that target. Or if you know how much you can pay per month and how long your bank will carry your note, you can quickly get the figure for how much of a down payment you'd need to make, or how much you can spend on your car. If you're working on your taxes (or someone else's taxes), the same template will also give you amortization figures.

Don't worry. A standard calculator, of course, is included in this app. Just choose the Calculator template to get a calculator with both math and trig functions, as well as a history. You can tap away on this like you would any ol' calculator.

But this app isn't just about car loans. You find more than 50 templates included in this app, some for traders, some for accountants, some for super math people, and some that are for mere mortals. I like the Area Conversion that allows me to fill in one of 11 units of measure and, with a single tap, get that converted to the other ten units of measure. A currency converter is also available that uses the most recent exchange rates (if you have a connection to the Internet when you use it). You find a depreciation template, an inflation calculator, several loan-related calculations, mortgage tools, a sales-tax template, and much more. You can even access a tip calculator that will divide your bill among multiple people!

For sure, a lot of what this app offers is pretty specialized, but I'd hazard that many will be glad to have this app on iPad if it's needed just once. If you do financial transactions for a living, however, this might be a must-have app for you. Real estate agents, accountants, investors, bankers, and anyone on the other side of those transactions will find it useful.

Daily Stocks

by 13apps

$69.99

What you can do with it: Get a variety of daily technical reports and scans for the markets.

Let me show you another specialty app for investors, called Daily Stocks. Though pricey, this app provides the user with technical scans of the market (up to 91 such technical scans as of this writing) and is designed to highlight trends in the marketplace based on some highly technical analytical techniques. Those trends, in turn, can help serious investors identify both opportunities and risks in the markets. This kind of information is mainly the domain of fairly serious traders, so if your eyes start to glaze over as I talk about it, I understand! I think it's important to talk about it here, however, because it's an example of an iPad app for serious investors.

Daily Stocks works just fine in landscape and portrait modes, but landscape mode shows you a little more information. As you can see in Figure 5-5, the left side of the screen offers charts for the three major U.S. indices and five global indices.

Figure 5-5: Looking at the Japanese Candlesticks tab.

It's the right two-thirds of the screen, however, that's dedicated to the real purpose of this app. At the top of the screen in the green bar are three tabs, labeled JC (Japanese Candlesticks), OS (Overextended Stocks), and SS (Stock Scans). These are three different styles of reports, and each offers very different information.

A *candlestick* in the trading world is a kind of bar graph. It shows the opening price of a stock and its closing price, with the color telling you whether it was a winning day (opening on the bottom, closing on the top) or a losing day (opening at the top, closing at the bottom).

In Daily Stocks, a red candlestick represents a losing day, and a green candlestick represents a winning day. Simple, eh? And more informative to traders than other graphs.

The JC tab offers ten Bullish trends, ten Bearish trends, and three Indecision trends. These are all attempts to understand where the market is headed based on patterns that have been identified in the past. In other words, they are far from perfect (but their adherents tend to feel strongly about them).

Those names you see, like Falling Three Method or Engulfing, are all English approximations of the original Japanese names the patterns were given.

In any event, the trends with more information are shaded darker gray, and a tap gives you a new screen with a definition of what the trend is supposed to identify and a list of the stocks that matched the pattern to begin with.

Overextended Stocks (OS) are stocks that have broken above their resistance levels (Overbought) or below their support levels (Oversold) or that have traveled beyond their Simple Moving Average (SMA). The OS tab gives you a list of the ten most oversold or overbought stocks compared to their SMA over the last 9 to 200 days. You can tap through one of those ten stocks in any of the SMA views to get several graphs and charts.

Lastly, the Stock Scans (SS) tab gives you more than 56 reports of stocks that have met some specific criteria (such as new 52-week highs or lows, various volume levels, crossover reports, and many more).

These are all very technical reports and scans, and if you're not an active — and, frankly, a serious — trader, you probably don't need this app. Most of this stuff is over my head, and I've been covering (Apple-related) stock news for more than 13 years. If you're a serious trader, however, you should check out Daily Stocks.

Quick Hits

In addition to the apps provided previously in this chapter, here are several more apps in this category that you should check out.

Pocket Expense Lite

by Blue Tags

Free — Hybrid

I realized recently that I've stopped keeping track of my checking and savings accounts as well as credit cards balances. I just desperately check my balances online once in a while. Realizing I had to get back in control, I discovered this handy free app that makes my old paper check registers obsolete. What I like about Pocket Expense Lite is that it provides a one-stop solution for managing finances that's pretty darn easy to use. You can set up a variety of account types to help you keep track of balances and activity in one spot. If you like to set limits for yourself, use features to set budget goals and have Pocket Expense keep tabs on your spending. If you've ever missed making a bill payment and want to avoid the stress and overdue payments, you can use this handy app to track bill payments, alerting you when they're due and helping you to make payments on time. If you need to get an overview of your financial activity, use the easy-to-generate reports.

iSlick

by Lanuta

Free

If your idea of a wonderful day is one in which you shop 'til you drop, I guarantee you'll love iSlick. iSlick taps into its own social networking resources to provide tips on the best deals and free stuff out there, according to all those happy shoppers. (And if you're really into free stuff, note that a free version of iSlick itself is available.)

You like coupons? iSlick helps you find them. Crave the hottest deals? iSlick trolls around the Internet every day to find the best. Without iSlick, how would I have found out that Quiznos was giving away a free cookie on Valentine's Day, or that REI had a closeout special on headlamps, or that I could run to my nearest Bath & Body Works store and get a free travel-size item today only (a $5 value!). Connect your iSlick account to your Facebook account and you can let your friends in on your favorite deals, creating your very own shopping network.

Quick Sale for iPad

by IntelliXense

$9.99

Quick Sale for iPad is a handy app for anyone who needs to invoice on the go (at street fairs, at a client's location, on a business trip, at a trade show, and so on) or, for that matter, anyone who wants to interface with customers with an iPad in his hands instead of a computer. It is the future, after all. In any event, Quick Sale for iPad is a fairly complete invoicing solution for your iPad. It offers unlimited inventory items and services (including photos for each one, if you want, and barcode scanner support) that you can organize by category. It also offers reports and the ability to e-mail reports and invoices, and it integrates with Credit Card Terminal from Inner Fence for conducting credit card transactions! You can print invoices directly from your iPad to an AirPrint-compatible wireless printer.

If you're into saving money, check out the Lite version of this app, which is absolutely free. It offers several of the features described previously, and is a good way to see if the app is for you before buying.

Pageonce – Money & Bills

by Pageonce, Inc.

Free — Hybrid

Pageonce – Money & Bills is a personal finance service for the mobile market. This is a free, ad-supported, hybrid app that works on both iPhone and iPad. It allows you to track your bills and expenses, monitor your credit cards, check your bank account status, check in on your stocks, and even track your frequent-flyer mileage programs. The company also offers the ability to remotely destroy your data through the service's website if you ever lose your iPhone or iPad. A Premium version of the app ($12.99) is ad-free and offers additional features. If you like the free version, you'll probably be willing to pay for the paid version.

E*TRADE Mobile Pro for iPad

by E*TRADE FINANCIAL

Free

E*TRADE Mobile Pro for iPad is that company's conduit to all its online brokerage services. The thing I love most about this app is that it's in the top tier of well-designed iPad apps in the App Store. The developers made great use of the iPad's screen real estate, and they put a lot of thought into arranging the app's information panes to match the way people will actually use them. That's a touch I really appreciate. When it comes to using the app, you can buy and sell stocks and options, get financial news, watch the indices, and monitor your portfolio. The only thing that's wrong with this app is that most of its services are accessible only by E*TRADE customers. If you're not an E*TRADE customer, check out the StockWatch app I talk about earlier in the chapter.

Chapter 6: Entertainment Apps

In This Chapter

- Emoti HD for Facebook
- Netflix
- SoundHound
- Pandora Radio
- ArtRage
- Seline HD – Music Instrument
- Movies by Flixster
- IMDb Movies & TV
- Marvel Superheroes
- Gravilux and Uzu
- OverDrive Media Console
- Crystal Caliburn II

Finally! Finally, you're going to get some entertainment on the iPad! I've shown you some great iPad apps, but I saved the best, or at least some of the most fun apps, for last. "Entertainment" is one of those broad topics that means a lot of different things to different people, and so in this chapter, I picked several kinds of apps that I think are entertaining. I have a social networking helper, music apps, a way to watch movies and TV on your iPad, and a couple of super cool apps that might even entertain your inner nerd!

Many of the apps I talk about in this chapter are apps that were written for the iPad. Some apps, however, have been written by the developer to run as native apps on both the iPad and iPhone (or iPod touch). These are called *hybrid* apps, and you find a + symbol next to the price in the App Store for those apps. Hybrid apps have the advantage of allowing you to buy once and use on whatever iOS device you have.

Emoti HD for Facebook

by nodconcept, LLC

$2.99

What you can do with it: Make posts to Facebook with bright, colorful emoticon images to illustrate your mood or some other aspect of your posts.

Facebook is probably one of the most popular forms of entertainment on the planet today. The company has more than half a billion members these days, and a lot of people waste — I mean spend — countless hours every day posting updates about themselves and reading up on what friends and family are doing. I thought it would be a good idea to kick off this chapter with an app that can make this form of entertainment even more entertaining. Emoti HD is an app that allows you to post great-looking emoticons in your Facebook posts, images that can be informative for those reading your posts, but images that can also simply draw more attention to your posts.

In case you've been hiding in a cave for the last 10–15 years before you popped out to pick up an iPad and this book, an *emoticon* is one of those little sideways faces you can make out of text characters, like **:)** for a smiley face or **:(** for a sad face. Emoji, on the other hand, started in Japan as a system for including actual images for smiley (and other) faces through SMS text messages. Emoti (for iPhone) and Emoti HD's name is a juxtaposition of the two concepts.

As of this writing, Emoti HD has 186 emoticons. These high-quality images were custom-made by nodconcept, the app's developer, and they look absolutely great. They're colorful, and they just pop off the screen on both your iPad and Facebook in your browser. The app includes all the basic emoticons for happy, angry, sad, ecstatic, crying, proud, goofy, surprised, in love, and even sleeping. But there's much more, too. You find sports and thank-you emoticons, and emoticons to denote that it's raining, snowing, hot, or cold. You see military emoticons, food, music, gambling, and religious emoticons. You find gay-pride, graduation, and baby emoticons (It's a boy! It's a girl!), and even emoticons for the major holidays. That's a lot of emoticons, but the developer says that more are coming!

You can also use Emoti HD to post to Facebook without using an emoticon, too, making this app a one-stop shop for posting. On the first page of emoticons, you find a dotted box with the text *no emoti* in it. Tap that, make your post, and your post will have no image and look like a normal Facebook post.

On the left side of Figure 6-1, I'm making a post to my Facebook account about my current favorite band, The Spyrals, out of San Francisco. I could have used one of the music-themed images, but I chose one of the thumbs-up emoticons instead. It's kind of like having my own personal Like and Dislike tool.

Figure 6-1: Making a post to Facebook with Emoti HD (left) and rearranging the sheets of emoticons by tapping and holding one of the sheets (right).

To make a post, tap an emoticon and you get a keyboard and a spot to write your post. Write the post, tap the Share button, and you're done! On your first post, tap the Facebook Connect button to log in to Facebook from Emoti HD. If you need to change accounts, you can log out of the current account by tapping the From field in a new post. You can pick your destination (your own Wall, a friend's Wall, a Group, a Page, or a Fan Page) by tapping the second field (Wall in Figure 6-1). It's very easy to use, and it may even be the most direct way to make a Facebook post on your iPad.

I want to show you one more cool feature in Emoti HD. In the upper-right corner of the display is an icon with nine little squares. Tap that and you get all nine pages of emoticons so you can quickly jump to the one you want. This is a cool navigation feature that I wish was in more apps, but nodconcept upped it a notch by adding the ability to rearrange the pages so that you can put them in the order you want. If you tap and hold one of the pages in this view, like I did on the right in Figure 6-1, they start shaking just like apps do when you want to rearrange their order on your home screen. Just tap, hold, and drag a page to the position you want it! For instance, I'm not a big soccer fan (and the 2012 World Cup is over), so I moved that page of emoticons to the end. That's pretty slick!

All in all, this is a cool app with great-looking emoticons. If you post on Facebook and want a way to make your posts stand out, or if you just want to be able to better illustrate your point, Emoti HD is for you.

Netflix

by James Odell

Free (subscription required) — Hybrid

What you can do with it: You can stream TV shows and movies for instant viewing on your iPad, and you can also manage your online Netflix account and Instant Queue (but not your physical DVD subscription service). But note that you'll need an Internet connection for both features and that the catalog of movies and shows that comes with this app is smaller than the one you access through your computer.

Wooohoooo! TV and movies on your iPad! You can watch video content of all sorts on your iPad. You can buy and rent TV shows and movies through Apple's iTunes Store, too. You also find YouTube content, videos you get from your friends and family, and movies that you might have bought on DVD and transferred to your computer and iPad. Some websites offer video content, as well, though much of that is currently Flash-based and therefore unwatchable on your iPad. Netflix, however, is another great choice, but I guess I should begin with a basic look at what exactly Netflix is.

Netflix started life as a mail-based DVD rental service. For a monthly subscription, you can get DVDs of TV shows and movies delivered to your house. After you watch them, you can return them, and Netflix sends you the next DVD in your queue. Because you're paying a flat fee, the faster you watch and then return your Netflix DVDs in the mail, the more video entertainment you get for your dollar.

Netflix is a great way to catch up on TV shows you either got behind on or were late watching in the first place. Go back to the beginning of *Breaking Bad,* for instance, or *Mad Men,* or even whole TV shows that went off the air years ago, like *Buffy the Vampire Slayer!*

From there, Netflix started adding other services, including streaming movies and TV shows across the Internet. You can watch TV shows and movies on your Mac or PC, and with the Netflix app on your iPad, you can even watch them on your iOS device, so long as you have an Internet connection. In Figure 6-2, I have the Bruce Willis flick, *Surrogates,* pulled up. I can add it to my Instant Queue (a queue for those shows I want to stream), or I can just play it right now. I can also read up on the show, get cast information, and more.

Another very cool tool for using Netflix is the ability to rate movies. The company uses proprietary algorithms to suggest movies and TV shows you might like based on the shows that you've rated. The system works, more often than not, and gets better as you give it more information.

Figure 6-2: On a movie or TV show's entry, you can watch it instantly or add it to your Instant Queue (where available).

The video quality looks great on the iPad's display — especially if you have a third- or fourth-generation iPad with Retina display — and I think it's a great way to rent movies and TV shows. It's a hybrid app, too, and it works just as well on your iPhone.

Another option for watching TV shows and movies on your iPad is Hulu Plus. It's a free download, but it requires a $9.99 monthly subscription. Anyone can download the Hulu app and watch some programs for free. It's just not as useful without a Hulu Plus account. Yet another good TV solution for Mac users is EyeTV ($4.99) from Elgato Systems, which allows you to stream TV from your Mac to your iPad, though it requires additional hardware on your Mac.

SoundHound

by SoundHound, Inc.

Free — Hybrid

What you can do with it: If you like to follow music trends, SoundHound can help by sharing with you the most tweeted songs and providing an easy way to jump to iTunes to buy them. SoundHound is a social music site that hooks into major social networking sites.

I don't always get to keep up with the latest music because I'm so busy writing iPad books. But when I have the time, it's nice to have an app that can recommend sounds to check out to save me having to troll through iTunes and other music stores in search of music. SoundHound lets me know what music people are tweeting about. However, it also offers an Underplayed category, which includes the songs that individuals are playing more than the radio stations. This provides a way past whatever politics go on in the radio/recording industry straight to the music people actually enjoy listening to, with several gems along the way.

When you play a preview of a song, you can also view recent tweets about it, view associated videos, share the song with others, or buy it on iTunes. You can also use various features to easily follow a musician or group on Twitter (see Figure 6-3), check out their tour dates for live performances, and look into the music of similar artists. You can also tap into radio apps like Pandora Radio and Rdio to use them to look for more music.

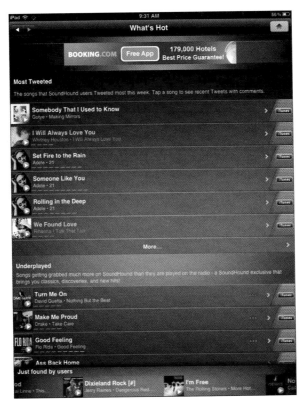

Figure 6-3: Follow tweets about the song you're previewing to see what others think.

One feature I like is a way to view the lyrics of songs (being a writer and someone who has written lyrics, I find that the impact a good lyric can have is often underrated). Another favorite feature is What's That Song. Play a song you have stored on your iPad and tap this button in the upper-right corner of SoundHound, and you can get information about the song and album, and bookmark the selection. You can also tap the microphone button and speak an artist or song title, and SoundHound searches and lists relevant songs or albums.

If details of a song include related video, just tap the Play button to play back video from sources such as YouTube. You might just see a live performance of a song or an artist interview you wouldn't have otherwise found. For example, I found no less than seven performances of one song by jazz artist Diana Krall on video and three others by other performers. This is a great way to find other artists who work in a genre you like but whom you might never stumble across otherwise.

If you're into music, be sure to check out GarageBand, which is available for iPad for $4.99, to mix up your own music. In fact, this mainstay Apple app is so much fun I cover it briefly in Book II, Chapter 2.

Pandora Radio

by Pandora Media, Inc.

Free — Hybrid

What you can do with it: Pandora offers live streaming radio through stations you set up around bands, songs, artists, or composers.

Pandora Radio is the self-titled app that brings the Pandora streaming radio service from your browser to your iPad (and other iOS devices). If you like music but don't know what Pandora is, I want you to stop reading, put this book down, and go download it from the App Store right now! Go on; I'll wait.

So I'm guessing that if you're still reading, you either already had it or have installed it now, so everyone's on the same page, right? Excellent! A lot of streaming radio stations are on the Internet, but Pandora came up with an approach of offering a wide variety of music to people in a way that they actually wanted to listen to it. Imagine that!

Here's how it works, in the online service as well as the iPad app: When you first launch Pandora, you're prompted to sign in with an existing account or create a new one. After you sign in, you can create a new station by simply searching for a band (or song or artist). When you do, Pandora starts playing a song by that band, a song that you can then give a thumbs-up or thumbs-down to. Pandora then looks at the songs you like (and don't like) and plays other songs it thinks you will like based on what people with similar tastes have said they like. This allows you to train your stations to play music you're probably going to really enjoy!

Rate as many songs as you can. The more data Pandora has, the more you'll like your stations!

You can create as many stations as you want (and even shuffle among them), each one starting with an artist, song, or composer. If a station gets out of control for you, delete it and start a new one. In Figure 6-4, I have stations for The Brian Jonestown Massacre, The Who, The Beatles, Led Zeppelin, Black Rebel Motorcycle Club, The Church, and a band called Jucifer.

Figure 6-4: Several radio stations set up (the list on the left) with information on the current song playing on the right.

In that figure, you see that I'm listening to "This Is The First Of Your Last Warning" from The Brian Jonestown Massacre. The album cover of that song is highlighted, and you can see the album covers of the songs that played before, allowing you to tap any of them to find out more. Note that I gave this song a thumbs-up, from the icon next to the name of the band. If I tap the Menu button directly below it, I can bookmark the song or artist, and I can also get taken straight to the song or artist in iTunes!

Which brings me to why I think Pandora is so cool: The stations and song ratings allow me to train those stations to play only songs I'm likely to like, but I'm still going to hear songs and bands I've never heard before! It's like having a personal DJ! I've found lots of new bands this way.

When you give a song a thumbs-down, Pandora immediately skips to the next song. However, there's a limit to how many songs you skip per hour (you're stuck with about eight). To get around this, jump to another station and when you return, the first station will have moved on from that ninth annoying song.

Another feature I really like is the band histories you get with each song — I just love learning more about bands.

Pandora is free, but the free service limits you to 40 hours of listening per month, a limit relating to a royalty agreement between the station and rights holders. For most users, 40 hours per month will probably be enough, but for $36 per year, you can have unlimited listening time, no ads, and a desktop app for listening to Pandora without a browser on your Mac or PC. The only real advantage to iPad users is the lack of ads and the unlimited listening; plus you're supporting a cool service (and the rights holders of all those songs).

As I said previously, if you like music, you should have Pandora on your iPad. It offers you a great way to hear favorite and new music alike, and you can build stations around all your favorite bands.

ArtRage

by Ambient Design, Ltd.

$2.99

What you can do with it: ArtRage lets you use your fingers to manipulate various artist's tools, photos, and backgrounds to create digital works of art.

I dabble in mixed-media artwork, so it was great fun to find ArtRage, an app that makes creating art on the iPad a lot of fun. Just pick your weapon (that is, your brush, crayon, paint roller, pastel chalk, or whatever) and use your finger to draw, paint, airbrush, and otherwise do the digital equivalent of finger painting.

The color wheel lets you choose any color you can imagine by tapping it; then you can use the different tools to create your art using those colors. When you're satisfied with your masterpiece, you can save it in your ArtRage gallery, and then save it to a photo album, print it, or send it via e-mail.

You find settings for how hard you have to press the screen to make your mark, how blending works, and even the texture of your canvas from smooth to crumpled or even foil.

You can change orientation of the piece as well, and even set the texture of paint you're laying down (a thick gloss to thin and dry on the brush, for example).

One very cool feature is the ability to grab items from your iPad Photos Camera Roll and insert the pictures in your artwork. Imagine the possibilities using other apps, both preinstalled on iPad or purchased from the App Store. For example, by using Photo Booth to take a picture of myself with an odd effect applied, and then inserting it on a tinfoil canvas and brushing on a bit of color, I create the weird and wonderful piece of art you see in Figure 6-5.

Figure 6-5: The foil background preset adds sparkle!

Quick Hits

Here are several more apps you should check out, which give you some alternatives to the apps I cover in more detail throughout this chapter.

Seline Ultimate – Music Instrument with MIDI

by Ilya Plavunov

$.99 — Hybrid

I picked Seline Ultimate to show you because it's one of the first musical instrument apps that takes a totally new approach to turning your iPad into an instrument. Rather than trying to bring an analog instrument to your digital iPad, Seline plays on an interface designed from the ground up for the iPad, called ioGrid. It allows you to play melodies with your hands while automatically generated backing tracks drone underneath what you're playing. The app has two effects and 20 main instrument voices (plus nine drone voices), and you can record what you play! It's fun, it's cool, and I recommend it.

Movies by Flixster

by Jeffrey Grossman

Free — Hybrid

Look up an intriguing movie and you get critic and viewer reviews, as well as photos and information about the cast and director. But what I really like about this app is that you can tap the Showtimes button and find out where this picture is playing near you, and when. You can then get a map to theaters to find your way there. You can comment on a movie on Facebook, or play a trailer. Tap a link to go to Rotten Tomatoes, the review site run by Flixster. You can also look up the latest movies by the most popular, by title, or by rating.

IMDb Movies & TV

by IMDb/Amazon

Free — Hybrid

I use IMDb all the time. The abbreviation stands for Internet Movie Database, but the site includes information about movies and TV shows, and the actors, directors, and even crew who make those shows for people to watch. I watch a lot of TV while I work, which means I watch on my computer. I often see someone and wonder where I saw the actor, or struggle at coming up with the actor's name, and I can look on IMDb to find out. I've also settled any number of bets (or at least debates) with friends and family by looking someone or something up on the service.

With IMDb Movies & TV on your iPad, you get an enormous amount of data about TV and movies, plus you get what I think is a huge bonus: an interface that's far superior to the service's browser-based home. Although the IMDb app takes you to the website if you ask it to, the reality is that it's easier to use the context-oriented menus and buttons on the iPad than it is to click around in a browser on your computer. It's a free hybrid app, too, so you can't really go wrong with it.

Marvel Comics

by Marvel Entertainment

Free — Hybrid

If you're a big fan of comic books, this app provides you with a way to download and navigate hundreds of Marvel Comics. You can choose a guided view that gives you one panel at a time through a comic, or device controls that allow you to move around and through pages of comic books.

If you download a comic, its data will update automatically without you having to perform an update to the app. This app has been updated for iOS 6 and iPhone 5.

Okay, so you won't do anything practical, like improve your vocabulary (unless *zap* counts) or practice playing a musical instrument, but you'll be very popular at those comic book conventions. Finally, if you're a big comic collector, you should know that both Bookman and ComicBookLover are superb ways to enjoy your collection on the iPad.

Gravilux and Uzu

by Scott Snibbe and Jason K. Smith (respectively)

$1.99 each — Hybrid

Gravilux and Uzu are two particle visualizers for the iPad (Gravilux is a hybrid app, too), but they both work in different ways, and they're both too cool for words.

With Gravilux, you "draw with stars" as your finger becomes the very embodiment of gravity itself. Where you touch your iPad's screen, the stars must react to your immense gravitational pull.

With Uzu, particles careen around on your screen, but they obey rules and patterns according to how many fingers touch it. (There are ten sets of parameters for up to ten fingers, not all of which have to be your own!)

On the other hand, Gravilux has more settings for you to toggle on and off. (Double-tap a corner of your screen to pull up the settings bar.)

Both apps look great on your iPad, and both are frightfully fun. If you download them, just be sure not to forget to feed your pets and/or kids, and you should be fine!

OverDrive Media Console

by OverDrive

Free

If you're head over heels in love with e-books, you just have to get OverDrive Media Console. This is a very useful app for both researchers and readers of popular fiction alike. OverDrive is a leading publisher of e-content, and this handy app helps you find e-books from retail stores. But the real bonus here is access to libraries — thousands of them.

OverDrive Media Console supports popular e-book, Adobe, and audiobook formats. If you're requesting content from a library, you need your library card number and PIN, which, of course, may limit your access to remote sources. If you're an international type, you'll be happy to know that the app offers access to libraries in dozens of countries, so if you happen to have a library card in, say, Ankara, Turkey, you have access.

Crystal Caliburn II

By LittleWing

$3.99

This is the number one paid iPad simulation game in Japan, and it's been optimized for iOS 6. The creators claim that the ball motion is pretty close to a physical pinball machine, even emulating the feel of ramps and their various slopes as the ball runs down or up them, and I, for one, agree. There's even support for multiple balls in play at the same time.

In case you want some education with your pinball, Caliburn was the original name of Excalibur, the sword that King Arthur pulled out of the stone, and the game is designed around that theme. The game involves Camelot and Merlin, and your achievements are described in terms of chivalry related to how many times you've visited Camelot, Avalon, and so on.

Index

D

E

Math & Science

Algebra I For Dummies,
2nd Edition
978-0-470-55964-2

Biology For Dummies,
2nd Edition
978-0-470-59875-7

Chemistry For Dummies,
2nd Edition
978-1-1180-0730-3

Geometry For Dummies,
2nd Edition
978-0-470-08946-0

Pre-Algebra Essentials
For Dummies
978-0-470-61838-7

Microsoft Office

Excel 2010 For Dummies
978-0-470-48953-6

Office 2010 All-in-One
For Dummies
978-0-470-49748-7

Office 2011 for Mac
For Dummies
978-0-470-87869-9

Word 2010
For Dummies
978-0-470-48772-3

Music

Guitar For Dummies,
2nd Edition
978-0-7645-9904-0

Clarinet For Dummies
978-0-470-58477-4

iPod & iTunes
For Dummies,
9th Edition
978-1-118-13060-5

Pets

Cats For Dummies,
2nd Edition
978-0-7645-5275-5

Dogs All-in One
For Dummies
978-0470-52978-2

Saltwater Aquariums
For Dummies
978-0-470-06805-2

Religion & Inspiration

The Bible For Dummies
978-0-7645-5296-0

Catholicism For Dummies,
2nd Edition
978-1-118-07778-8

Spirituality For Dummies,
2nd Edition
978-0-470-19142-2

Self-Help & Relationships

Happiness For Dummies
978-0-470-28171-0

Overcoming Anxiety
For Dummies,
2nd Edition
978-0-470-57441-6

Seniors

Crosswords For Seniors
For Dummies
978-0-470-49157-7

iPad 2 For Seniors
For Dummies, 3rd Edition
978-1-118-17678-8

Laptops & Tablets
For Seniors For Dummies,
2nd Edition
978-1-118-09596-6

Smartphones & Tablets

BlackBerry For Dummies,
5th Edition
978-1-118-10035-6

Droid X2 For Dummies
978-1-118-14864-8

HTC ThunderBolt
For Dummies
978-1-118-07601-9

MOTOROLA XOOM
For Dummies
978-1-118-08835-7

Sports

Basketball For Dummies,
3rd Edition
978-1-118-07374-2

Football For Dummies,
2nd Edition
978-1-118-01261-1

Golf For Dummies,
4th Edition
978-0-470-88279-5

Test Prep

ACT For Dummies,
5th Edition
978-1-118-01259-8

ASVAB For Dummies,
3rd Edition
978-0-470-63760-9

The GRE Test For
Dummies, 7th Edition
978-0-470-00919-2

Police Officer Exam
For Dummies
978-0-470-88724-0

Series 7 Exam
For Dummies
978-0-470-09932-2

Web Development

HTML, CSS, & XHTML
For Dummies, 7th Editio
978-0-470-91659-9

Drupal For Dummies,
2nd Edition
978-1-118-08348-2

Windows 7

Windows 7
For Dummies
978-0-470-49743-2

Windows 7
For Dummies,
Book + DVD Bundle
978-0-470-52398-8

Windows 7 All-in-One
For Dummies
978-0-470-48763-1

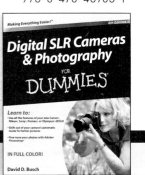